HOW NOT TO SUMMON A DEMON LORD

11

Story
YUKIYA MURASAKI

Art
NAOTO FUKUDA

Character Design
TAKAHIRO TSURUSAKI

CHARACTERS

INTRODUCTIONS

Race: Demon
Level: 150

A self-proclaimed Demon Lord from another world.

Thanks to the "Magic Deflection" effect of the Demon Lord's Ring, which Diablo received in-game, Rem and Shera's Enslavement Ritual backfired. Now *they're* the ones with Enslavement Collars. In the real world, Diablo was unpopular, didn't have a way with words, and couldn't interact with other people to save his life. But in this world, he's tall, handsome, and practically invincible! He still doesn't have a way with words, but he manages to make it through tough situations by acting like a Demon Lord.

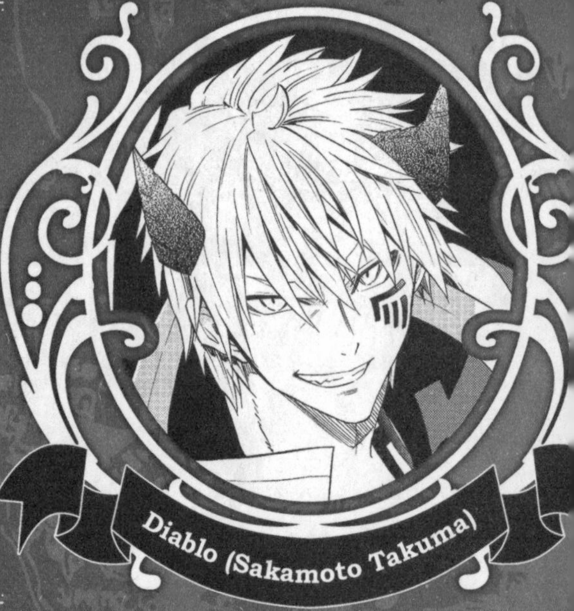
Diablo (Sakamoto Takuma)

STORY

Takuma Sakamoto is an elite gamer in the fantasy MMORPG *Cross Reverie*. He is so overwhelmingly strong that he is known as the "Demon Lord." One day, he's summoned to a world nearly identical to the game by two girls: Shera, an Elf, and Rem, a Pantherian. Thanks to a pair of Enslavement Collars, Takuma Sakamoto—now Diablo—has control over the girls…but he really sucks at talking to other people!! To hide this, Diablo begins behaving like his Demon Lord persona from the game. While demonstrating his power, built up through skills he acquired by playing *Cross Reverie*, Diablo sets out on an adventure with Shera and Rem.

In Zircon Tower, Diablo and his companions have hit rock bottom. Batutta—the Paladin captain behind the frontier city's deadly outbreak of Marked Death Disease—has captured Rem and Lumachina, and plans to use them for his nefarious scheme. But when Diablo ventures underground to save them, Batutta deals a debilitating blow to his left arm. Severely wounded, and unable to use his most powerful magic, has Diablo finally met his match?

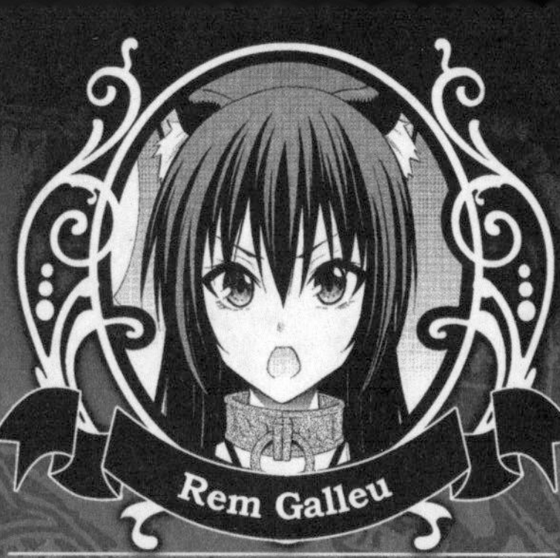
Rem Galleu

Race: Pantherian Level: 40
A Summoner and an Adventurer. She has a small, catlike body with fluffy ears and a tail. She's also flat as a board. The Demon Lord Krebskulm was trapped inside her body, but Diablo saved her from that fate. Rem is always calm, though she's a bit of a prude.

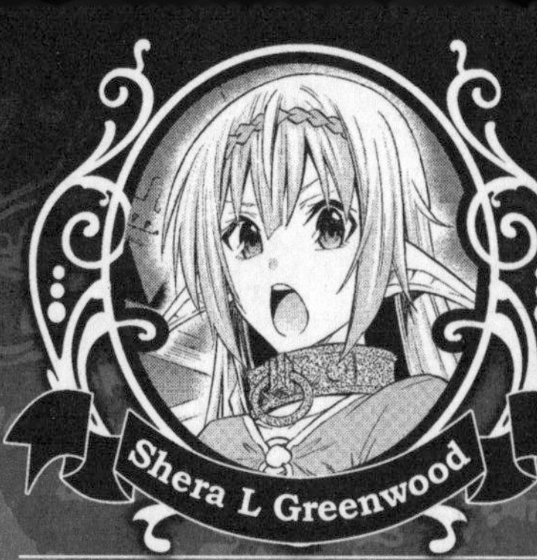
Shera L Greenwood

Race: Elf Level: 30
A Summoner and an Elf. She is slender and elegant, but also has an impressively large bosom that is at odds with the rest of her body. Her innocent and naive personality calms everyone around her. In reality, she is an Elvish princess from Greenwood, but she fled that kingdom to search for freedom.

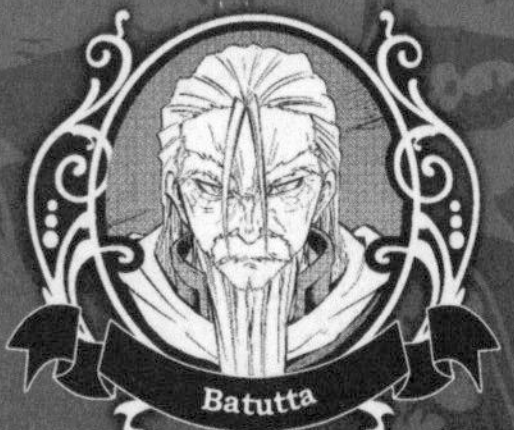
Batutta

A famous Paladin captain who spread the Marked Death Disease throughout Zircon Tower for his own selfish desires. A seasoned and formidable enemy.

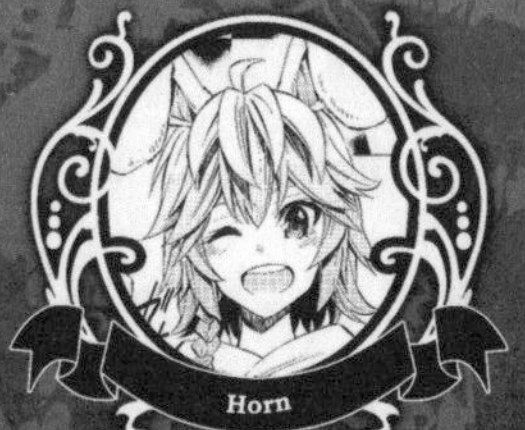
Horn

Race: Grasswalker
Horn lives in the frontier town of Zircon Tower, where he enthusiastically guides adventurers through dungeons.

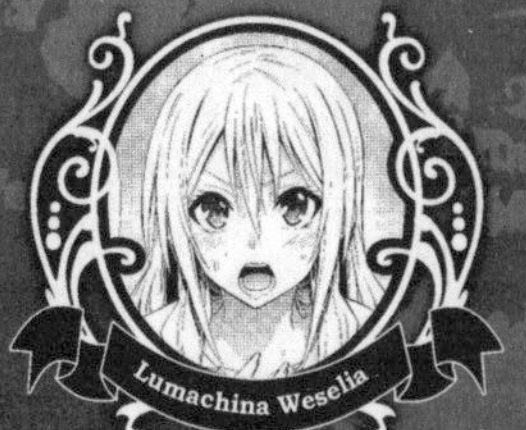
Lumachina Weselia

The High Priestess of the Church. Corruption within the Cardinal Council has put her life in danger. Lumachina believes that Diablo, who saved her, is God.

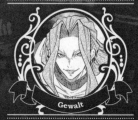

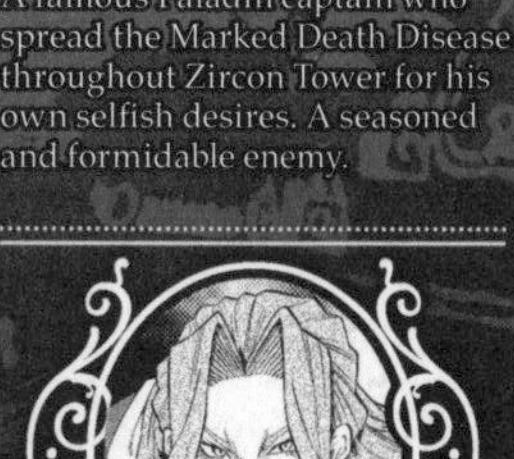
Gewalt

A Paladin hired to assassinate Lumachina. He speaks strangely, but he is also a skilled Summoner.

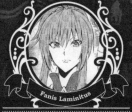

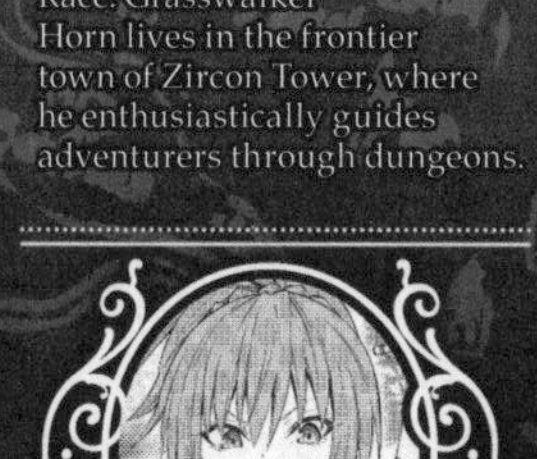
Fanis Laminitus

The governor of Zircon Tower and a powerful Magi-Gunner. She is blatantly condescending toward Diablo, the Church, and the king.

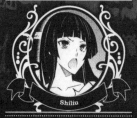

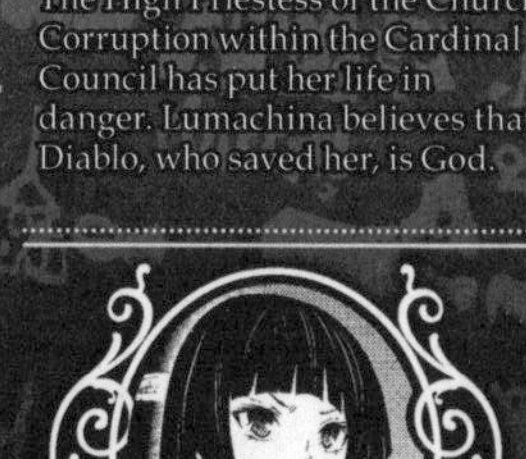
Shiliu

Batutta's maid. She looks prim and proper, but she is completely steeped in Batutta's evil plans.

HOW NOT TO SUMMON A
DEMON LORD
11

✣✣✣ CONTENTS ✣✣✣

50 CATCHING UP III

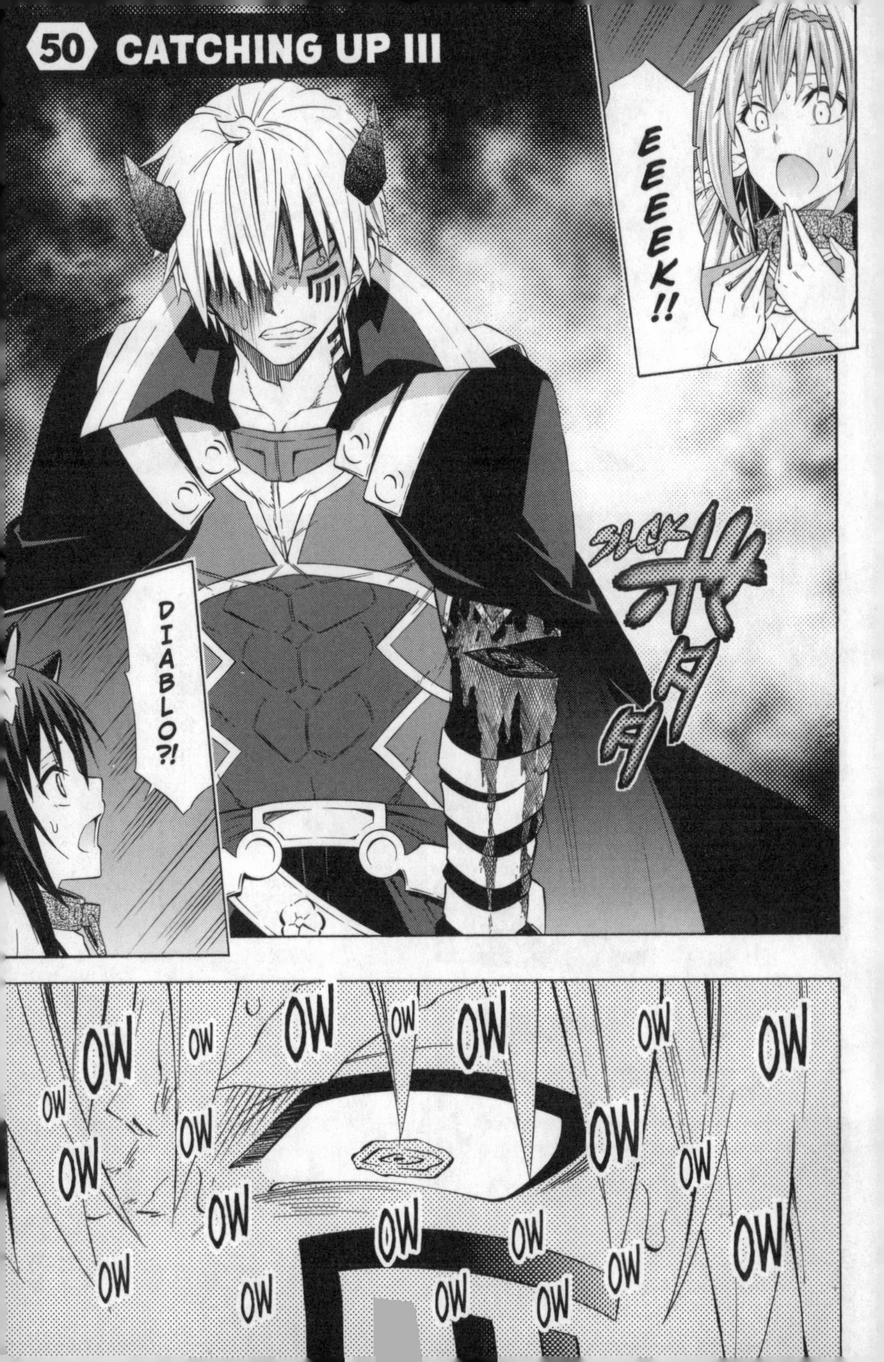
EEEEK!!
DIABLO?!
OW OW OW OW OW OW OW OW OW OW OW OW OW OW OW OW OW OW OW OW OW

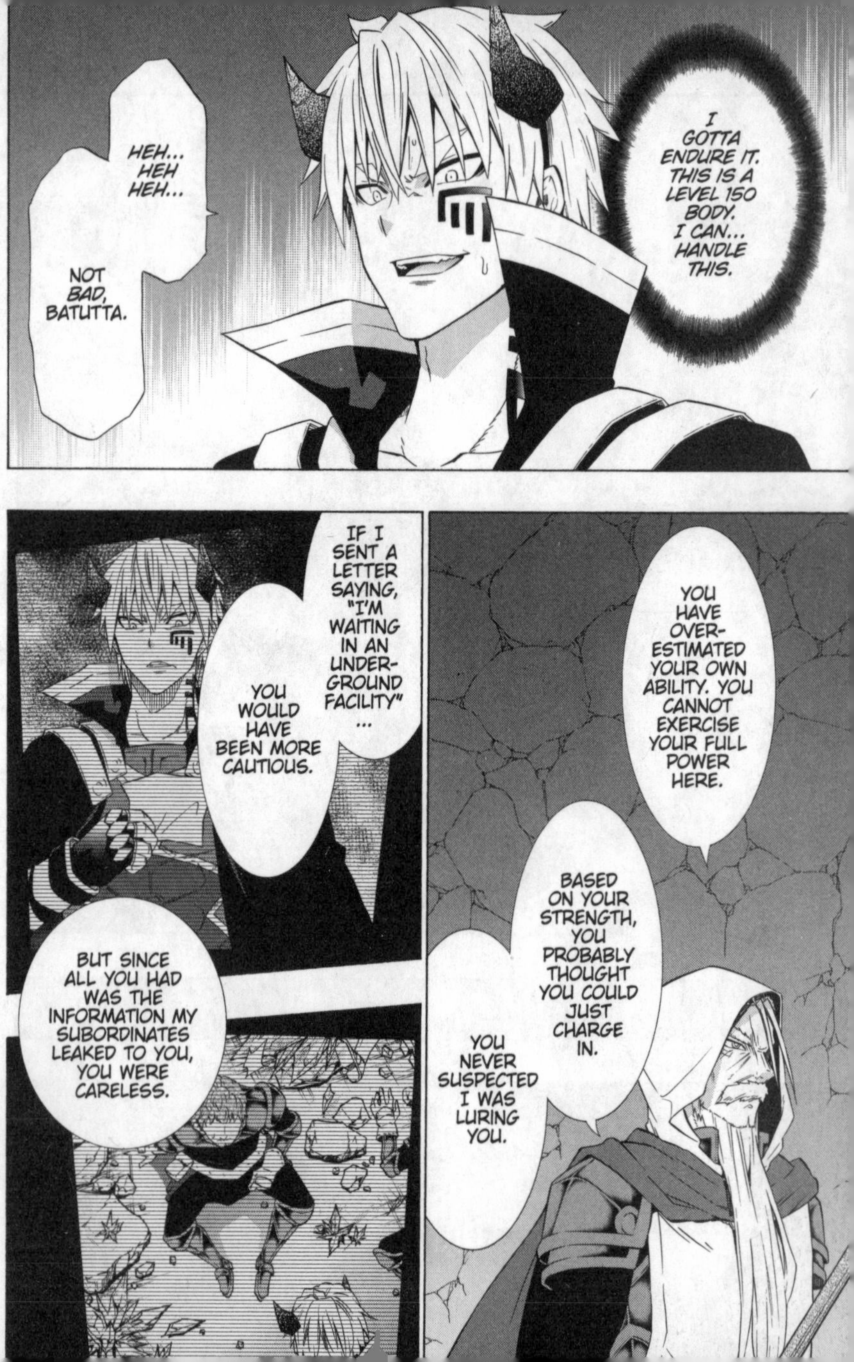
I GOTTA ENDURE IT. THIS IS A LEVEL 150 BODY. I CAN... HANDLE THIS.
HEH... HEH HEH...
NOT BAD, BATUTTA.
YOU HAVE OVER-ESTIMATED YOUR OWN ABILITY. YOU CANNOT EXERCISE YOUR FULL POWER HERE.
BASED ON YOUR STRENGTH, YOU PROBABLY THOUGHT YOU COULD JUST CHARGE IN.
YOU NEVER SUSPECTED I WAS LURING YOU.
IF I SENT A LETTER SAYING, "I'M WAITING IN AN UNDER-GROUND FACILITY"...
YOU WOULD HAVE BEEN MORE CAUTIOUS.
BUT SINCE ALL YOU HAD WAS THE INFORMATION MY SUBORDINATES LEAKED TO YOU, YOU WERE CARELESS.

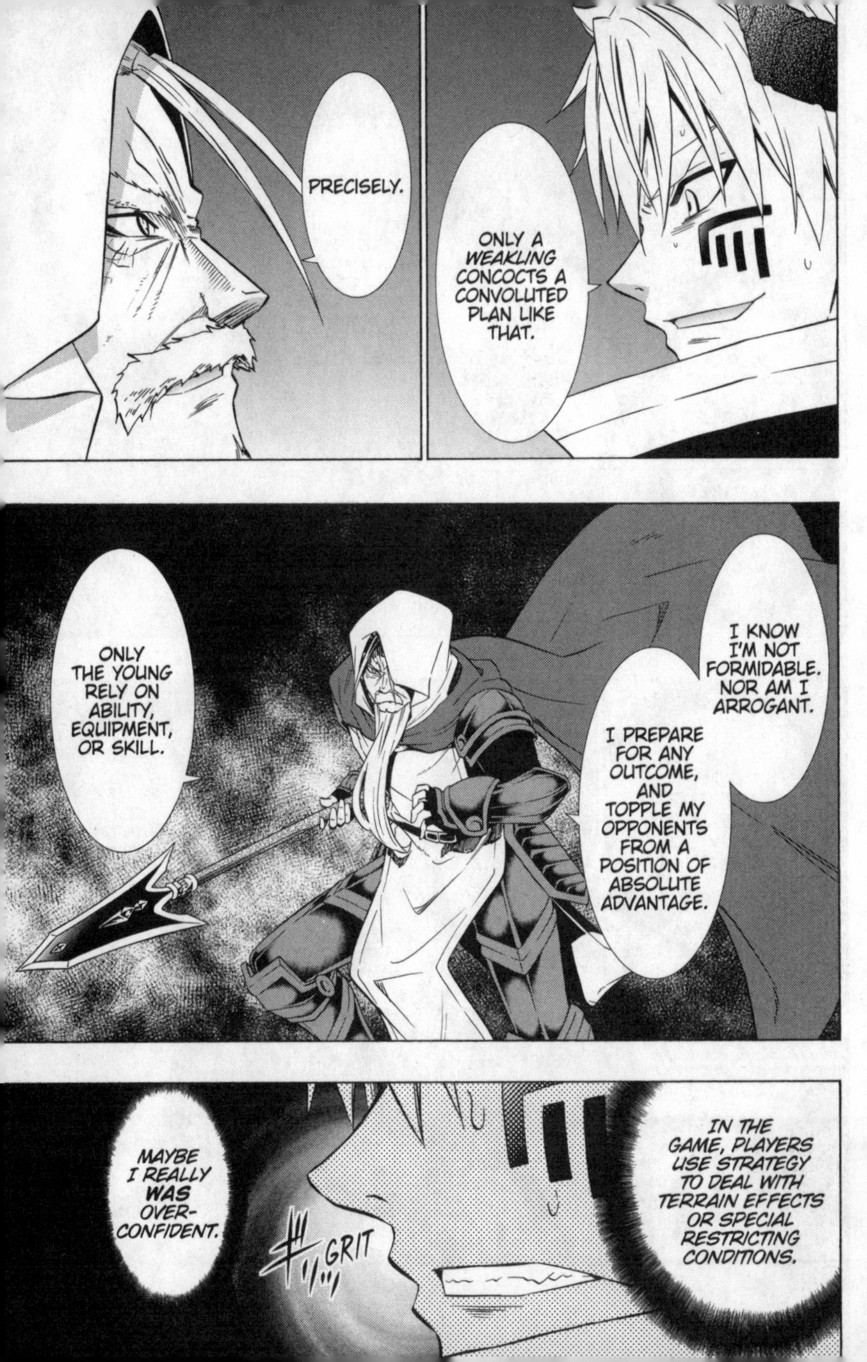
ONLY A WEAKLING CONCOCTS A CONVOLUTED PLAN LIKE THAT.
PRECISELY.
I KNOW I'M NOT FORMIDABLE. NOR AM I ARROGANT.
I PREPARE FOR ANY OUTCOME, AND TOPPLE MY OPPONENTS FROM A POSITION OF ABSOLUTE ADVANTAGE.
ONLY THE YOUNG RELY ON ABILITY, EQUIPMENT, OR SKILL.
IN THE GAME, PLAYERS USE STRATEGY TO DEAL WITH TERRAIN EFFECTS OR SPECIAL RESTRICTING CONDITIONS.
GRIT
MAYBE I REALLY WAS OVER-CONFIDENT.

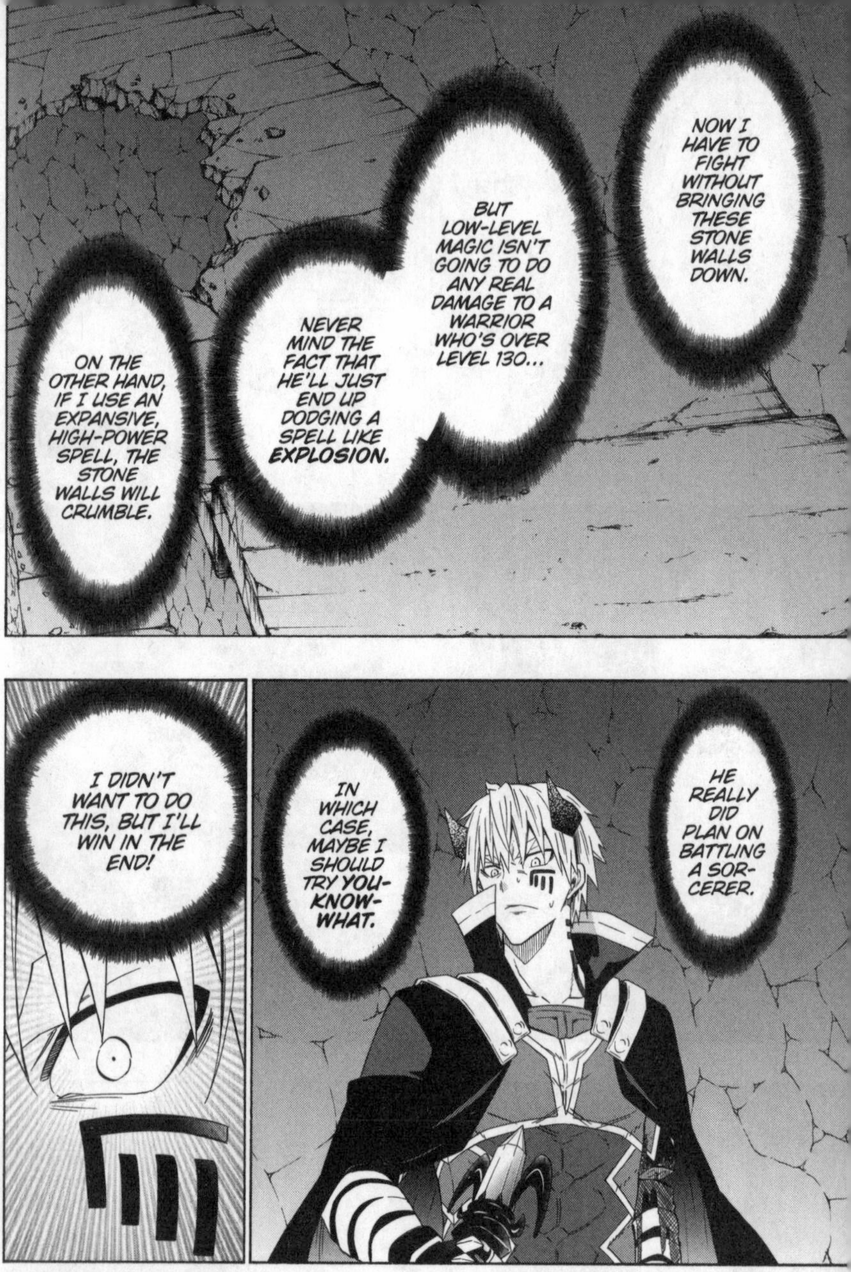
NOW I HAVE TO FIGHT WITHOUT BRINGING THESE STONE WALLS DOWN.
BUT LOW-LEVEL MAGIC ISN'T GOING TO DO ANY REAL DAMAGE TO A WARRIOR WHO'S OVER LEVEL 130...
NEVER MIND THE FACT THAT HE'LL JUST END UP DODGING A SPELL LIKE **EXPLOSION**.
ON THE OTHER HAND, IF I USE AN EXPANSIVE, HIGH-POWER SPELL, THE STONE WALLS WILL CRUMBLE.
HE REALLY DID PLAN ON BATTLING A SOR-CERER.
IN WHICH CASE, MAYBE I SHOULD TRY **YOU-KNOW-WHAT**.
I DIDN'T WANT TO DO THIS, BUT I'LL WIN IN THE END!

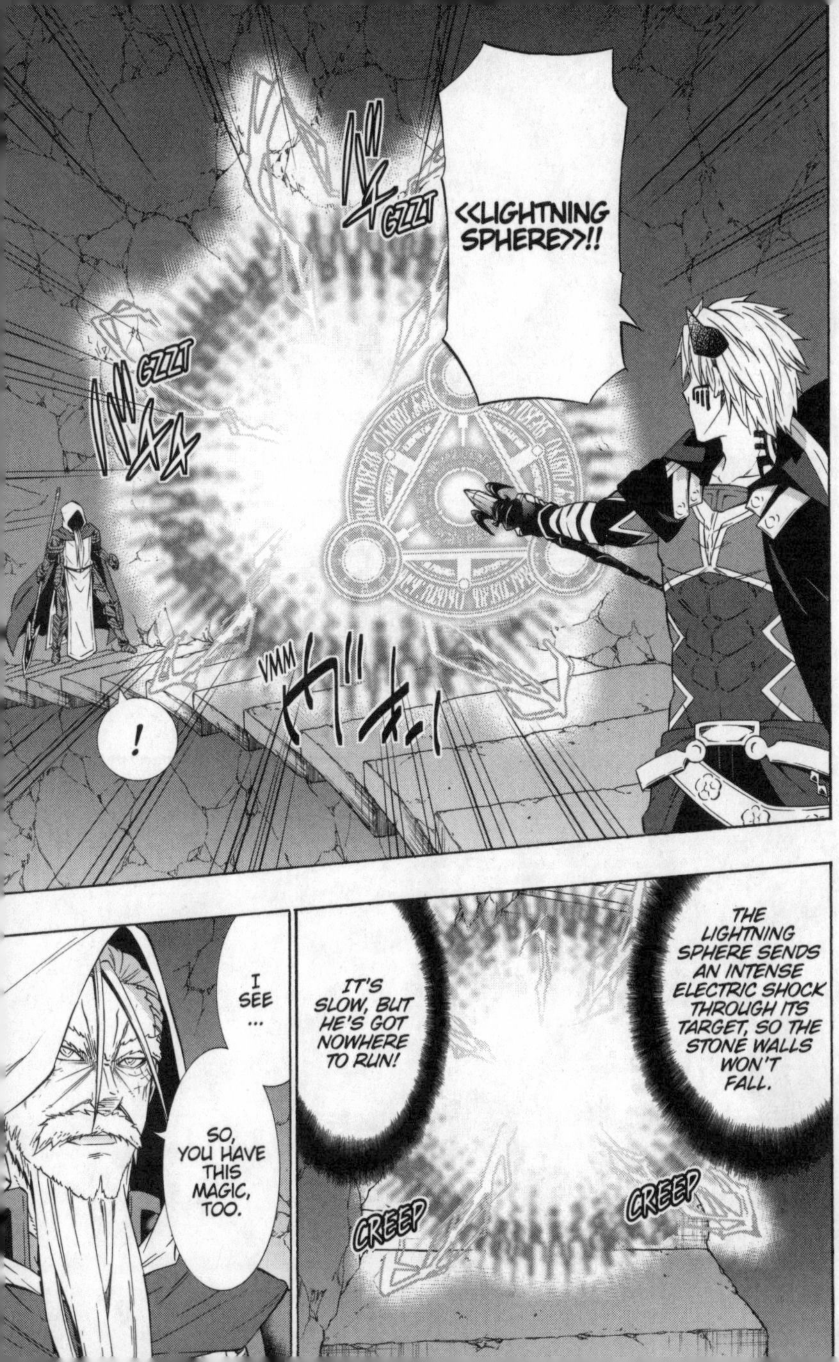

<<LIGHTNING SPHERE>>!!
GZZZT
GZZZT
VMM
!
THE LIGHTNING SPHERE SENDS AN INTENSE ELECTRIC SHOCK THROUGH ITS TARGET, SO THE STONE WALLS WON'T FALL.
IT'S SLOW, BUT HE'S GOT NOWHERE TO RUN!
CREEP
CREEP
I SEE ...
SO, YOU HAVE THIS MAGIC, TOO.

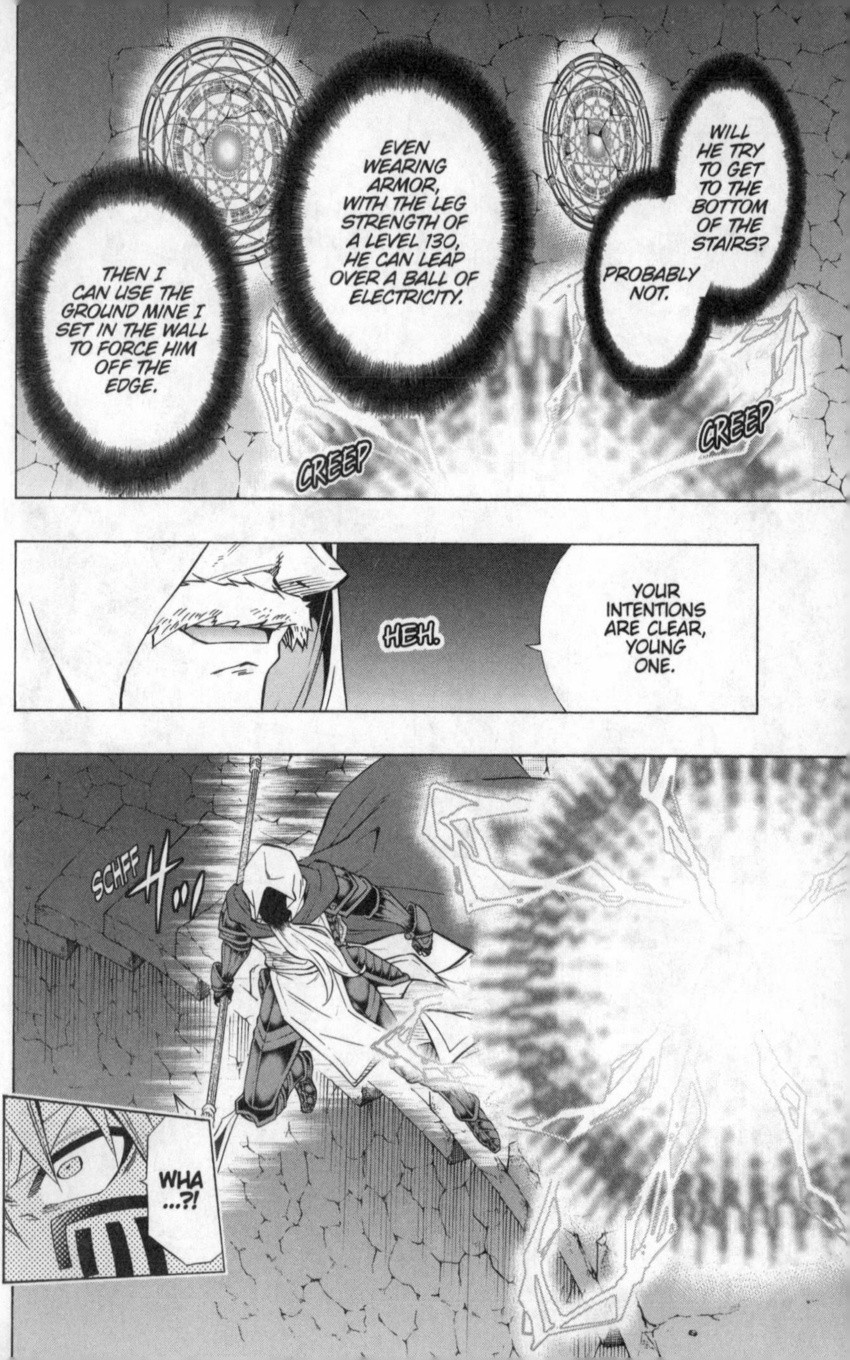
WILL HE TRY TO GET TO THE BOTTOM OF THE STAIRS?
PROBABLY NOT.
EVEN WEARING ARMOR, WITH THE LEG STRENGTH OF A LEVEL 130, HE CAN LEAP OVER A BALL OF ELECTRICITY.
THEN I CAN USE THE GROUND MINE I SET IN THE WALL TO FORCE HIM OFF THE EDGE.
CREEP
CREEP
YOUR INTENTIONS ARE CLEAR, YOUNG ONE.
HEH.
SCHFF
WHA ...?!

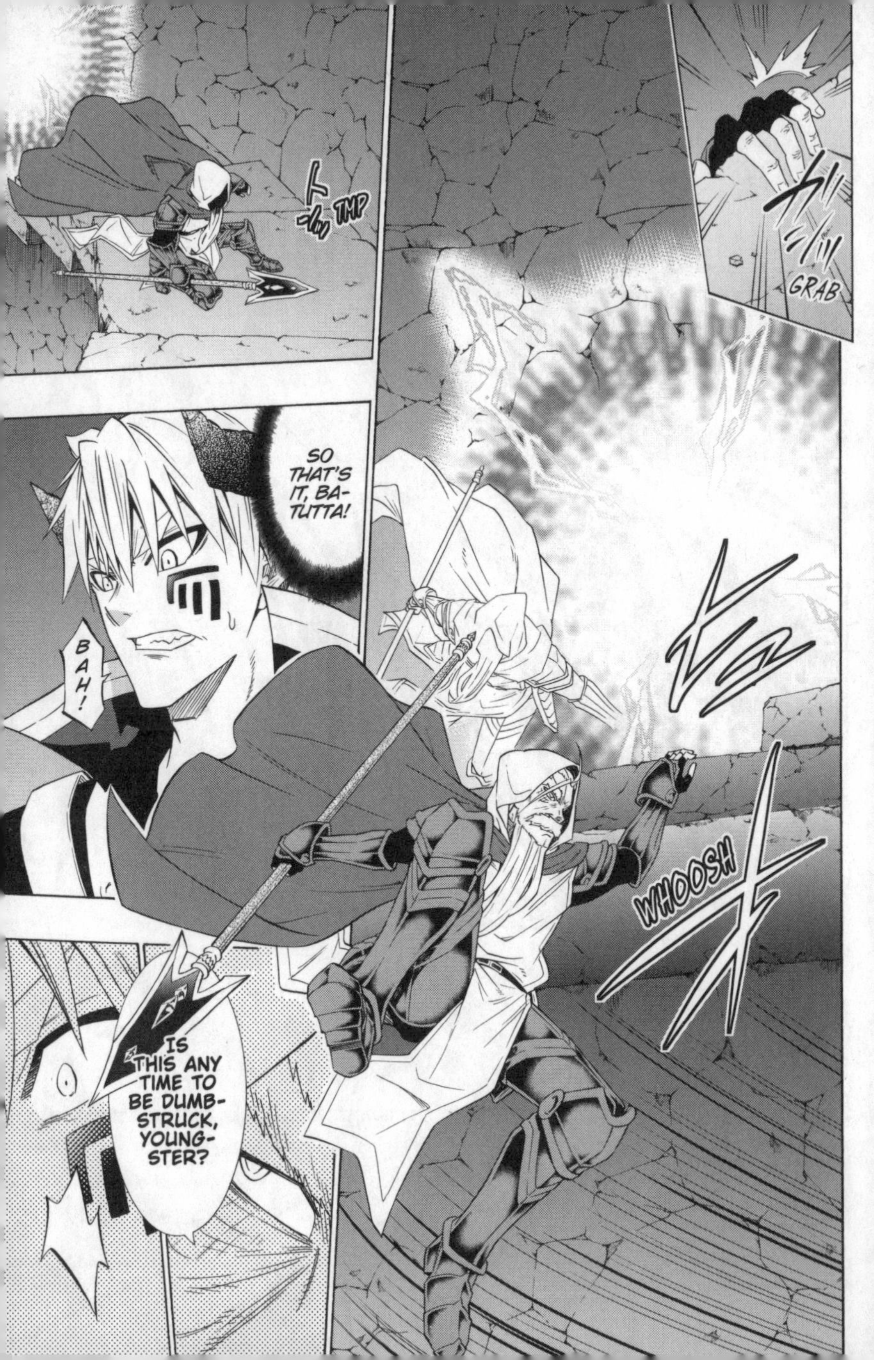
GRAB
TMP
WHOOSH
IS THIS ANY TIME TO BE DUMB-STRUCK, YOUNG-STER?
SO THAT'S IT, BA-TUTTA!
BAH!

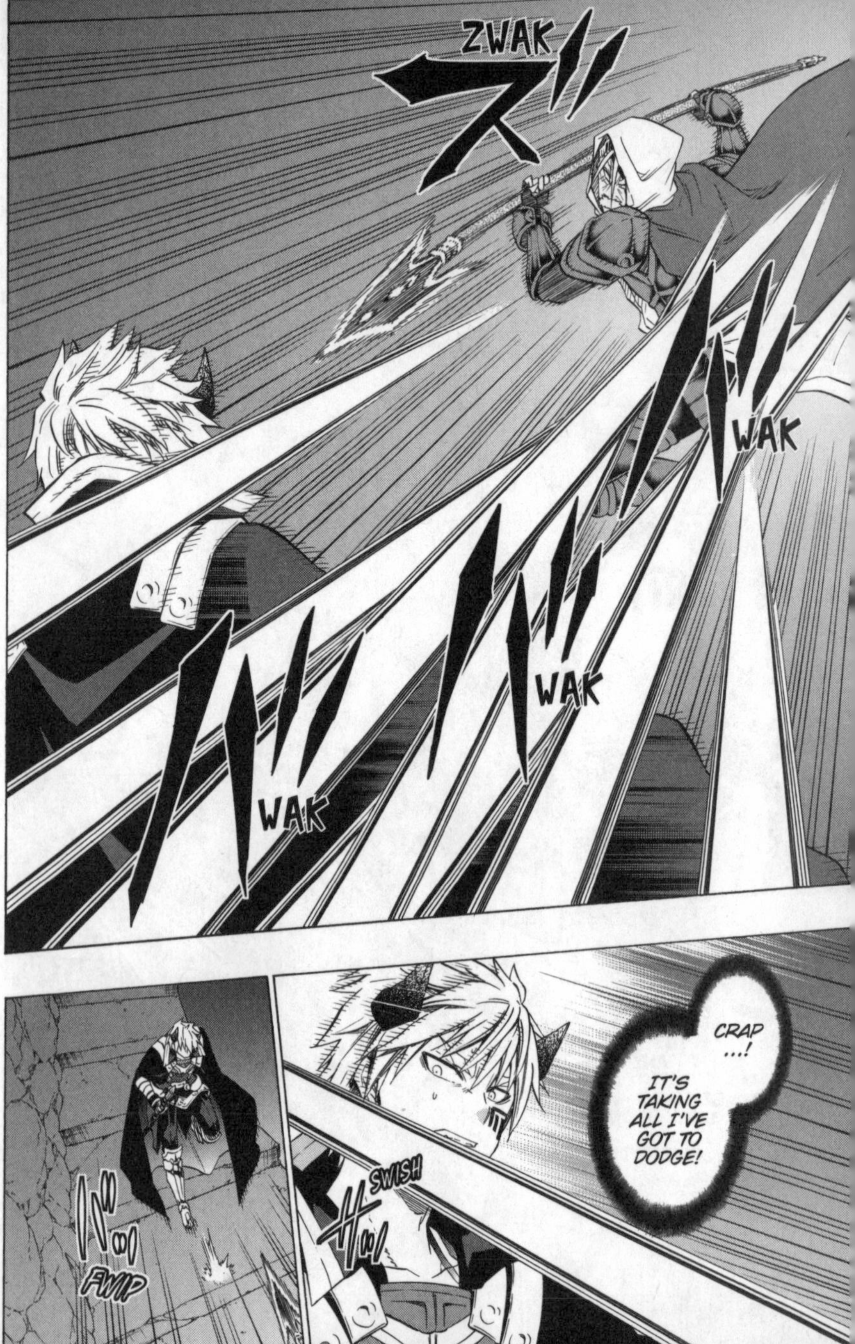
ZWAK
WAK
WAK
WAK
CRAP ...!
IT'S TAKING ALL I'VE GOT TO DODGE!
SWISH
FWIP

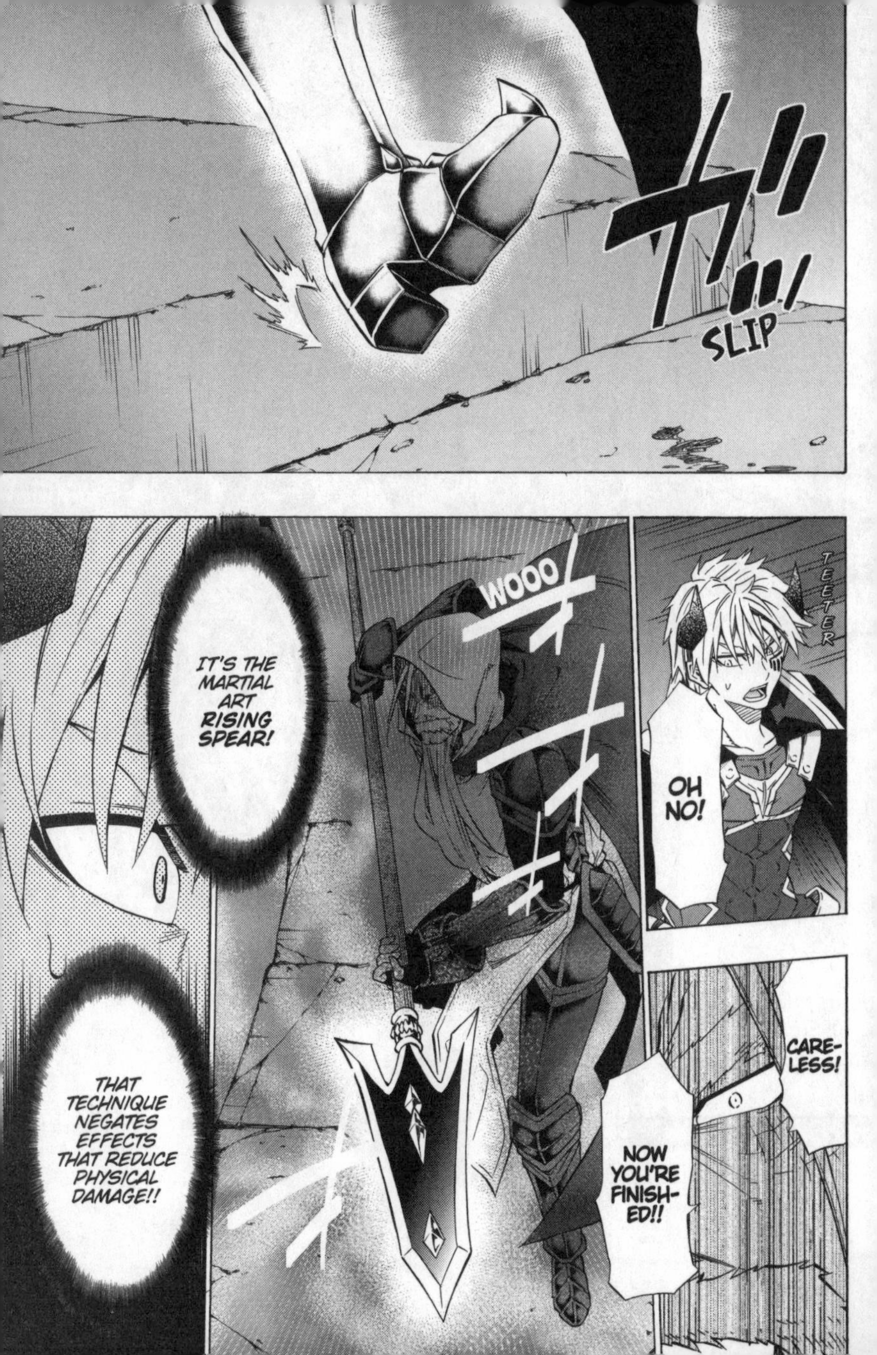
SLIP
TEETER
OH NO!
CARE-LESS!
NOW YOU'RE FINISH-ED!!
WOOO
IT'S THE MARTIAL ART RISING SPEAR!
THAT TECHNIQUE NEGATES EFFECTS THAT REDUCE PHYSICAL DAMAGE!!

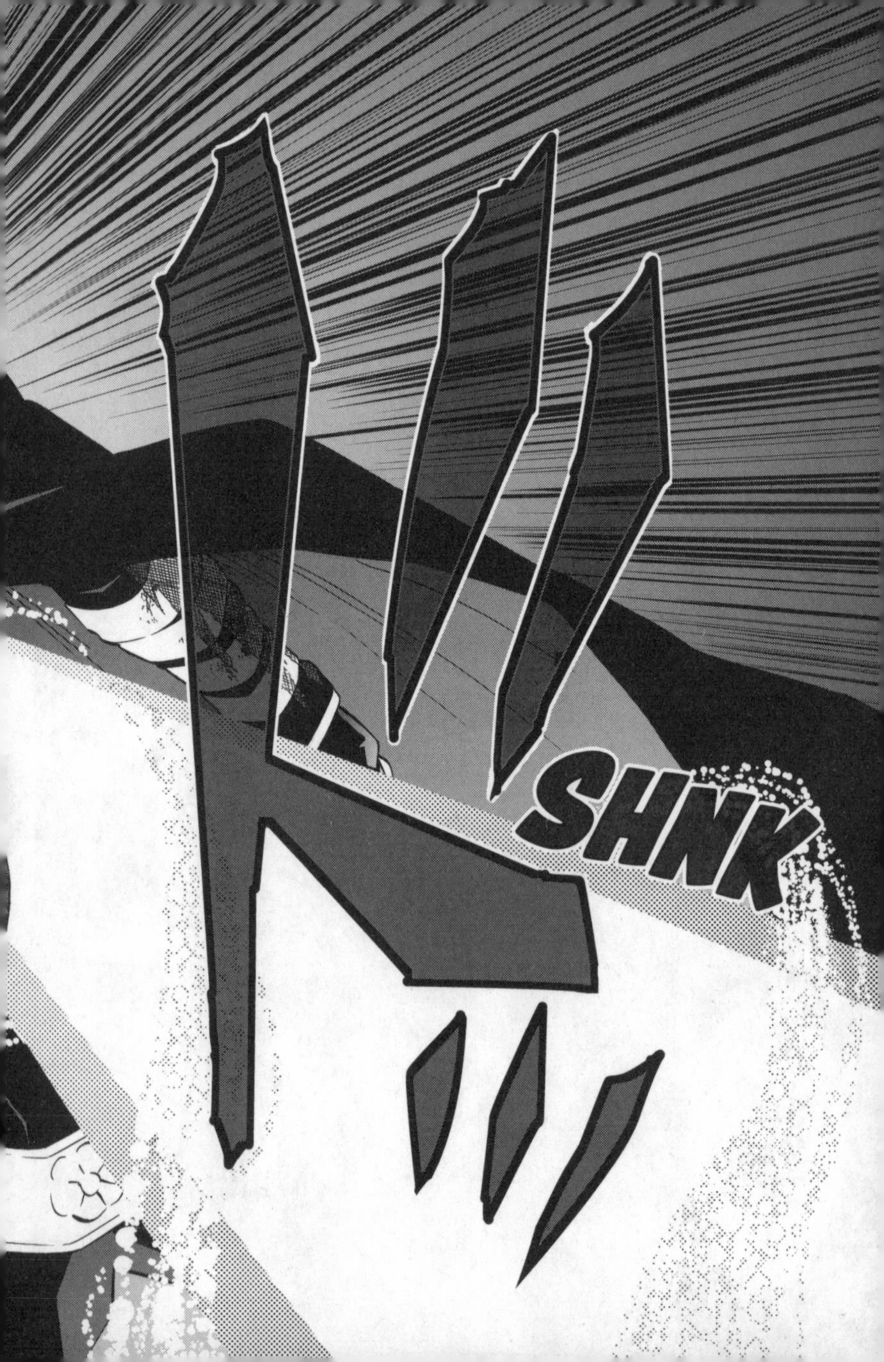
SHNK

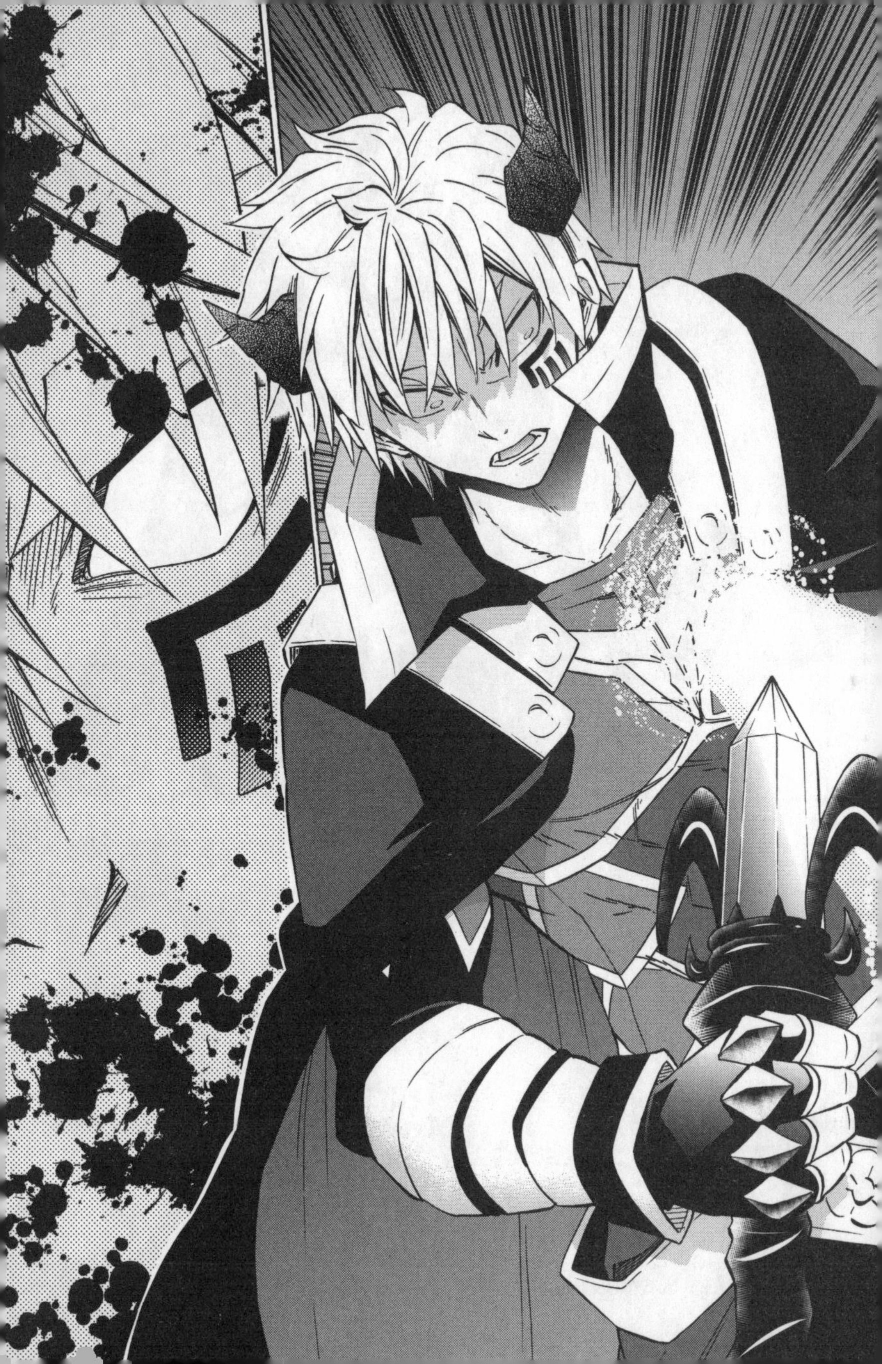

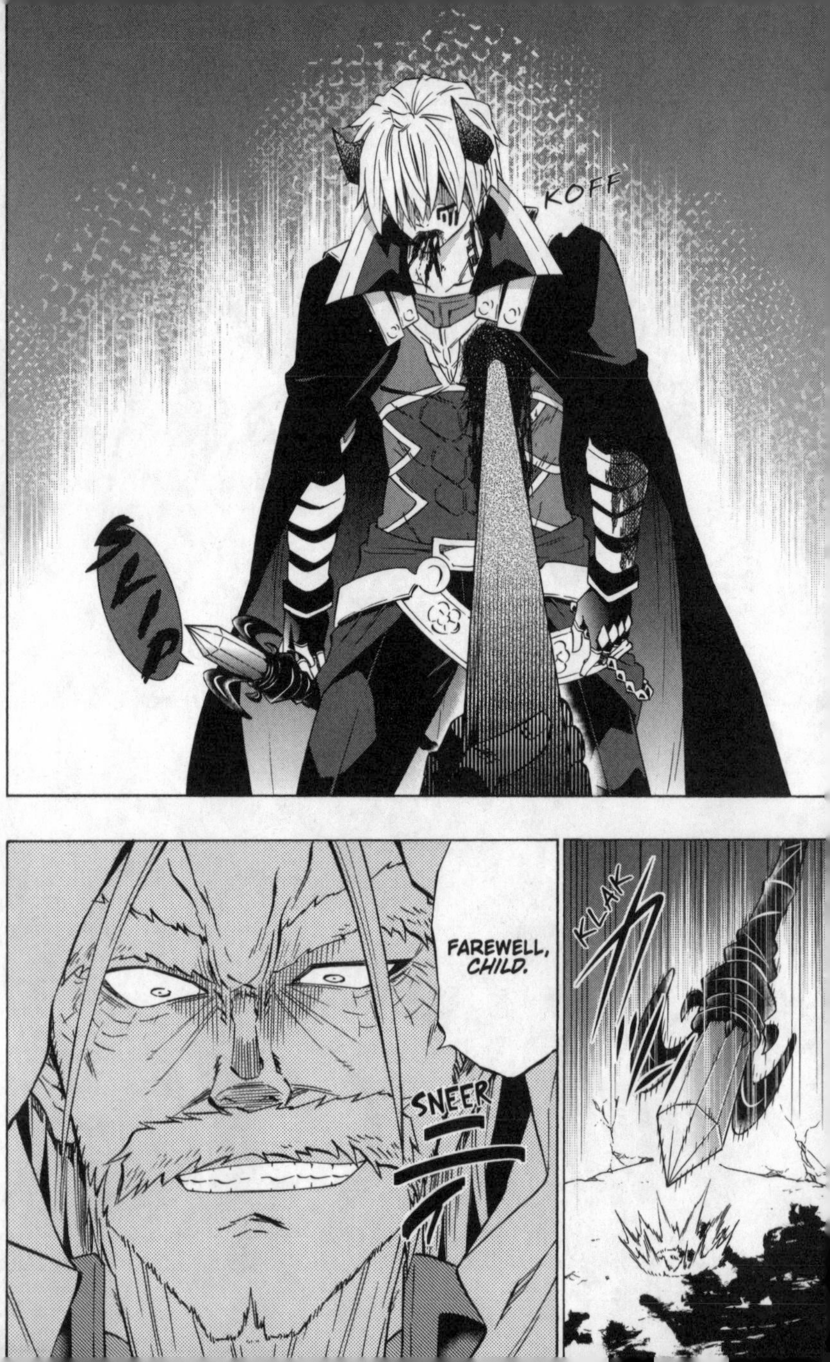
KOFF
SVIP
KLAK
FAREWELL, CHILD.
SNEER

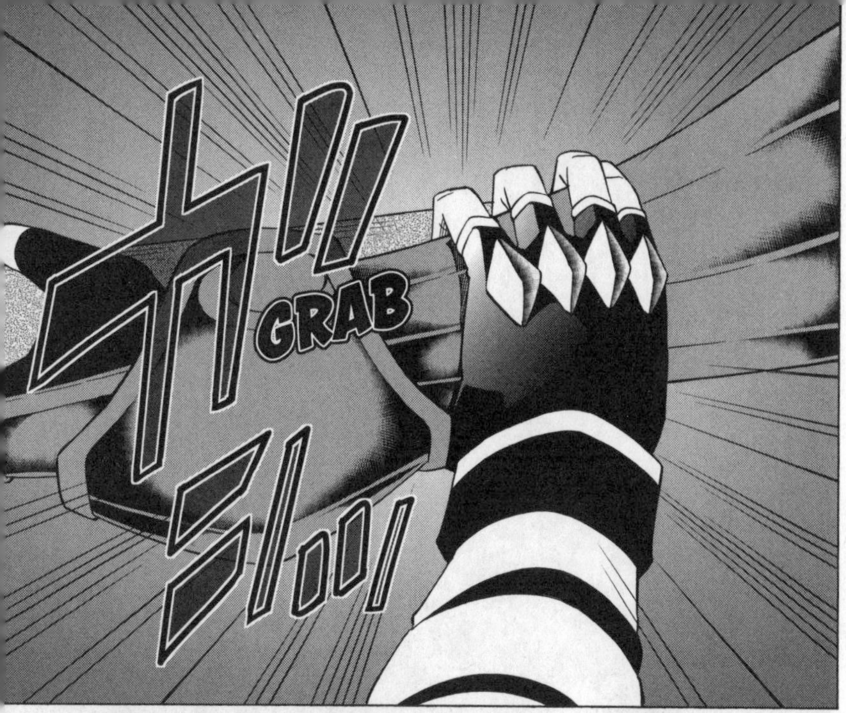
GRAB
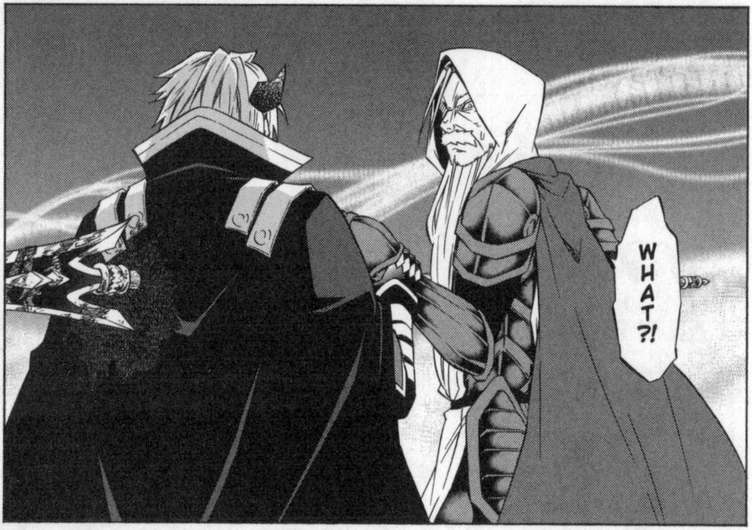
WHAT?!

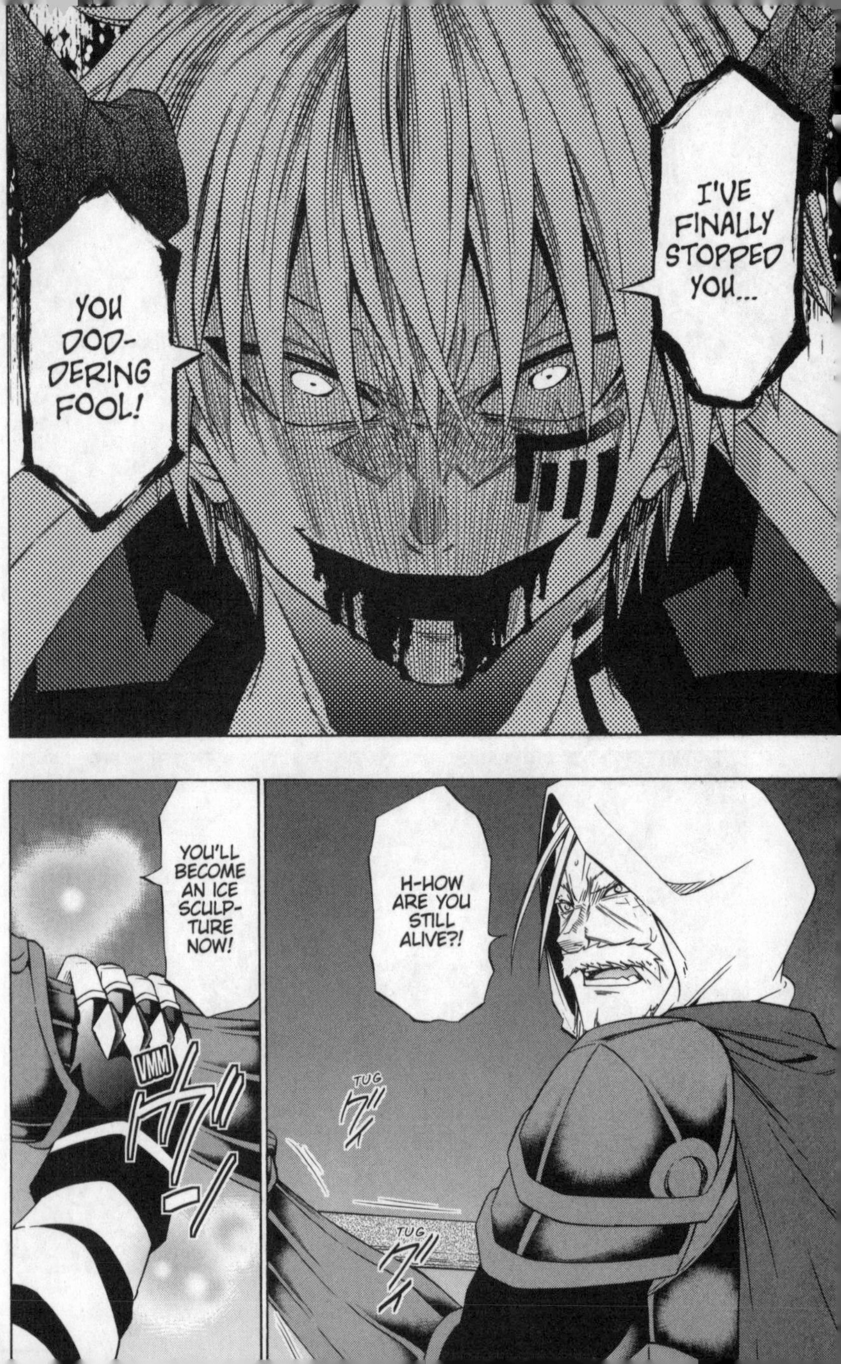
I'VE FINALLY STOPPED YOU...
YOU DOD-DERING FOOL!
H-HOW ARE YOU STILL ALIVE?!
TUG
TUG
YOU'LL BECOME AN ICE SCULP-TURE NOW!
VMM

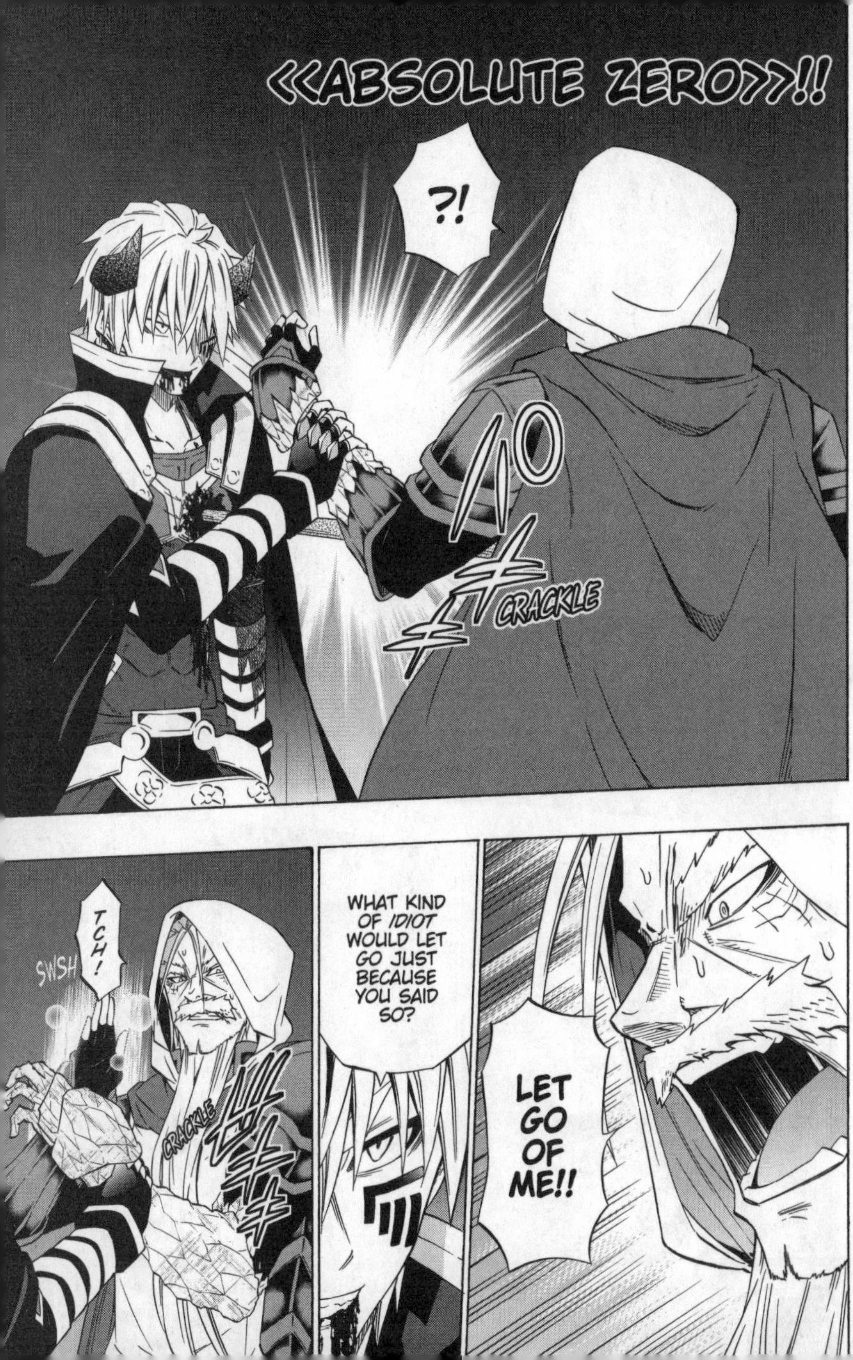
<<ABSOLUTE ZERO>>?!!
?!
CRACKLE
LET GO OF ME!!
WHAT KIND OF *IDIOT* WOULD LET GO JUST BECAUSE YOU SAID SO?
TCH!
SWSH
CRACKLE

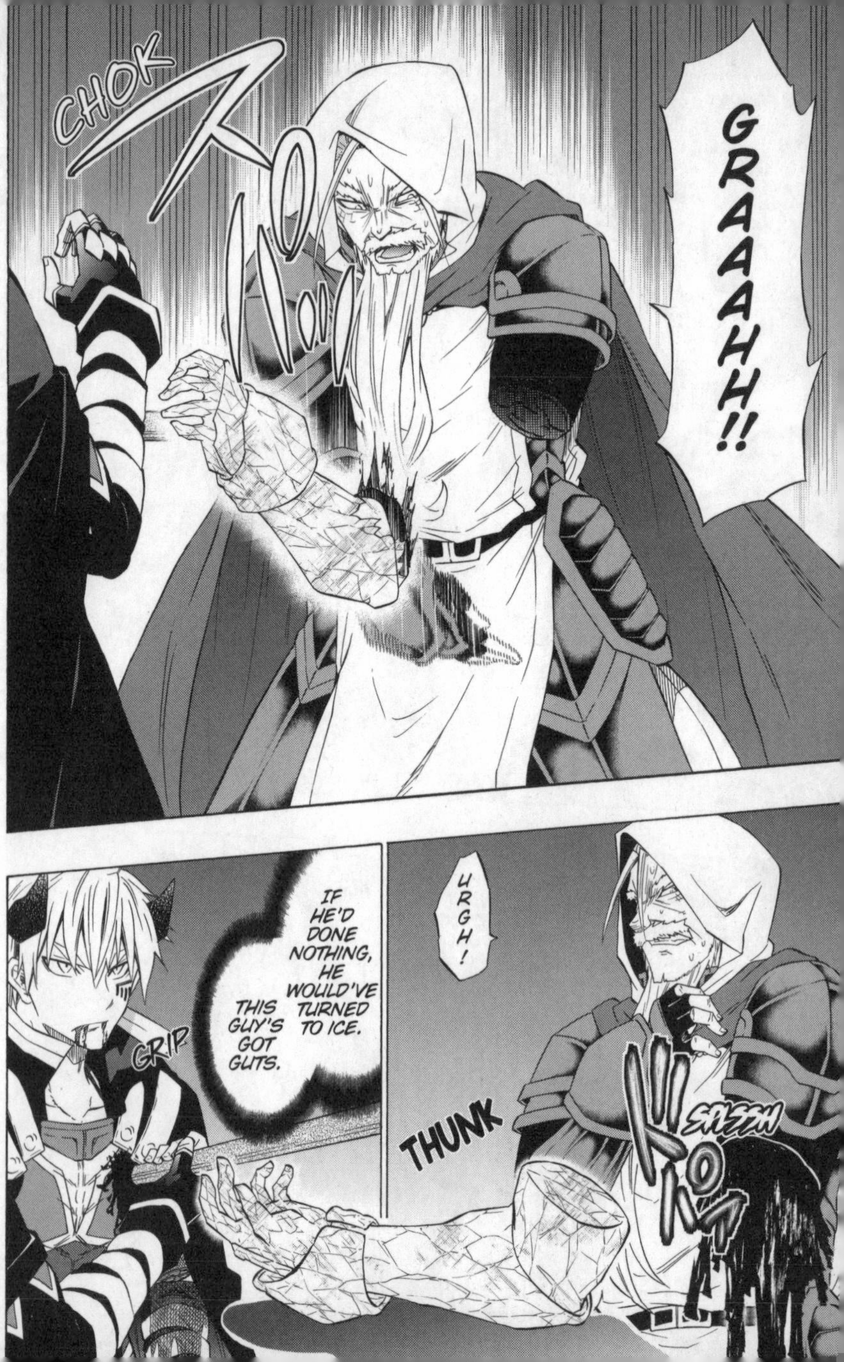
CHOK
GRAAAAHH!!
URGH!
THUNK
IF HE'D DONE NOTHING, HE WOULD'VE TURNED TO ICE.
THIS GUY'S GOT GUTS.
GRIP

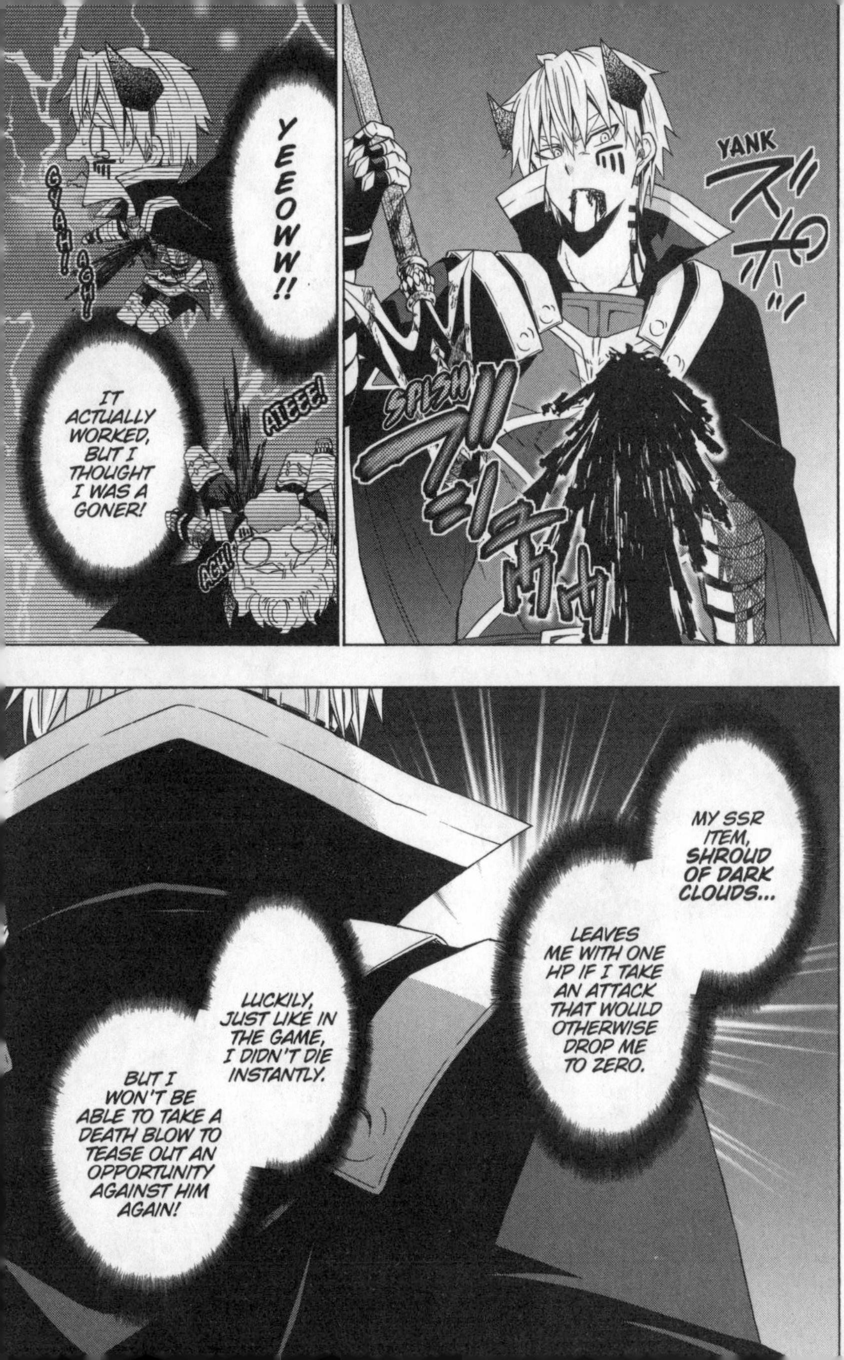
YANK
SPLISH
YEEOWW!!
GYAAH! AGH!
AIEEE!
IT ACTUALLY WORKED, BUT I THOUGHT I WAS A GONER!
ACH!
MY SSR ITEM, SHROUD OF DARK CLOUDS...
LEAVES ME WITH ONE HP IF I TAKE AN ATTACK THAT WOULD OTHERWISE DROP ME TO ZERO.
LUCKILY, JUST LIKE IN THE GAME, I DIDN'T DIE INSTANTLY.
BUT I WON'T BE ABLE TO TAKE A DEATH BLOW TO TEASE OUT AN OPPORTUNITY AGAINST HIM AGAIN!

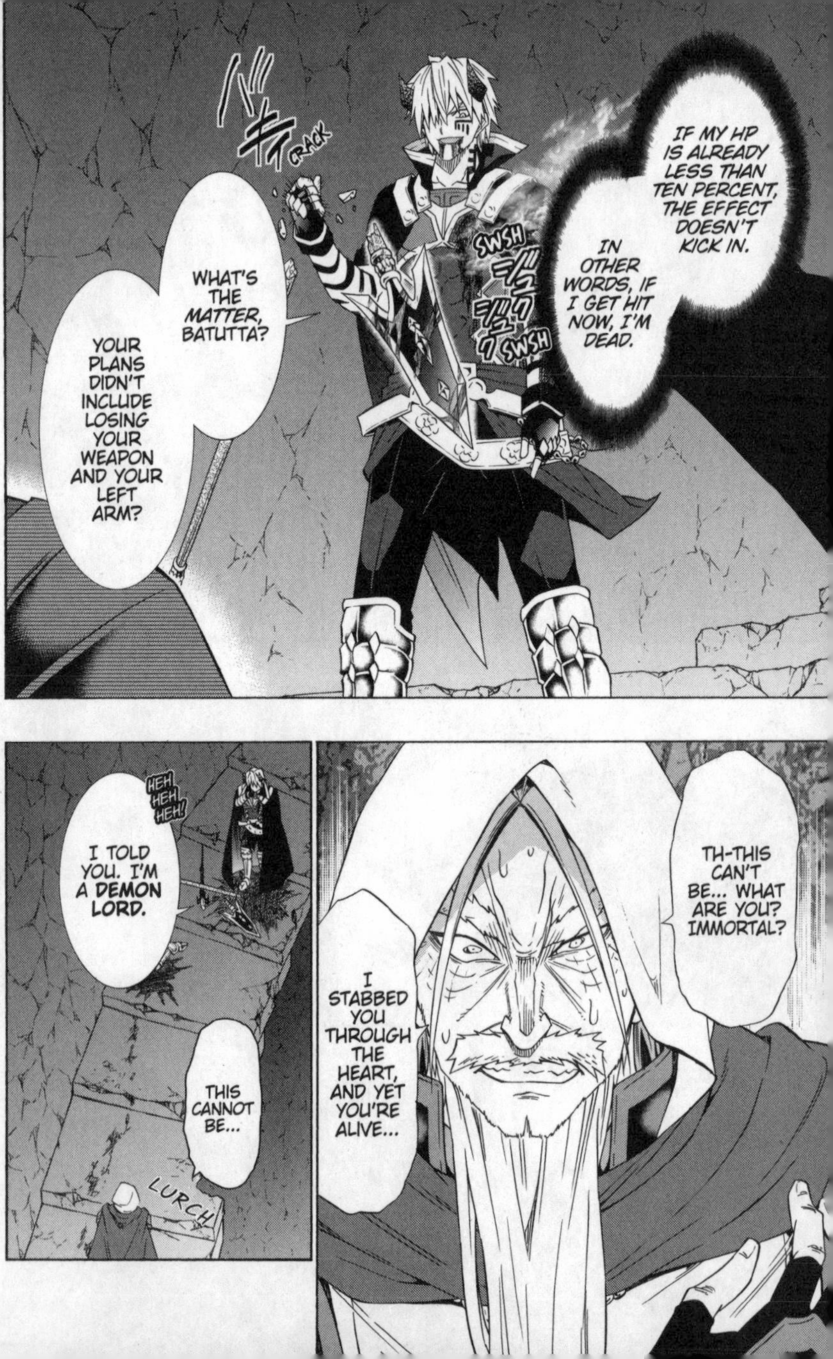
IF MY HP IS ALREADY LESS THAN TEN PERCENT, THE EFFECT DOESN'T KICK IN.
IN OTHER WORDS, IF I GET HIT NOW, I'M DEAD.
SWSH
SWSH
CRACK
WHAT'S THE MATTER, BATUTTA?
YOUR PLANS DIDN'T INCLUDE LOSING YOUR WEAPON AND YOUR LEFT ARM?
TH-THIS CAN'T BE... WHAT ARE YOU? IMMORTAL?
I STABBED YOU THROUGH THE HEART, AND YET YOU'RE ALIVE...
HEH HEH HEH!
I TOLD YOU. I'M A DEMON LORD.
THIS CANNOT BE...
LURCH

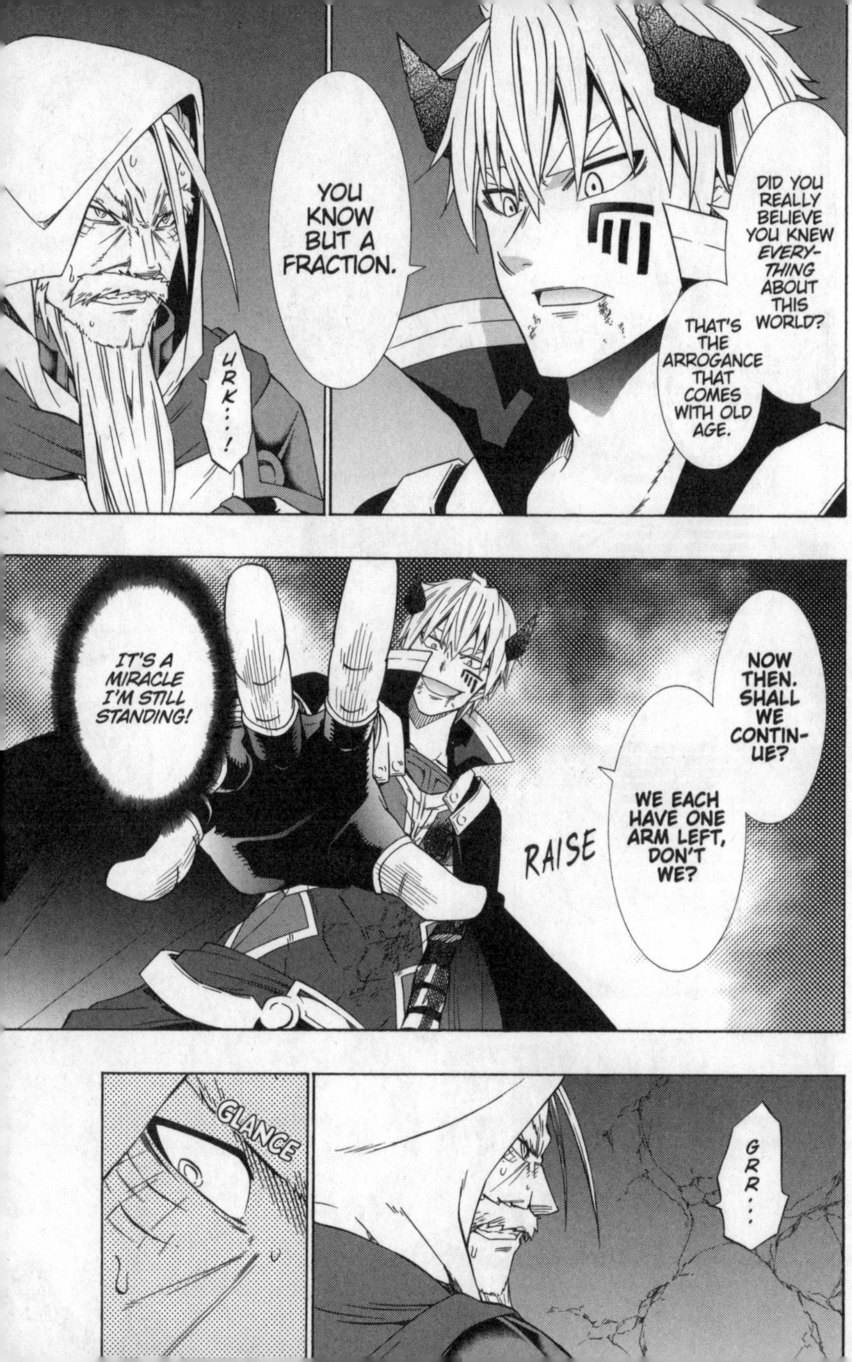
DID YOU REALLY BELIEVE YOU KNEW *EVERYTHING* ABOUT THIS WORLD?
THAT'S THE ARROGANCE THAT COMES WITH OLD AGE.
YOU KNOW BUT A FRACTION.
URK...!
NOW THEN. SHALL WE CONTINUE?
WE EACH HAVE ONE ARM LEFT, DON'T WE?
RAISE
IT'S A MIRACLE I'M STILL STANDING!
GRR...
GLANCE

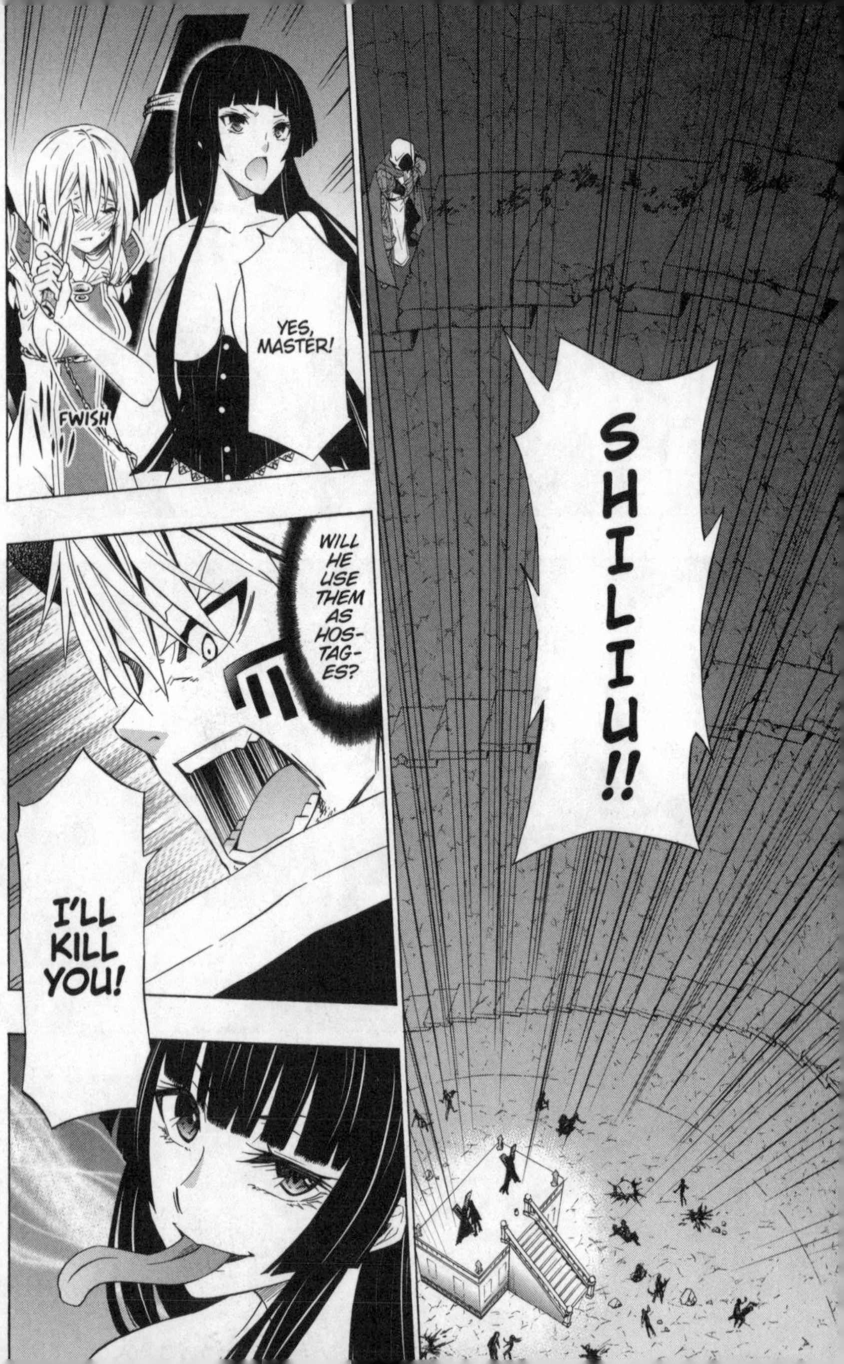
SHILIU!!
YES, MASTER!
FWISH
WILL HE USE THEM AS HOS-TAG-ES?
I'LL KILL YOU!

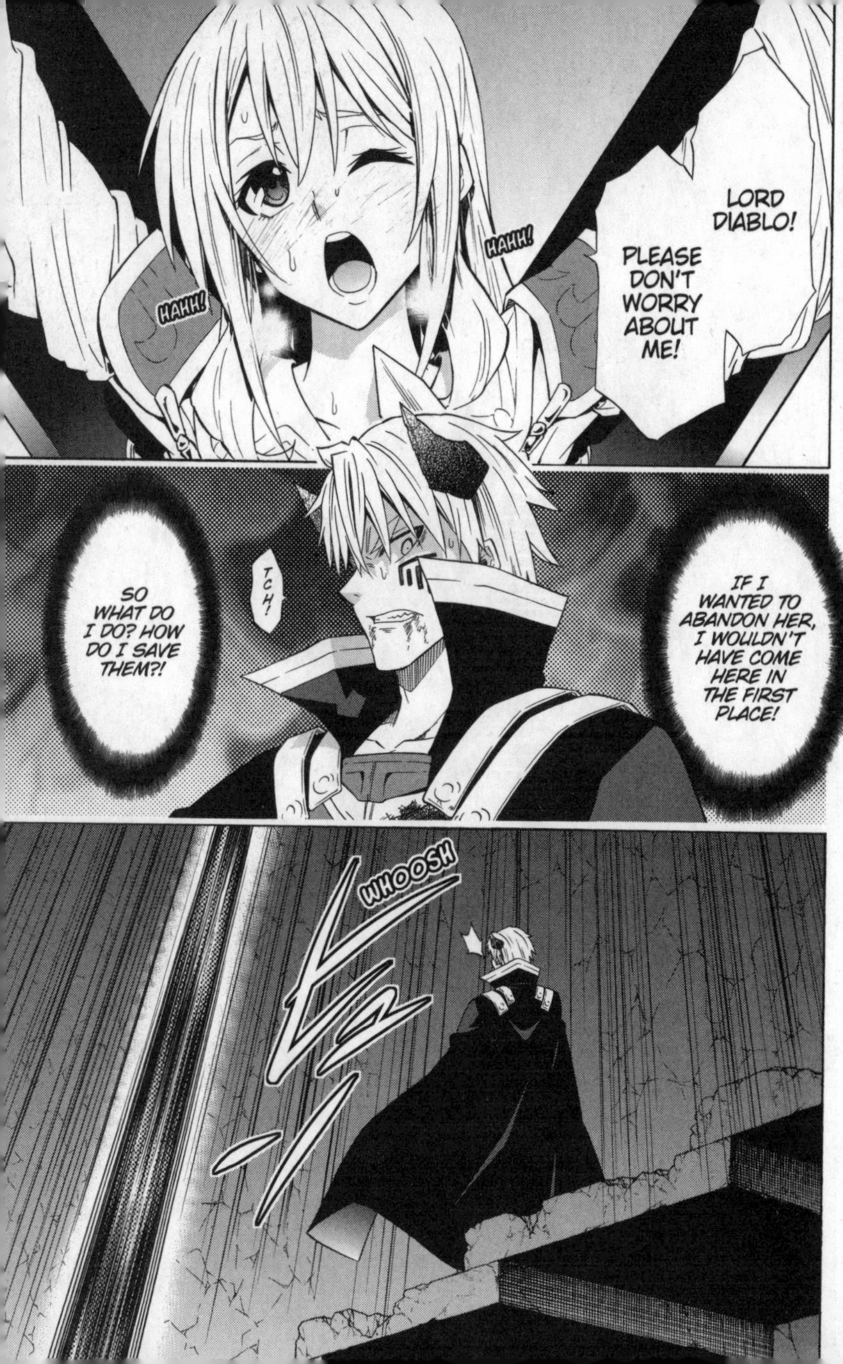
LORD DIABLO!
PLEASE DON'T WORRY ABOUT ME!
HAHH!
HAHH!
IF I WANTED TO ABANDON HER, I WOULDN'T HAVE COME HERE IN THE FIRST PLACE!
TCH!
SO WHAT DO I DO? HOW DO I SAVE THEM?!
WHOOSH

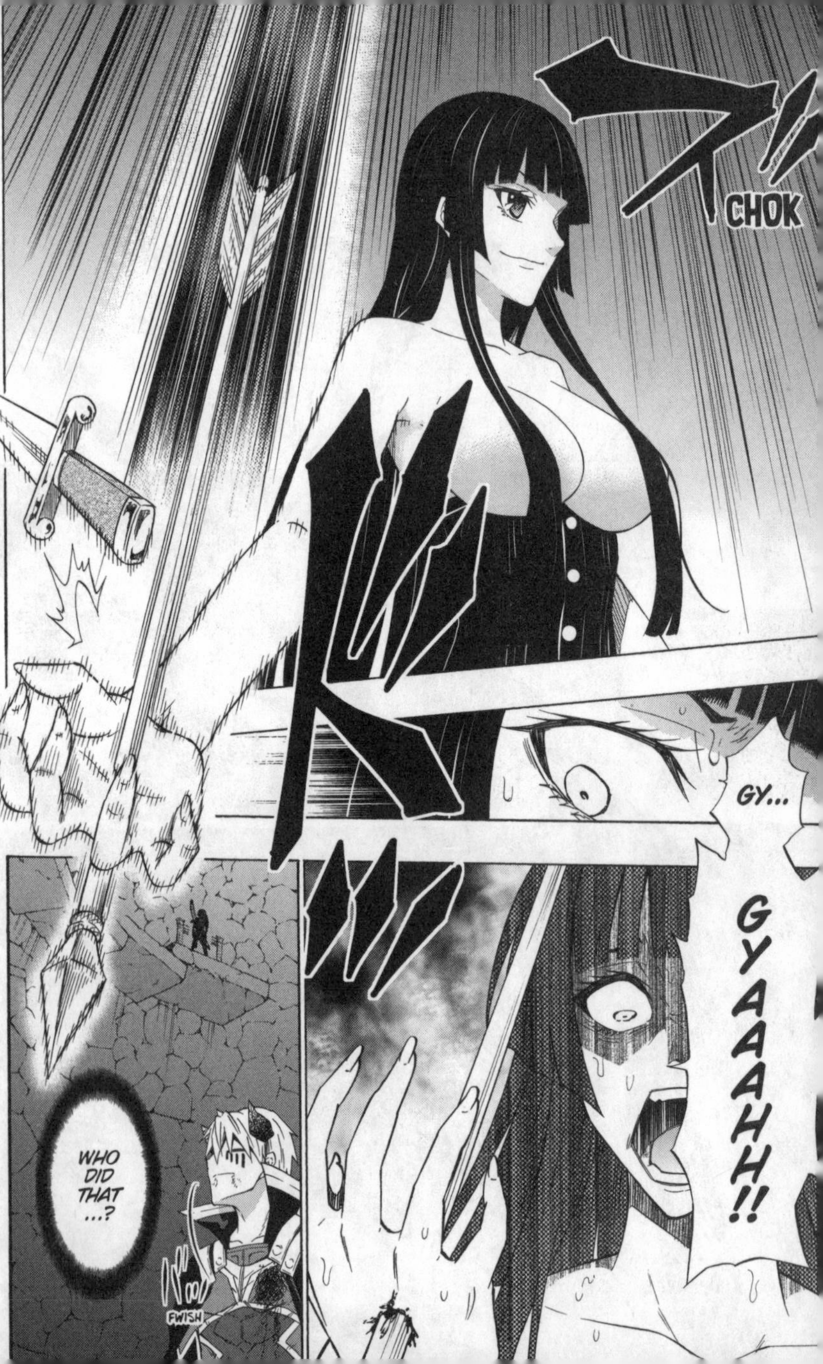

CHOK
GY...
GYAAAAHH!!
WHO DID THAT ...?
FWISH

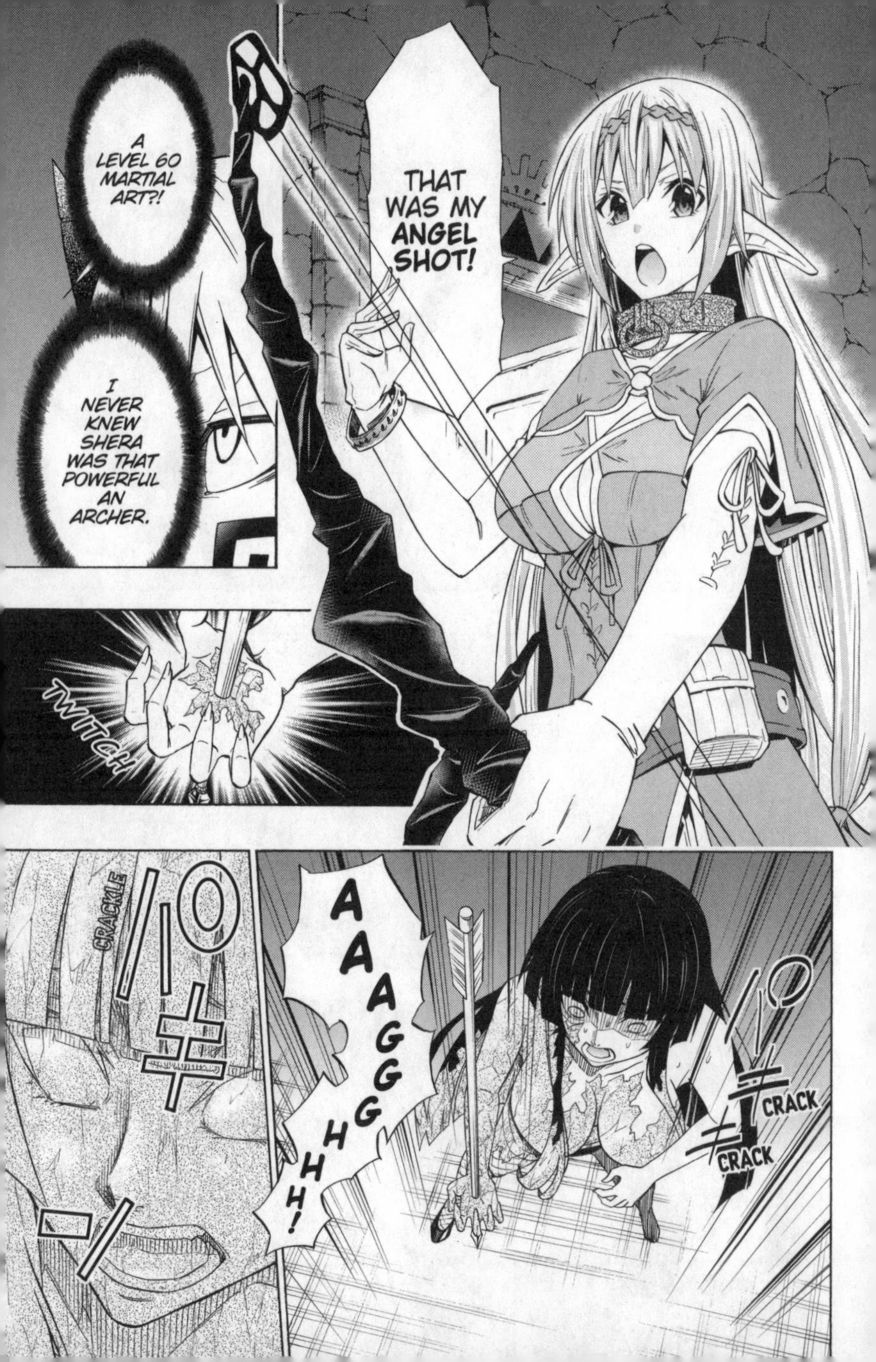
THAT WAS MY ANGEL SHOT!
A LEVEL 60 MARTIAL ART?!
I NEVER KNEW SHERA WAS THAT POWERFUL AN ARCHER.
TWITCH
AAAGGGHHH!
CRACK
CRACK
CRACKLE

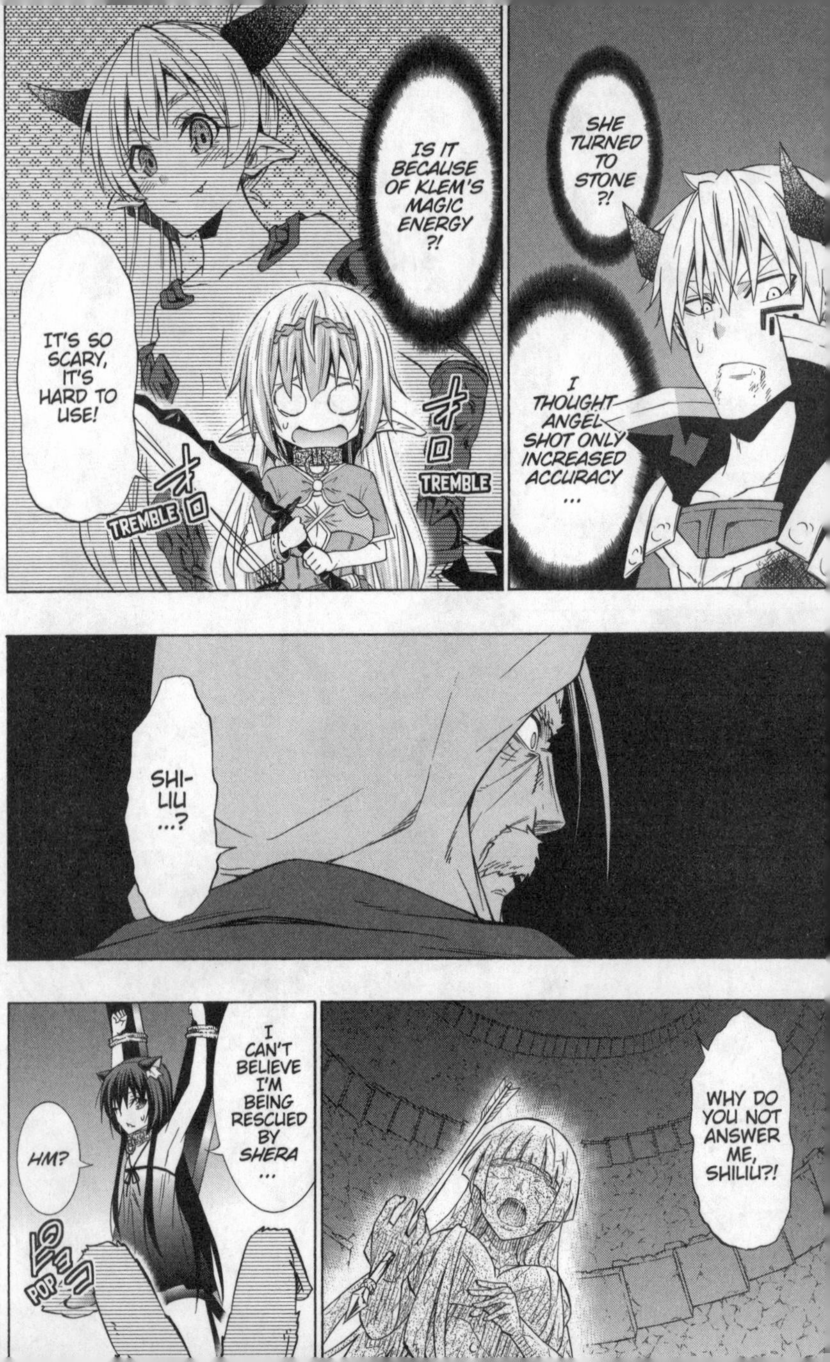
SHE TURNED TO STONE?!
I THOUGHT ANGEL SHOT ONLY INCREASED ACCURACY...
IS IT BECAUSE OF KLEM'S MAGIC ENERGY?!
TREMBLE
IT'S SO SCARY, IT'S HARD TO USE!
TREMBLE
SHI-LIU...?
WHY DO YOU NOT ANSWER ME, SHILIU?!
I CAN'T BELIEVE I'M BEING RESCUED BY SHERA...
HM?
POP

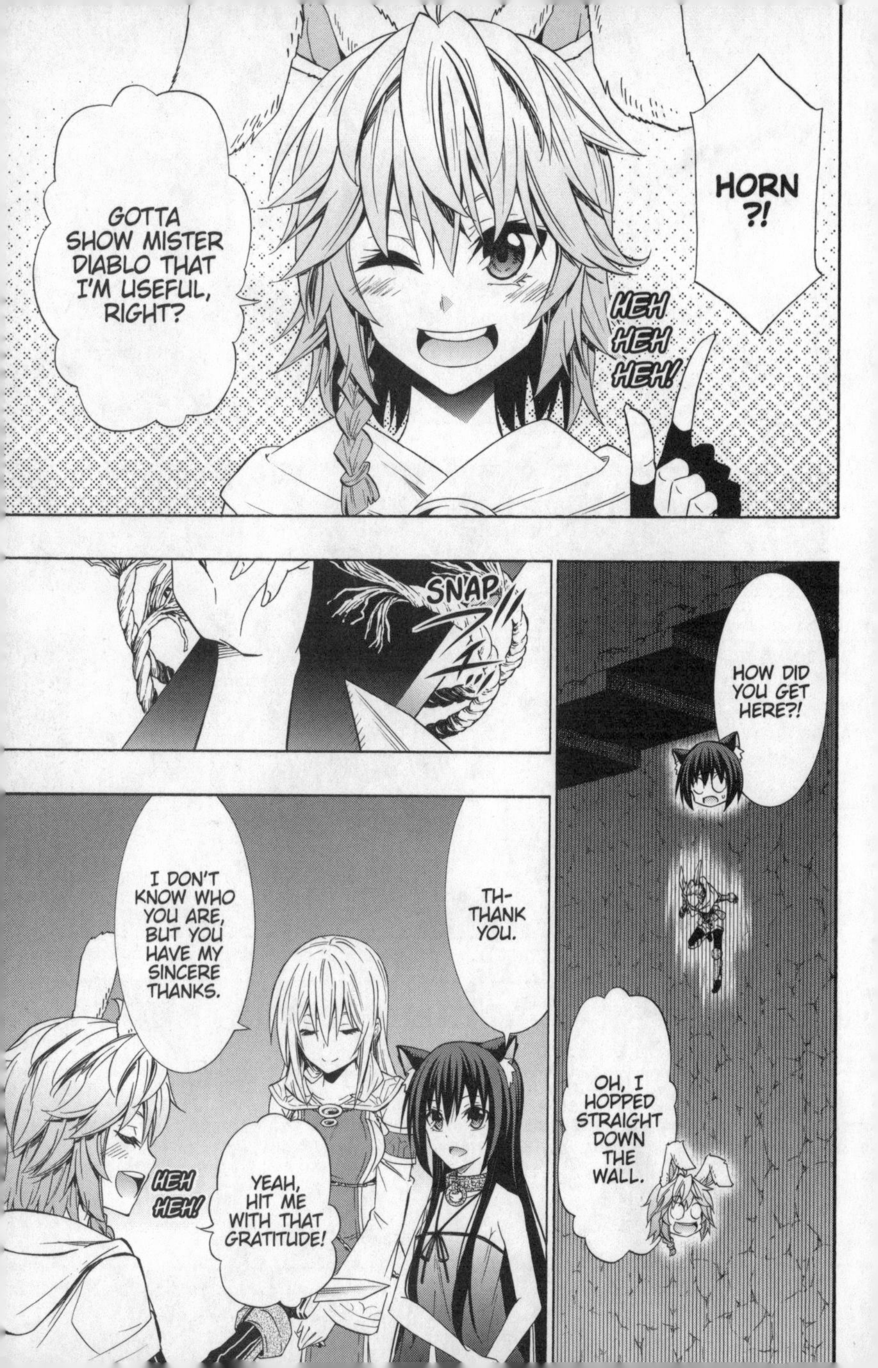
HORN ?!
HEH HEH HEH!
GOTTA SHOW MISTER DIABLO THAT I'M USEFUL, RIGHT?
HOW DID YOU GET HERE?!
OH, I HOPPED STRAIGHT DOWN THE WALL.
SNAP
TH- THANK YOU.
I DON'T KNOW WHO YOU ARE, BUT YOU HAVE MY SINCERE THANKS.
YEAH, HIT ME WITH THAT GRATITUDE!
HEH HEH!

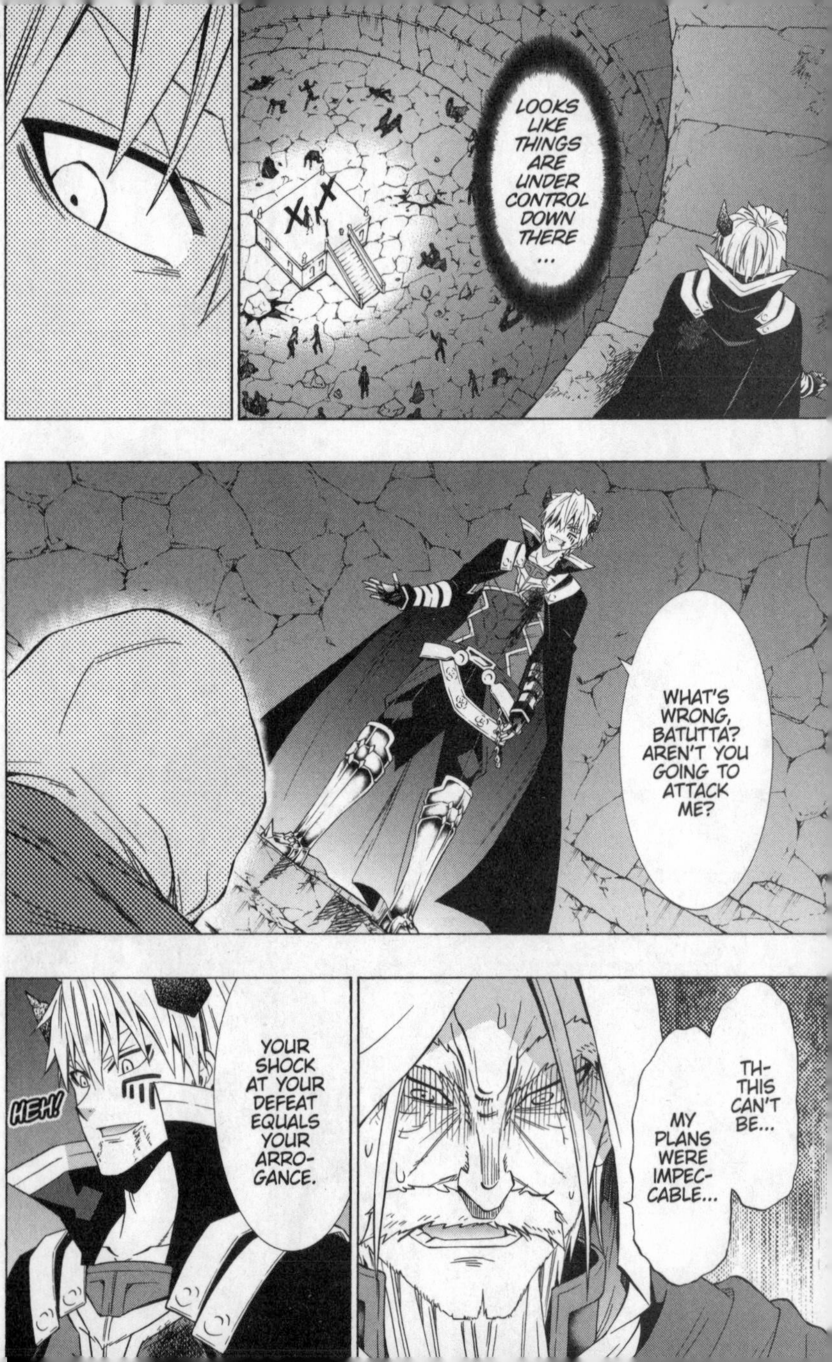
LOOKS LIKE THINGS ARE UNDER CONTROL DOWN THERE ...
WHAT'S WRONG, BATUTTA? AREN'T YOU GOING TO ATTACK ME?
TH-THIS CAN'T BE...
MY PLANS WERE IMPECCABLE...
YOUR SHOCK AT YOUR DEFEAT EQUALS YOUR ARROGANCE.
HEH!

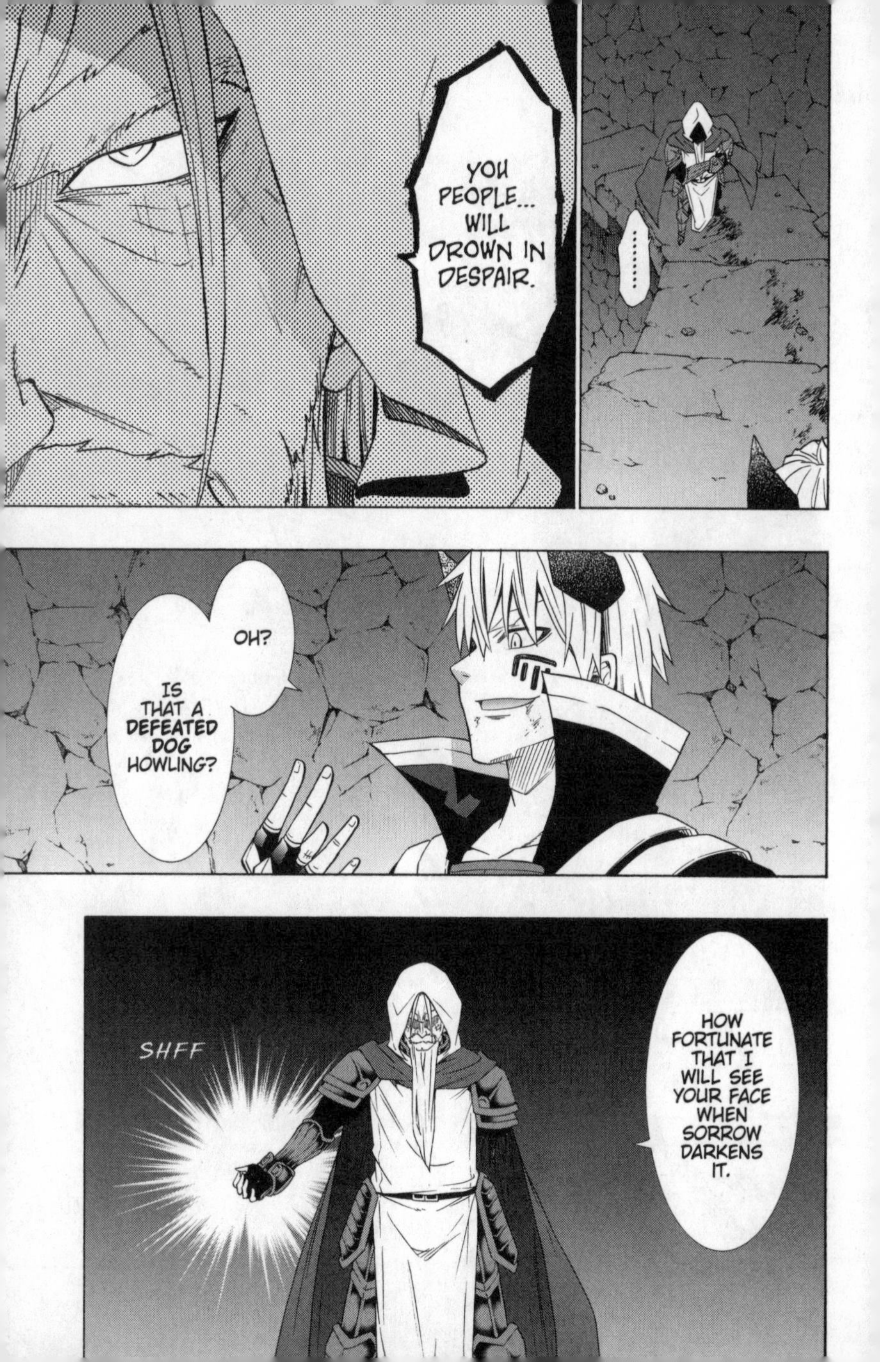
......
YOU PEOPLE... WILL DROWN IN DESPAIR.
OH?
IS THAT A DEFEATED DOG HOWLING?
HOW FORTUNATE THAT I WILL SEE YOUR FACE WHEN SORROW DARKENS IT.
SHFF

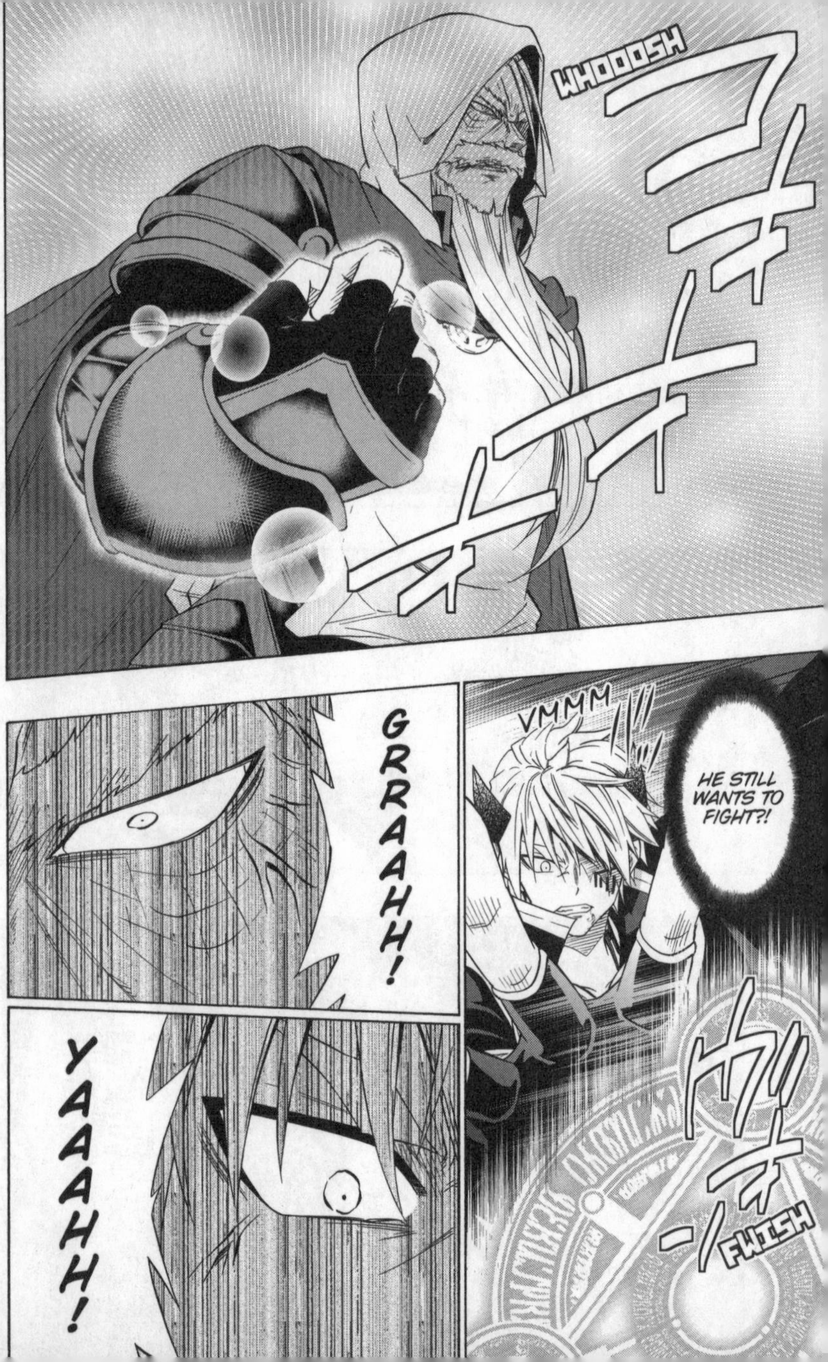
WHOOOSH
VMMM
HE STILL WANTS TO FIGHT?!
FWISH
GRRAAHH!
YAAAAHH!

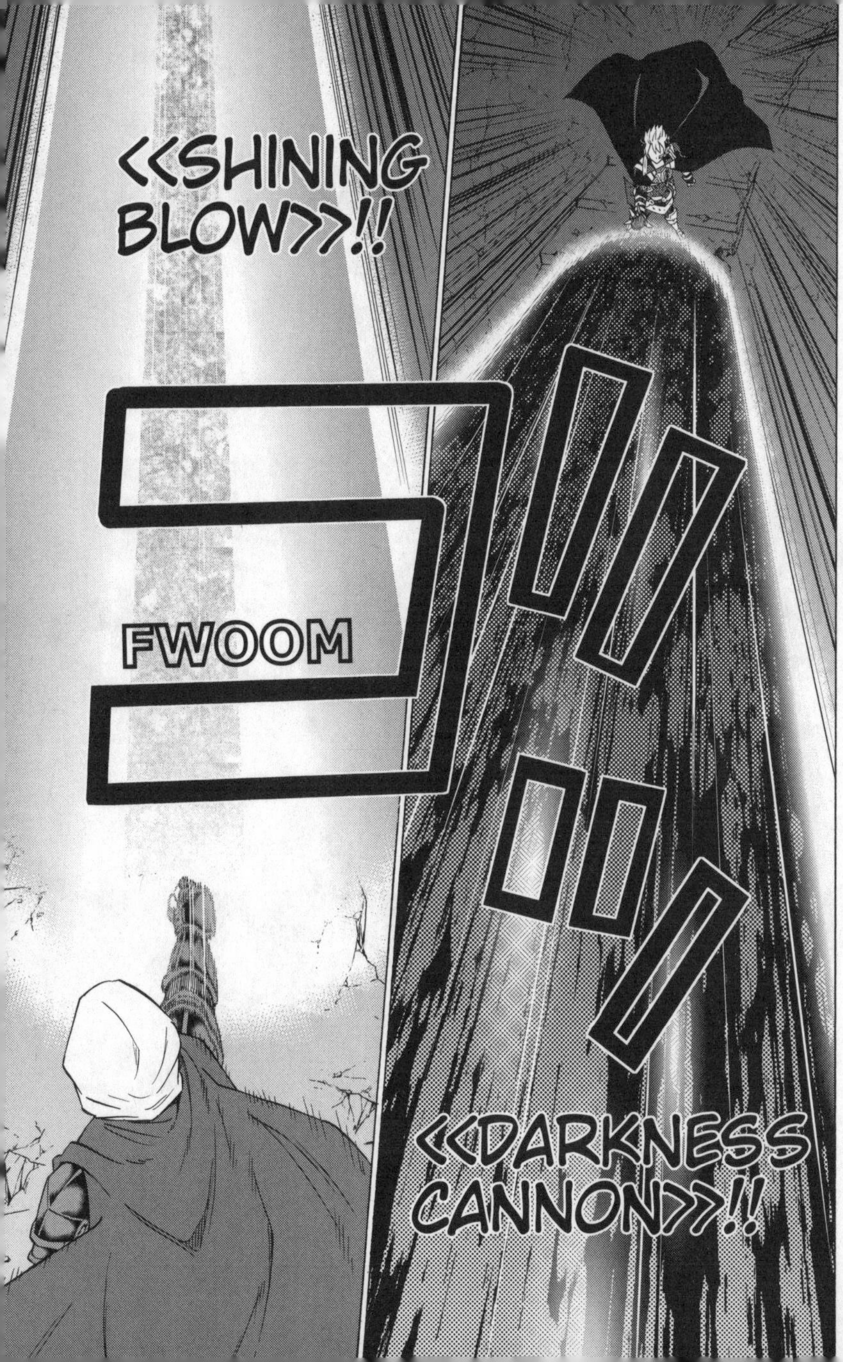
<<DARKNESS CANNON>>!!
<<SHINING BLOW>>!!
FWOOM

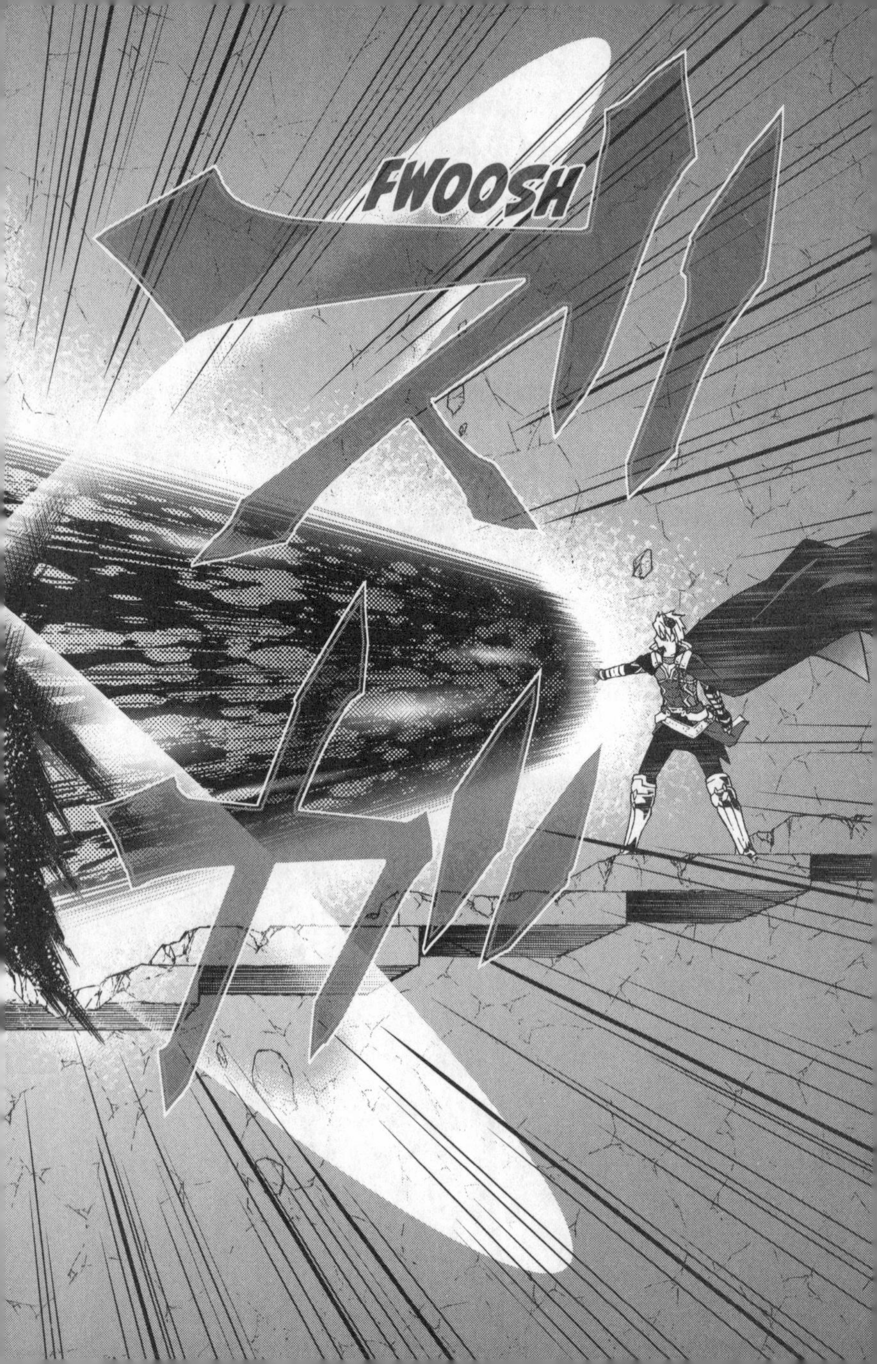
FWOOSH

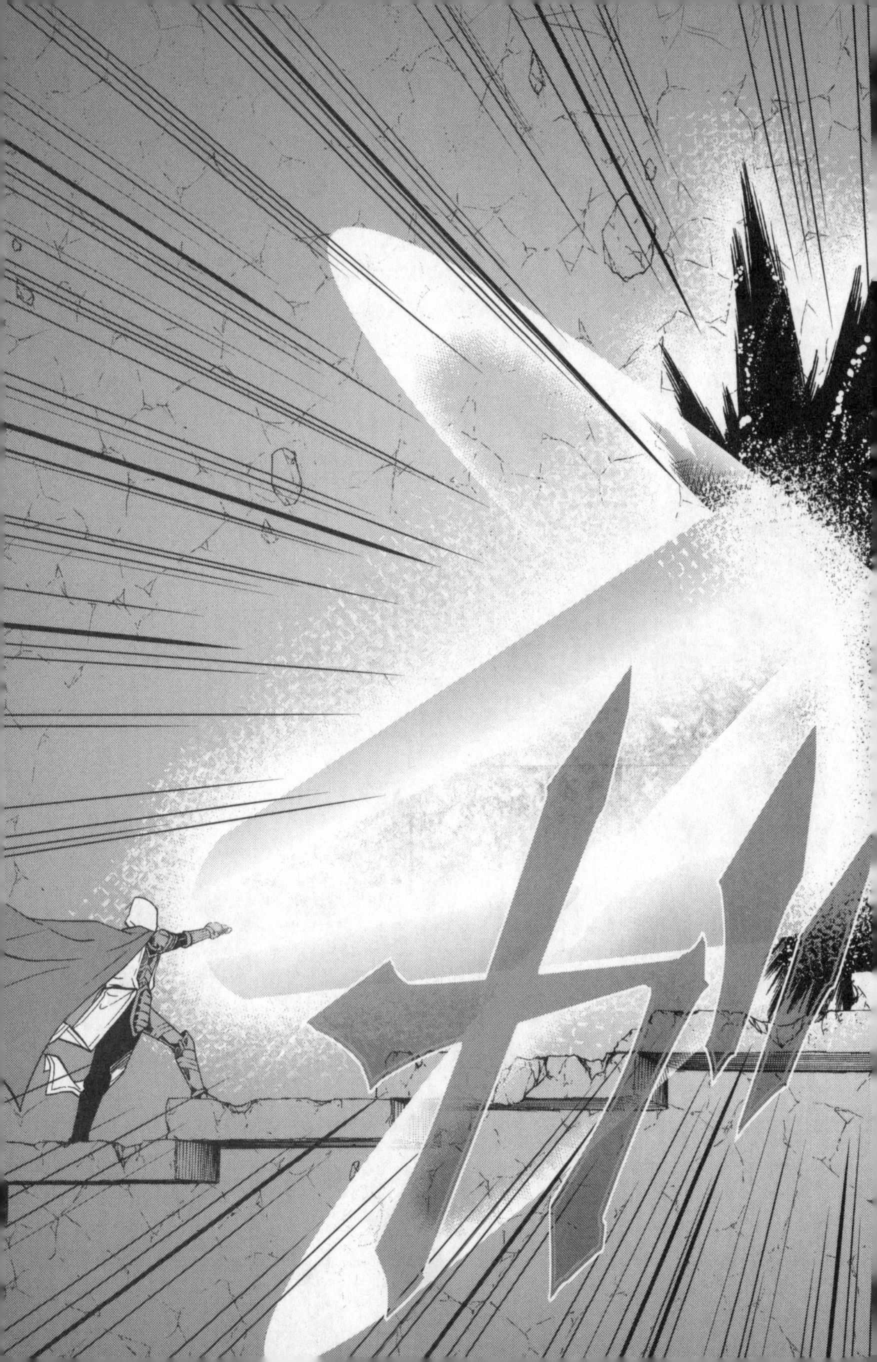

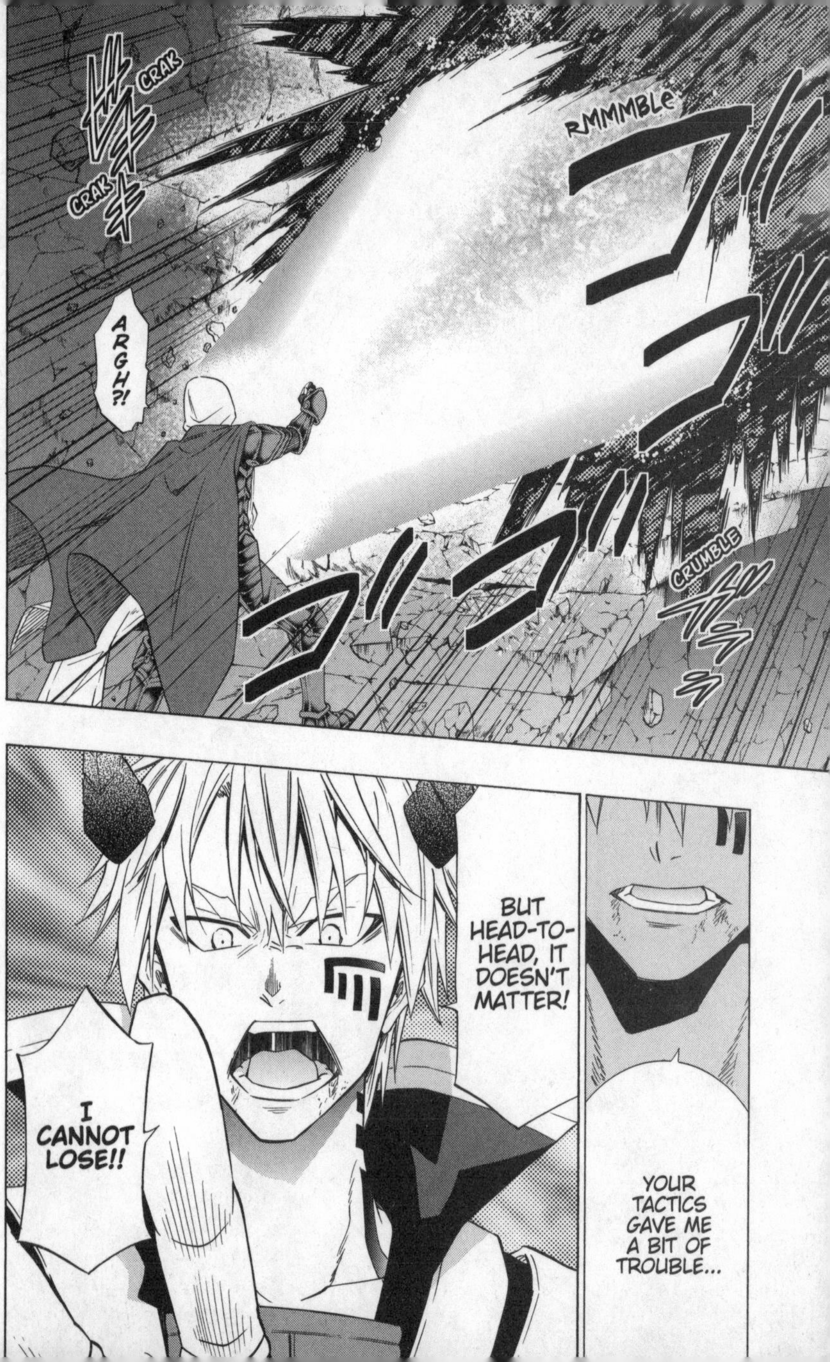
RMMMBLE
CRUMBLE
CRAK
CRAK
ARGH?!
YOUR TACTICS GAVE ME A BIT OF TROUBLE...
BUT HEAD-TO-HEAD, IT DOESN'T MATTER!
I CANNOT LOSE!!

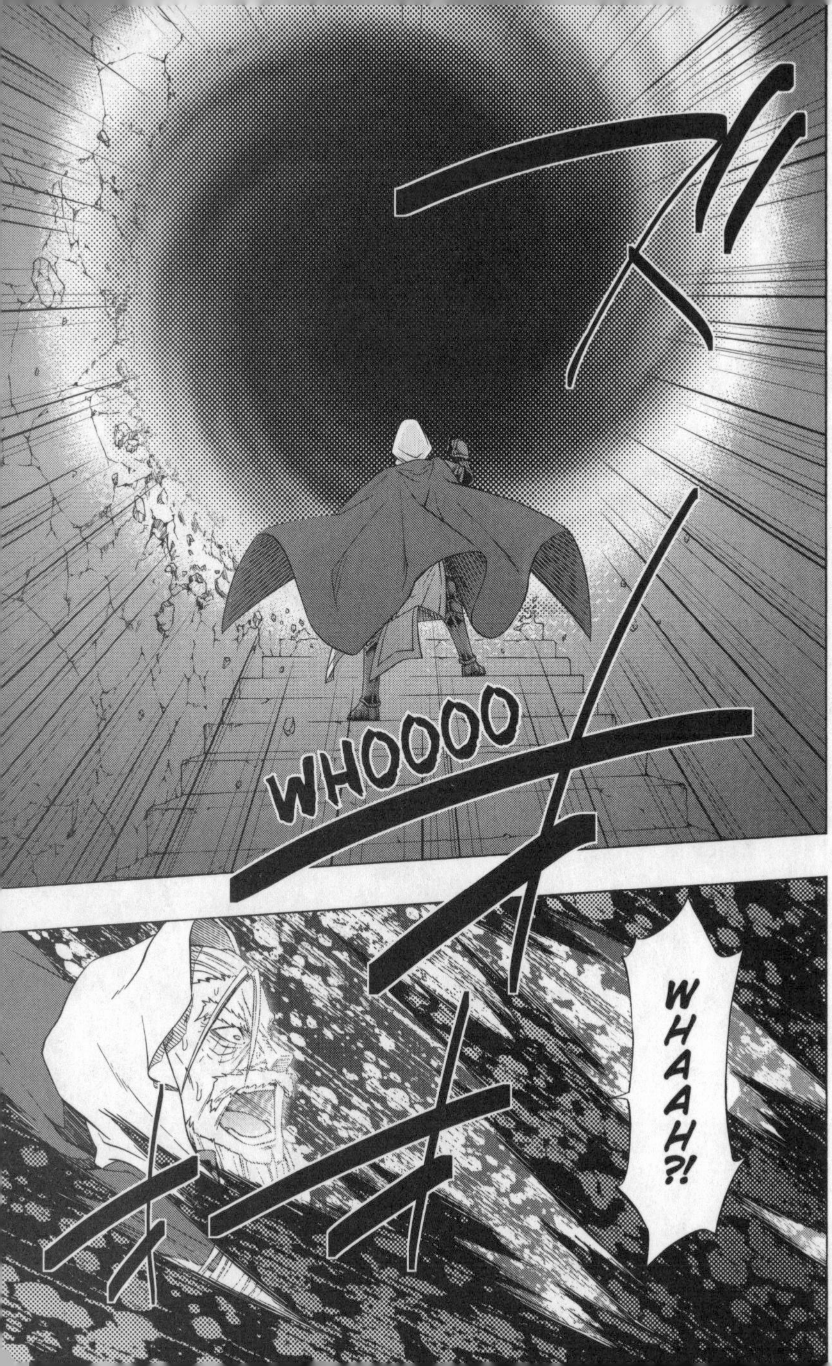
WHOOOO
WHAAAH?!

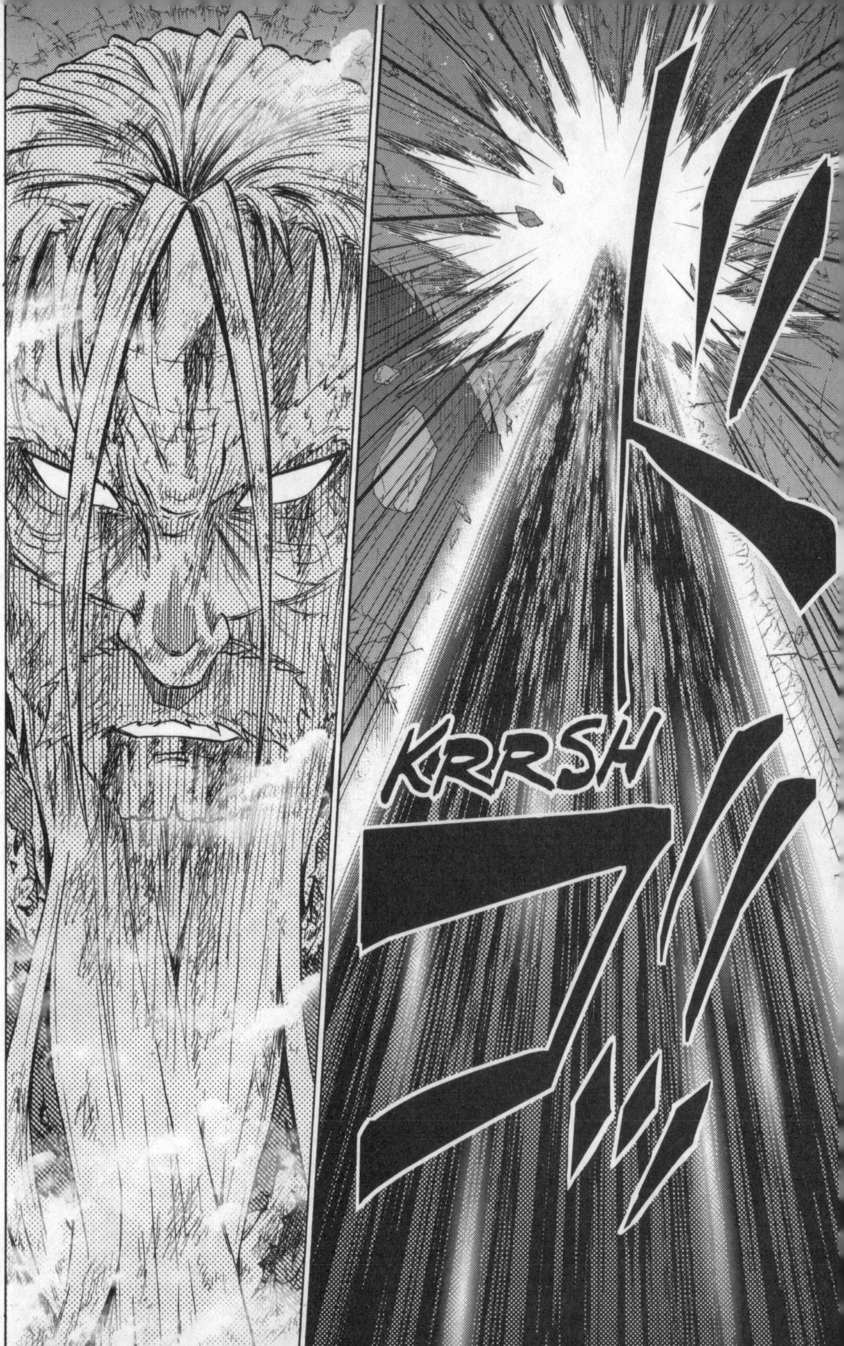
KRRSH

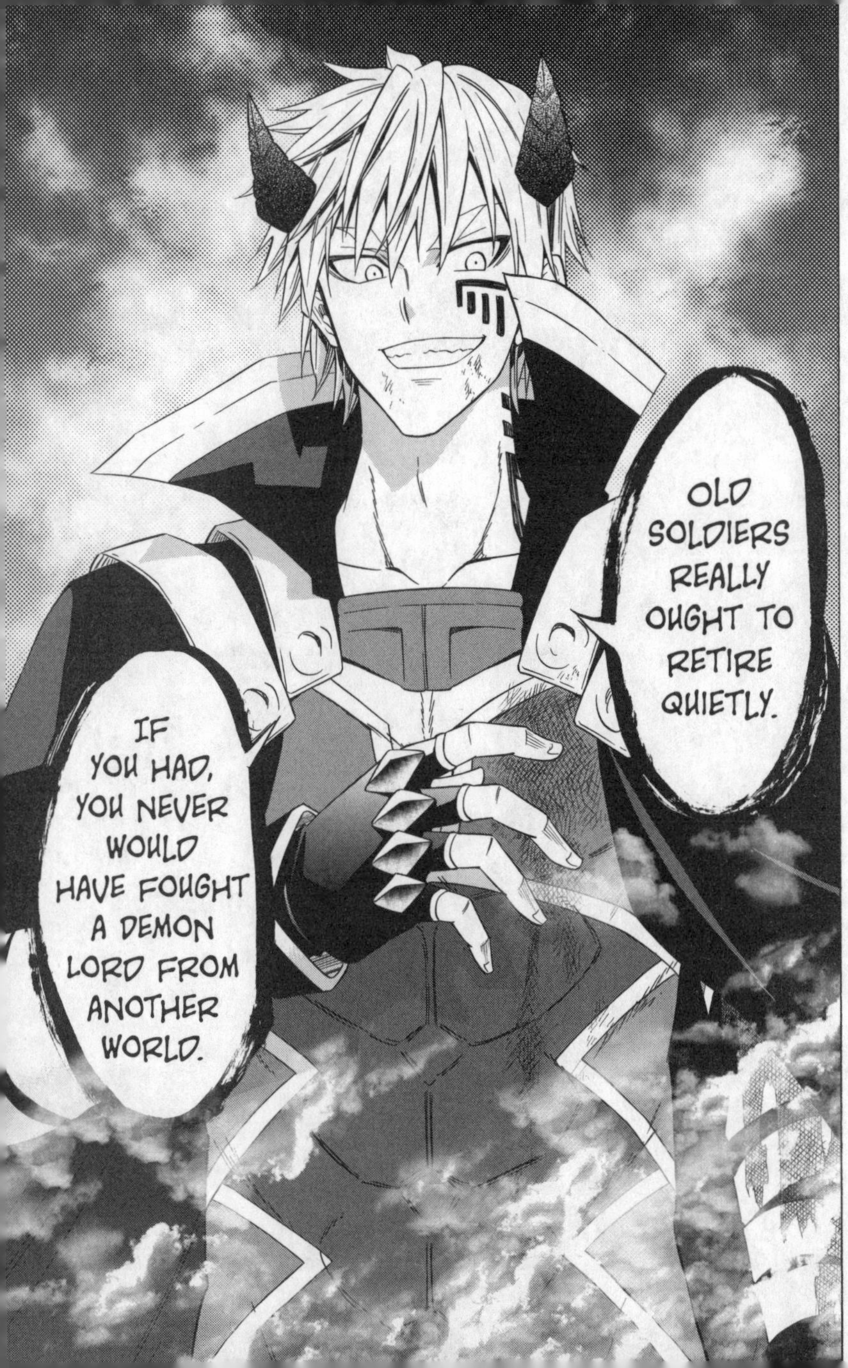
OLD SOLDIERS REALLY OUGHT TO RETIRE QUIETLY.
IF YOU HAD, YOU NEVER WOULD HAVE FOUGHT A DEMON LORD FROM ANOTHER WORLD.

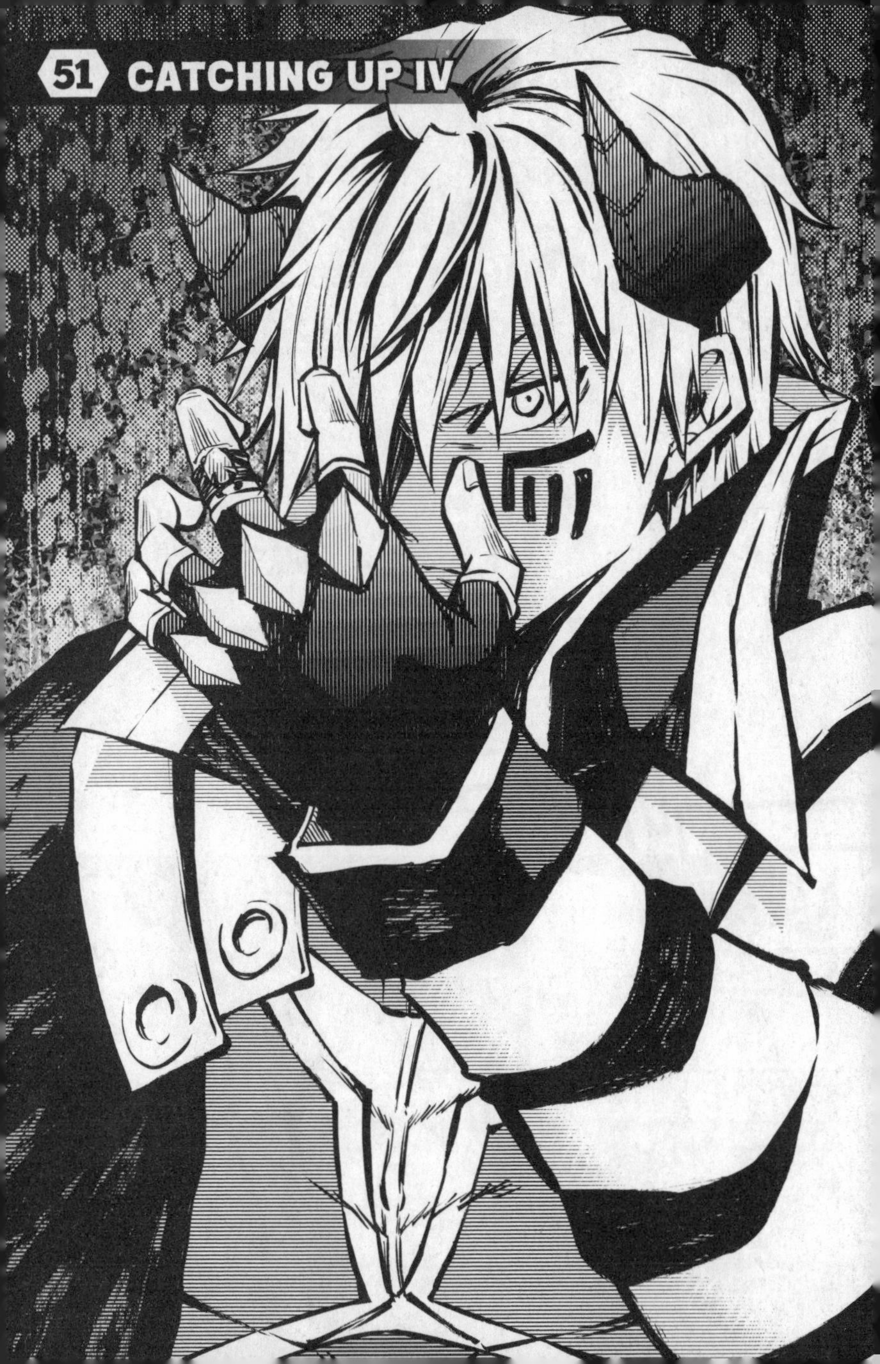
51
CATCHING UP IV

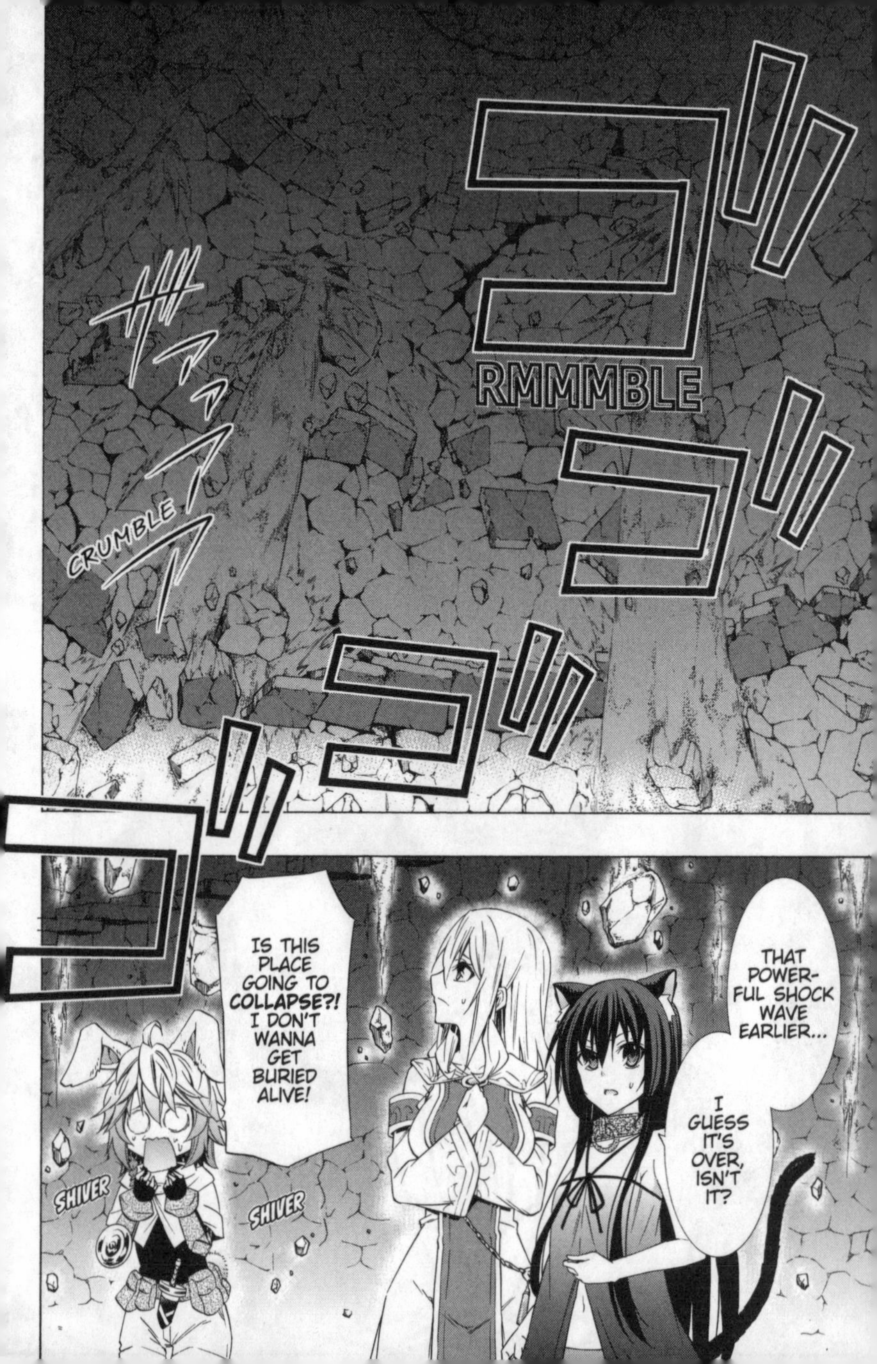
RMMMBLE
CRUMBLE
THAT POWER-FUL SHOCK WAVE EARLIER...
I GUESS IT'S OVER, ISN'T IT?
IS THIS PLACE GOING TO COLLAPSE?! I DON'T WANNA GET BURIED ALIVE!
SHIVER
SHIVER

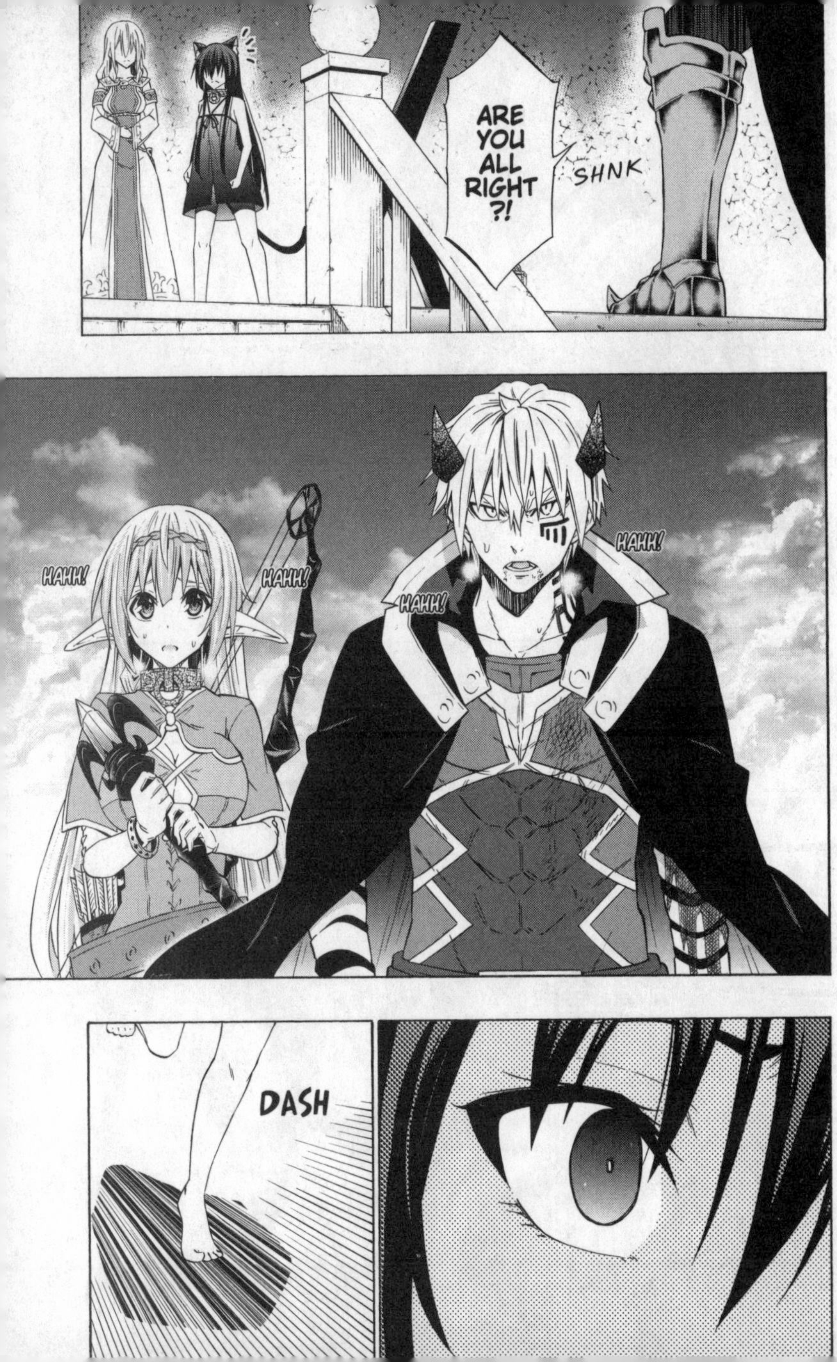
SHNK
ARE YOU ALL RIGHT?!
HAHH!
HAHH!
HAHH!
HAHH!
DASH

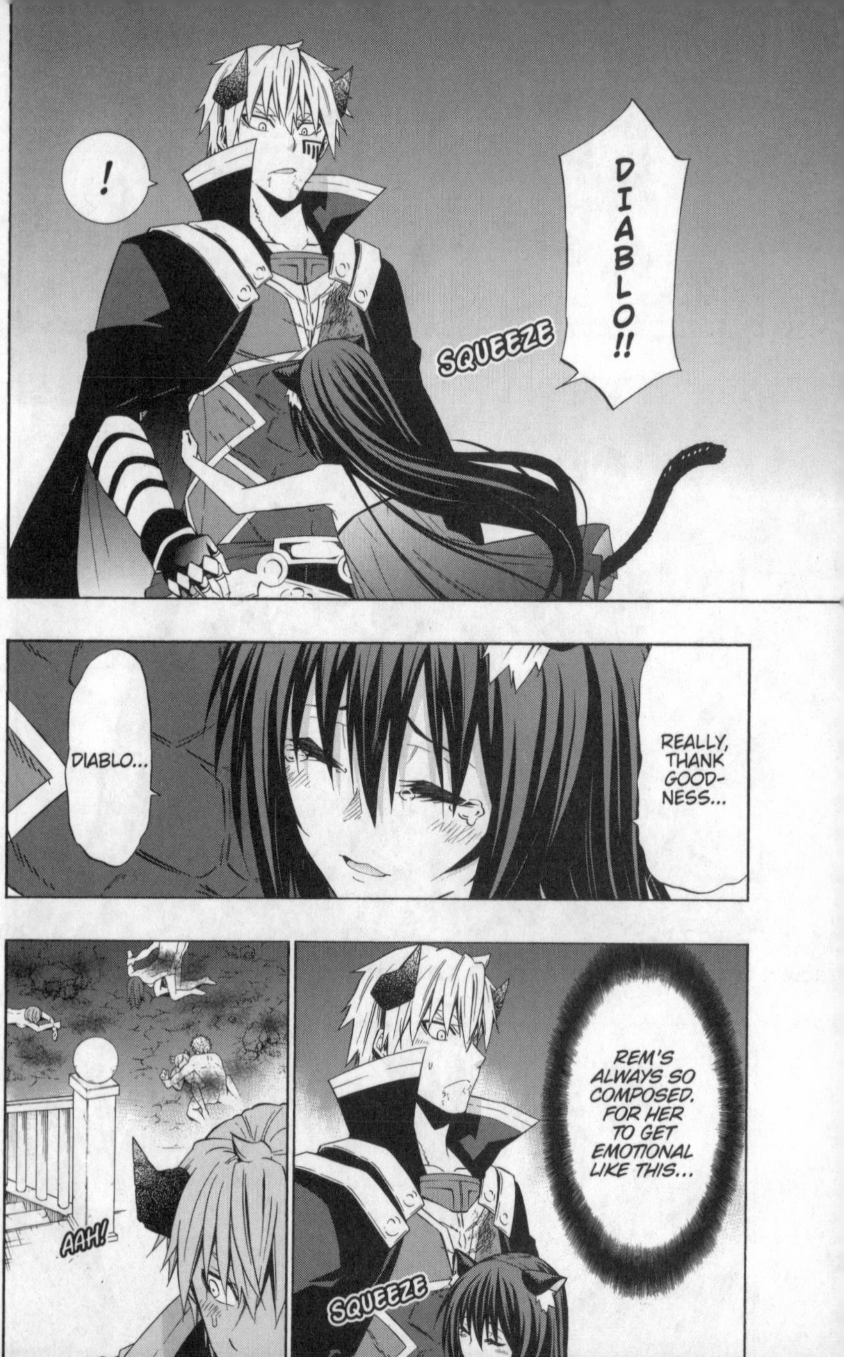
DIABLO!!
SQUEEZE
!
REALLY, THANK GOODNESS...
DIABLO...
REM'S ALWAYS SO COMPOSED. FOR HER TO GET EMOTIONAL LIKE THIS...
SQUEEZE
AAH!

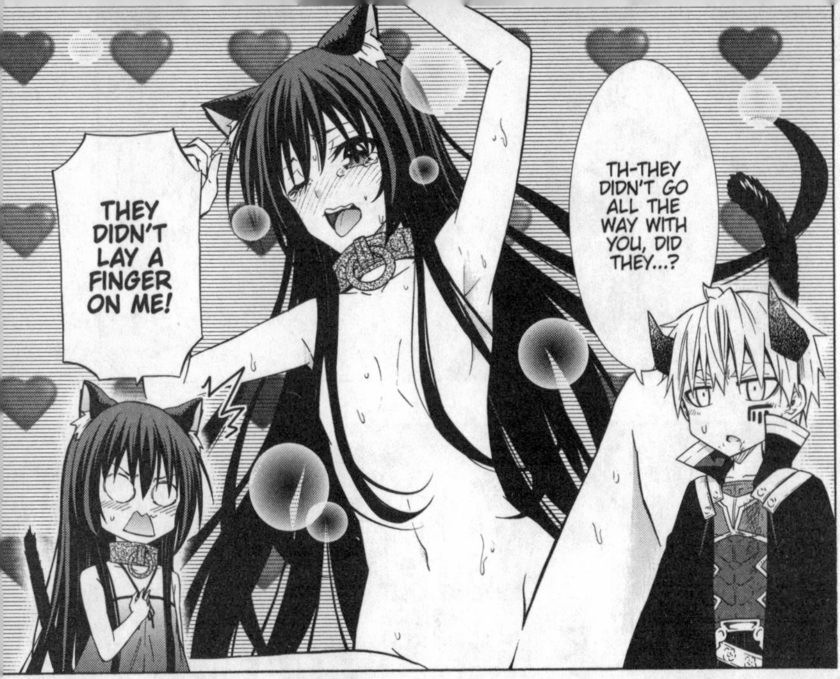
TH-THEY DIDN'T GO ALL THE WAY WITH YOU, DID THEY...?
THEY DIDN'T LAY A FINGER ON ME!

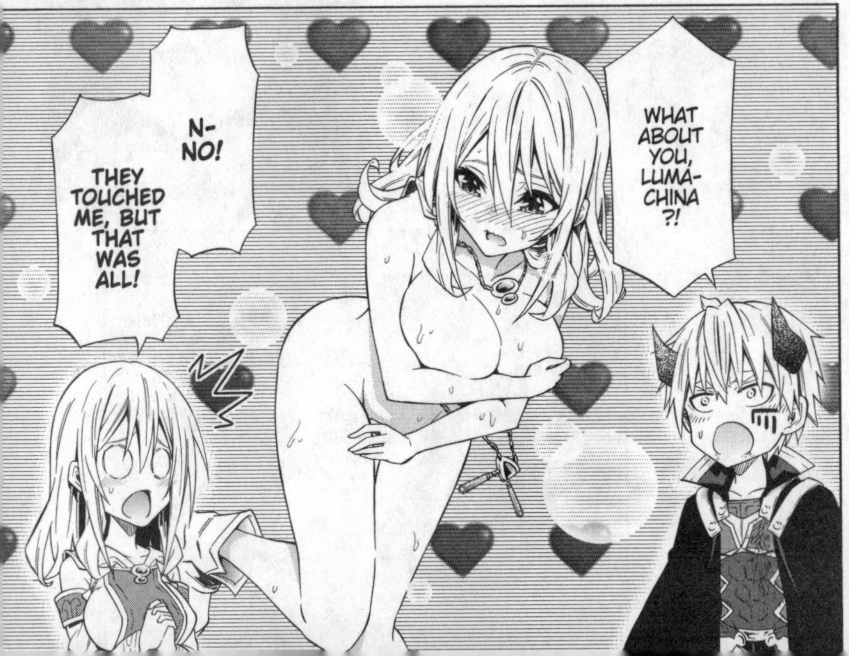
WHAT ABOUT YOU, LUMA-CHINA?!
N-NO!
THEY TOUCHED ME, BUT THAT WAS ALL!

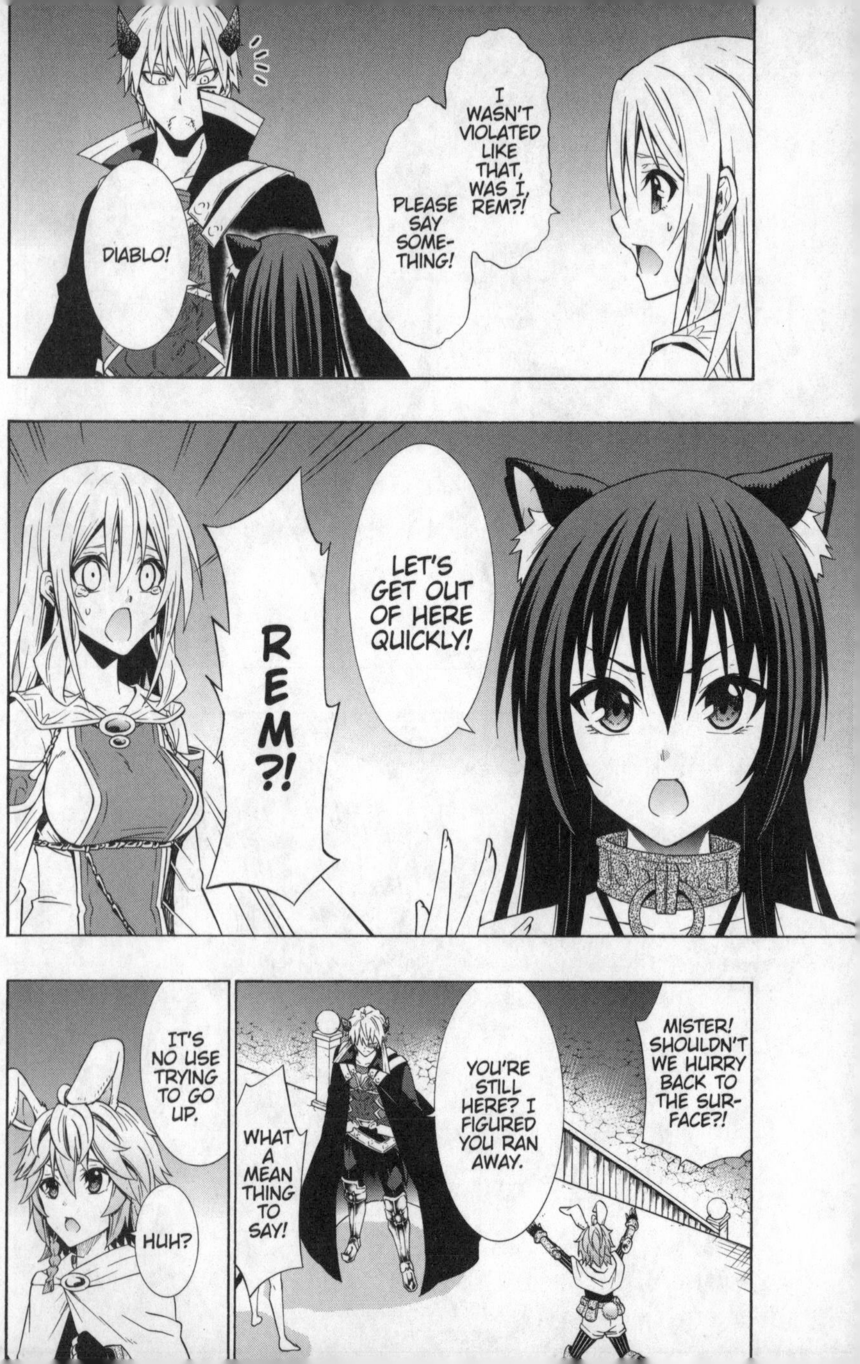
I WASN'T VIOLATED LIKE THAT, WAS I, REM?!
PLEASE SAY SOMETHING!
DIABLO!
LET'S GET OUT OF HERE QUICKLY!
REM?!
MISTER! SHOULDN'T WE HURRY BACK TO THE SURFACE?!
YOU'RE STILL HERE? I FIGURED YOU RAN AWAY.
WHAT A MEAN THING TO SAY!
IT'S NO USE TRYING TO GO UP.
HUH?

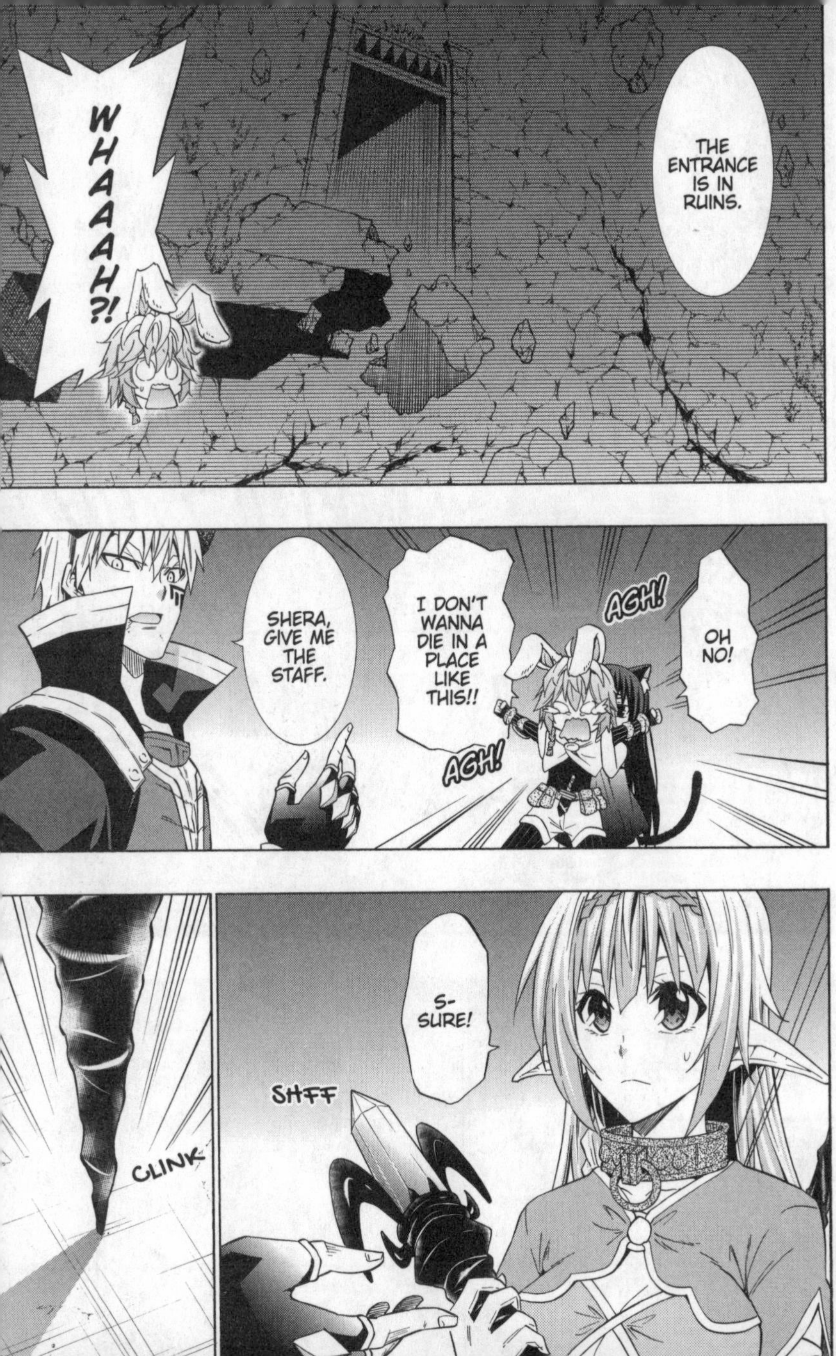
THE ENTRANCE IS IN RUINS.
WHAAAAH?!
OH NO!
AGH!
I DON'T WANNA DIE IN A PLACE LIKE THIS!!
AGH!
SHERA, GIVE ME THE STAFF.
S-SURE!
SHFF
CLINK

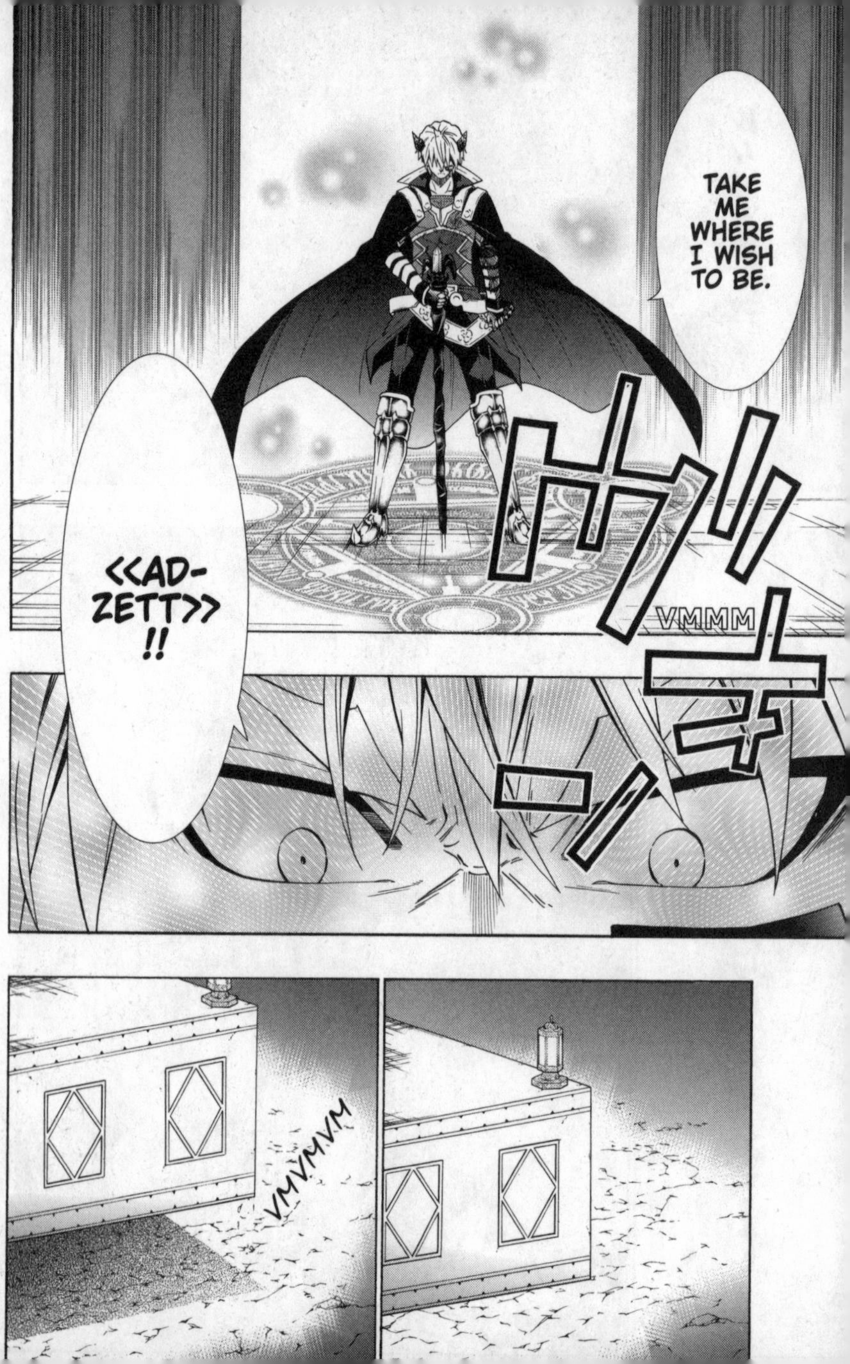
TAKE ME WHERE I WISH TO BE.
<<AD-ZETT>>!!
VMMM
VMVMVM

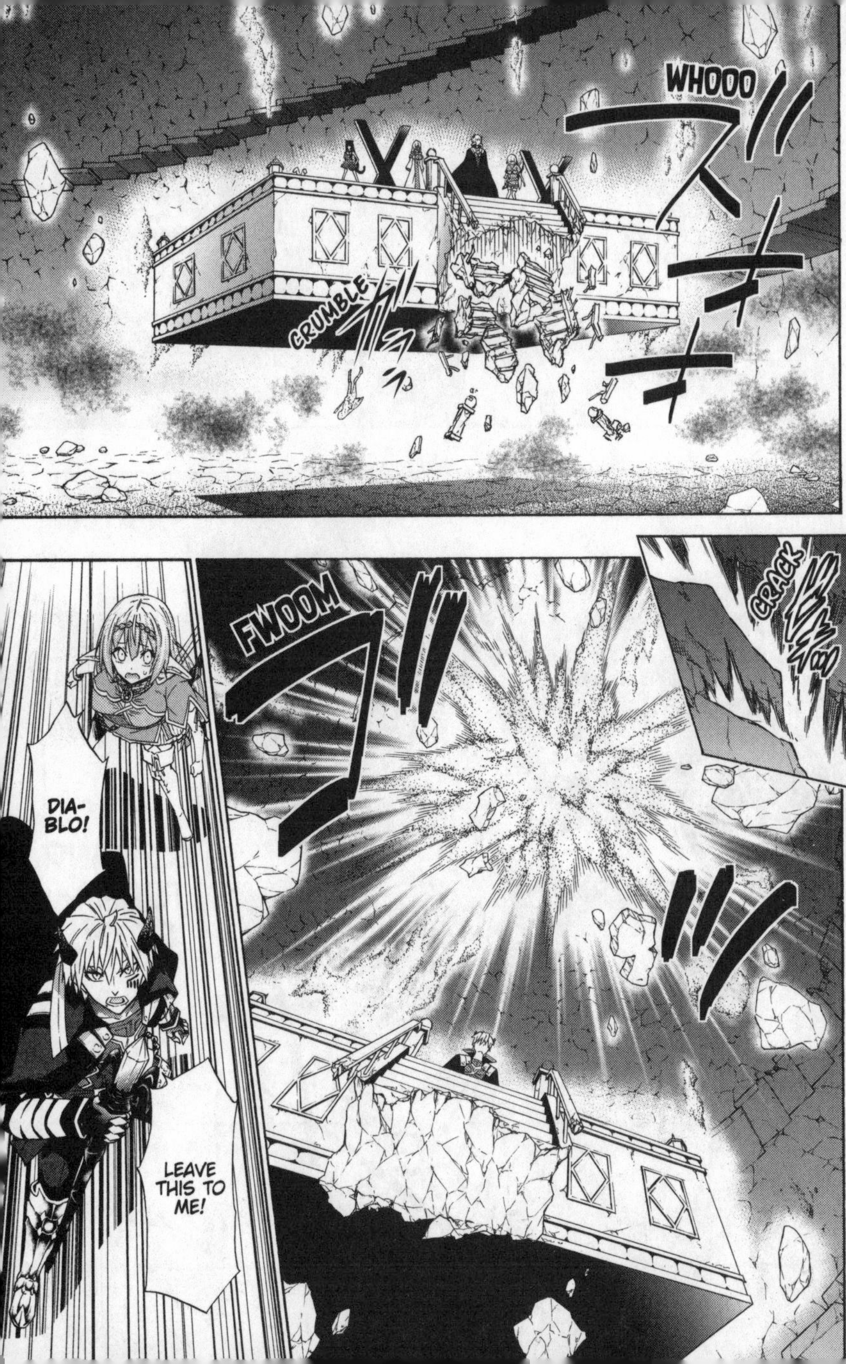
WHOOO
CRUMBLE
CRACK
FWOOM
DIA-
BLO!
LEAVE
THIS TO
ME!

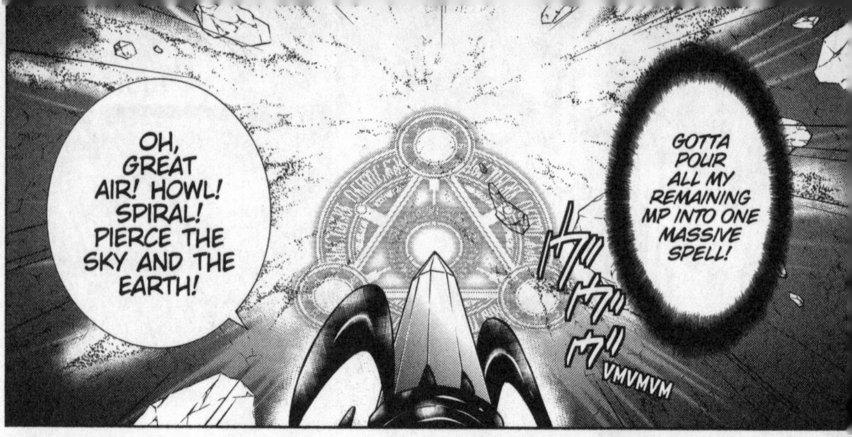
GOTTA POUR ALL MY REMAINING MP INTO ONE MASSIVE SPELL!
OH, GREAT AIR! HOWL! SPIRAL! PIERCE THE SKY AND THE EARTH!
VMVMVM
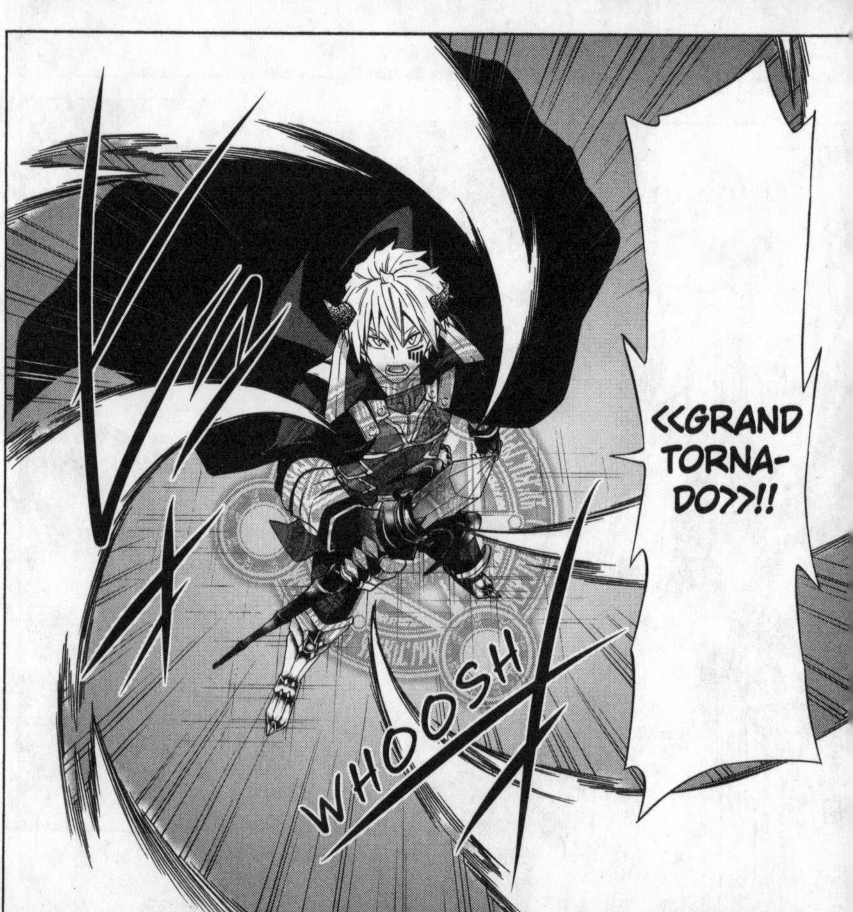
<<GRAND TORNA-DO>>!!
WHOOSH

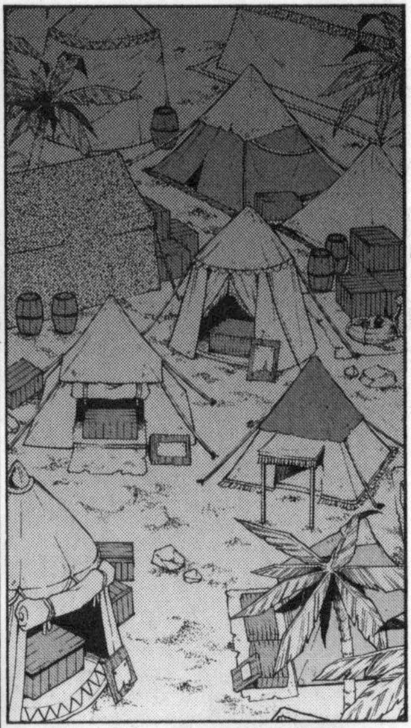

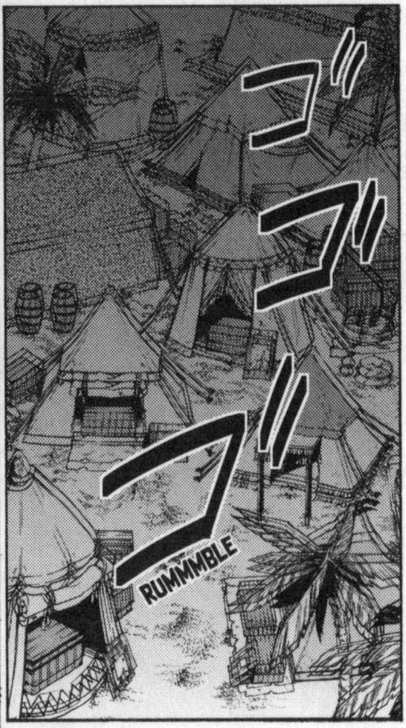
ゴゴゴ
RUMMMBLE

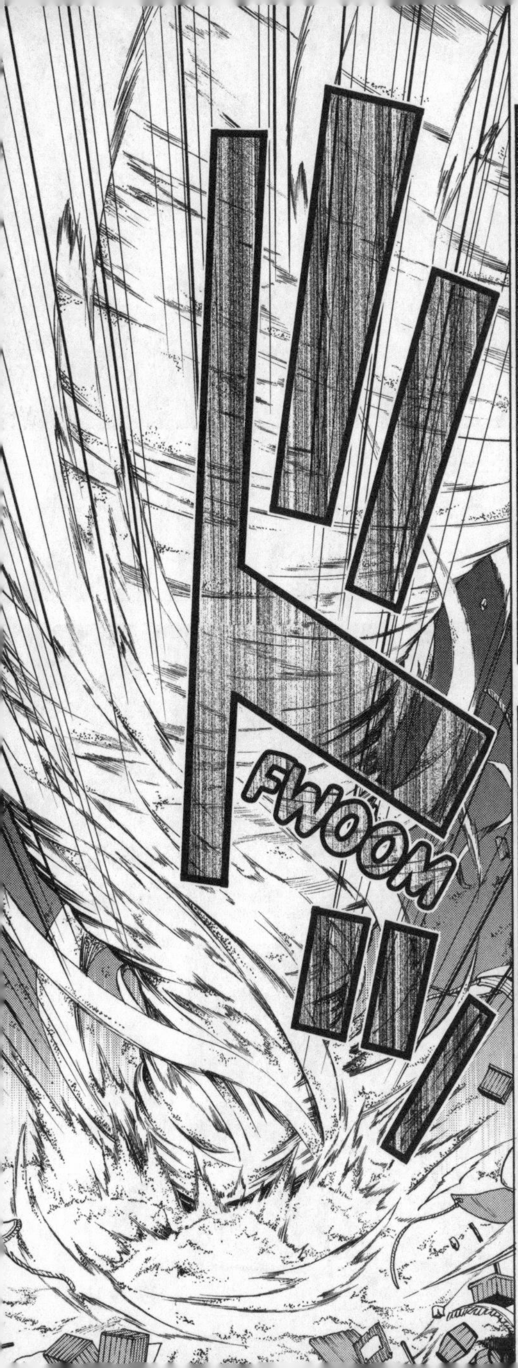
FWOOM

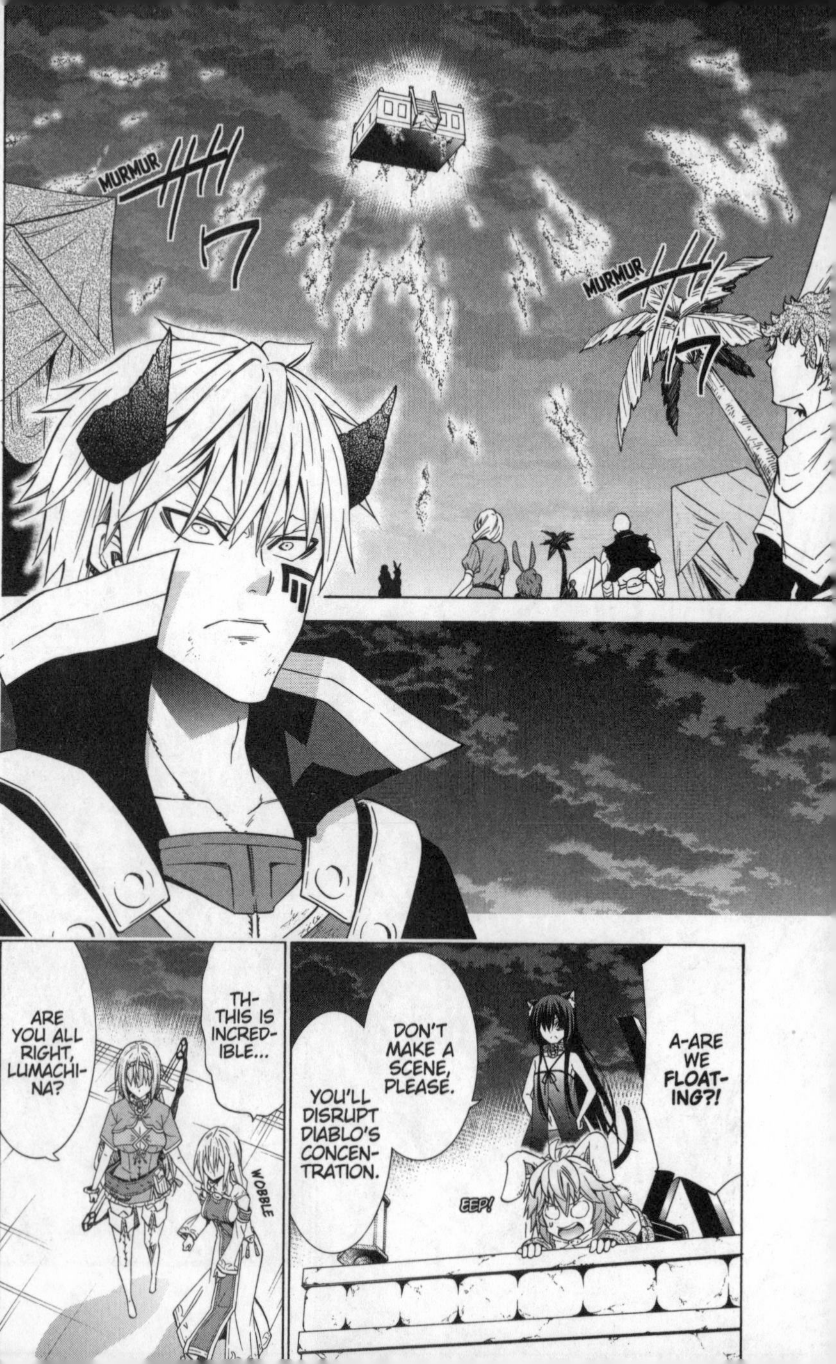
MURMUR
MURMUR
A-ARE WE FLOATING?!
DON'T MAKE A SCENE, PLEASE.
YOU'LL DISRUPT DIABLO'S CONCENTRATION.
EEP!
TH-THIS IS INCREDIBLE...
ARE YOU ALL RIGHT, LUMACHINA?
WOBBLE

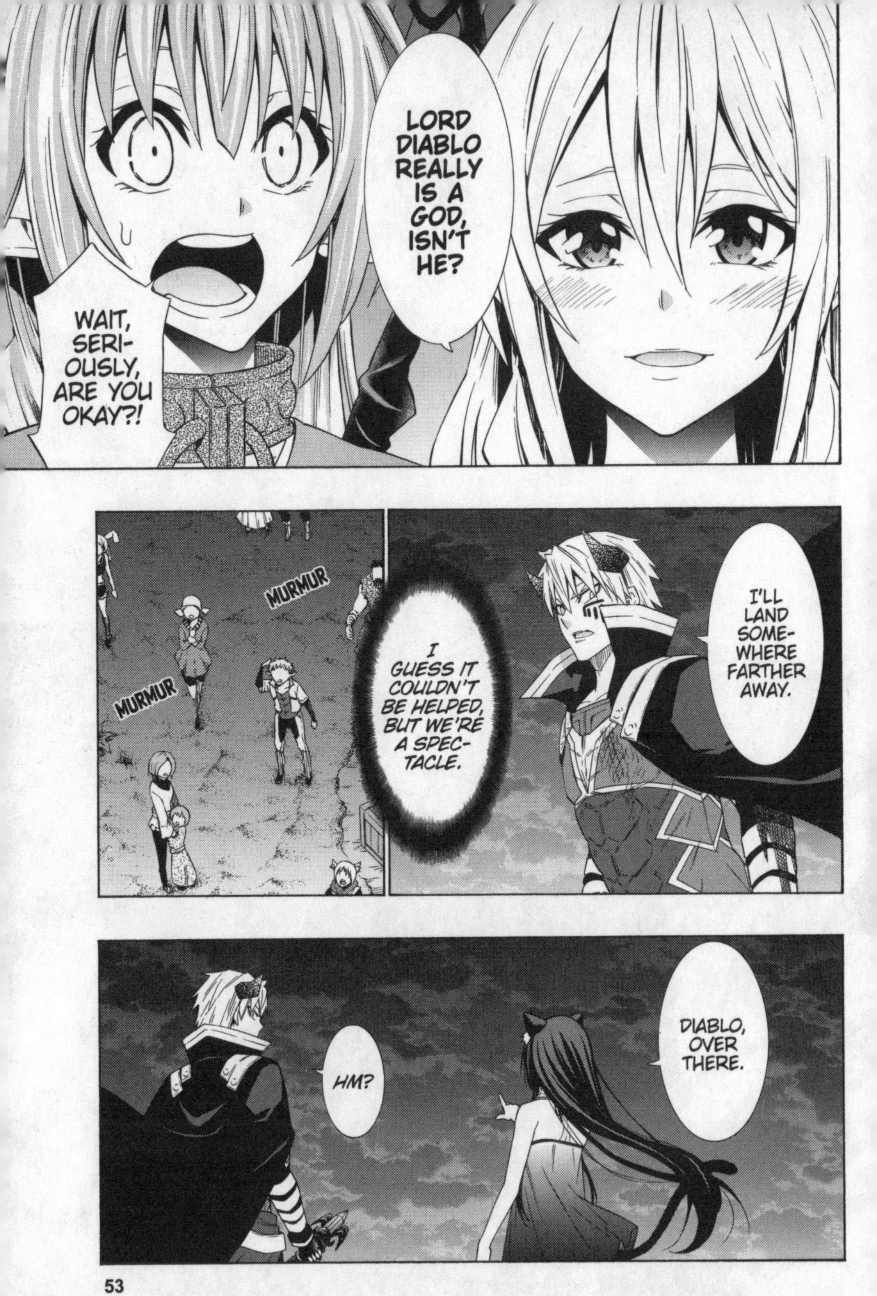
LORD DIABLO REALLY IS A GOD, ISN'T HE?
WAIT, SERI-OUSLY, ARE YOU OKAY?!
I'LL LAND SOME-WHERE FARTHER AWAY.
I GUESS IT COULDN'T BE HELPED, BUT WE'RE A SPEC-TACLE.
MURMUR
MURMUR
DIABLO, OVER THERE.
HM?

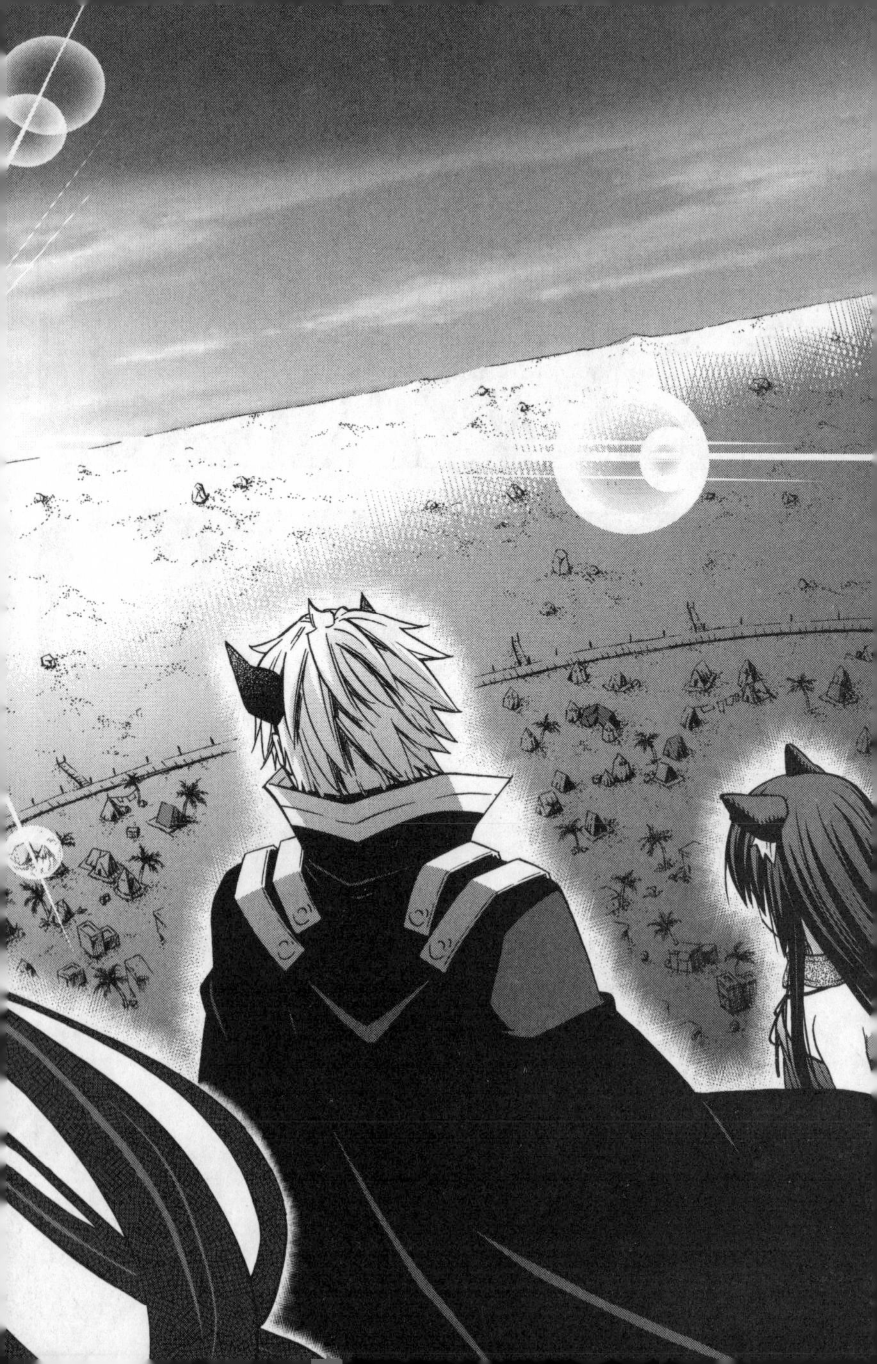

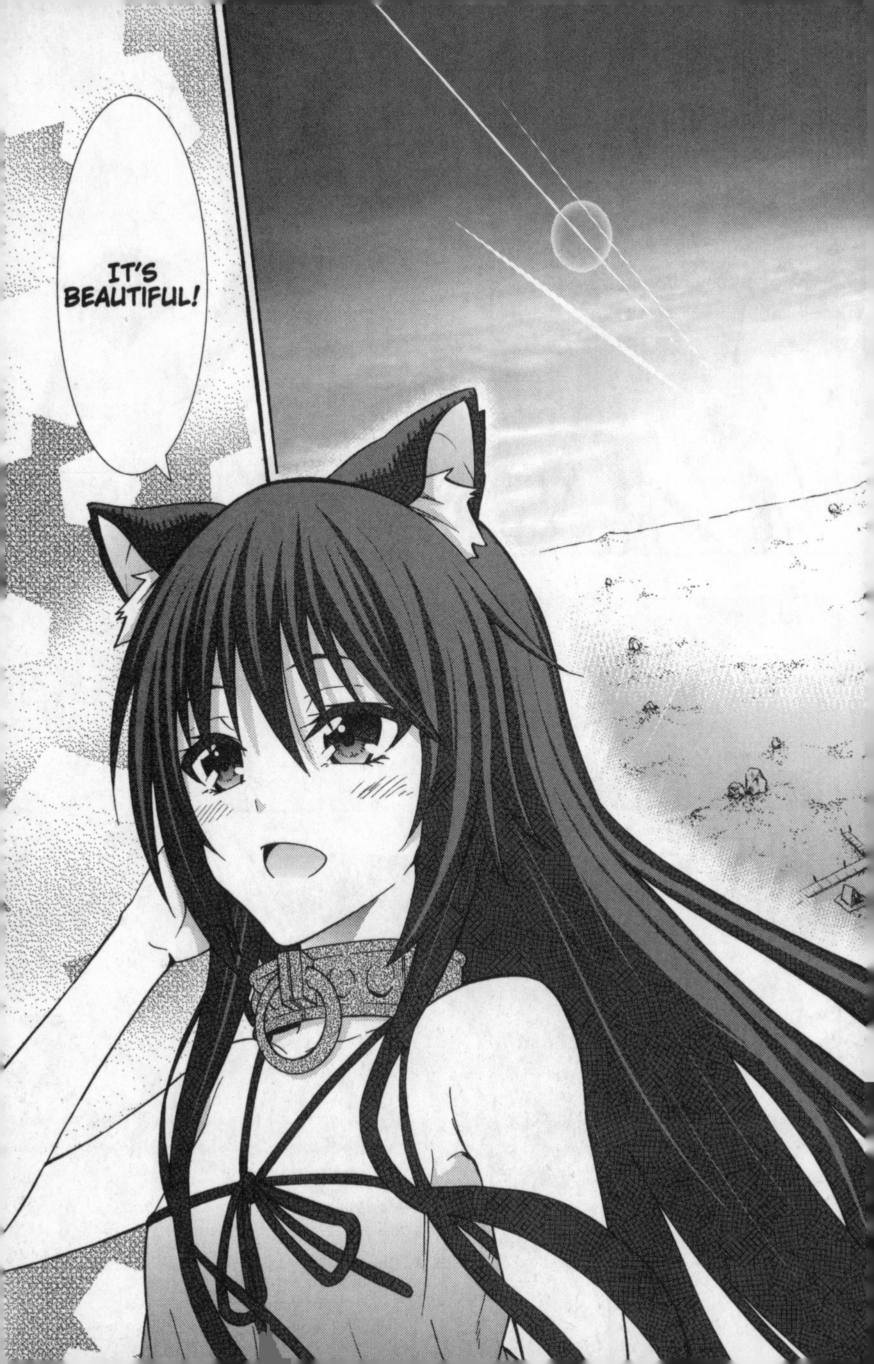
IT'S BEAUTIFUL!

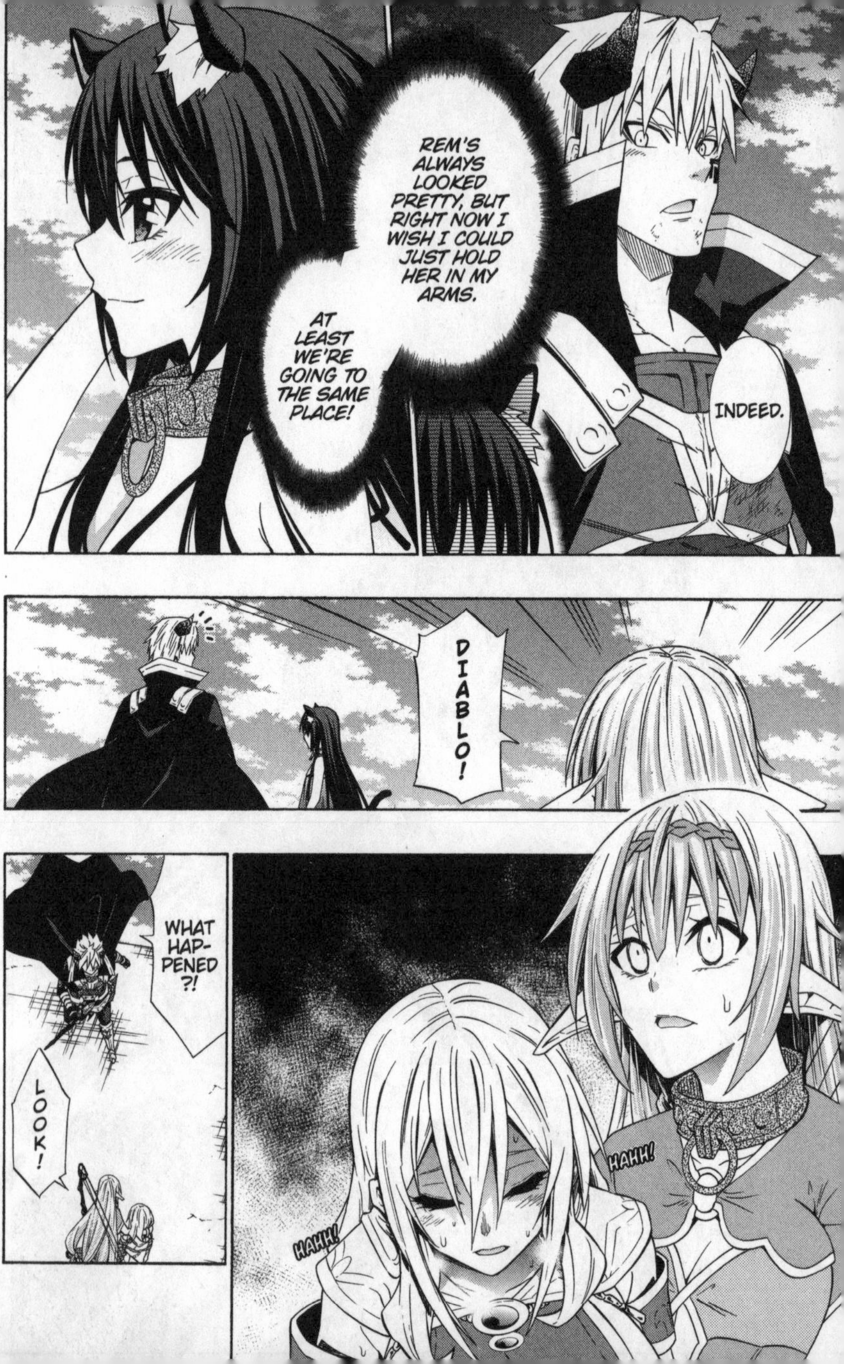
INDEED.
REM'S ALWAYS LOOKED PRETTY, BUT RIGHT NOW I WISH I COULD JUST HOLD HER IN MY ARMS.
AT LEAST WE'RE GOING TO THE SAME PLACE!
DIABLO!
HAHH!
HAHH!
WHAT HAP-PENED?!
LOOK!

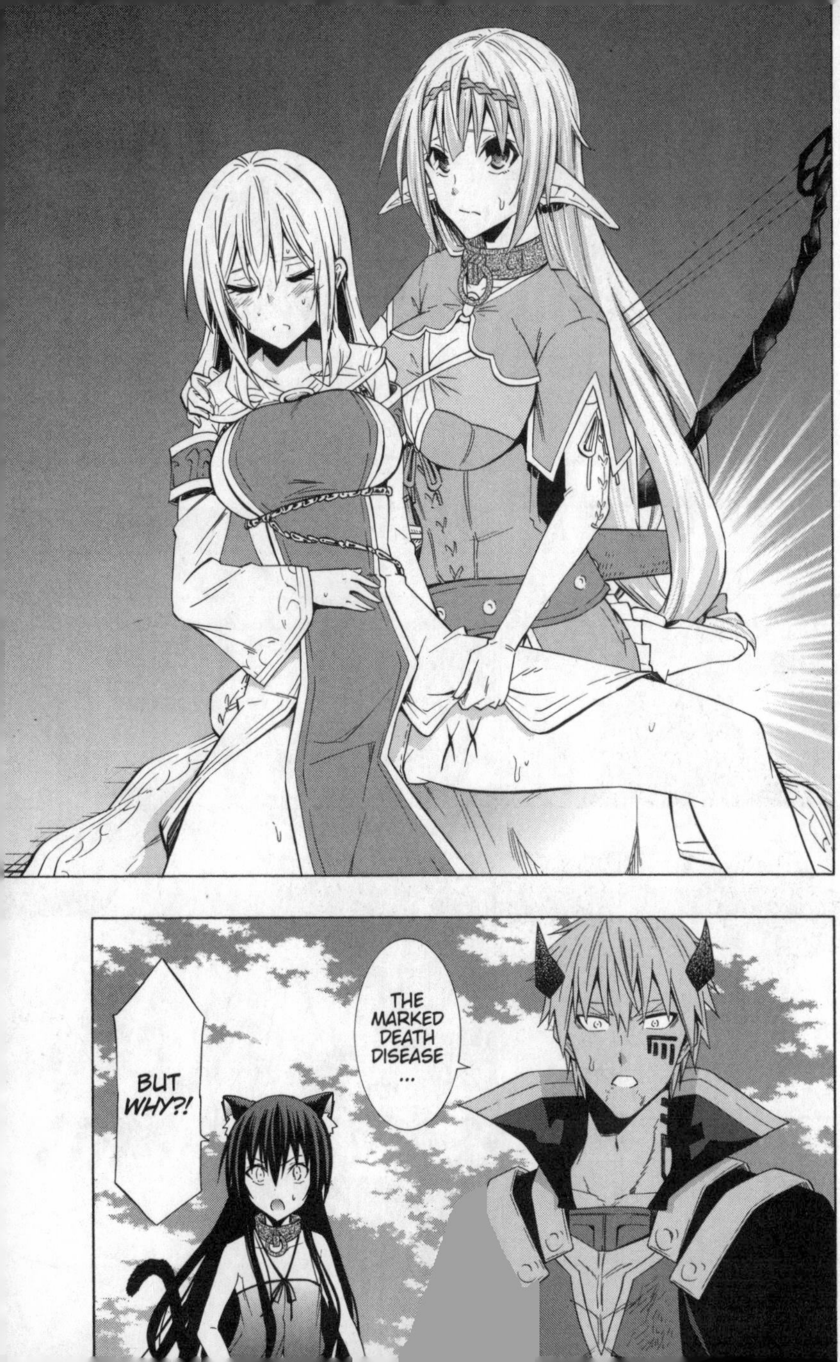
THE MARKED DEATH DISEASE...
BUT WHY?!

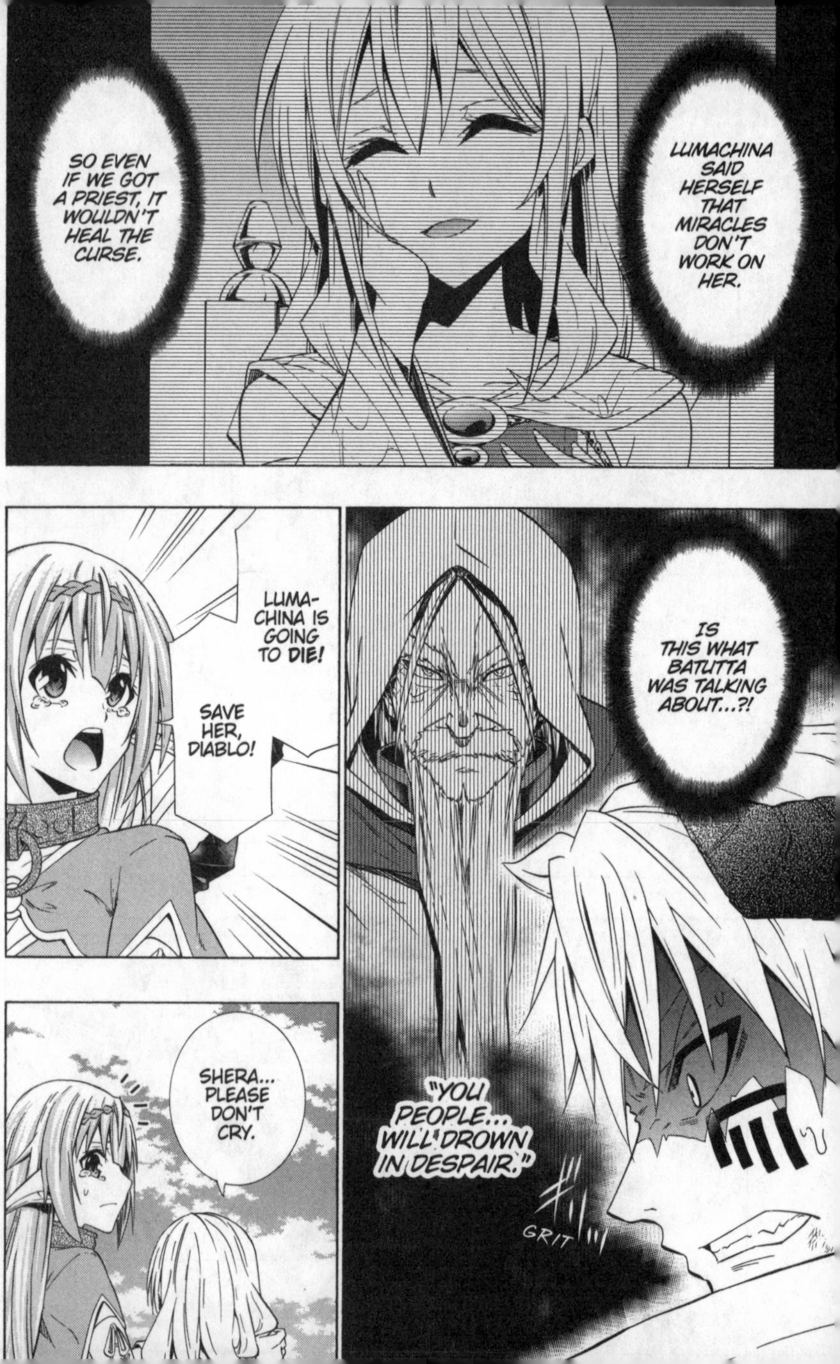
LUMACHINA SAID HERSELF THAT MIRACLES DON'T WORK ON HER.
SO EVEN IF WE GOT A PRIEST, IT WOULDN'T HEAL THE CURSE.
IS THIS WHAT BATUTTA WAS TALKING ABOUT...?!
"YOU PEOPLE... WILL DROWN IN DESPAIR."
GRIT
LUMA-CHINA IS GOING TO DIE!
SAVE HER, DIABLO!
SHERA... PLEASE DON'T CRY.

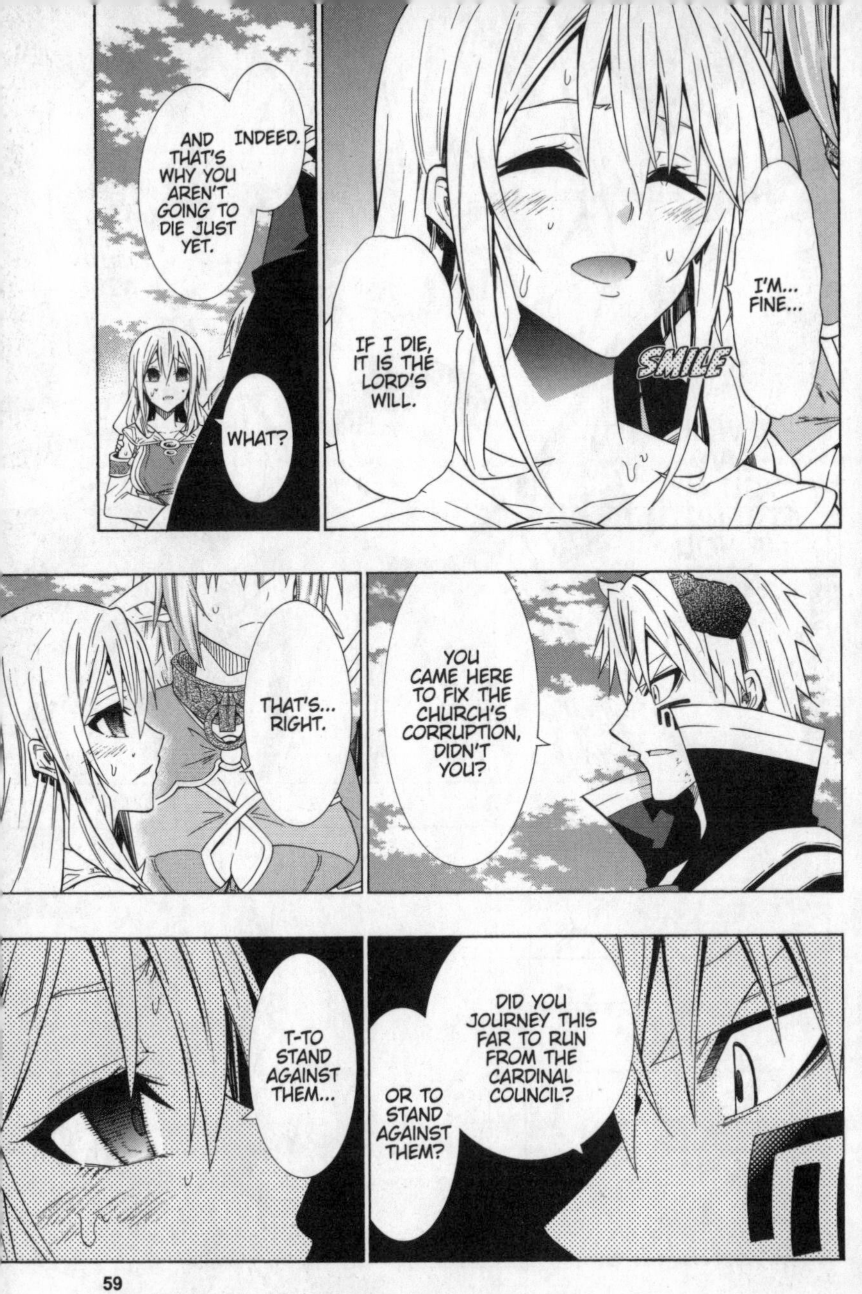
I'M... FINE...
SMILE
IF I DIE, IT IS THE LORD'S WILL.
INDEED. AND THAT'S WHY YOU AREN'T GOING TO DIE JUST YET.
WHAT?
YOU CAME HERE TO FIX THE CHURCH'S CORRUPTION, DIDN'T YOU?
THAT'S... RIGHT.
DID YOU JOURNEY THIS FAR TO RUN FROM THE CARDINAL COUNCIL?
OR TO STAND AGAINST THEM?
T-TO STAND AGAINST THEM...

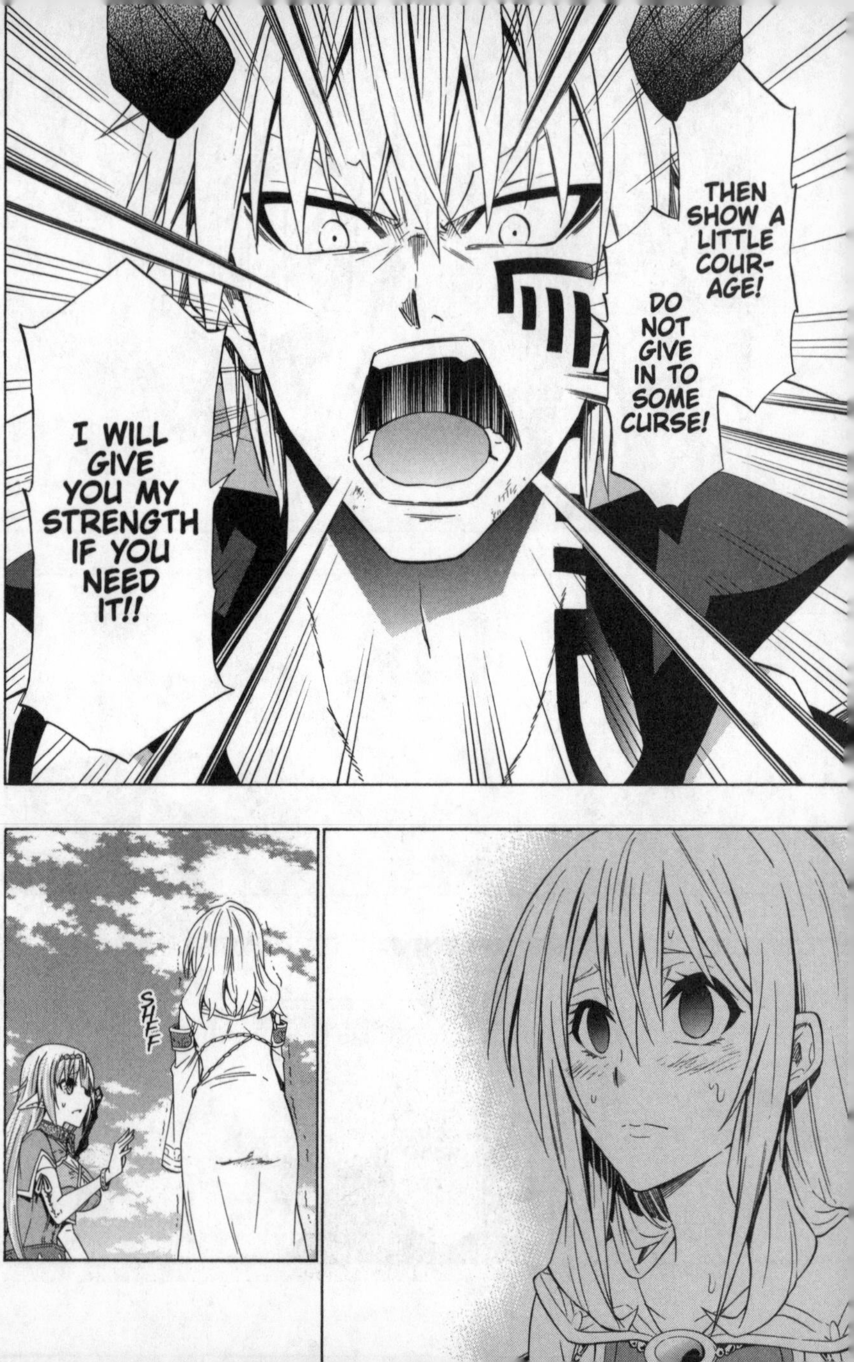
THEN SHOW A LITTLE COURAGE!
DO NOT GIVE IN TO SOME CURSE!
I WILL GIVE YOU MY STRENGTH IF YOU NEED IT!!
SHFF

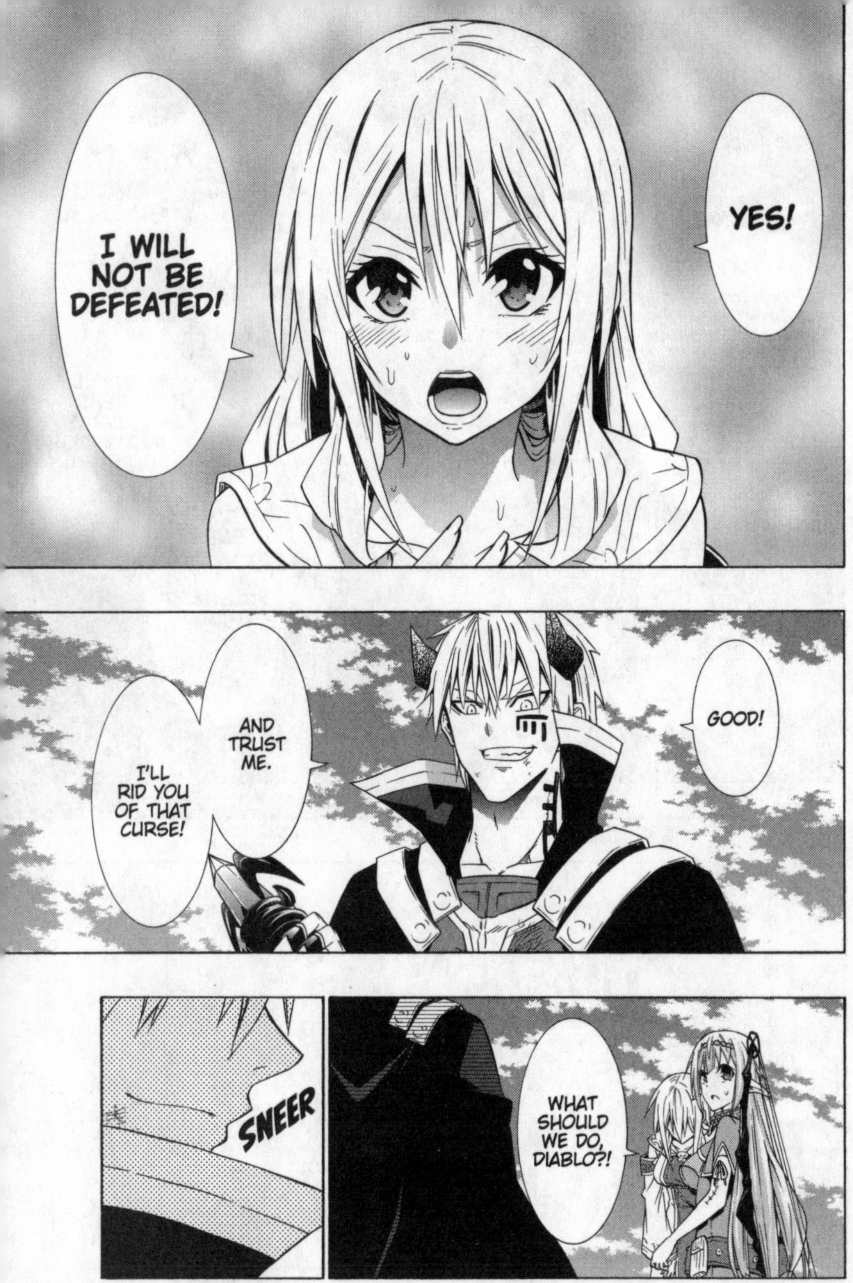
YES!
I WILL NOT BE DEFEATED!
GOOD!
AND TRUST ME.
I'LL RID YOU OF THAT CURSE!
WHAT SHOULD WE DO, DIABLO?!
SNEER

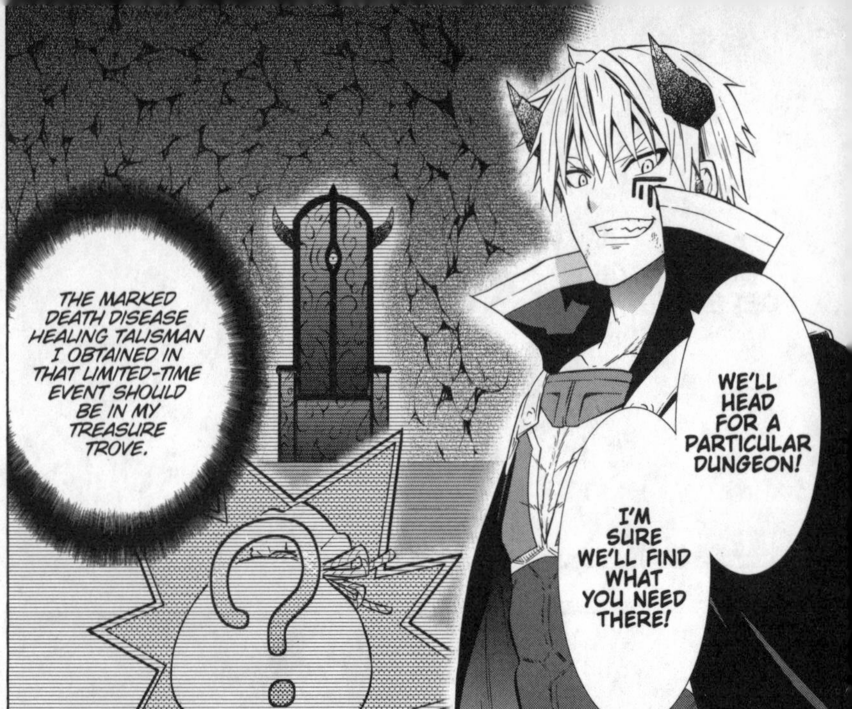
WE'LL HEAD FOR A PARTICULAR DUNGEON!
I'M SURE WE'LL FIND WHAT YOU NEED THERE!
THE MARKED DEATH DISEASE HEALING TALISMAN I OBTAINED IN THAT LIMITED-TIME EVENT SHOULD BE IN MY TREASURE TROVE.
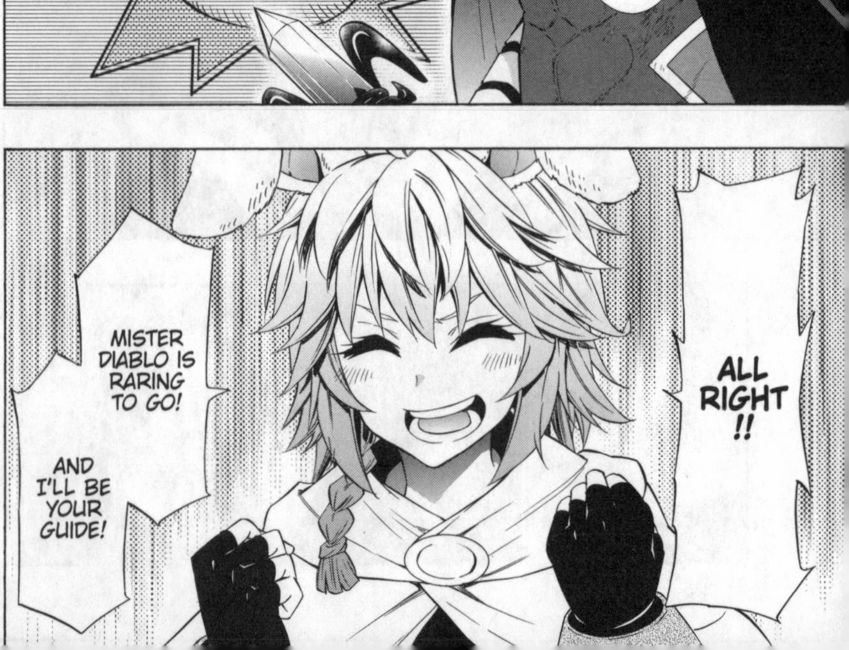
ALL RIGHT !!
MISTER DIABLO IS RARING TO GO!
AND I'LL BE YOUR GUIDE!

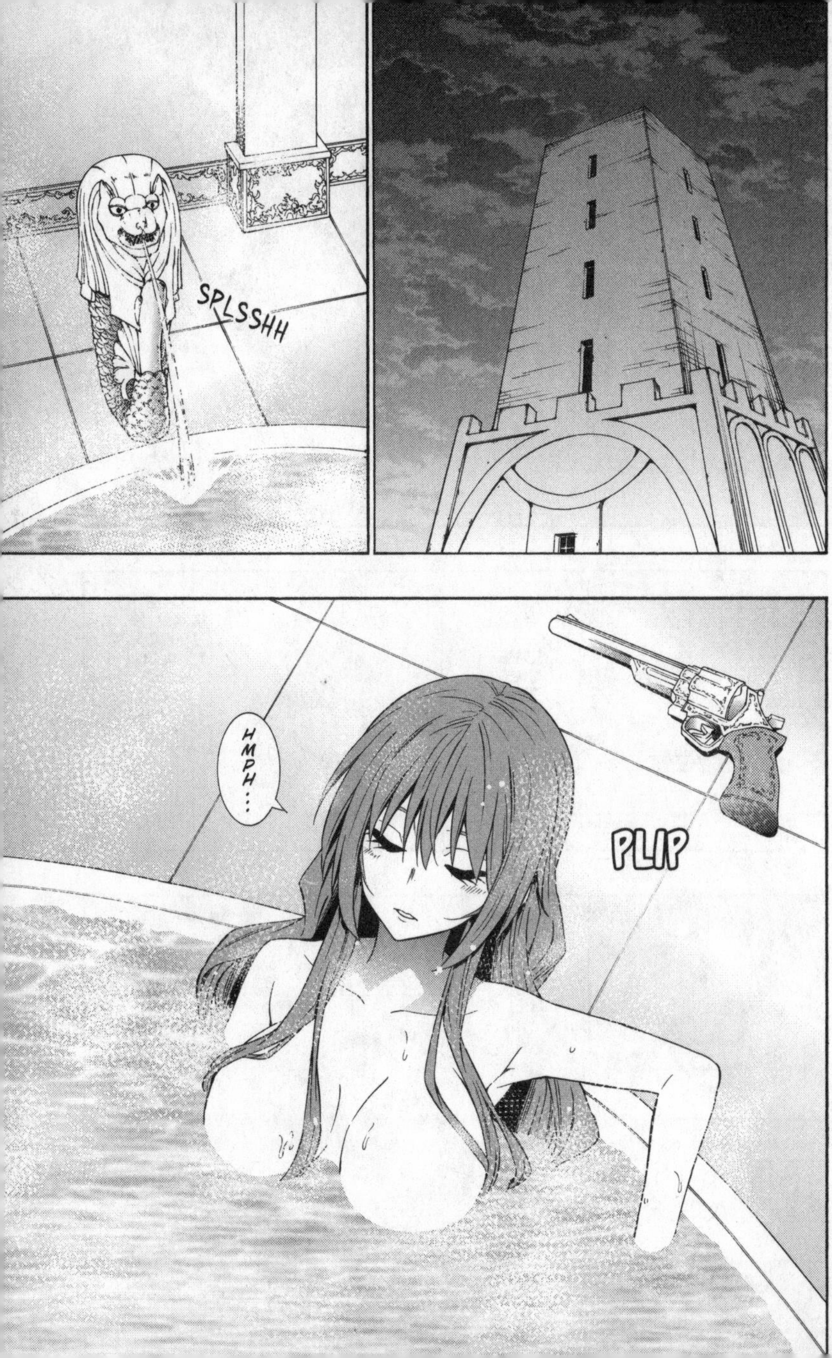
SPLSSHH
HMPH...
PLIP

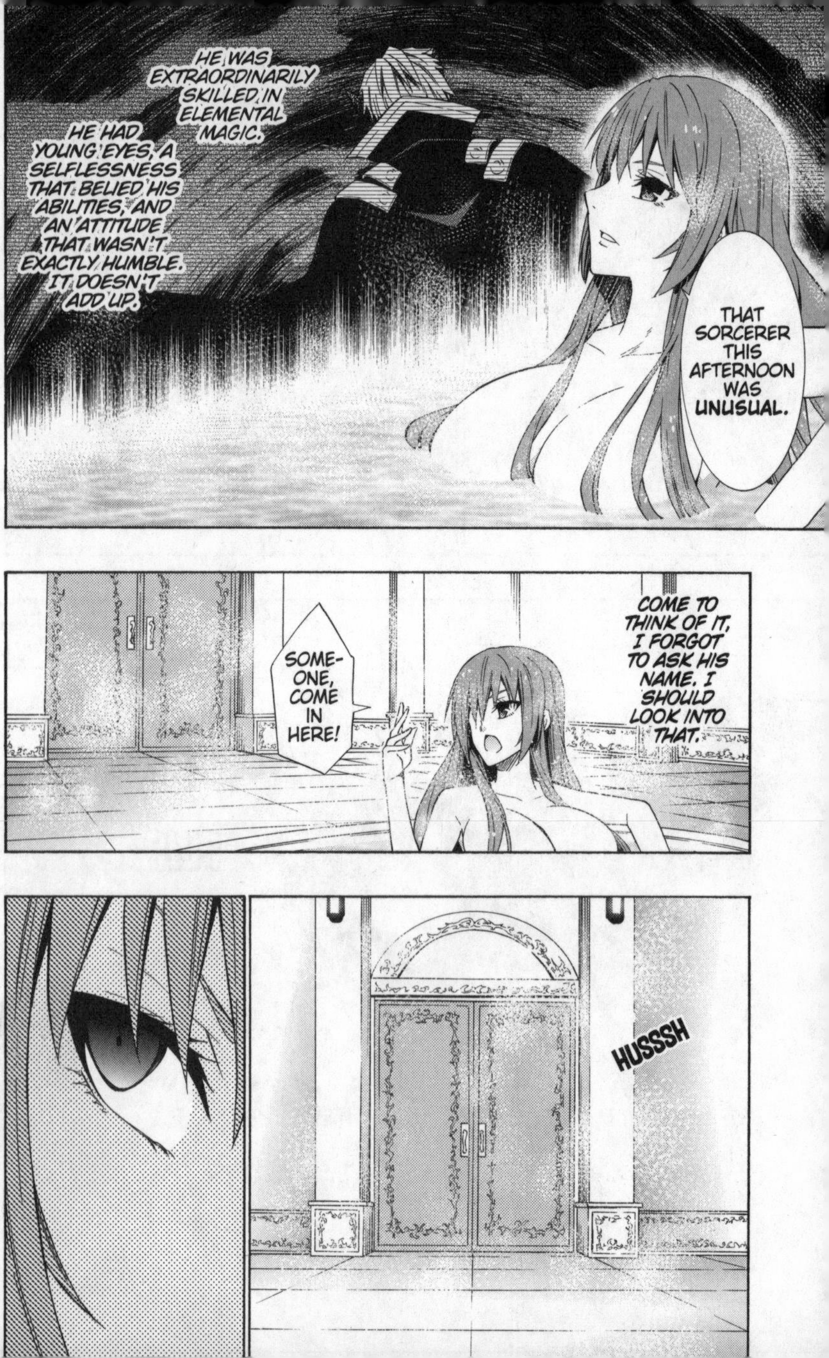
THAT SORCERER THIS AFTERNOON WAS UNUSUAL.
HE WAS EXTRAORDINARILY SKILLED IN ELEMENTAL MAGIC.
HE HAD YOUNG EYES, A SELFLESSNESS THAT BELIED HIS ABILITIES, AND AN ATTITUDE THAT WASN'T EXACTLY HUMBLE. IT DOESN'T ADD UP.
COME TO THINK OF IT, I FORGOT TO ASK HIS NAME. I SHOULD LOOK INTO THAT.
SOME-ONE, COME IN HERE!
HUSSSH

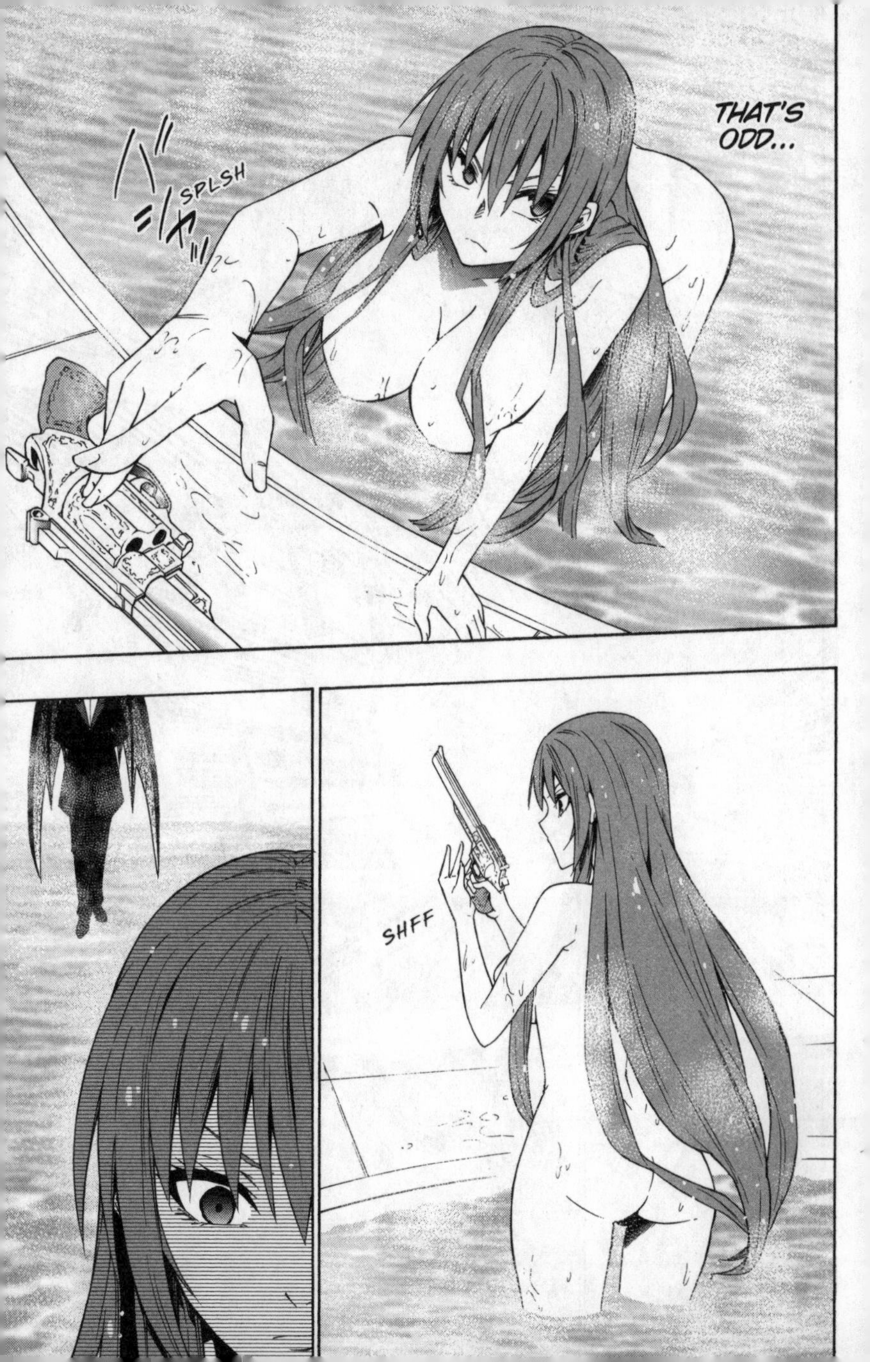
THAT'S ODD...
SPLSH
SHFF

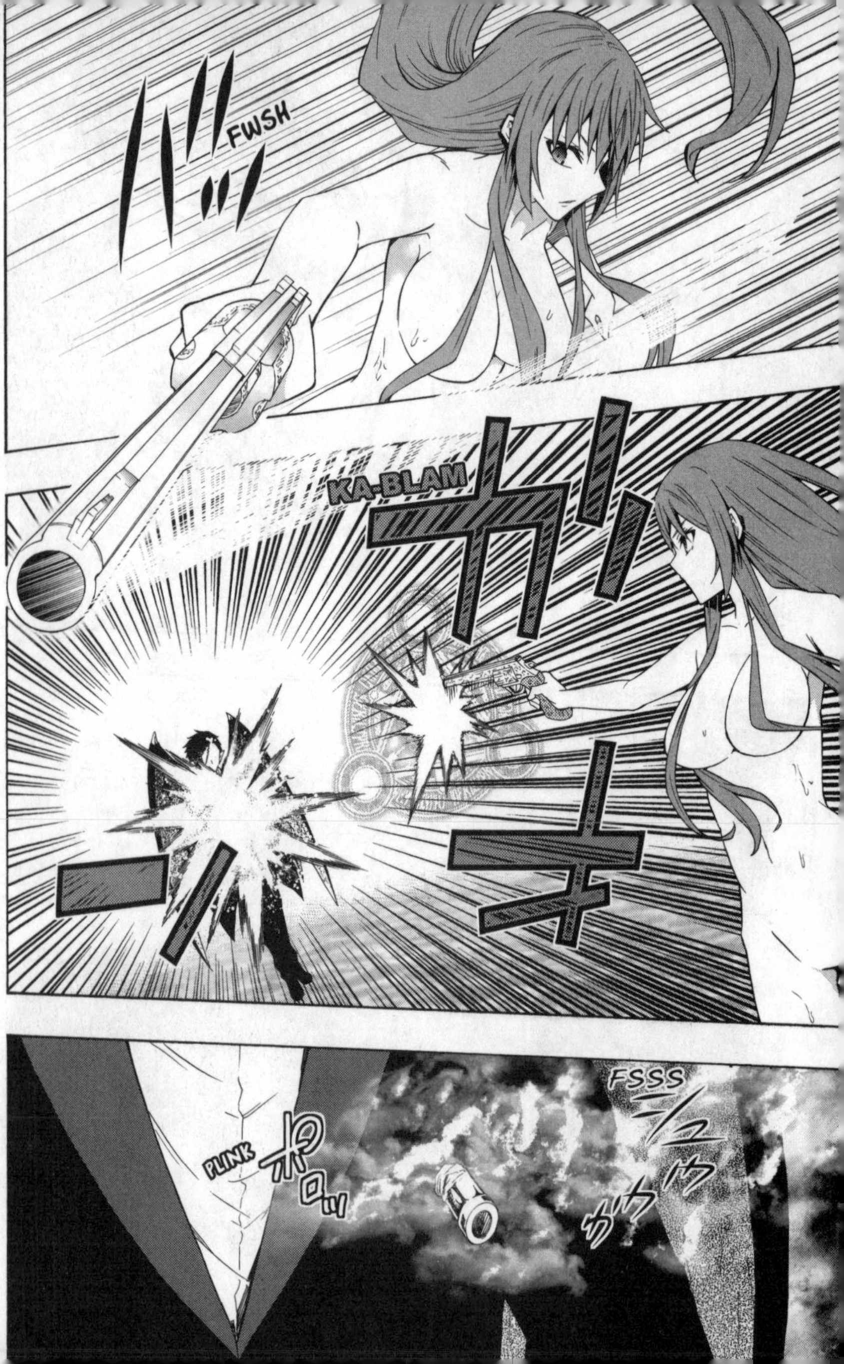
FWSH
KA-BLAM
FSSS
PLINK

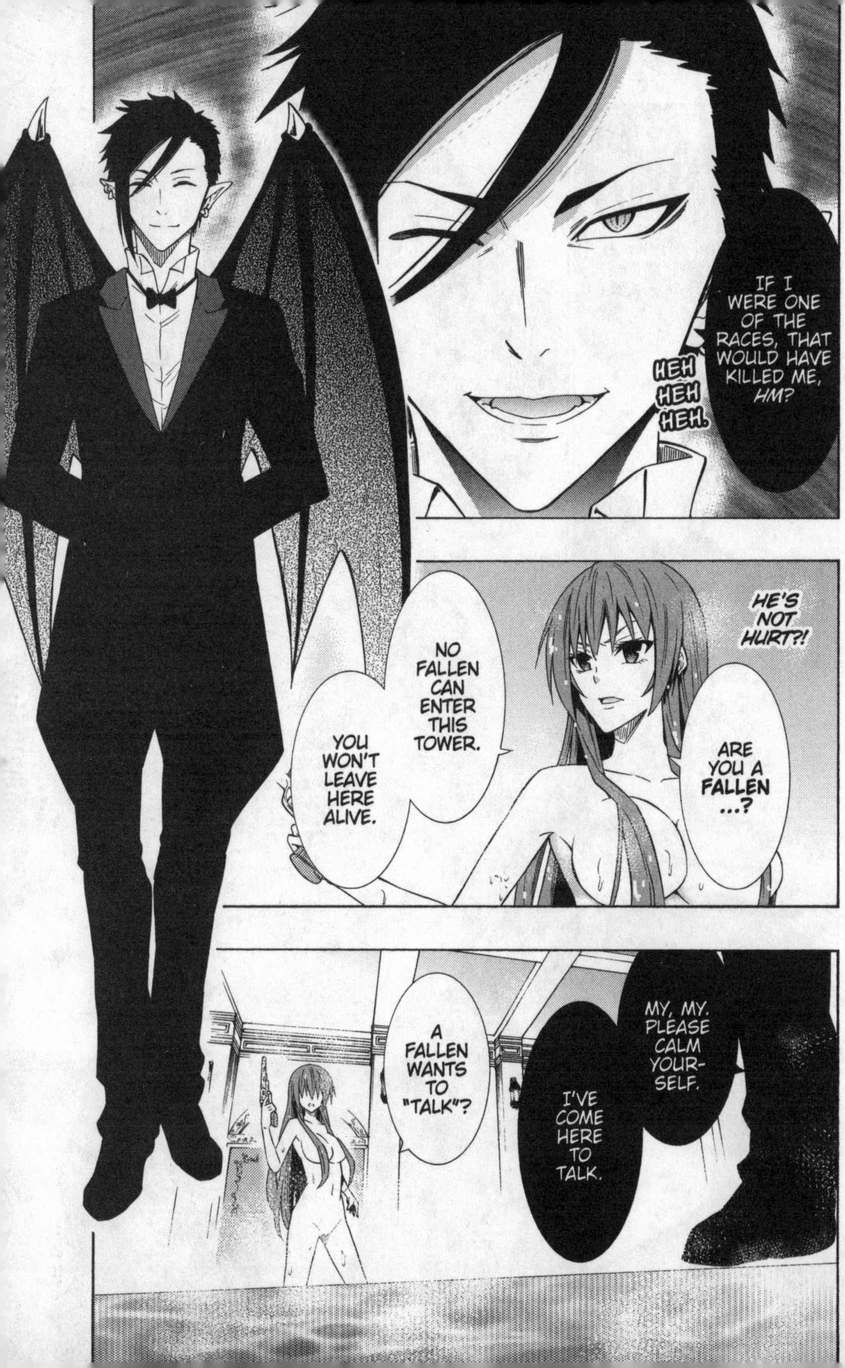
IF I WERE ONE OF THE RACES, THAT WOULD HAVE KILLED ME, *HM?*
HEH HEH HEH.
HE'S NOT HURT?!
ARE YOU A FALLEN ...?
NO FALLEN CAN ENTER THIS TOWER.
YOU WON'T LEAVE HERE ALIVE.
MY, MY. PLEASE CALM YOUR-SELF.
I'VE COME HERE TO TALK.
A FALLEN WANTS TO "TALK"?

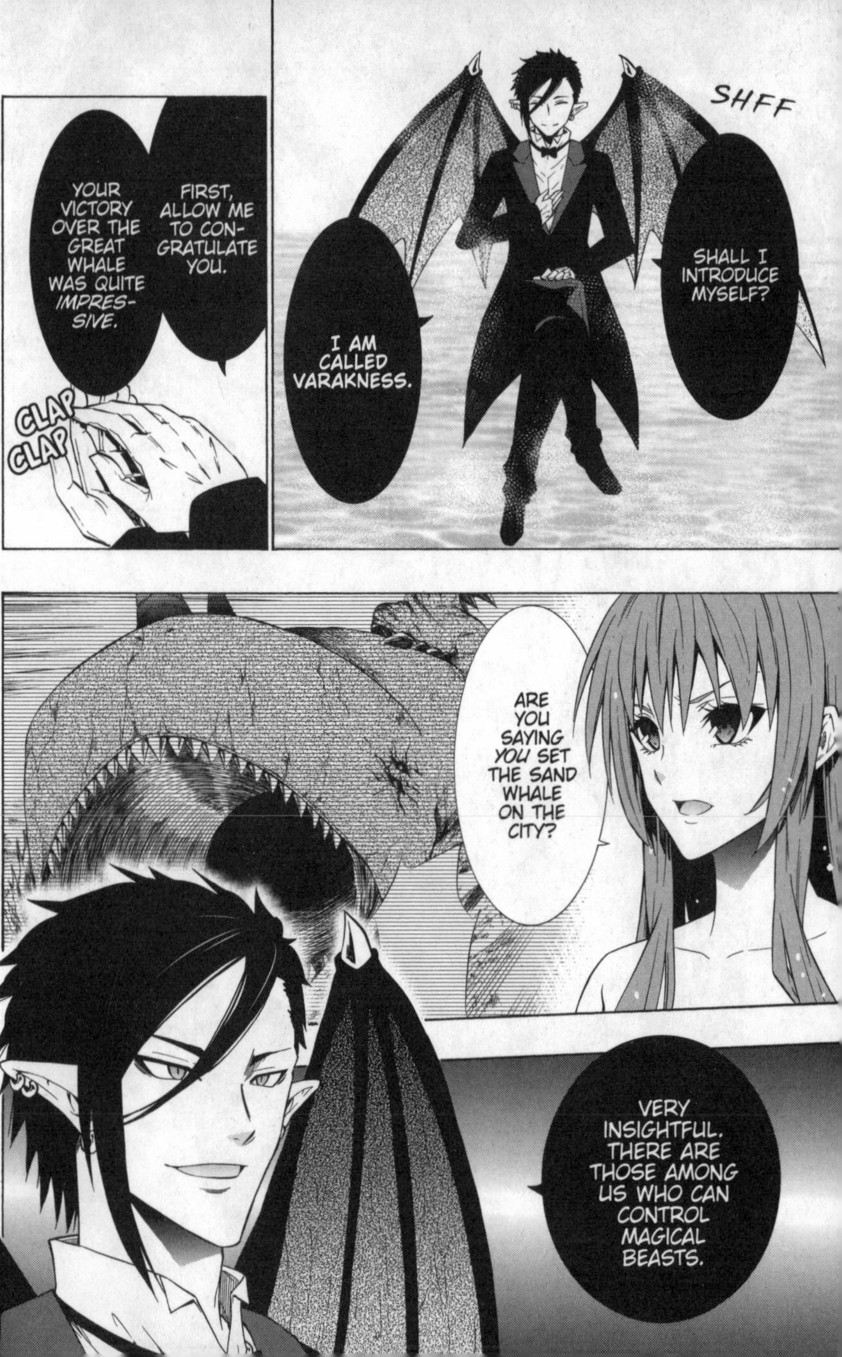
SHFF
SHALL I INTRODUCE MYSELF?
I AM CALLED VARAKNESS.
FIRST, ALLOW ME TO CONGRATULATE YOU.
YOUR VICTORY OVER THE GREAT WHALE WAS QUITE *IMPRESSIVE.*
CLAP CLAP
ARE YOU SAYING *YOU* SET THE SAND WHALE ON THE CITY?
VERY INSIGHTFUL. THERE ARE THOSE AMONG US WHO CAN CONTROL MAGICAL BEASTS.

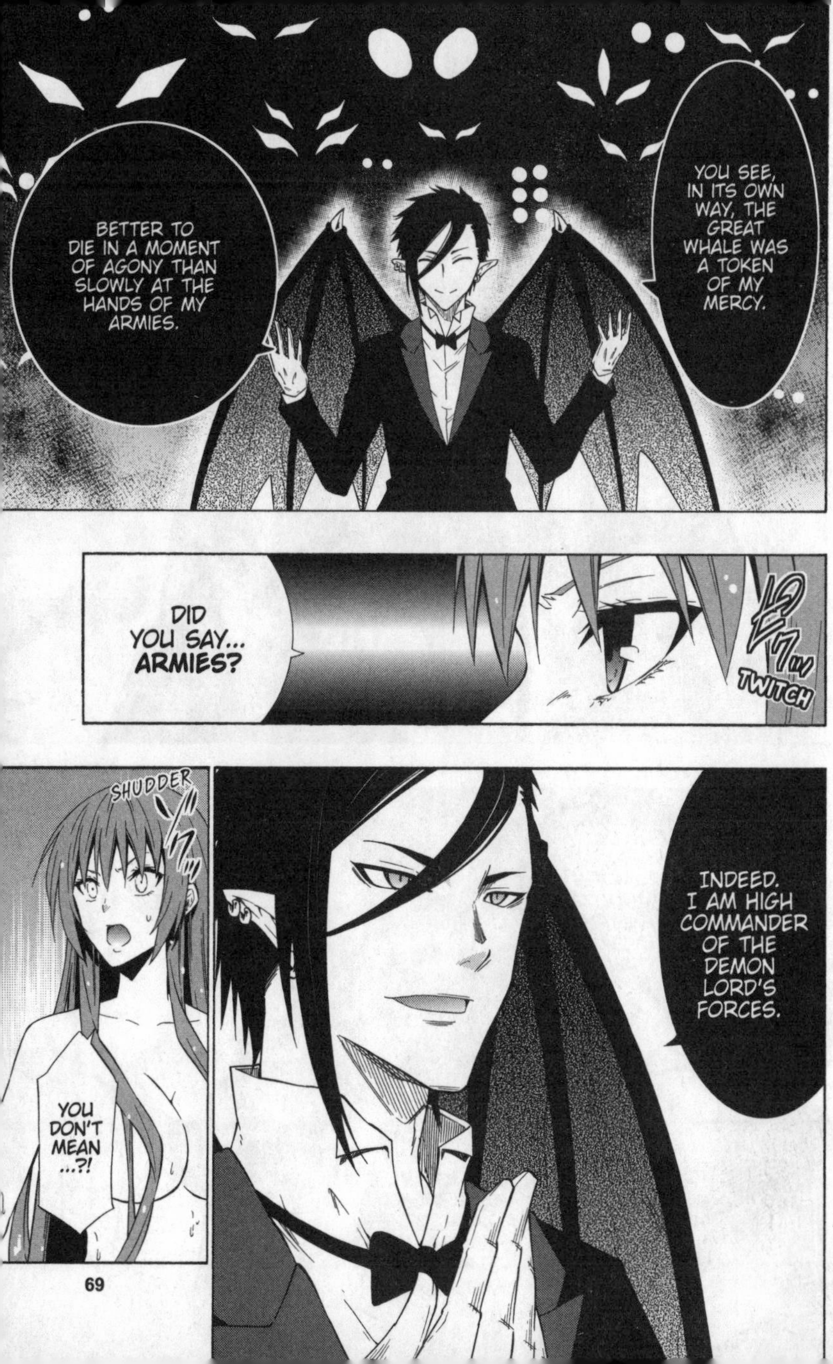
YOU SEE, IN ITS OWN WAY, THE GREAT WHALE WAS A TOKEN OF MY MERCY.
BETTER TO DIE IN A MOMENT OF AGONY THAN SLOWLY AT THE HANDS OF MY ARMIES.
TWITCH
DID YOU SAY... ARMIES?
INDEED. I AM HIGH COMMANDER OF THE DEMON LORD'S FORCES.
SHUDDER
YOU DON'T MEAN ...?!

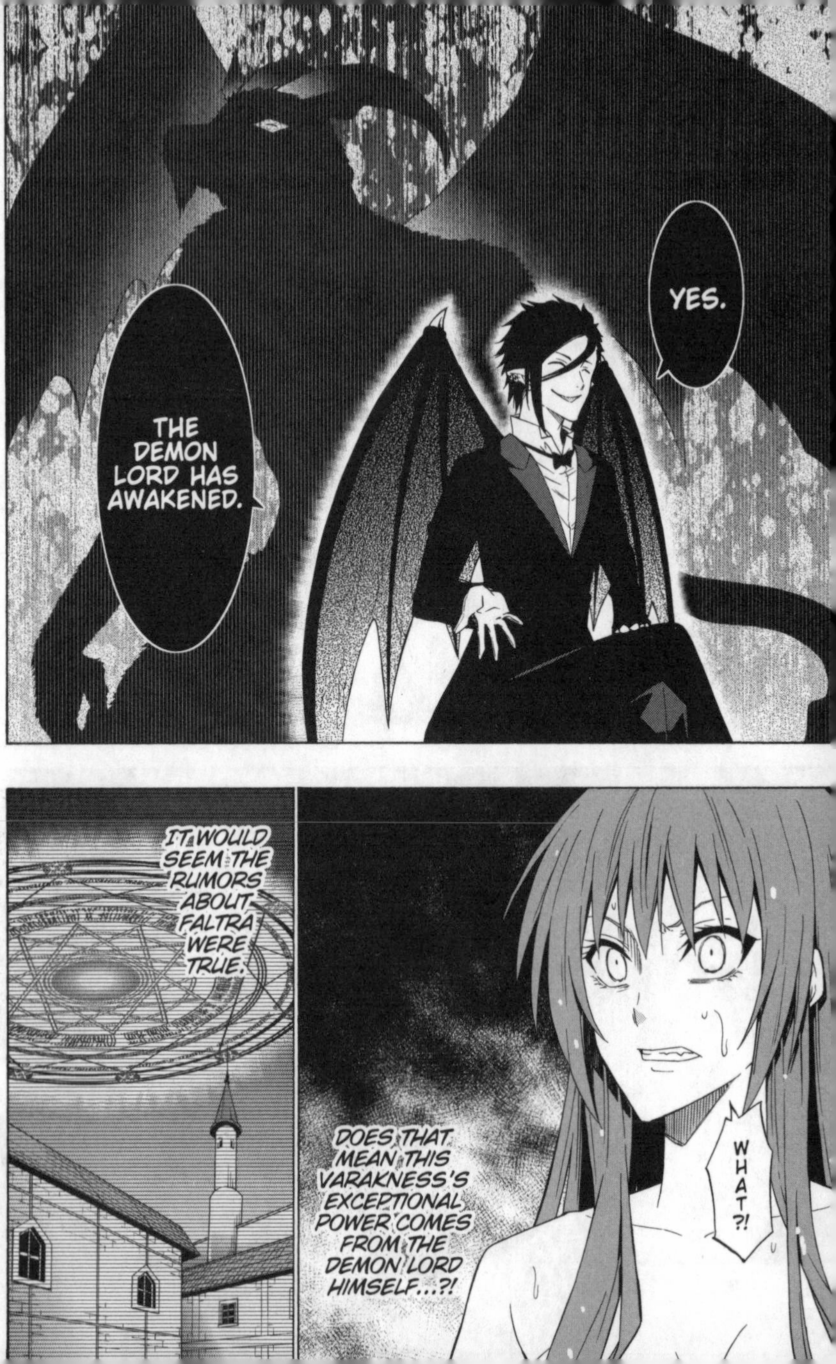
YES.
THE DEMON LORD HAS AWAKENED.
WHAT?!
DOES THAT MEAN THIS VARAKNESS'S EXCEPTIONAL POWER COMES FROM THE DEMON LORD HIMSELF...?!
IT WOULD SEEM THE RUMORS ABOUT FALTRA WERE TRUE.

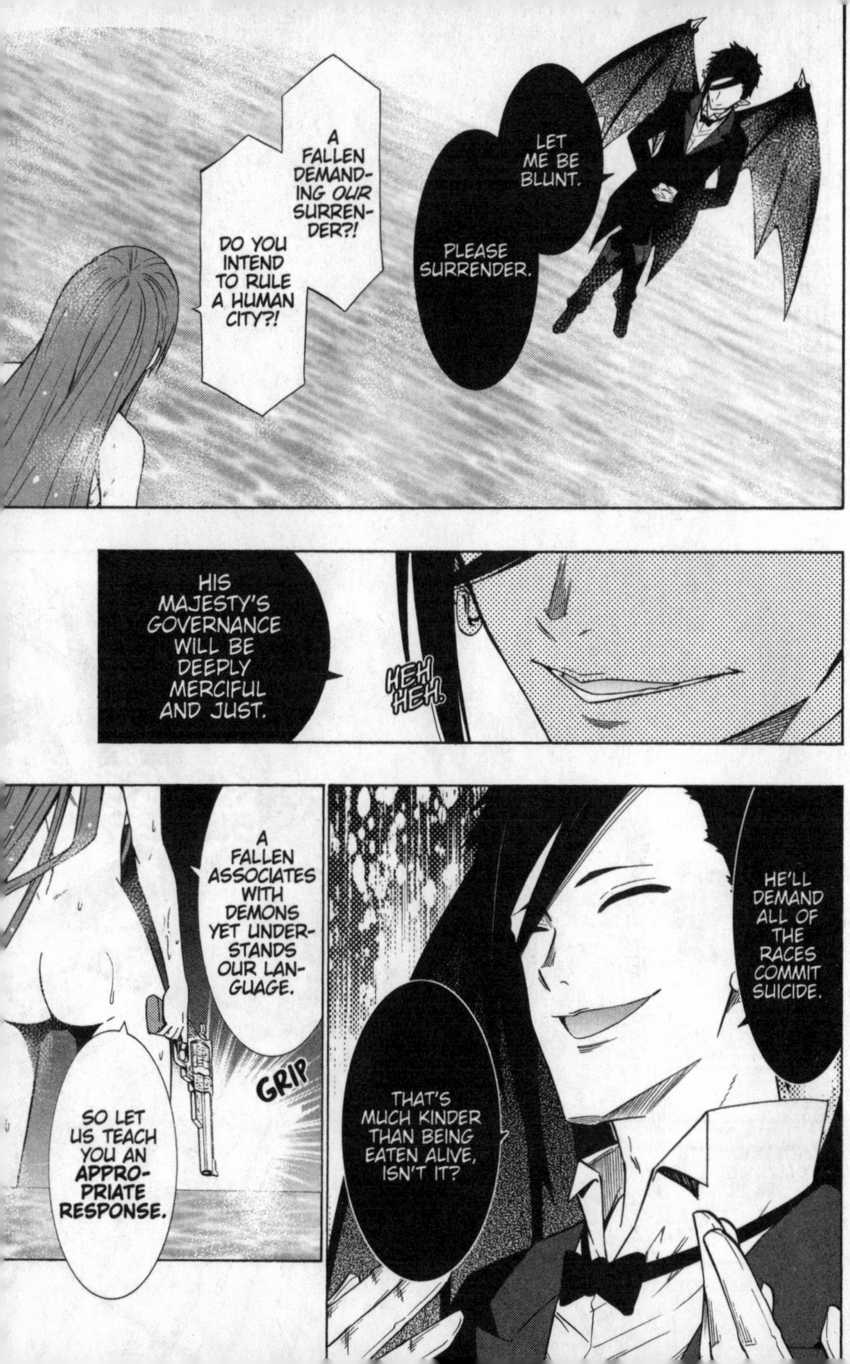
LET ME BE BLUNT.
PLEASE SURRENDER.
A FALLEN DEMANDING OUR SURRENDER?!
DO YOU INTEND TO RULE A HUMAN CITY?!
HIS MAJESTY'S GOVERNANCE WILL BE DEEPLY MERCIFUL AND JUST.
HEH HEH.
HE'LL DEMAND ALL OF THE RACES COMMIT SUICIDE.
THAT'S MUCH KINDER THAN BEING EATEN ALIVE, ISN'T IT?
A FALLEN ASSOCIATES WITH DEMONS YET UNDERSTANDS OUR LANGUAGE.
GRIP
SO LET US TEACH YOU AN APPROPRIATE RESPONSE.

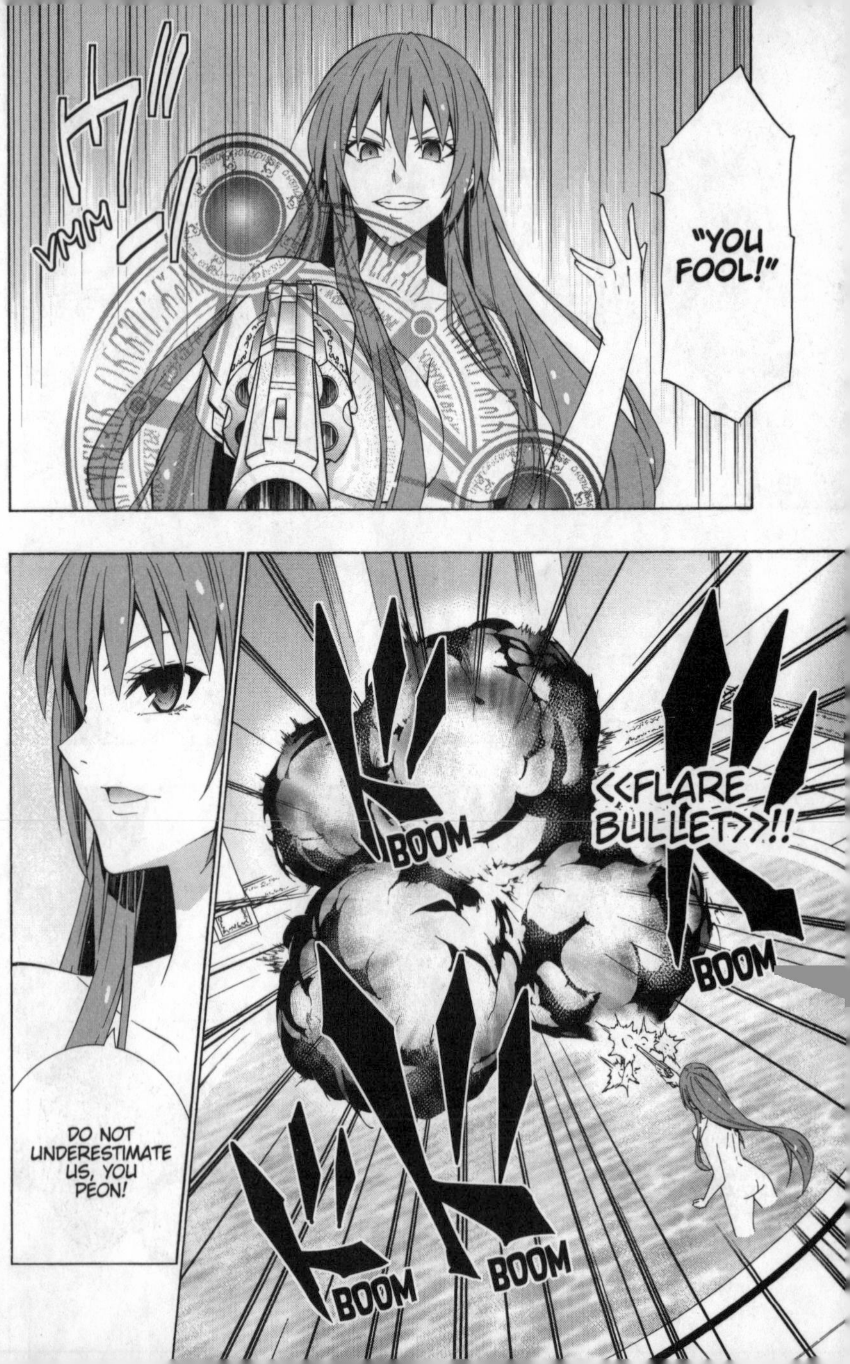
"YOU FOOL!"
VMM
<<FLARE BULLET>>!!
BOOM
BOOM
BOOM
BOOM
DO NOT UNDERESTIMATE US, YOU PEON!

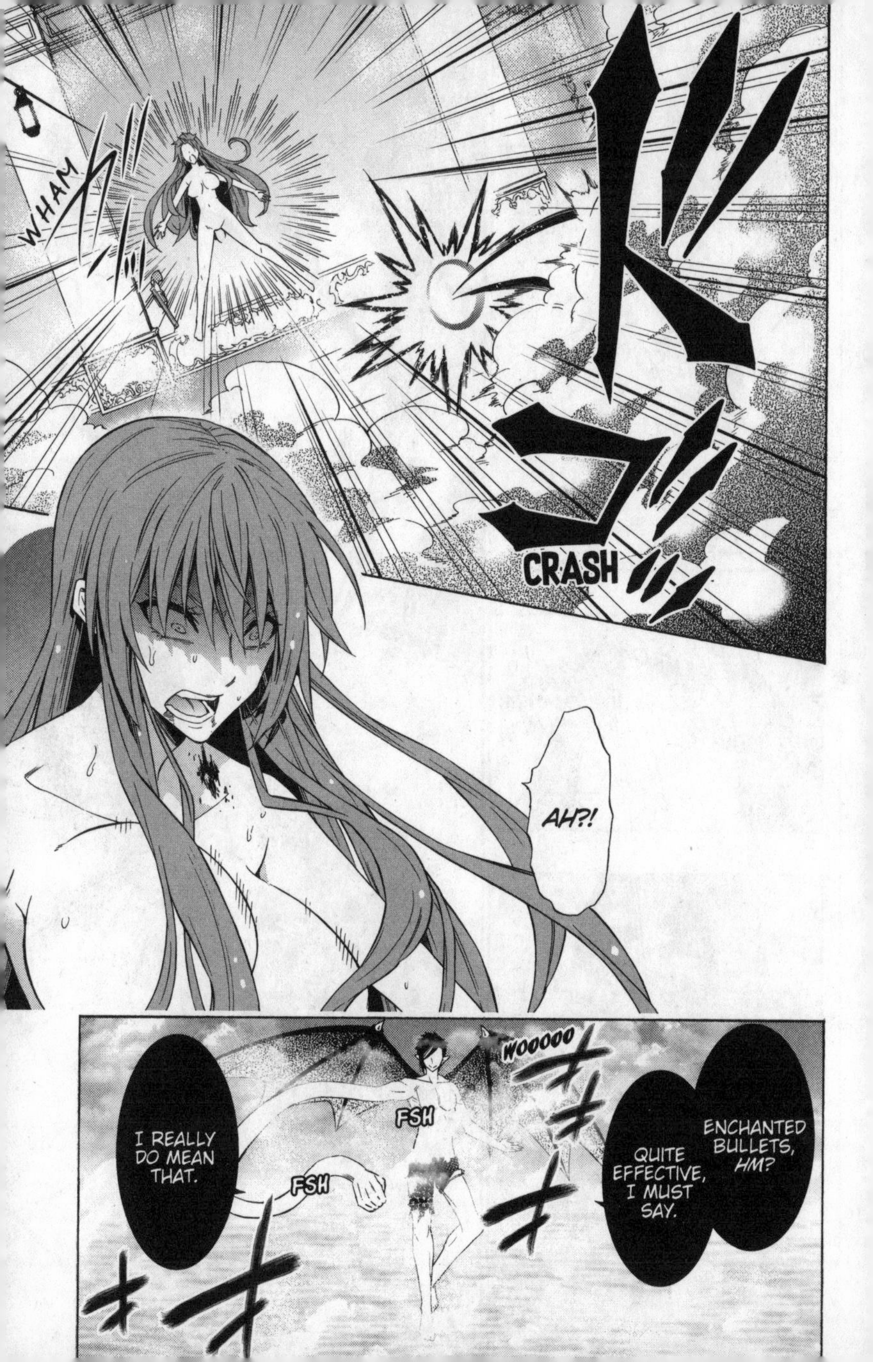
CRASH
WHAM
AH?!
ENCHANTED BULLETS, HM?
QUITE EFFECTIVE, I MUST SAY.
WOOOOO
FSH
FSH
I REALLY DO MEAN THAT.

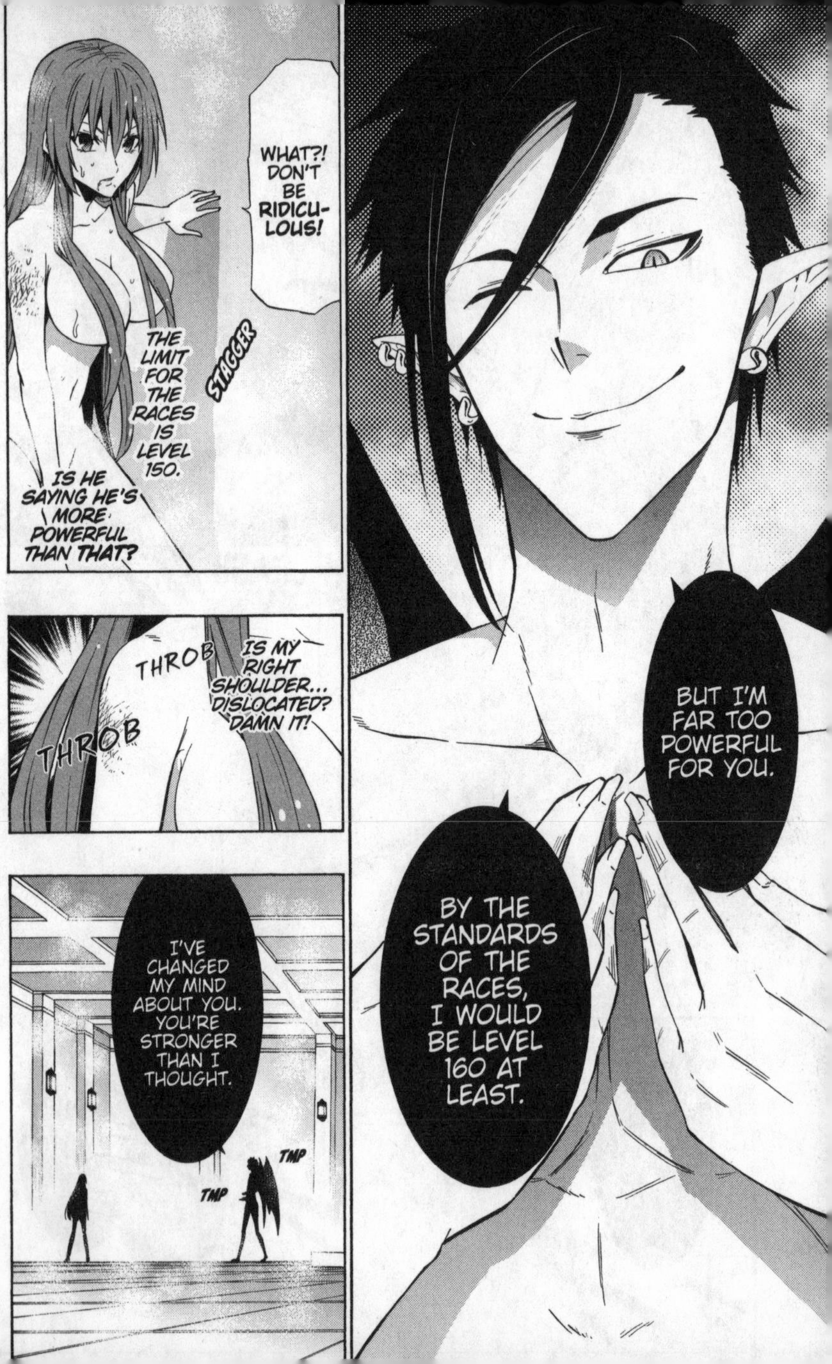

BUT I'M FAR TOO POWERFUL FOR YOU.
BY THE STANDARDS OF THE RACES, I WOULD BE LEVEL 160 AT LEAST.
WHAT?! DON'T BE RIDICU-LOUS!
STAGGER
THE LIMIT FOR THE RACES IS LEVEL 150.
IS HE SAYING HE'S MORE POWERFUL THAN THAT?
IS MY RIGHT SHOULDER... DISLOCATED? DAMN IT!
THROB
THROB
I'VE CHANGED MY MIND ABOUT YOU. YOU'RE STRONGER THAN I THOUGHT.
TMP
TMP

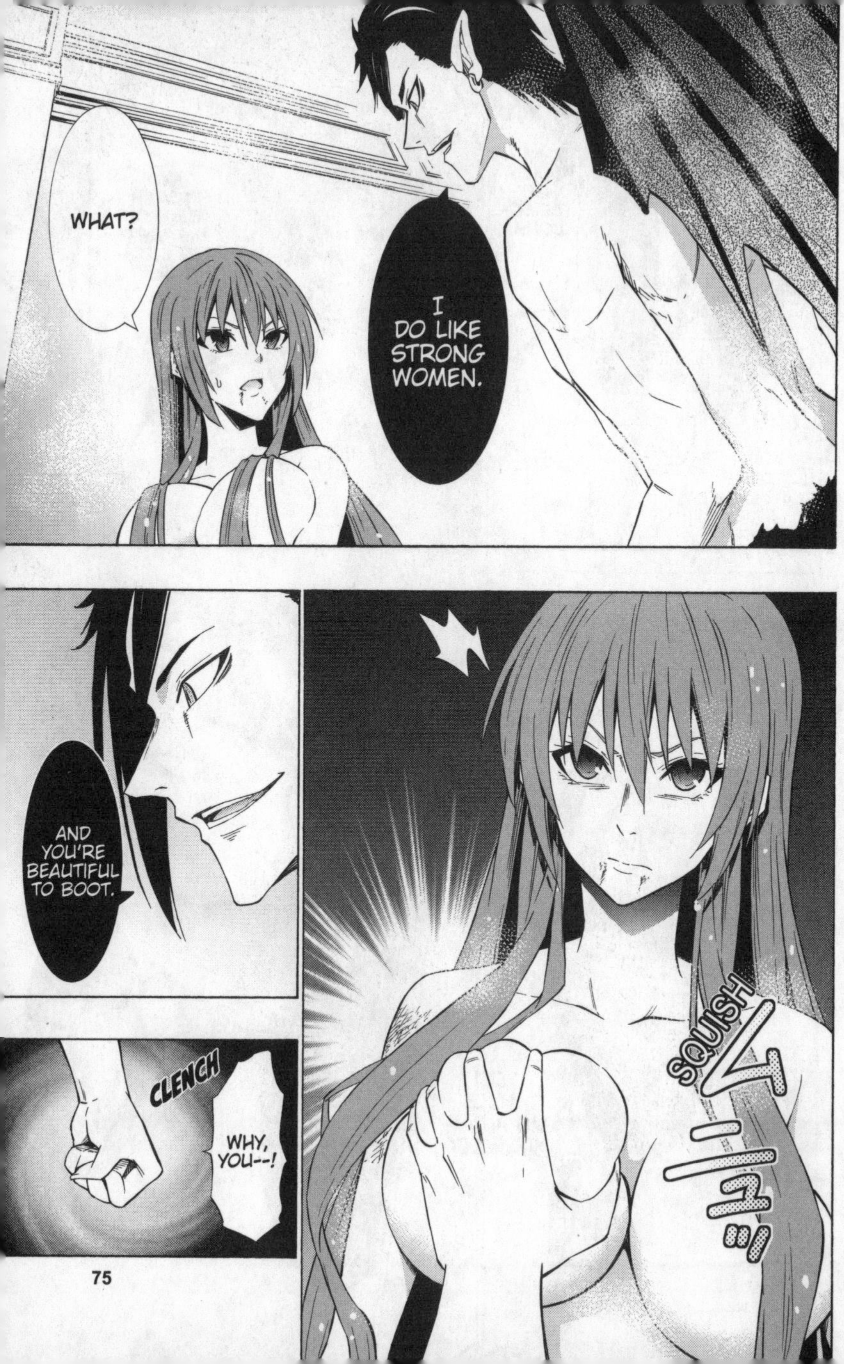
I DO LIKE STRONG WOMEN.
WHAT?
SQUISH
AND YOU'RE BEAUTIFUL TO BOOT.
CLENCH
WHY, YOU--!

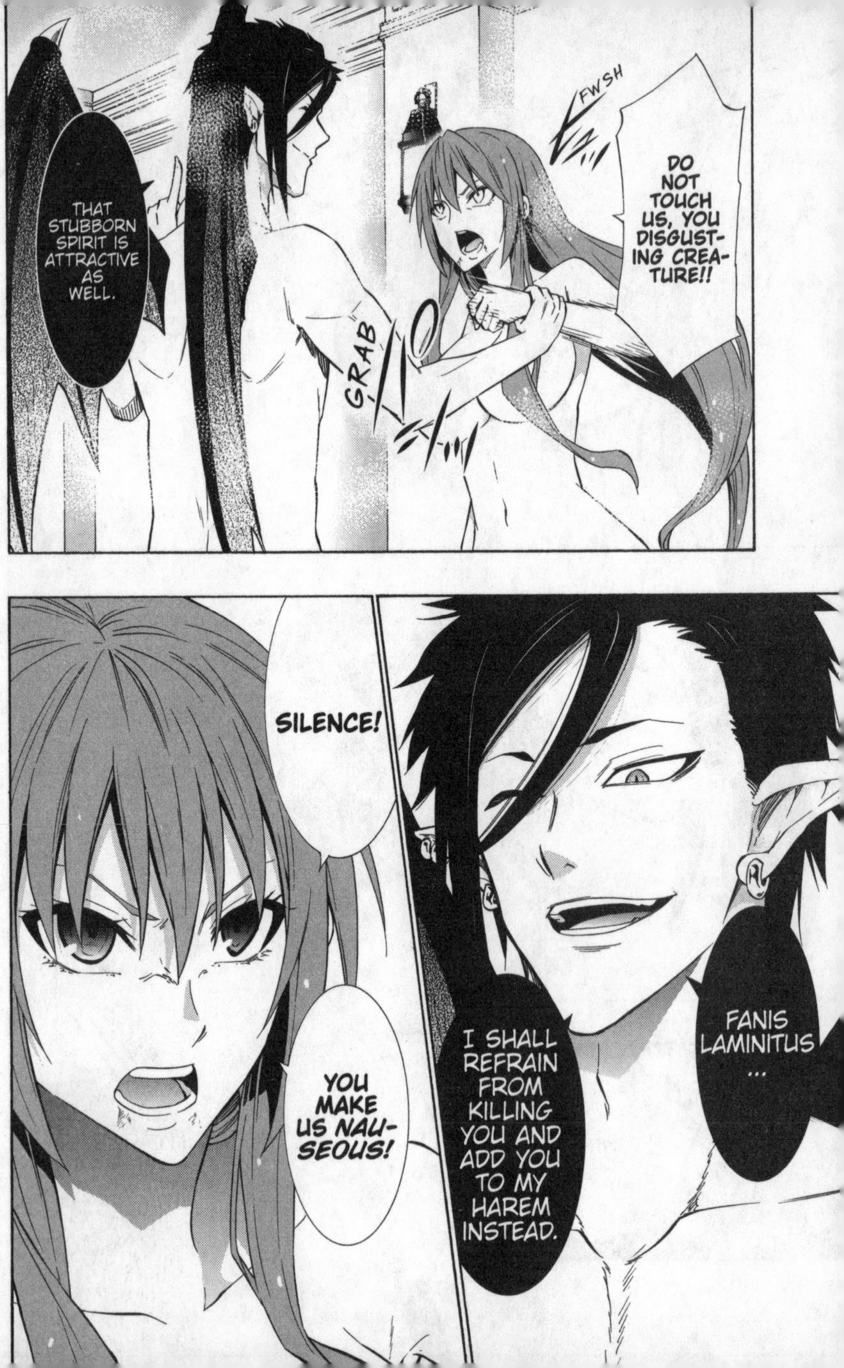
FWSH
DO NOT TOUCH US, YOU DISGUST-ING CREA-TURE!!
GRAB
THAT STUBBORN SPIRIT IS ATTRACTIVE AS WELL.
FANIS LAMINITUS ...
I SHALL REFRAIN FROM KILLING YOU AND ADD YOU TO MY HAREM INSTEAD.
SILENCE!
YOU MAKE US NAU-SEOUS!

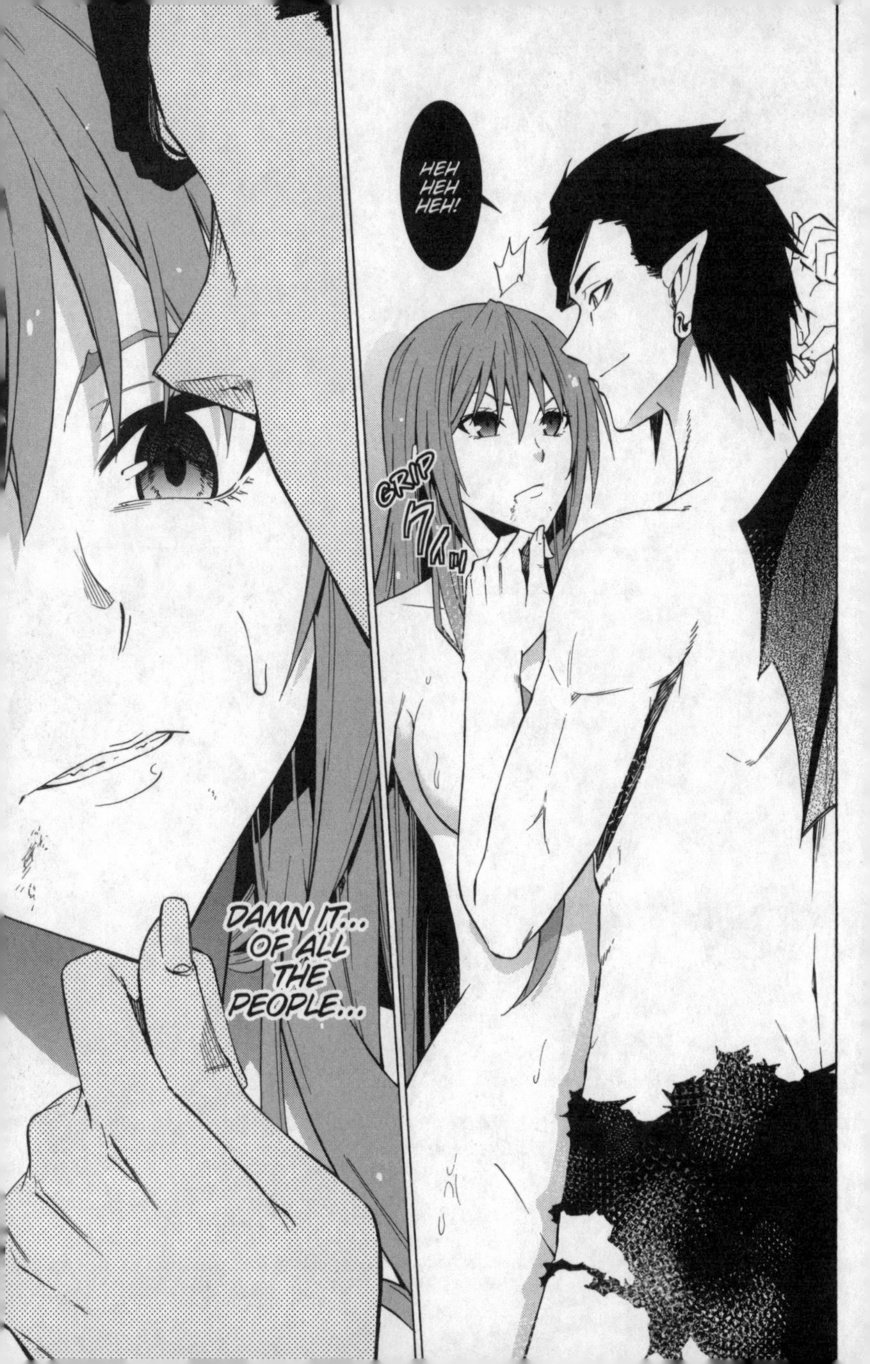
HEH HEH HEH!
GRIP
DAMN IT... OF ALL THE PEOPLE...

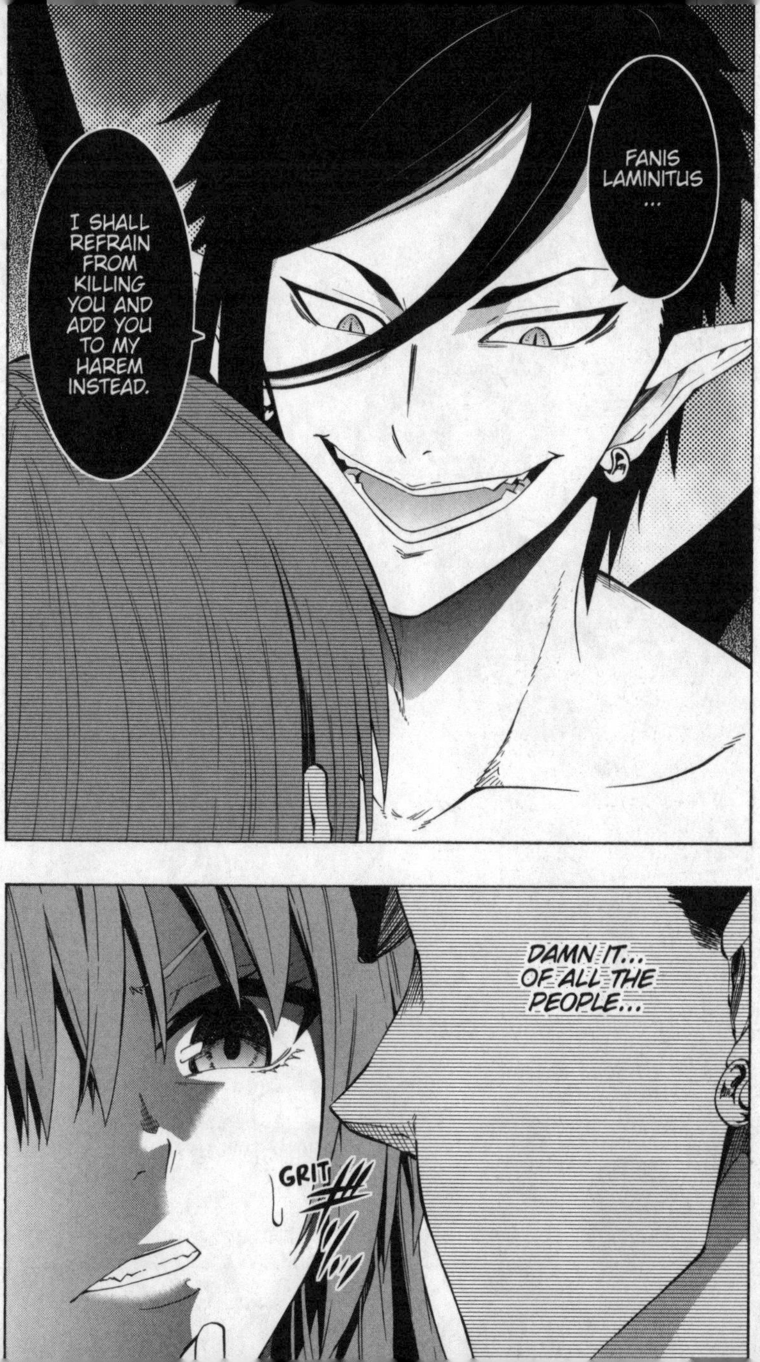
FANIS LAMINITUS ...
I SHALL REFRAIN FROM KILLING YOU AND ADD YOU TO MY HAREM INSTEAD.
DAMN IT... OF ALL THE PEOPLE...
GRIT

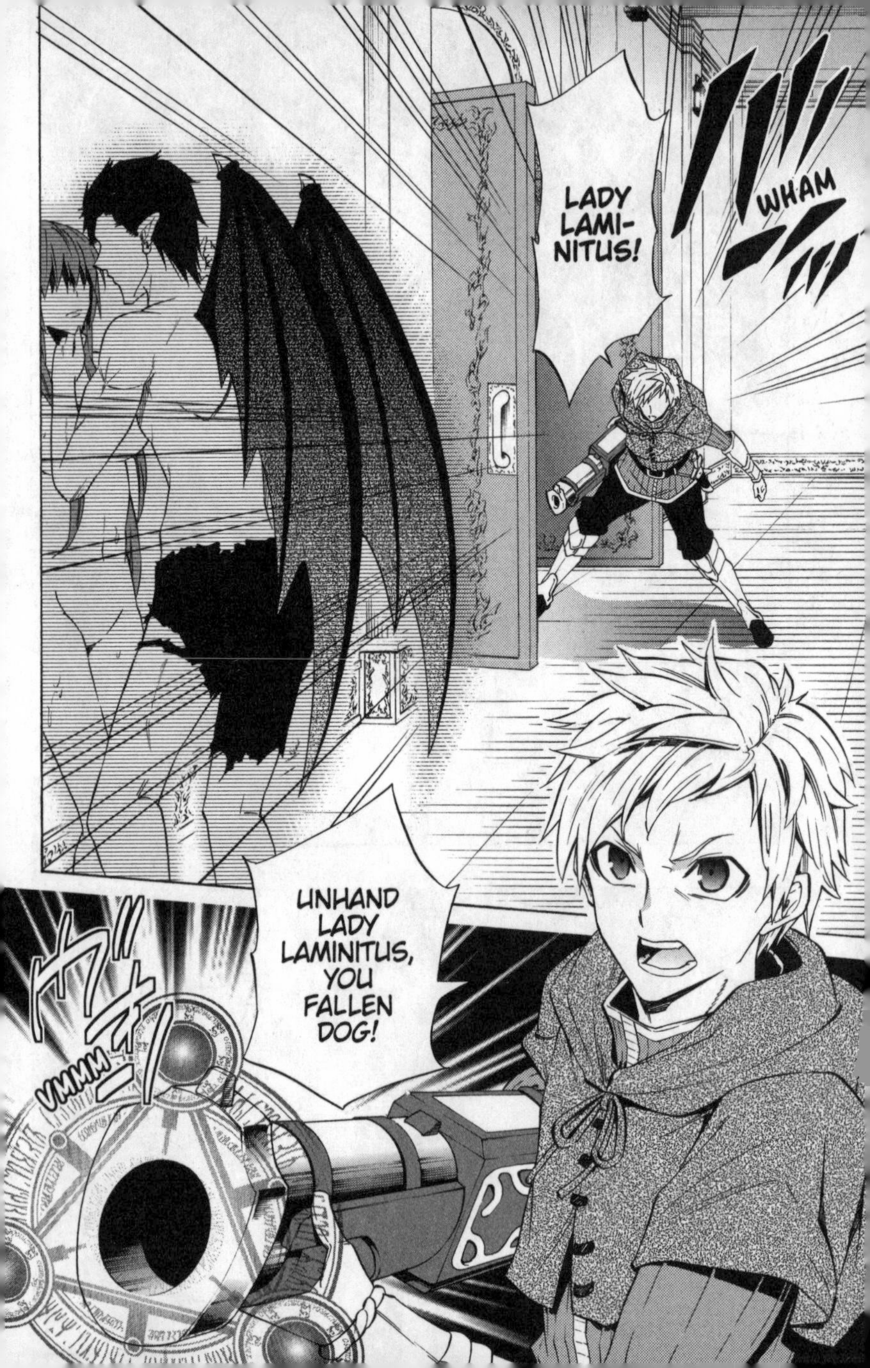
WHAM
LADY LAMINITUS!
UNHAND LADY LAMINITUS, YOU FALLEN DOG!
VMMM

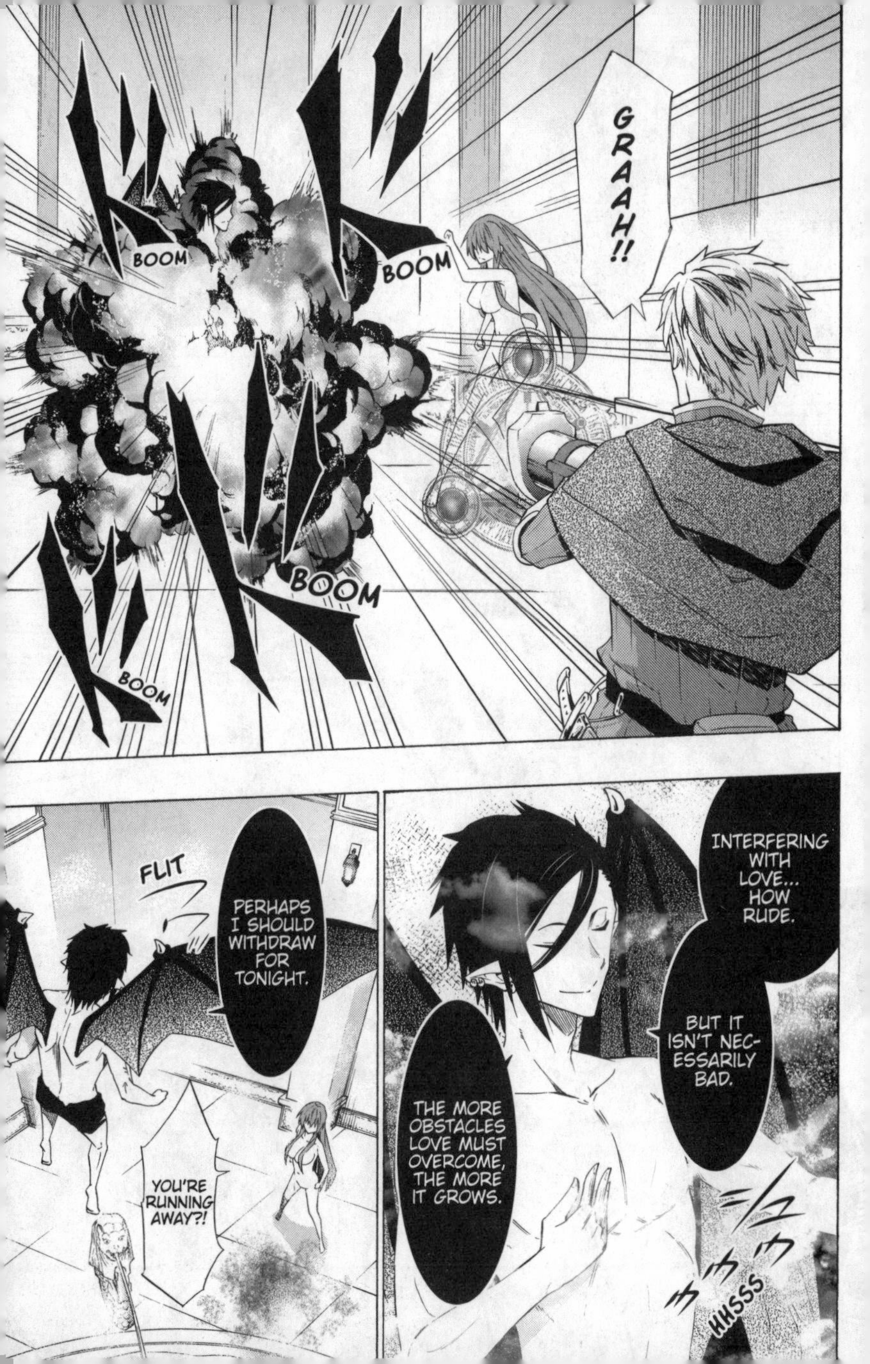
GRAAH!!
BOOM
BOOM
BOOM
BOOM
INTERFERING WITH LOVE... HOW RUDE.
BUT IT ISN'T NEC-ESSARILY BAD.
THE MORE OBSTACLES LOVE MUST OVERCOME, THE MORE IT GROWS.
HHSSS
FLIT
PERHAPS I SHOULD WITHDRAW FOR TONIGHT.
YOU'RE RUNNING AWAY?!

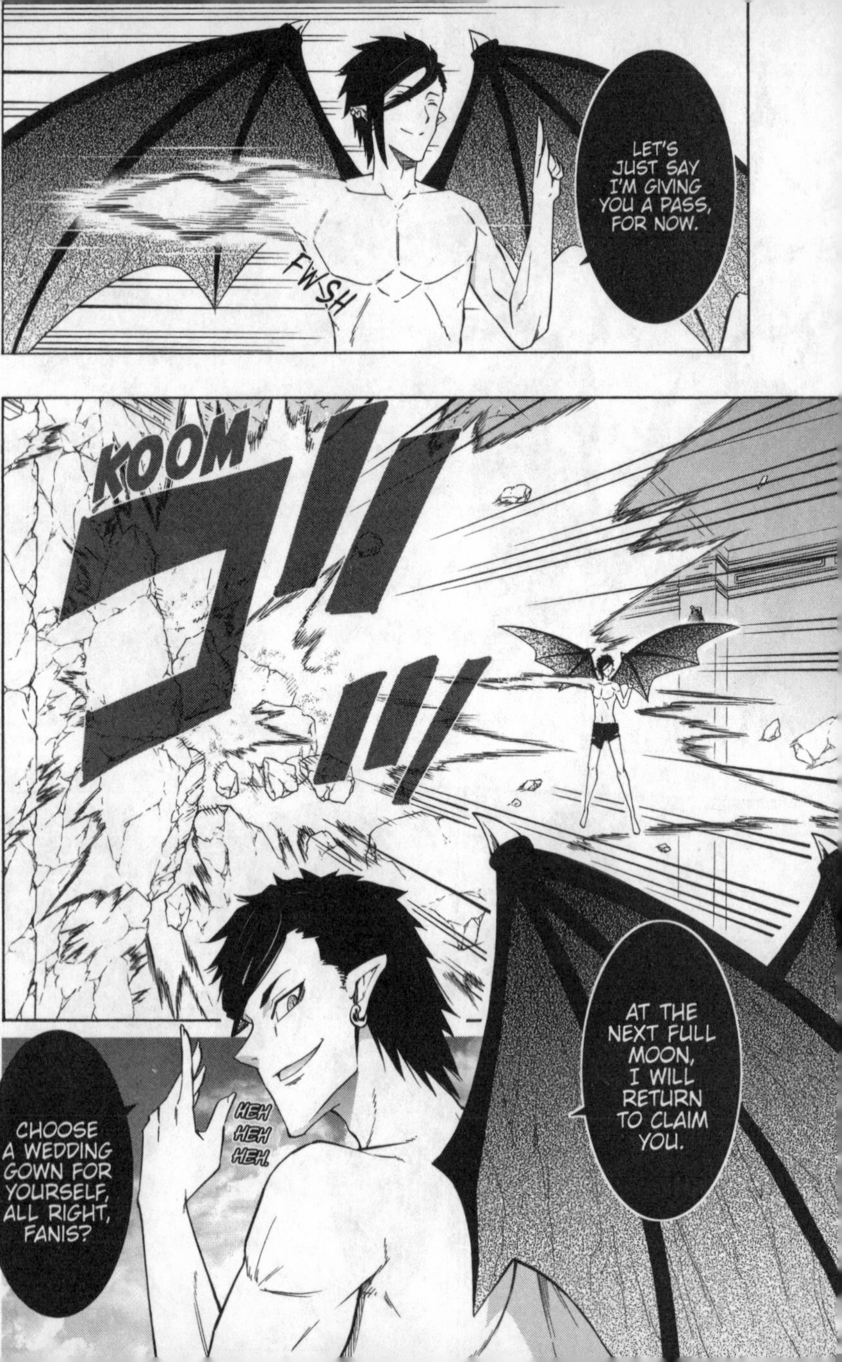
LET'S JUST SAY I'M GIVING YOU A PASS, FOR NOW.
FWSH
KOOM
AT THE NEXT FULL MOON, I WILL RETURN TO CLAIM YOU.
HEH HEH HEH.
CHOOSE A WEDDING GOWN FOR YOURSELF, ALL RIGHT, FANIS?

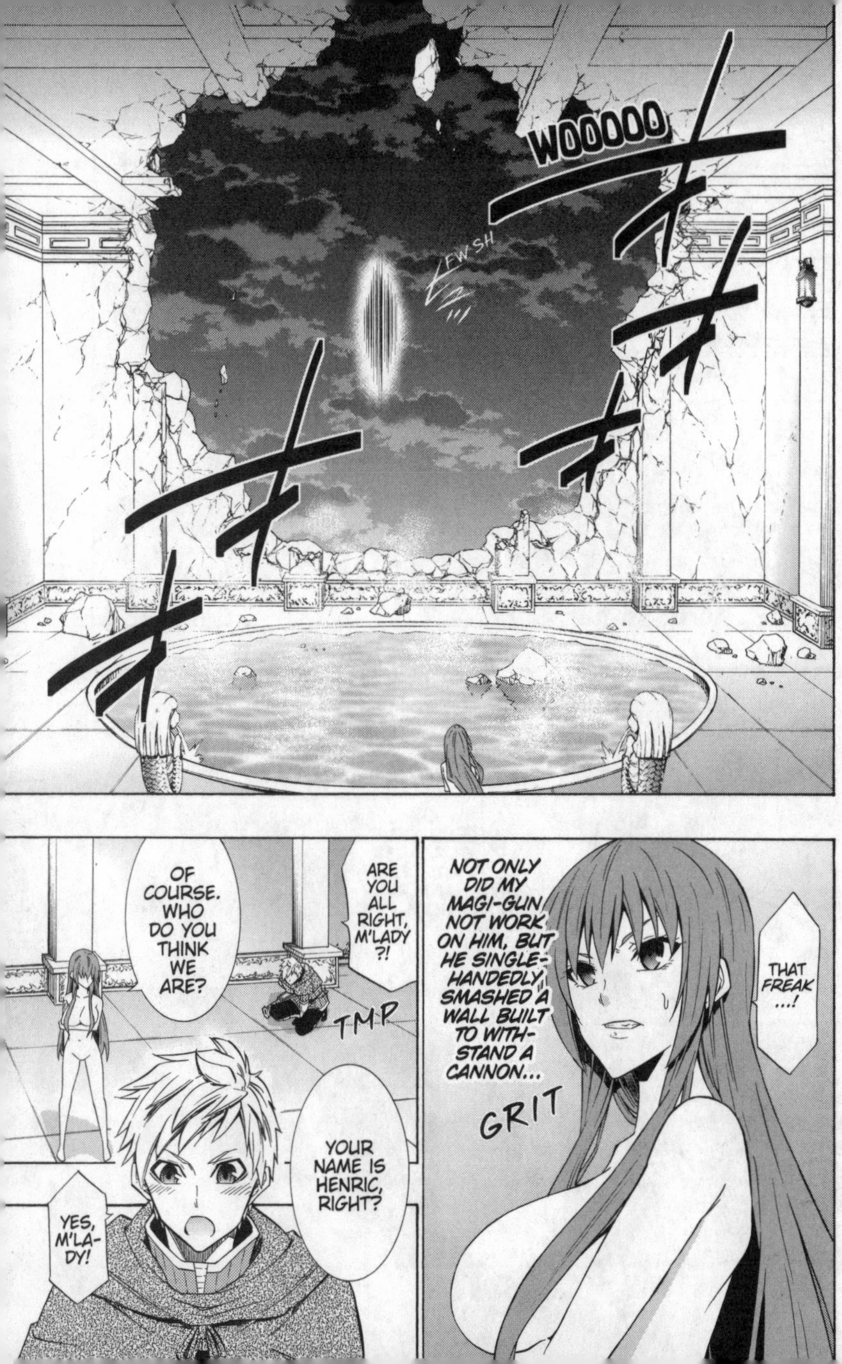
WOOOOO
FWSH
THAT FREAK...!
NOT ONLY DID MY MAGI-GUN NOT WORK ON HIM, BUT HE SINGLE-HANDEDLY SMASHED A WALL BUILT TO WITH-STAND A CANNON...
GRIT
ARE YOU ALL RIGHT, M'LADY?!
OF COURSE. WHO DO YOU THINK WE ARE?
TMP
YOUR NAME IS HENRIC, RIGHT?
YES, M'LADY!

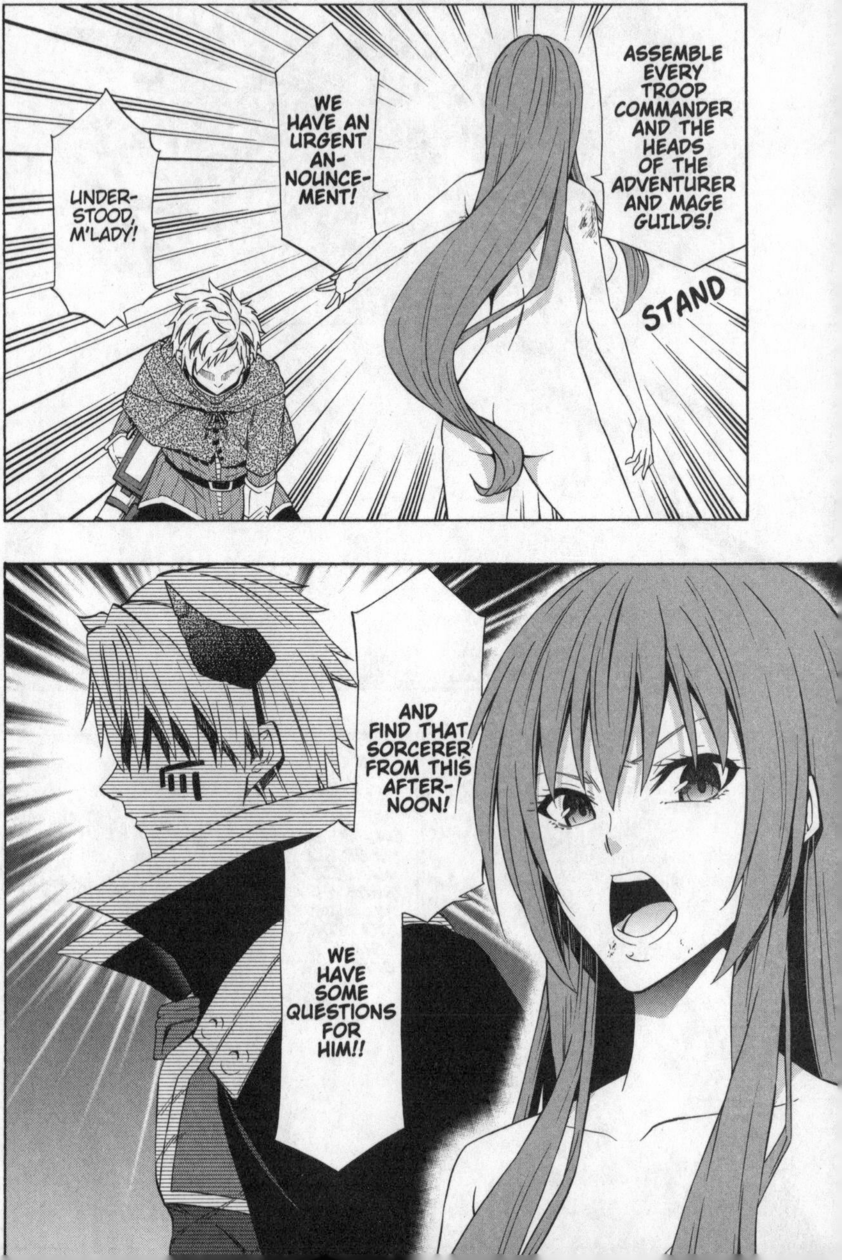
ASSEMBLE EVERY TROOP COMMANDER AND THE HEADS OF THE ADVENTURER AND MAGE GUILDS!
STAND
WE HAVE AN URGENT ANNOUNCEMENT!
UNDERSTOOD, M'LADY!
AND FIND THAT SORCERER FROM THIS AFTERNOON!
WE HAVE SOME QUESTIONS FOR HIM!!

52 REACHING A DUNGEON

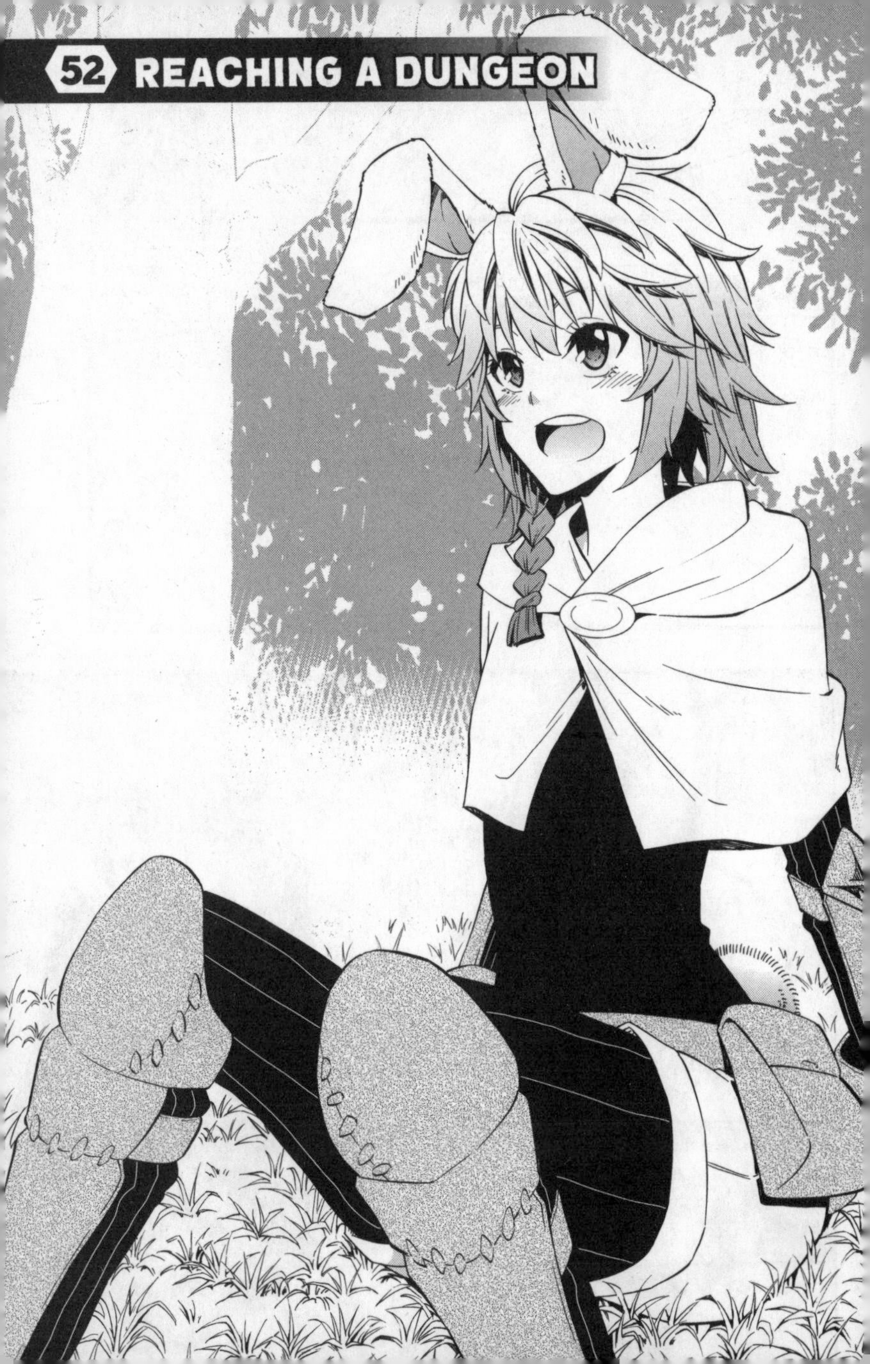

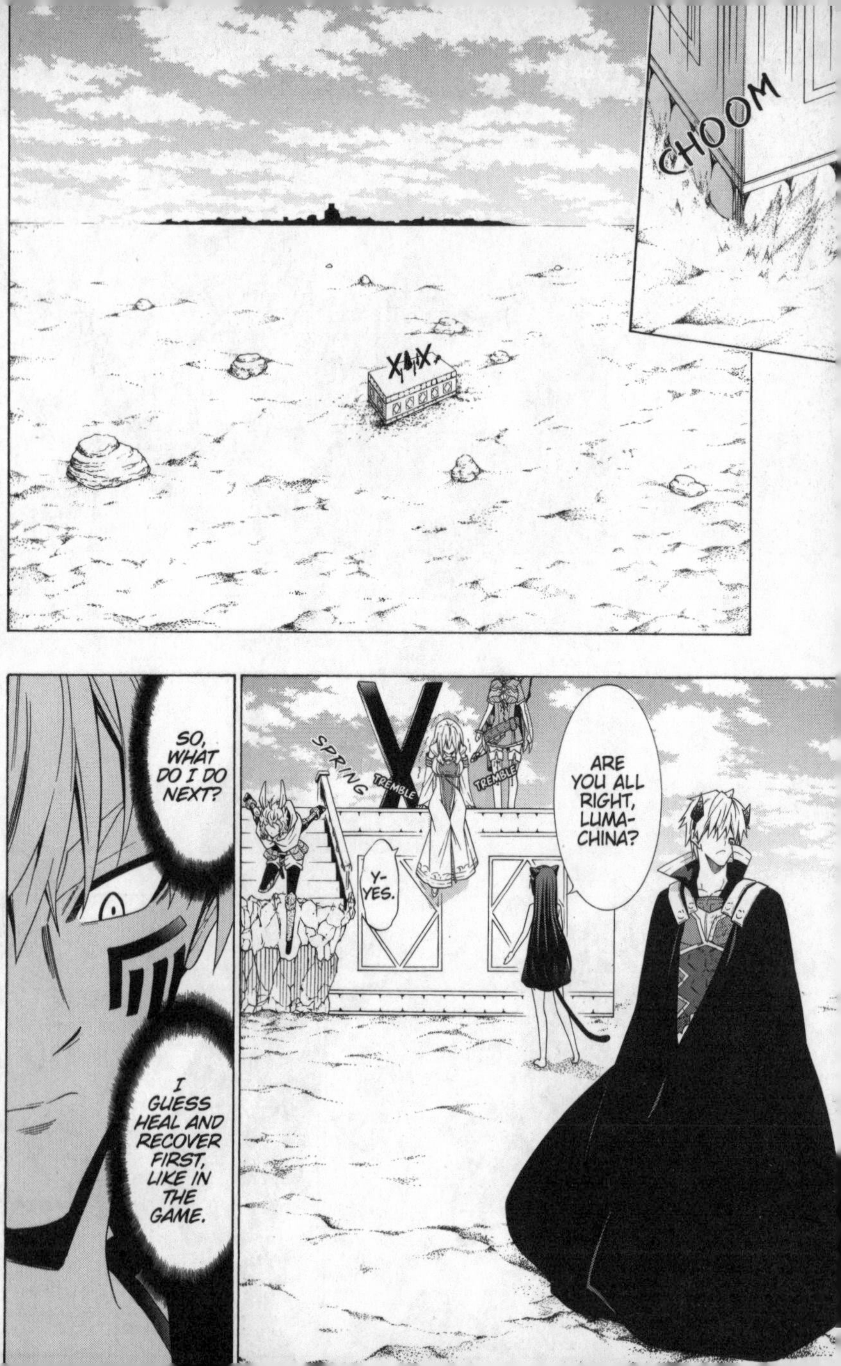
CHOOM
ARE YOU ALL RIGHT, LUMA-CHINA?
TREMBLE
TREMBLE
SPRING
Y-YES.
SO, WHAT DO I DO NEXT?
I GUESS HEAL AND RECOVER FIRST, LIKE IN THE GAME.

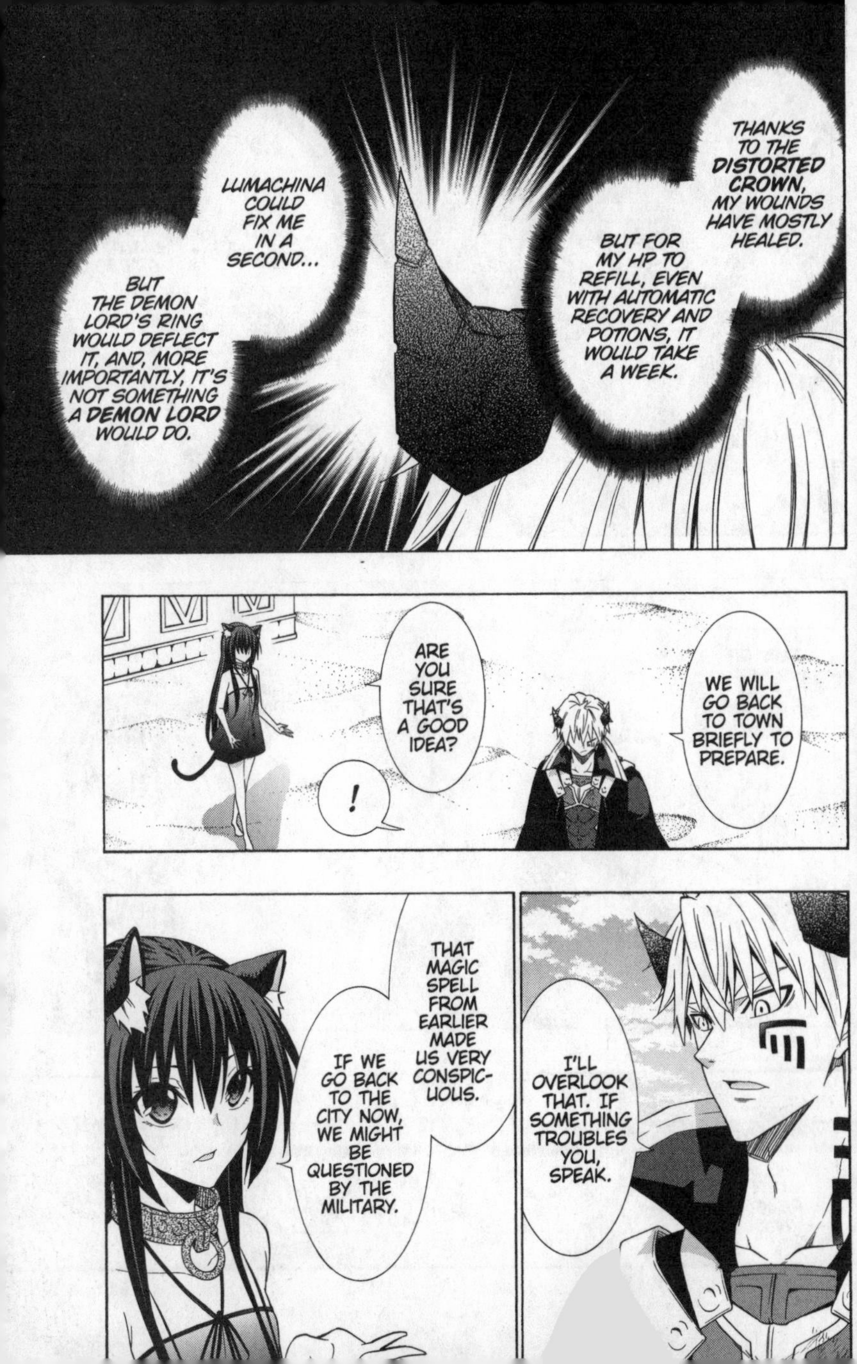
THANKS TO THE DISTORTED CROWN, MY WOUNDS HAVE MOSTLY HEALED.
BUT FOR MY HP TO REFILL, EVEN WITH AUTOMATIC RECOVERY AND POTIONS, IT WOULD TAKE A WEEK.
LUMACHINA COULD FIX ME IN A SECOND...
BUT THE DEMON LORD'S RING WOULD DEFLECT IT, AND, MORE IMPORTANTLY, IT'S NOT SOMETHING A DEMON LORD WOULD DO.
WE WILL GO BACK TO TOWN BRIEFLY TO PREPARE.
ARE YOU SURE THAT'S A GOOD IDEA?
!
I'LL OVERLOOK THAT. IF SOMETHING TROUBLES YOU, SPEAK.
THAT MAGIC SPELL FROM EARLIER MADE US VERY CONSPICUOUS.
IF WE GO BACK TO THE CITY NOW, WE MIGHT BE QUESTIONED BY THE MILITARY.

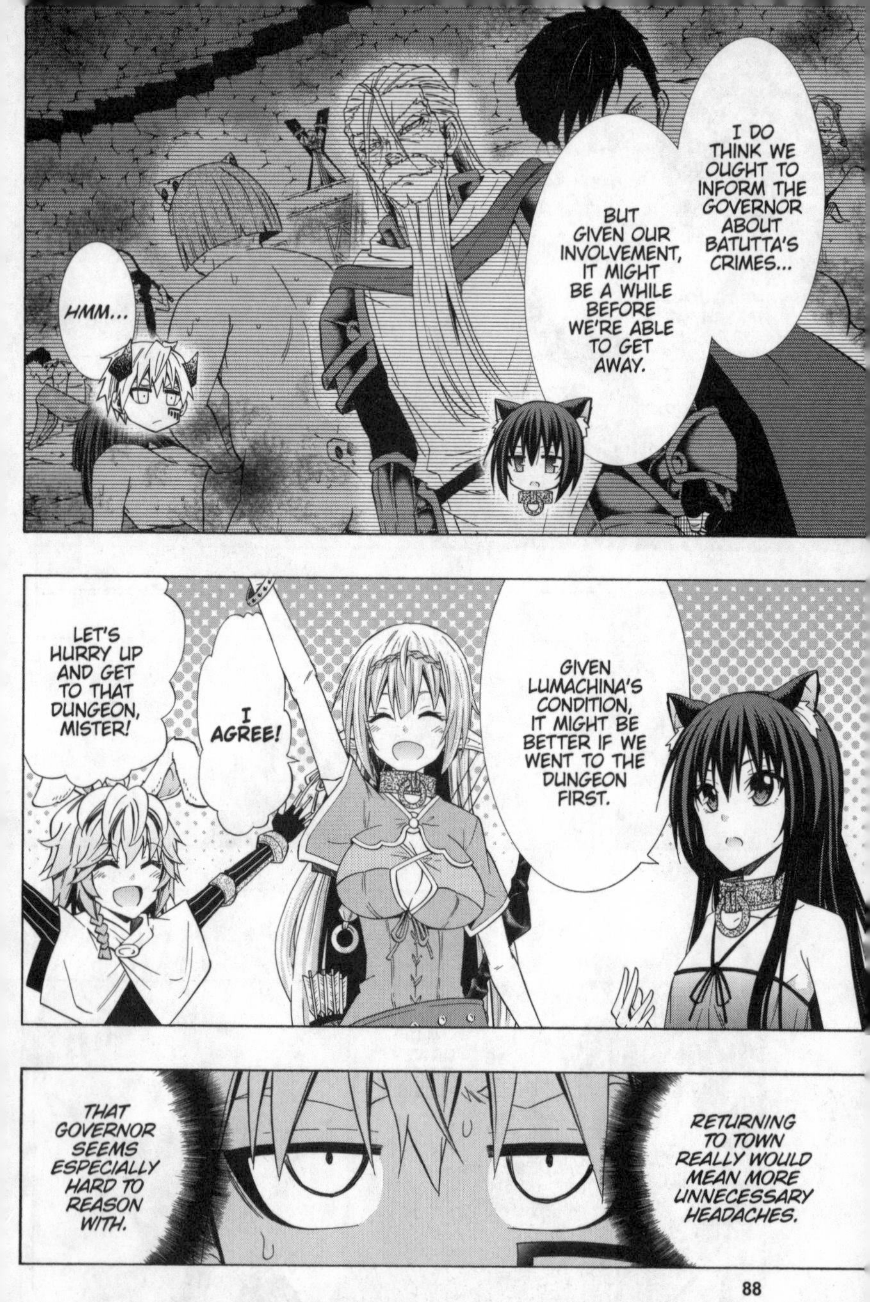
I DO THINK WE OUGHT TO INFORM THE GOVERNOR ABOUT BATUTTA'S CRIMES...
BUT GIVEN OUR INVOLVEMENT, IT MIGHT BE A WHILE BEFORE WE'RE ABLE TO GET AWAY.
HMM...
GIVEN LUMACHINA'S CONDITION, IT MIGHT BE BETTER IF WE WENT TO THE DUNGEON FIRST.
I AGREE!
LET'S HURRY UP AND GET TO THAT DUNGEON, MISTER!
RETURNING TO TOWN REALLY WOULD MEAN MORE UNNECESSARY HEADACHES.
THAT GOVERNOR SEEMS ESPECIALLY HARD TO REASON WITH.

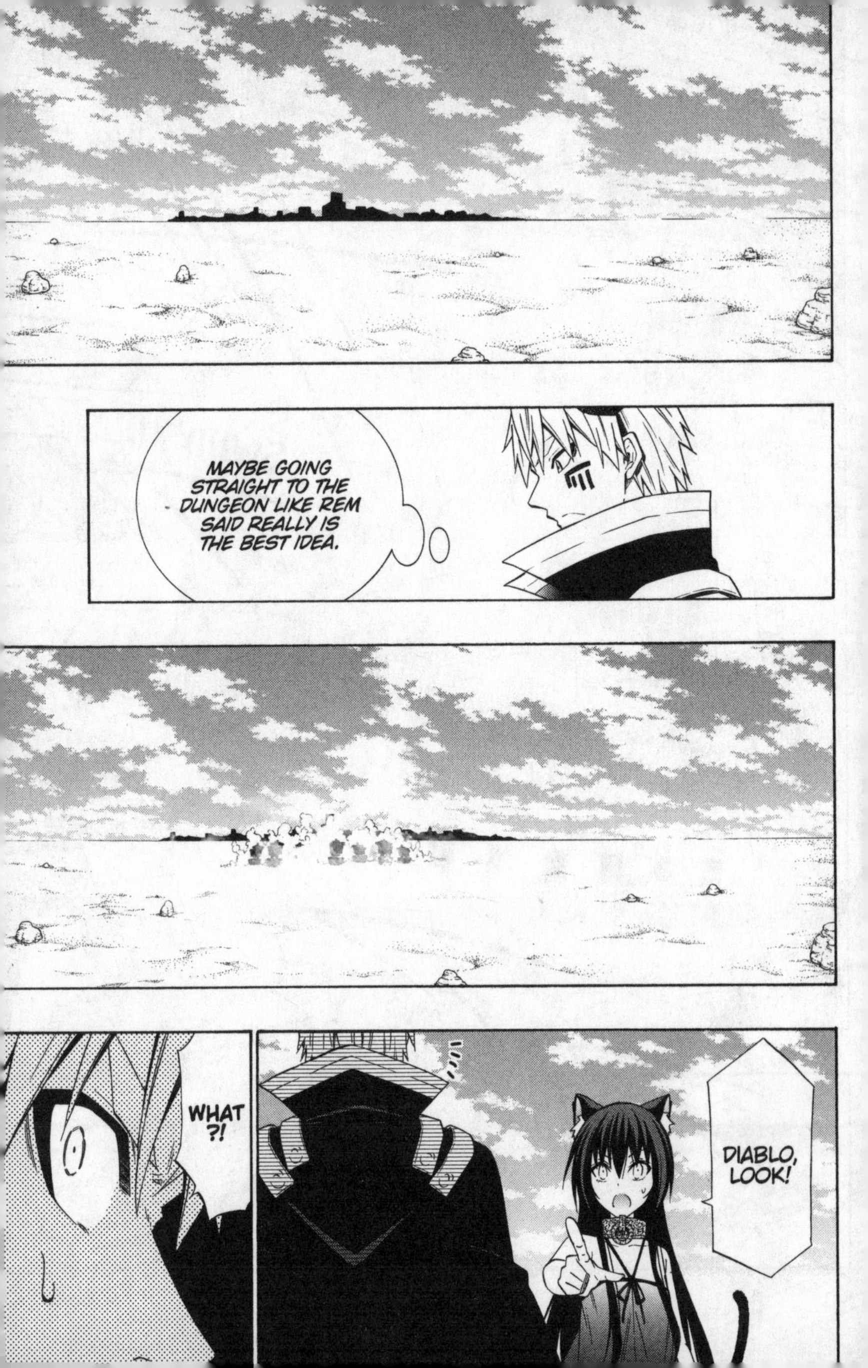
MAYBE GOING STRAIGHT TO THE DUNGEON LIKE REM SAID REALLY IS THE BEST IDEA.
DIABLO, LOOK!
WHAT ?!

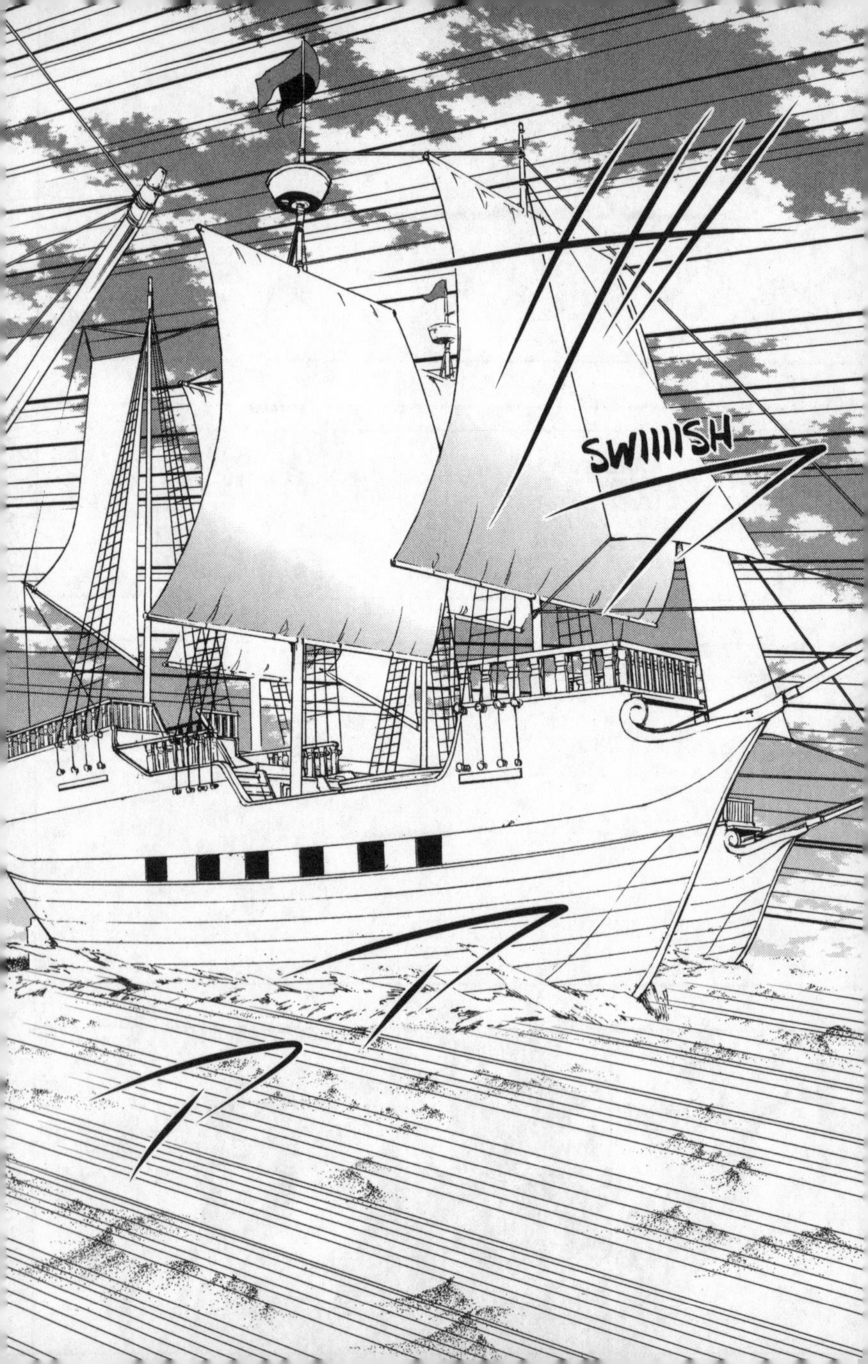
SWIIIISH

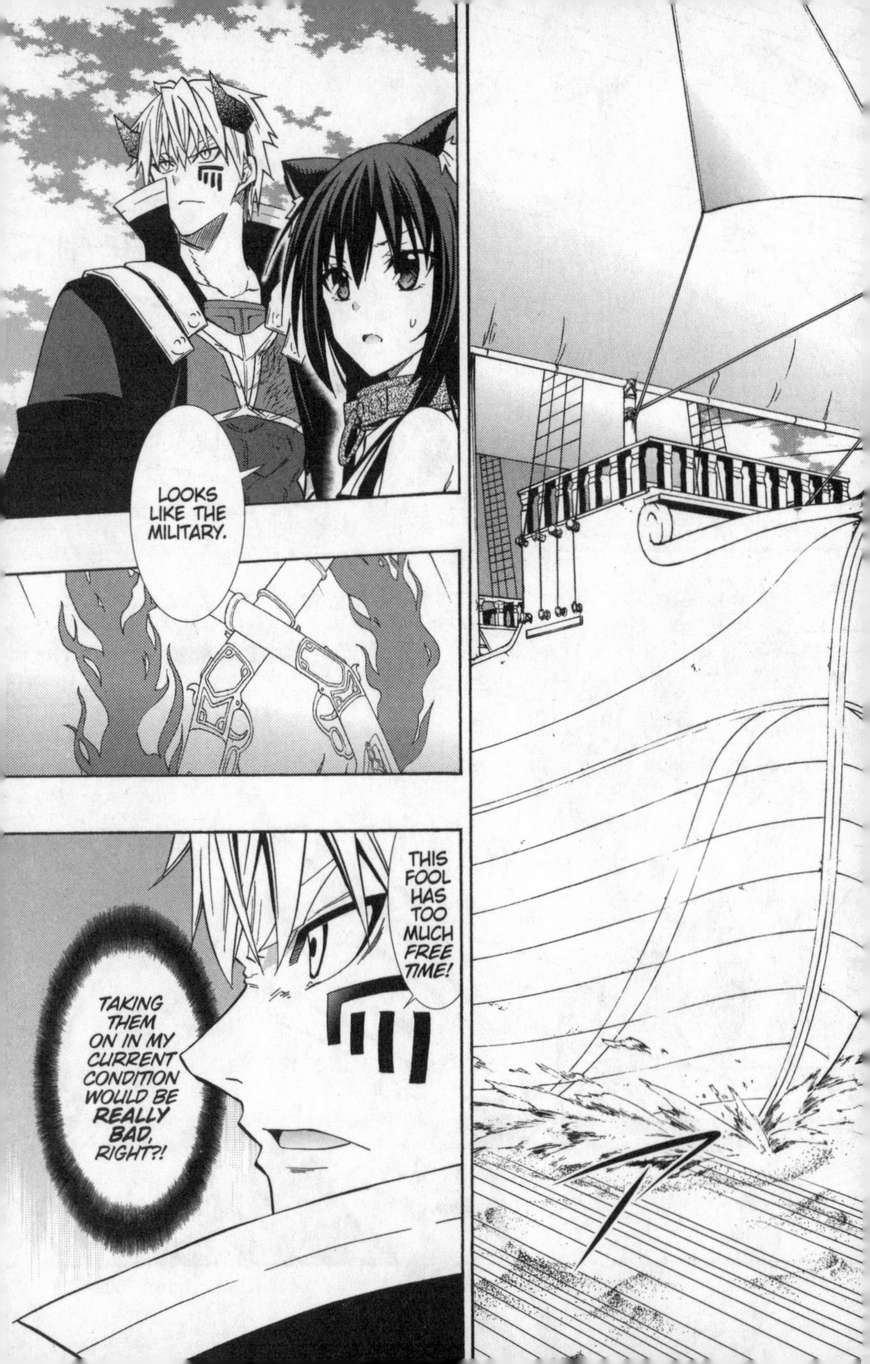
LOOKS LIKE THE MILITARY.
THIS FOOL HAS TOO MUCH FREE TIME!
TAKING THEM ON IN MY CURRENT CONDITION WOULD BE REALLY BAD, RIGHT?!

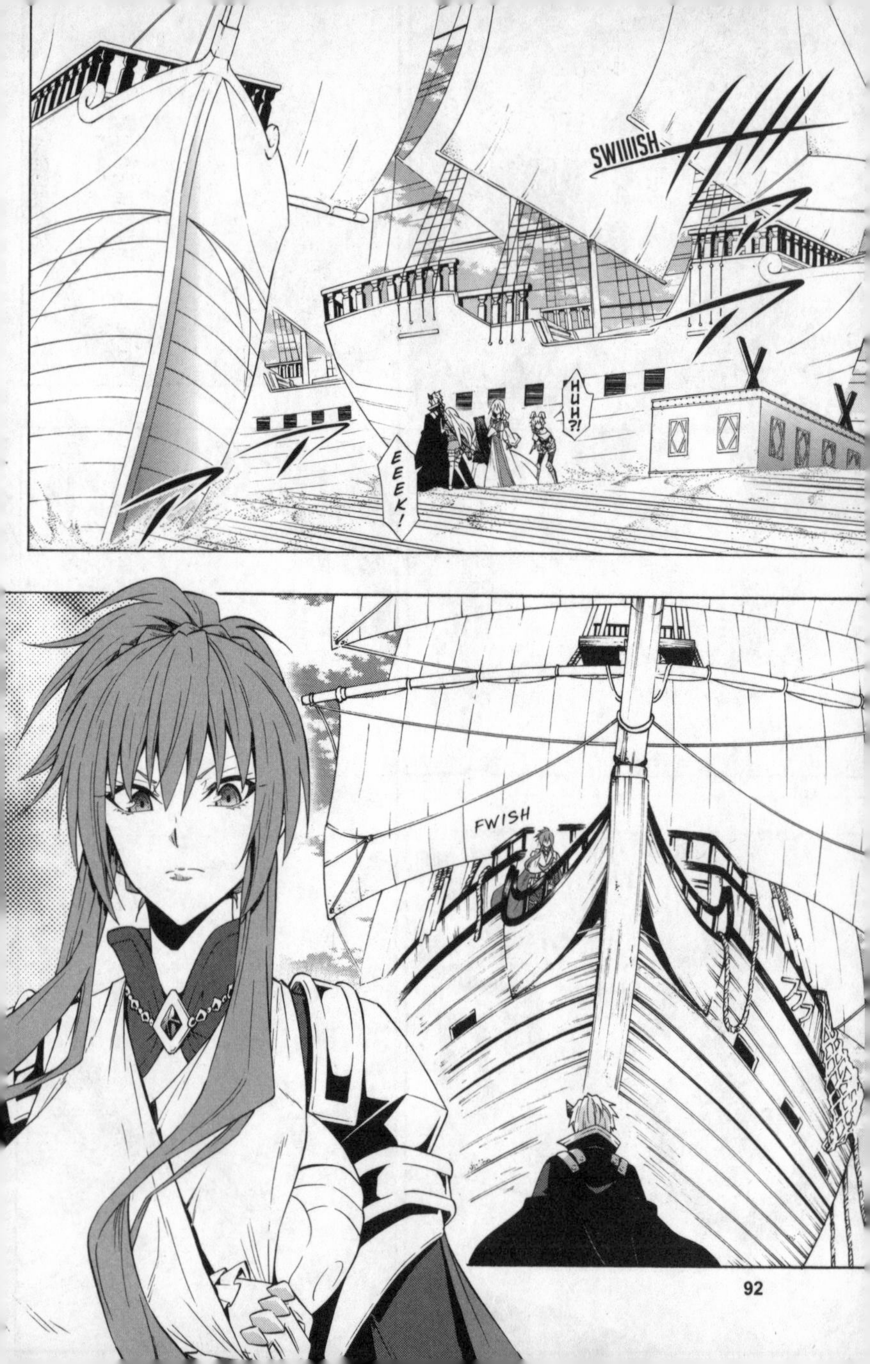
SWIIIISH
HUH?!
EEEK!
FWISH

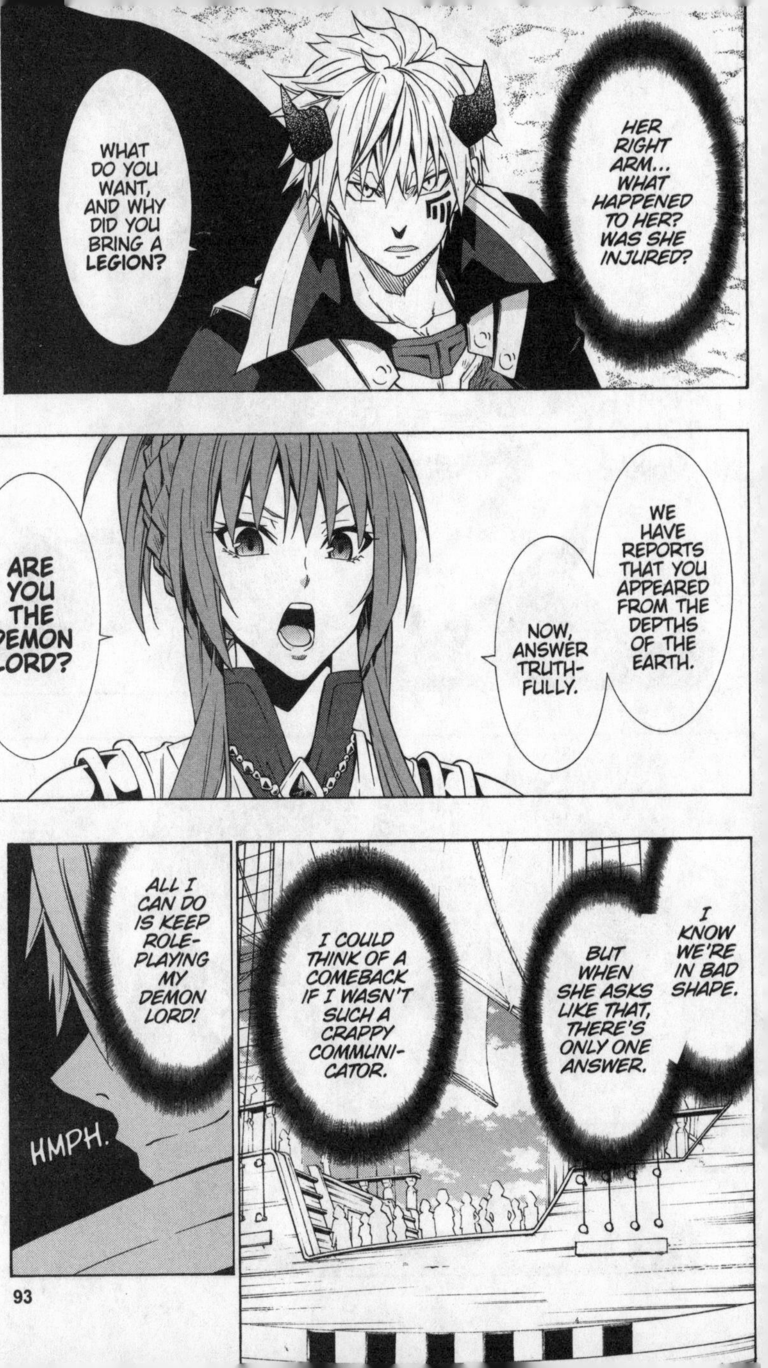
HER RIGHT ARM... WHAT HAPPENED TO HER? WAS SHE INJURED?
WHAT DO YOU WANT, AND WHY DID YOU BRING A LEGION?
WE HAVE REPORTS THAT YOU APPEARED FROM THE DEPTHS OF THE EARTH.
NOW, ANSWER TRUTH-FULLY.
ARE YOU THE DEMON LORD?
I KNOW WE'RE IN BAD SHAPE.
BUT WHEN SHE ASKS LIKE THAT, THERE'S ONLY ONE ANSWER.
I COULD THINK OF A COMEBACK IF I WASN'T SUCH A CRAPPY COMMUNI-CATOR.
ALL I CAN DO IS KEEP ROLE-PLAYING MY DEMON LORD!
HMPH.

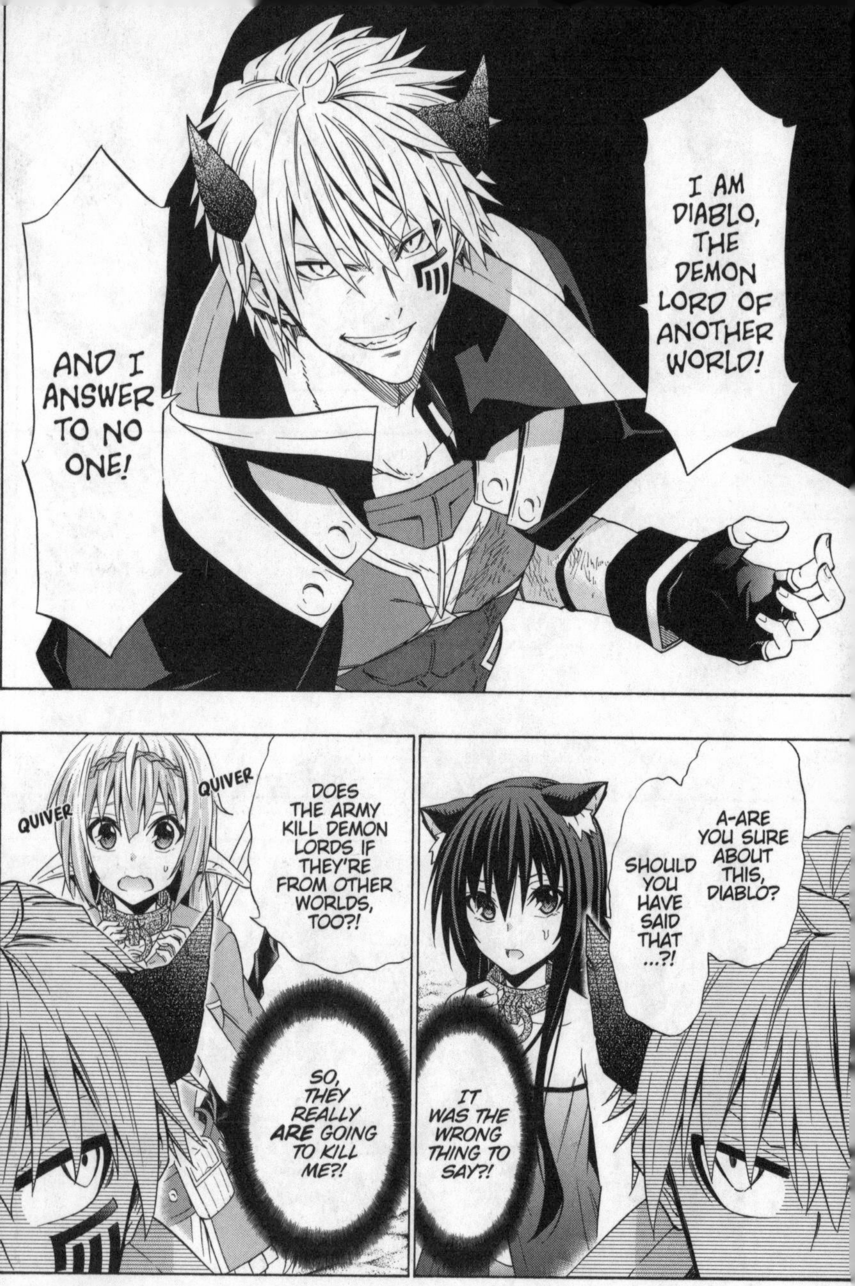
I AM DIABLO, THE DEMON LORD OF ANOTHER WORLD!
AND I ANSWER TO NO ONE!
A-ARE YOU SURE ABOUT THIS, DIABLO?
SHOULD YOU HAVE SAID THAT ...?!
IT WAS THE WRONG THING TO SAY?!
DOES THE ARMY KILL DEMON LORDS IF THEY'RE FROM OTHER WORLDS, TOO?!
QUIVER
QUIVER
SO, THEY REALLY ARE GOING TO KILL ME?!

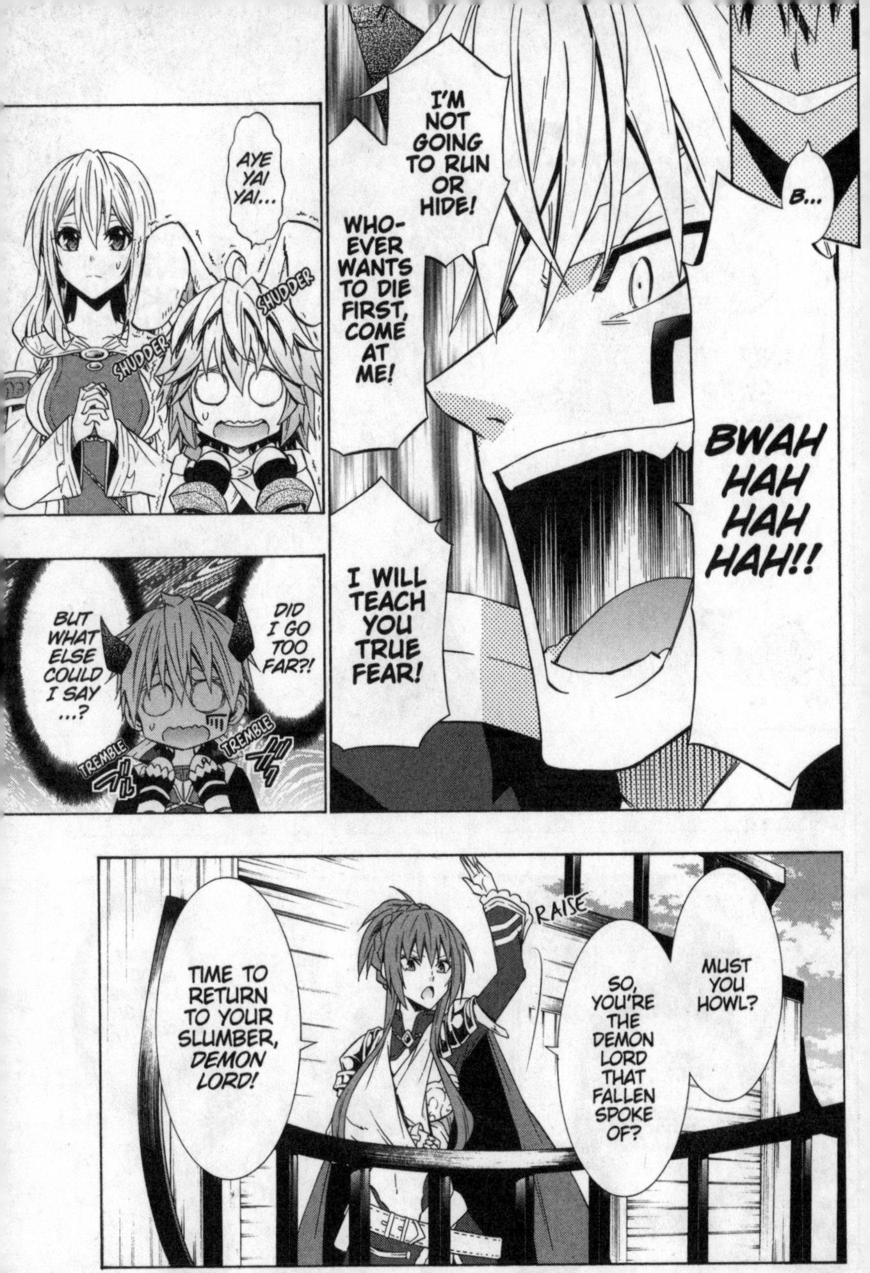
B...
BWAH HAH HAH HAH!!
I'M NOT GOING TO RUN OR HIDE!
WHO-EVER WANTS TO DIE FIRST, COME AT ME!
I WILL TEACH YOU TRUE FEAR!
AYE YAI YAI...
SHUDDER
SHUDDER
DID I GO TOO FAR?!
BUT WHAT ELSE COULD I SAY ...?
TREMBLE
TREMBLE
MUST YOU HOWL?
SO, YOU'RE THE DEMON LORD THAT FALLEN SPOKE OF?
RAISE
TIME TO RETURN TO YOUR SLUMBER, DEMON LORD!

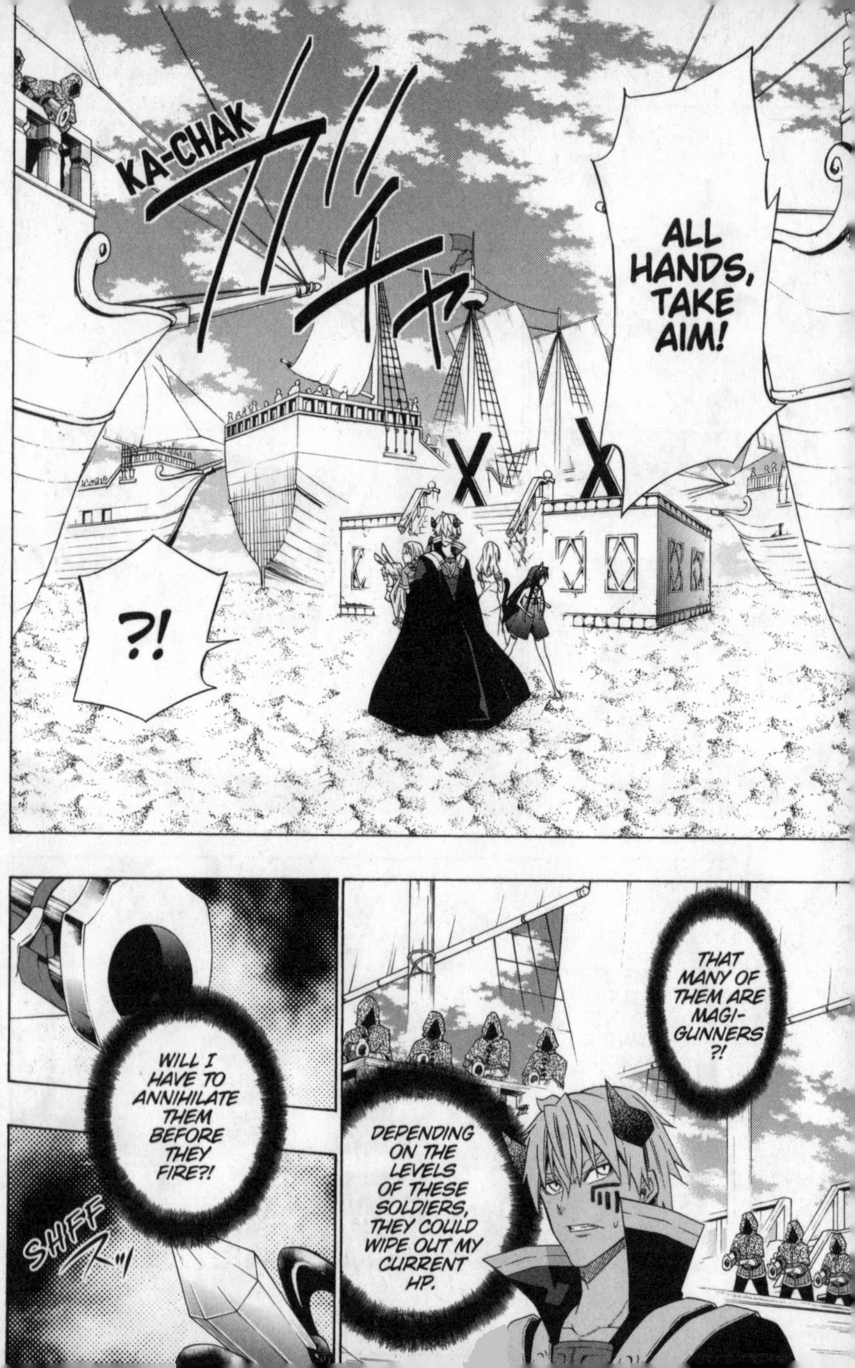

ALL HANDS, TAKE AIM!
KA-CHAK
?!
THAT MANY OF THEM ARE MAGI-GUNNERS?!
DEPENDING ON THE LEVELS OF THESE SOLDIERS, THEY COULD WIPE OUT MY CURRENT HP.
WILL I HAVE TO ANNIHILATE THEM BEFORE THEY FIRE?!
SHFF

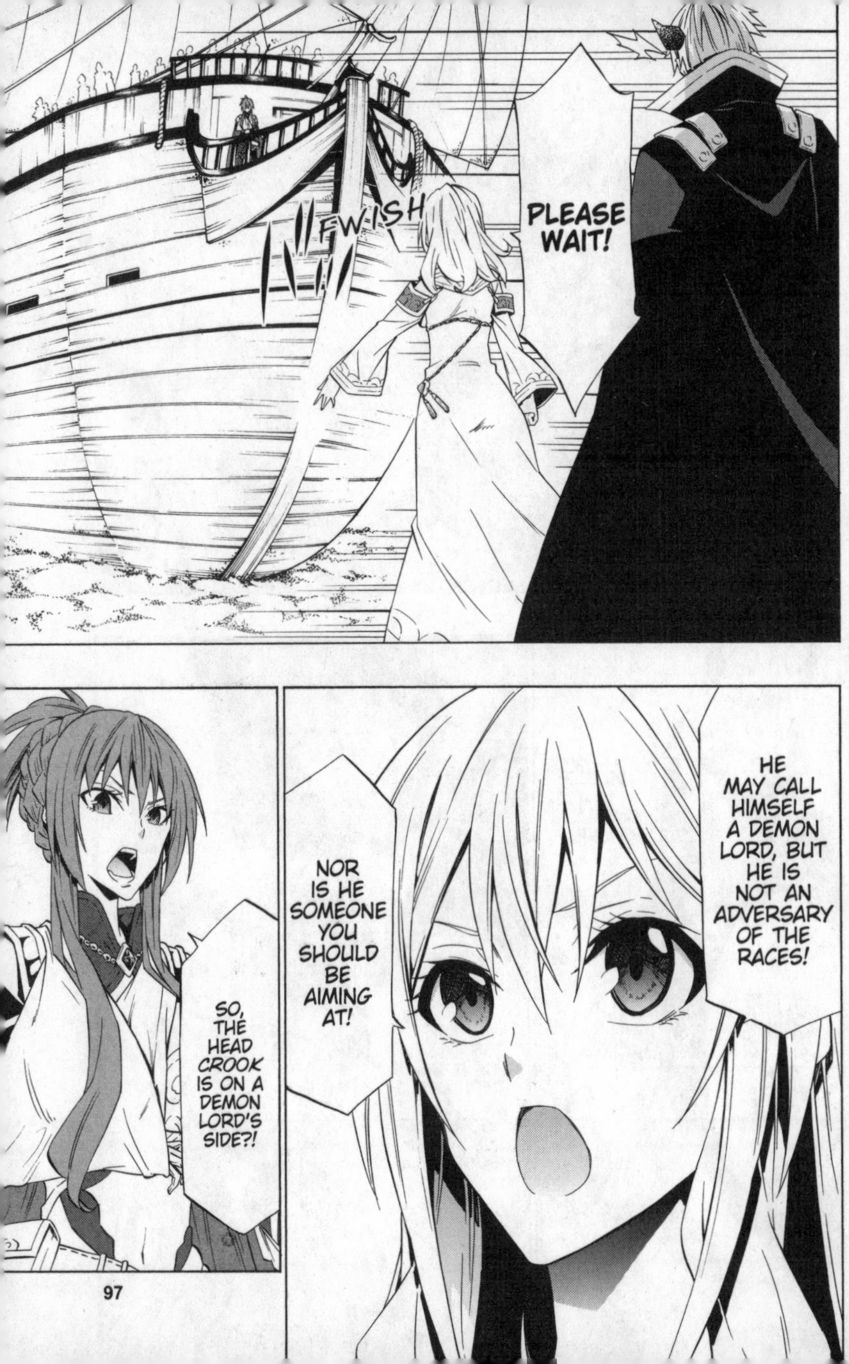
PLEASE WAIT!
FWISH
HE MAY CALL HIMSELF A DEMON LORD, BUT HE IS NOT AN ADVERSARY OF THE RACES!
NOR IS HE SOMEONE YOU SHOULD BE AIMING AT!
SO, THE HEAD CROOK IS ON A DEMON LORD'S SIDE?!

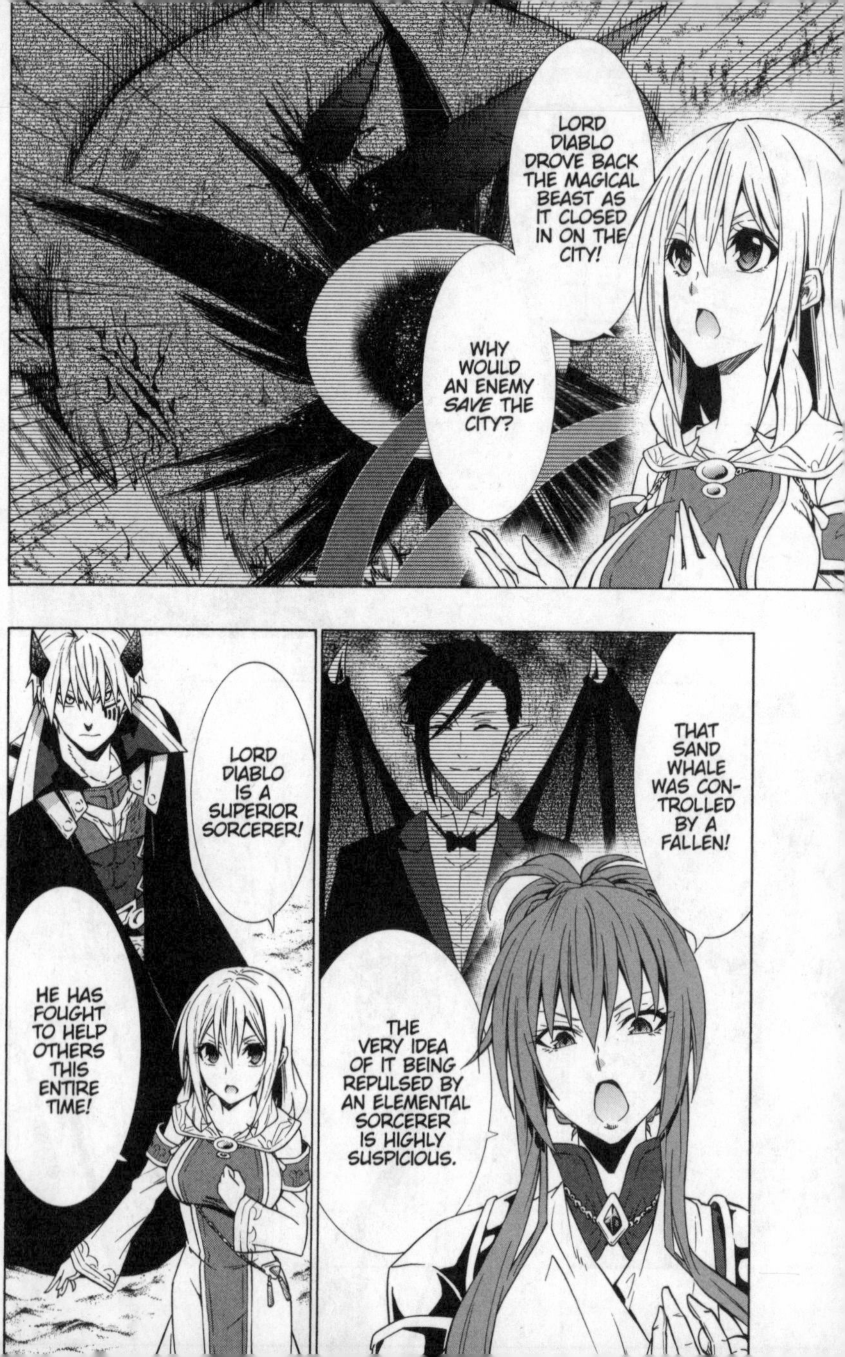
LORD DIABLO DROVE BACK THE MAGICAL BEAST AS IT CLOSED IN ON THE CITY!
WHY WOULD AN ENEMY *SAVE* THE CITY?
THAT SAND WHALE WAS CON-TROLLED BY A FALLEN!
THE VERY IDEA OF IT BEING REPULSED BY AN ELEMENTAL SORCERER IS HIGHLY SUSPICIOUS.
LORD DIABLO IS A SUPERIOR SORCERER!
HE HAS FOUGHT TO HELP OTHERS THIS ENTIRE TIME!

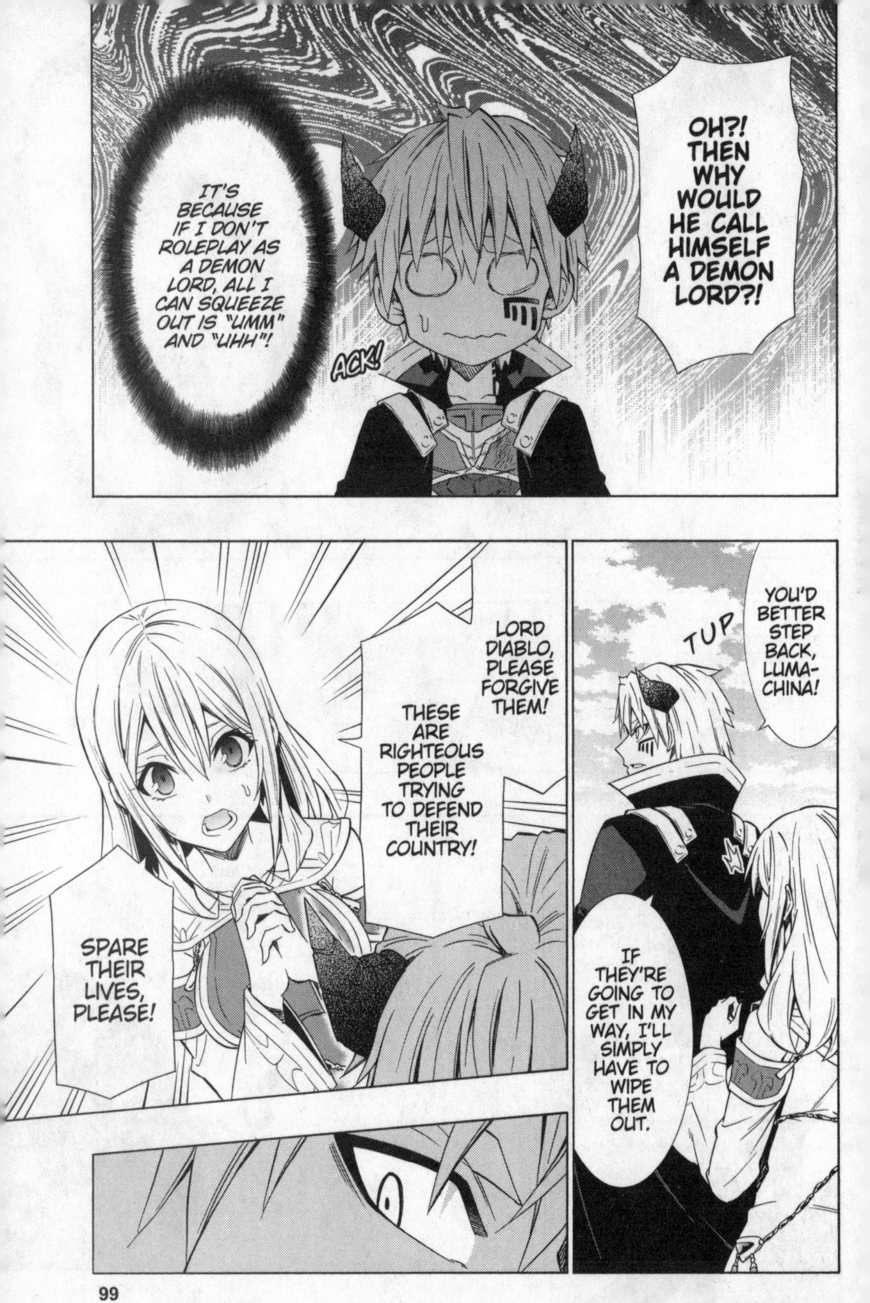
OH?! THEN WHY WOULD HE CALL HIMSELF A DEMON LORD?!
IT'S BECAUSE IF I DON'T ROLEPLAY AS A DEMON LORD, ALL I CAN SQUEEZE OUT IS "UMM" AND "UHH"!
ACK!
YOU'D BETTER STEP BACK, LUMA-CHINA!
TUP
IF THEY'RE GOING TO GET IN MY WAY, I'LL SIMPLY HAVE TO WIPE THEM OUT.
LORD DIABLO, PLEASE FORGIVE THEM!
THESE ARE RIGHTEOUS PEOPLE TRYING TO DEFEND THEIR COUNTRY!
SPARE THEIR LIVES, PLEASE!

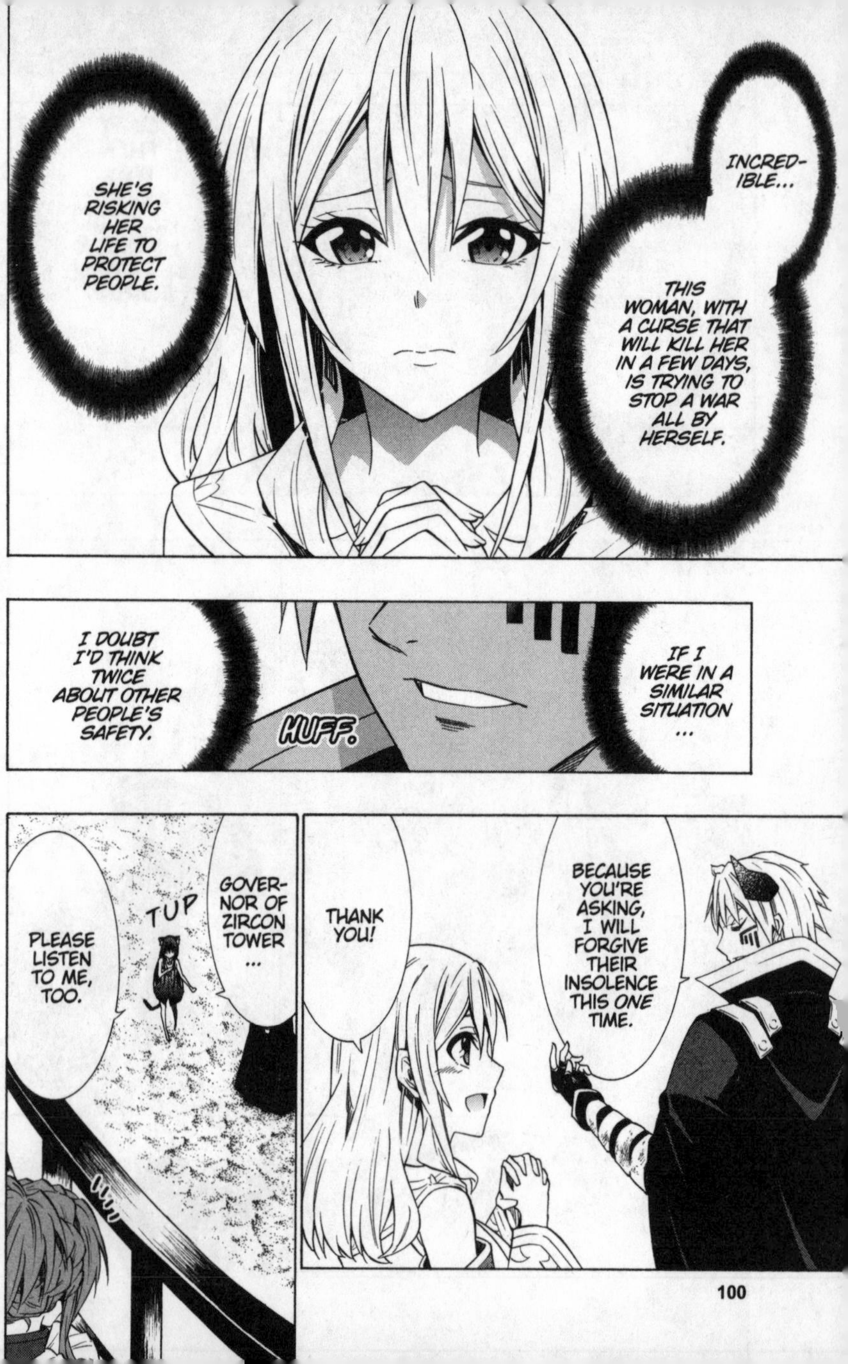
INCRED-IBLE...
THIS WOMAN, WITH A CURSE THAT WILL KILL HER IN A FEW DAYS, IS TRYING TO STOP A WAR ALL BY HERSELF.
SHE'S RISKING HER LIFE TO PROTECT PEOPLE.
IF I WERE IN A SIMILAR SITUATION...
HUFF.
I DOUBT I'D THINK TWICE ABOUT OTHER PEOPLE'S SAFETY.
BECAUSE YOU'RE ASKING, I WILL FORGIVE THEIR INSOLENCE THIS ONE TIME.
THANK YOU!
GOVER-NOR OF ZIRCON TOWER...
TUP
PLEASE LISTEN TO ME, TOO.

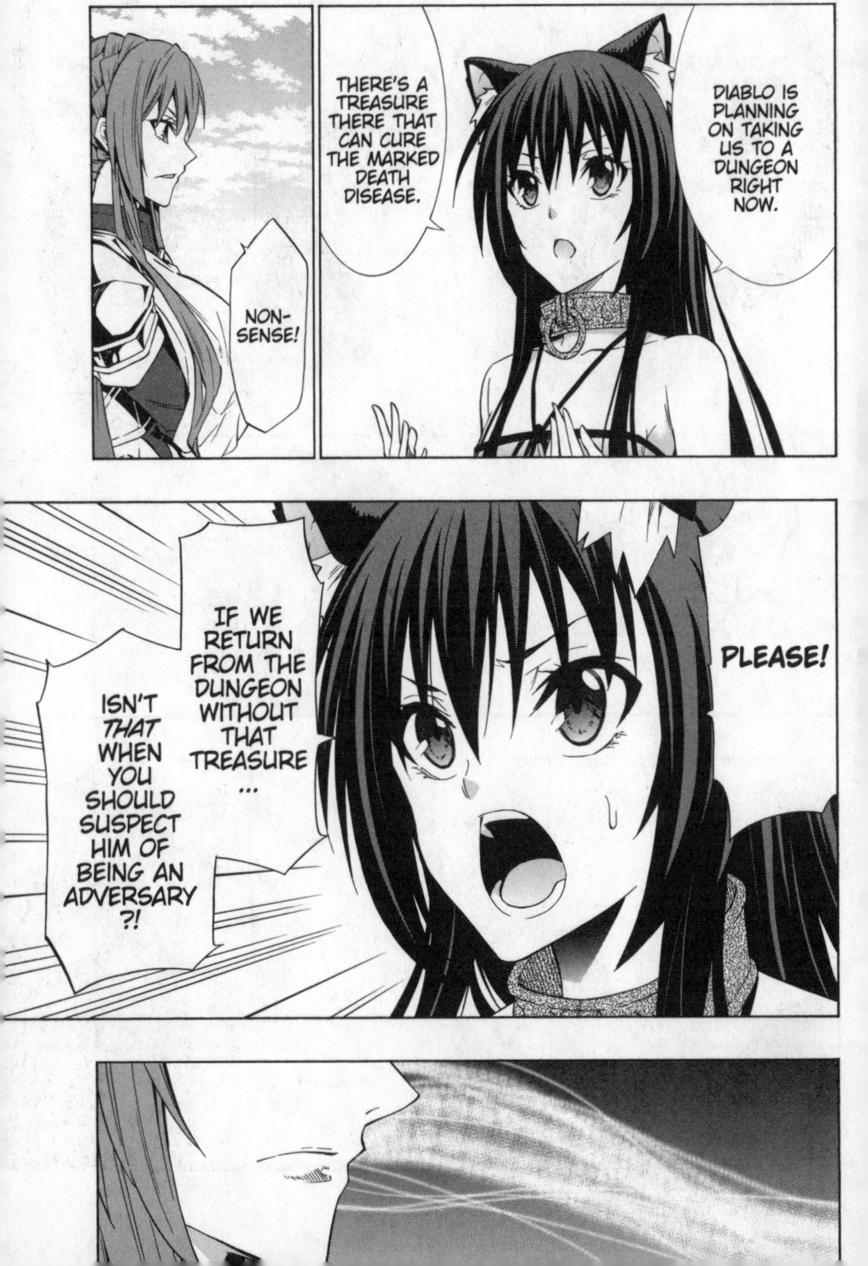
DIABLO IS PLANNING ON TAKING US TO A DUNGEON RIGHT NOW.
THERE'S A TREASURE THERE THAT CAN CURE THE MARKED DEATH DISEASE.
NON-SENSE!
PLEASE!
IF WE RETURN FROM THE DUNGEON WITHOUT THAT TREASURE ...
ISN'T *THAT* WHEN YOU SHOULD SUSPECT HIM OF BEING AN ADVERSARY?!

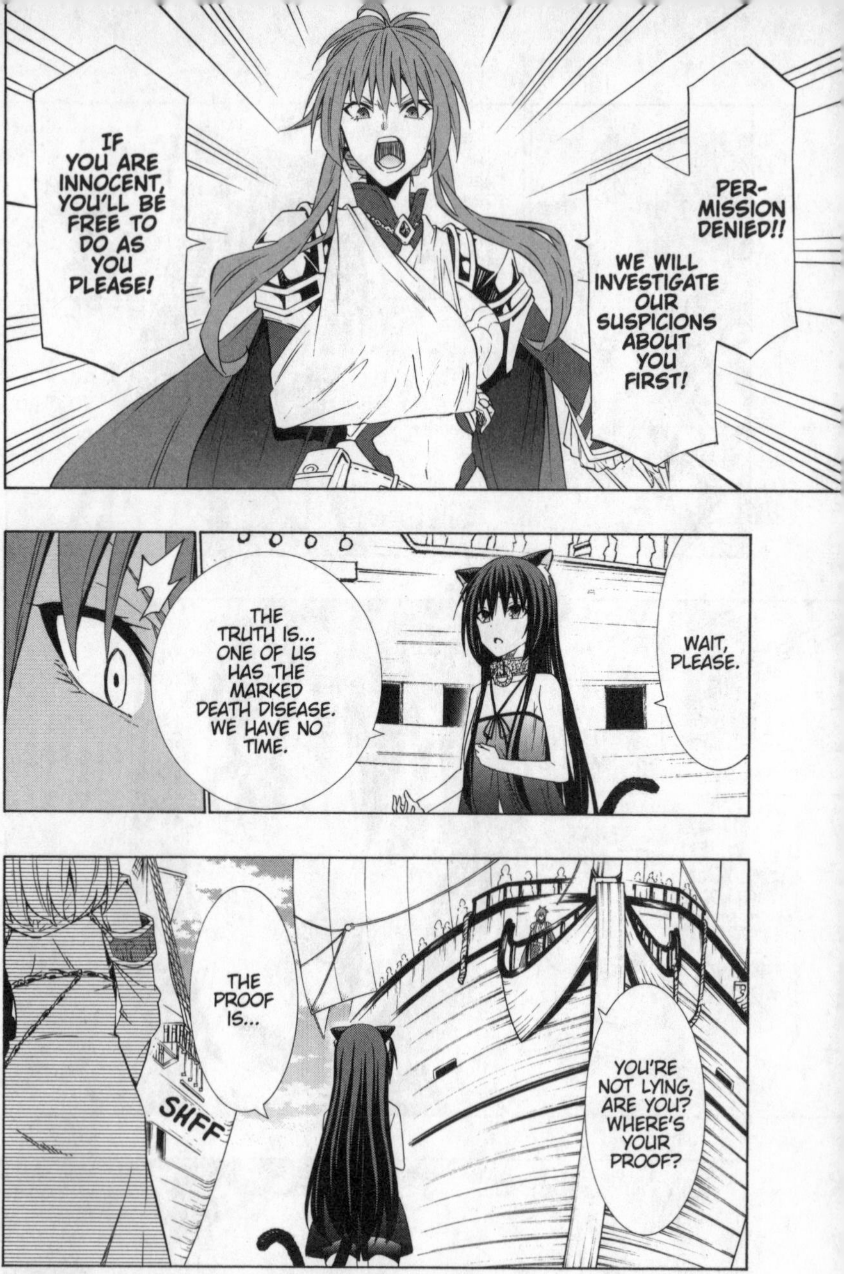
PER-MISSION DENIED!!
WE WILL INVESTIGATE OUR SUSPICIONS ABOUT YOU FIRST!
IF YOU ARE INNOCENT, YOU'LL BE FREE TO DO AS YOU PLEASE!
WAIT, PLEASE.
THE TRUTH IS... ONE OF US HAS THE MARKED DEATH DISEASE. WE HAVE NO TIME.
YOU'RE NOT LYING, ARE YOU? WHERE'S YOUR PROOF?
THE PROOF IS...
SHFF

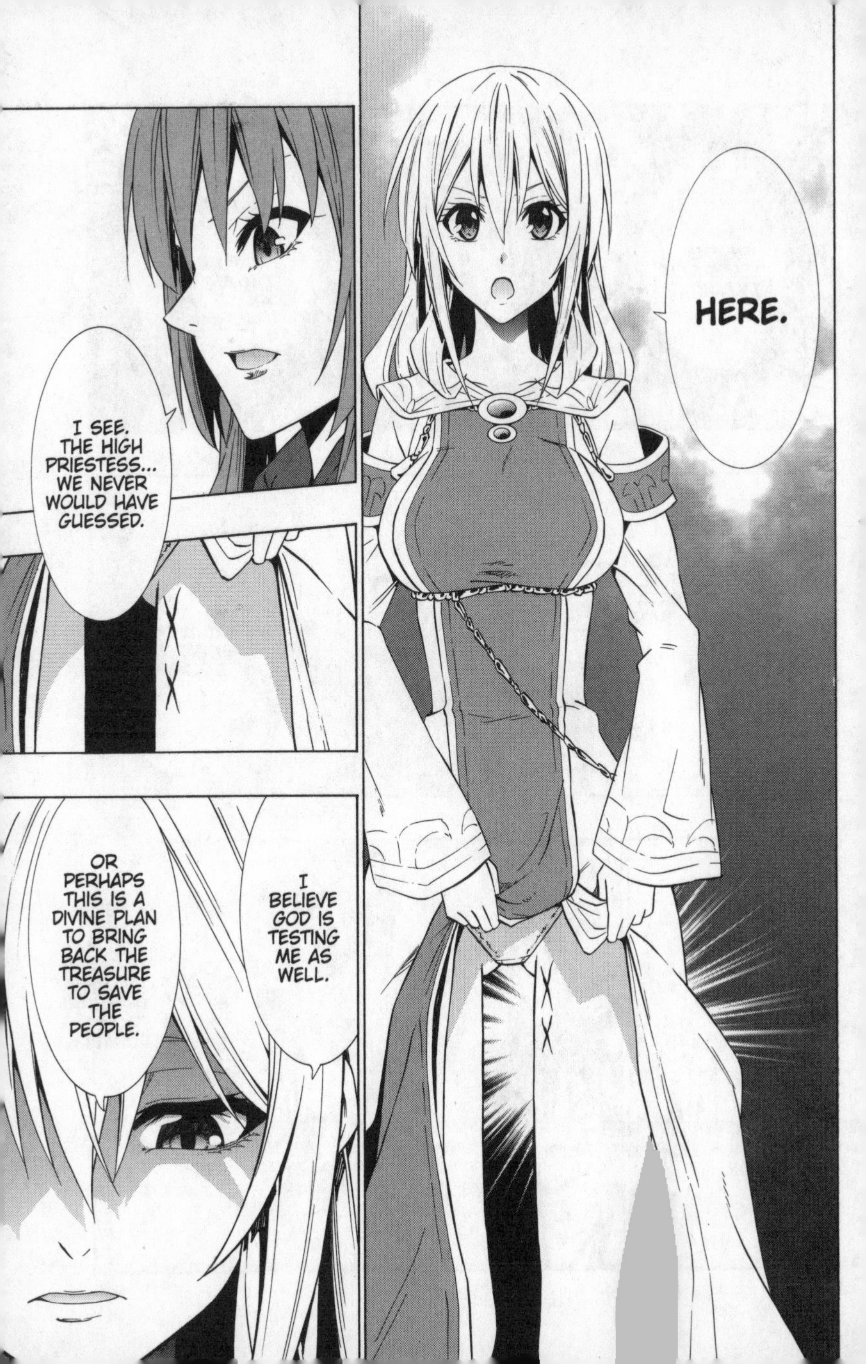
HERE.
I SEE. THE HIGH PRIESTESS... WE NEVER WOULD HAVE GUESSED.
I BELIEVE GOD IS TESTING ME AS WELL.
OR PERHAPS THIS IS A DIVINE PLAN TO BRING BACK THE TREASURE TO SAVE THE PEOPLE.

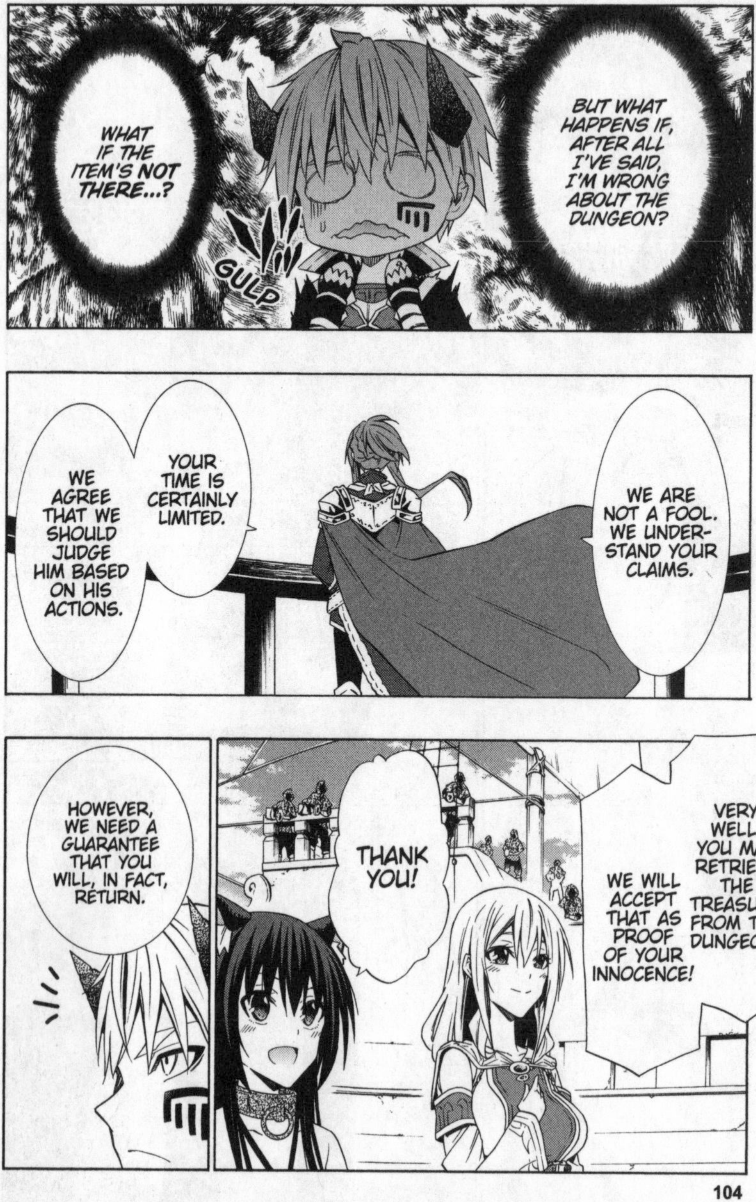
BUT WHAT HAPPENS IF, AFTER ALL I'VE SAID, I'M WRONG ABOUT THE DUNGEON?
WHAT IF THE ITEM'S NOT THERE...?
GULP
WE ARE NOT A FOOL. WE UNDER-STAND YOUR CLAIMS.
YOUR TIME IS CERTAINLY LIMITED.
WE AGREE THAT WE SHOULD JUDGE HIM BASED ON HIS ACTIONS.
VERY WELL! YOU MAY RETRIEVE THE TREASURE FROM THE DUNGEON!
WE WILL ACCEPT THAT AS PROOF OF YOUR INNOCENCE!
THANK YOU!
HOWEVER, WE NEED A GUARANTEE THAT YOU WILL, IN FACT, RETURN.

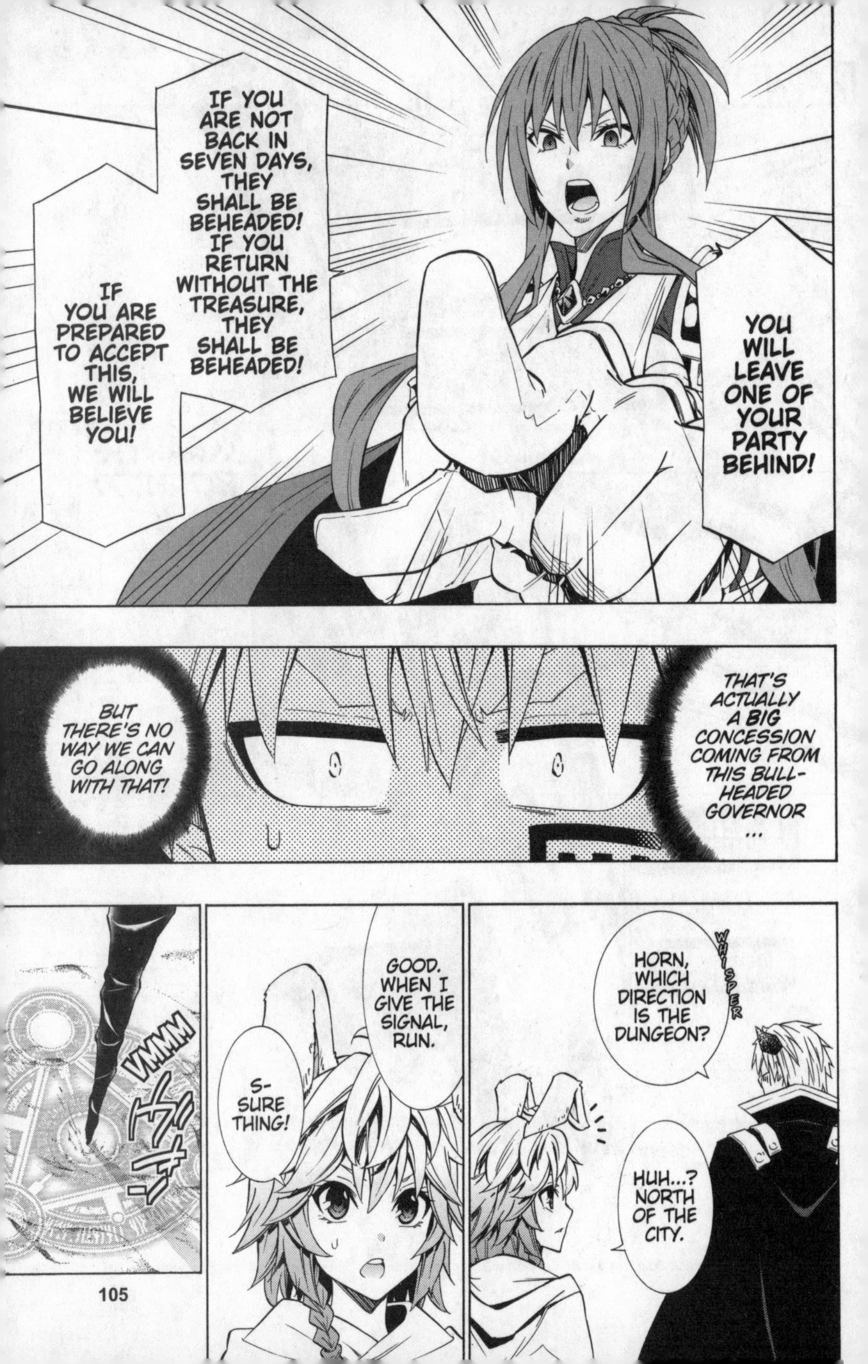
YOU WILL LEAVE ONE OF YOUR PARTY BEHIND!
IF YOU ARE NOT BACK IN SEVEN DAYS, THEY SHALL BE BEHEADED! IF YOU RETURN WITHOUT THE TREASURE, THEY SHALL BE BEHEADED!
IF YOU ARE PREPARED TO ACCEPT THIS, WE WILL BELIEVE YOU!
THAT'S ACTUALLY A BIG CONCESSION COMING FROM THIS BULL-HEADED GOVERNOR ...
BUT THERE'S NO WAY WE CAN GO ALONG WITH THAT!
WHISPER
HORN, WHICH DIRECTION IS THE DUNGEON?
HUH...? NORTH OF THE CITY.
GOOD. WHEN I GIVE THE SIGNAL, RUN.
S-SURE THING!
VMMM

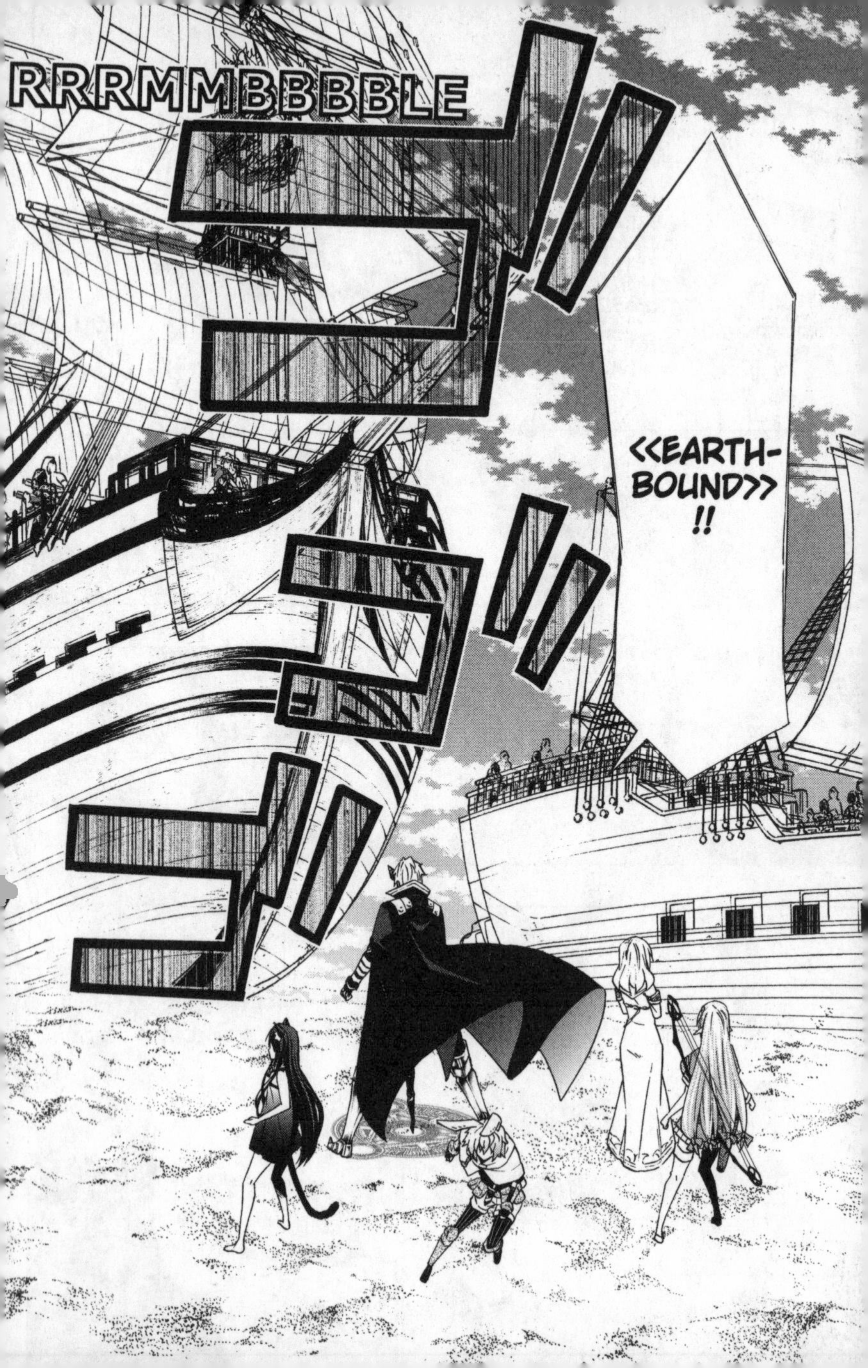
RRRMMBBBBLE
<<EARTH-BOUND>>!!

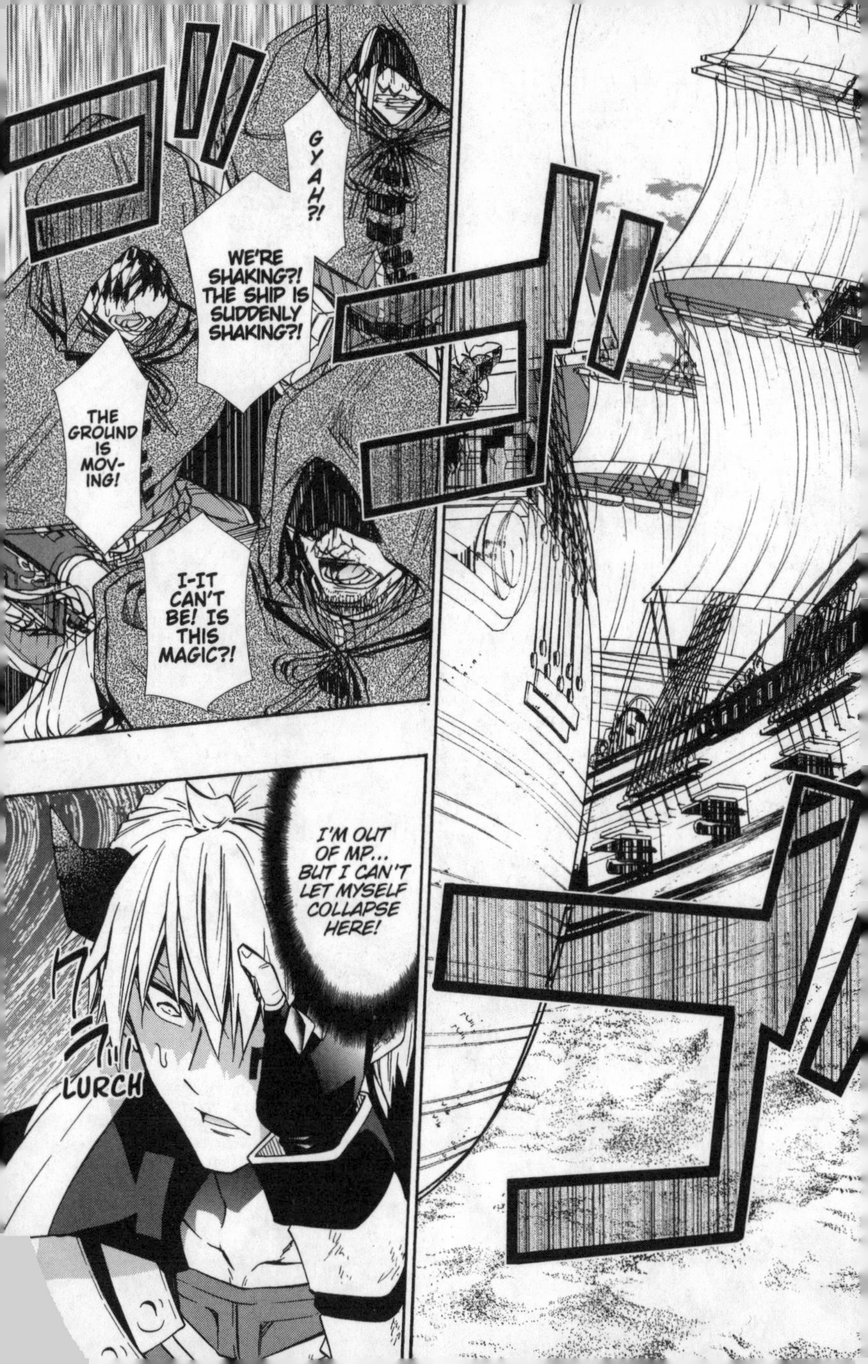
GYAH?!
WE'RE SHAKING?! THE SHIP IS SUDDENLY SHAKING?!
THE GROUND IS MOV-ING!
I-IT CAN'T BE! IS THIS MAGIC?!
I'M OUT OF MP... BUT I CAN'T LET MYSELF COLLAPSE HERE!
LURCH

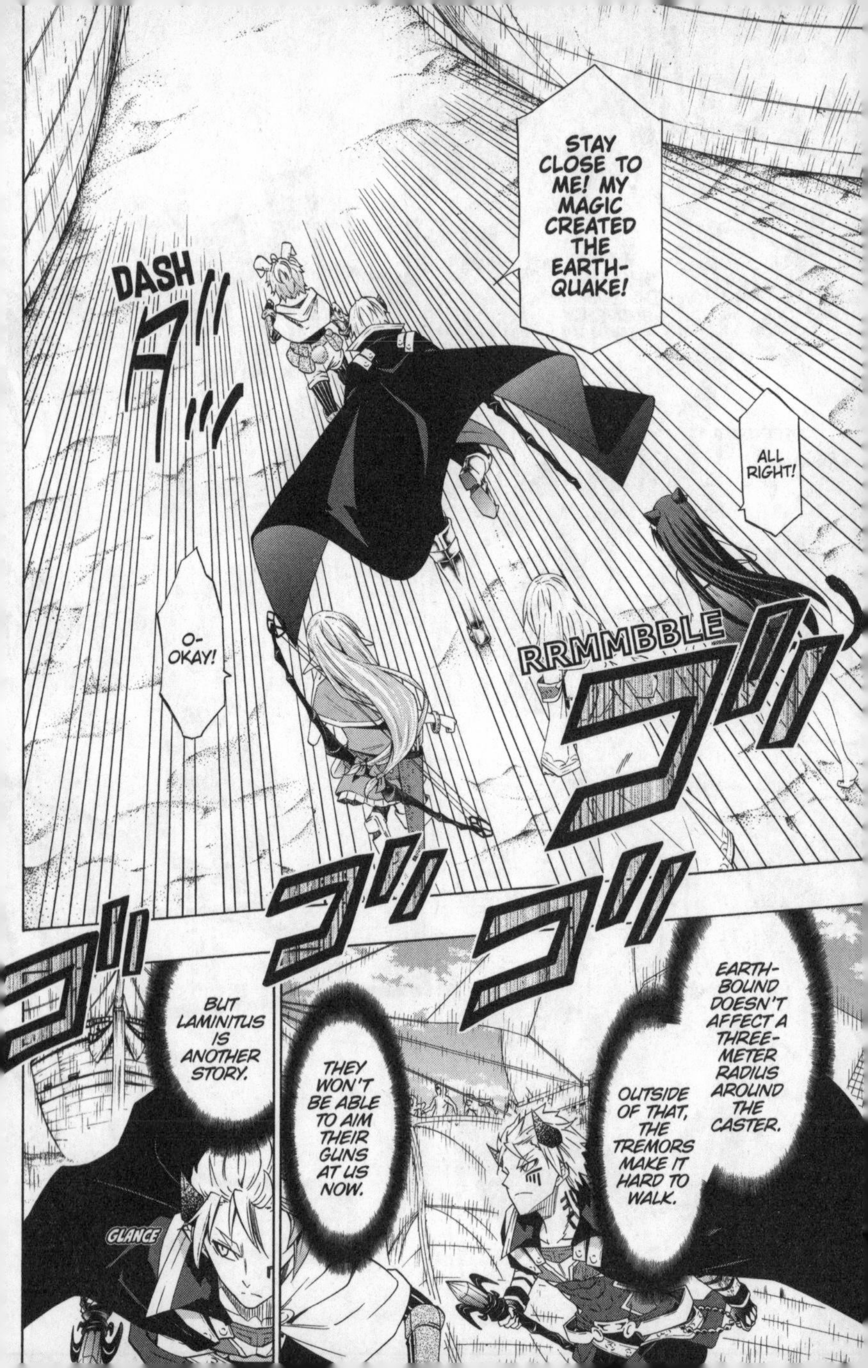
STAY CLOSE TO ME! MY MAGIC CREATED THE EARTH-QUAKE!
ALL RIGHT!
DASH
O-OKAY!
RRMMBBLE
EARTH-BOUND DOESN'T AFFECT A THREE-METER RADIUS AROUND THE CASTER.
OUTSIDE OF THAT, THE TREMORS MAKE IT HARD TO WALK.
THEY WON'T BE ABLE TO AIM THEIR GUNS AT US NOW.
BUT LAMINITUS IS ANOTHER STORY.
GLANCE

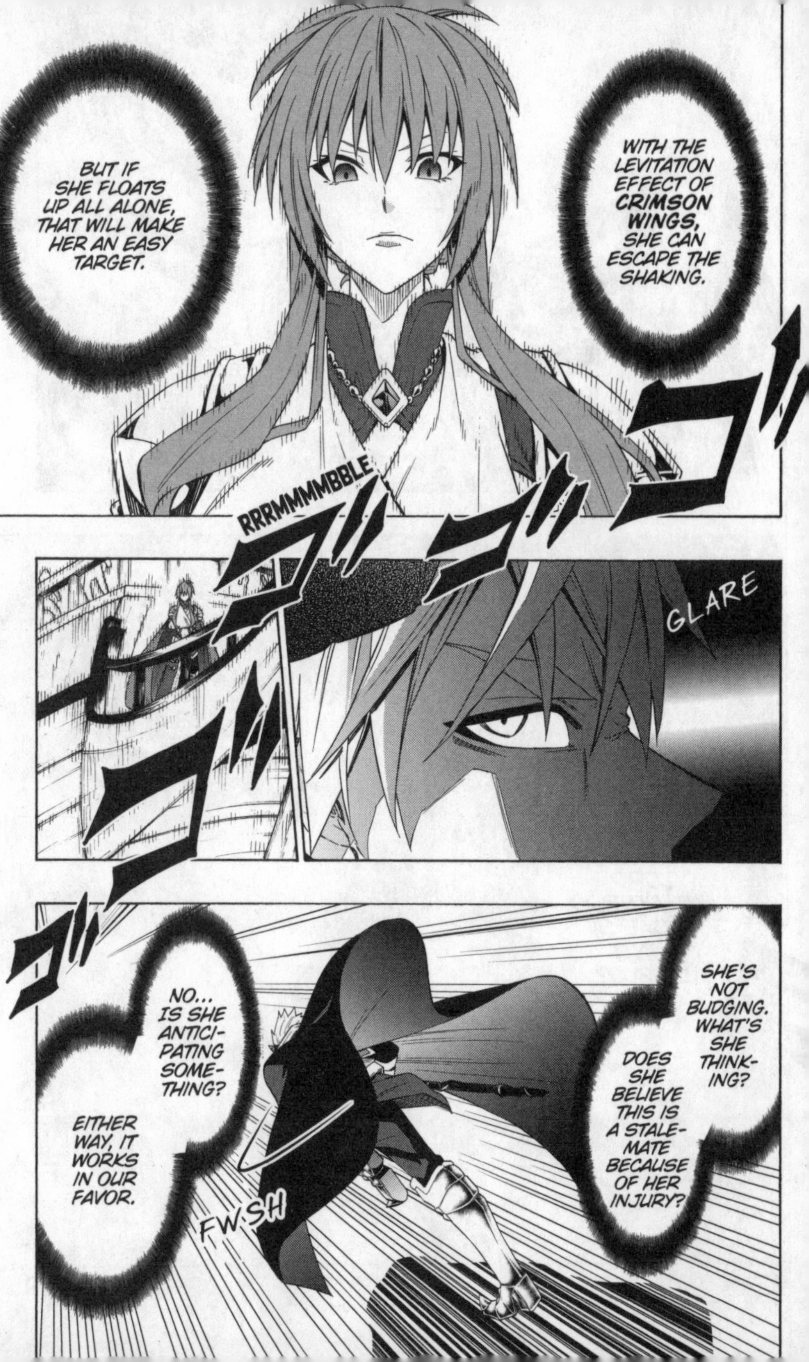
WITH THE LEVITATION EFFECT OF CRIMSON WINGS, SHE CAN ESCAPE THE SHAKING.
BUT IF SHE FLOATS UP ALL ALONE, THAT WILL MAKE HER AN EASY TARGET.
RRRMMMMBBLE
GLARE
SHE'S NOT BUDGING. WHAT'S SHE THINKING?
DOES SHE BELIEVE THIS IS A STALEMATE BECAUSE OF HER INJURY?
NO... IS SHE ANTICIPATING SOMETHING?
EITHER WAY, IT WORKS IN OUR FAVOR.
FWSH

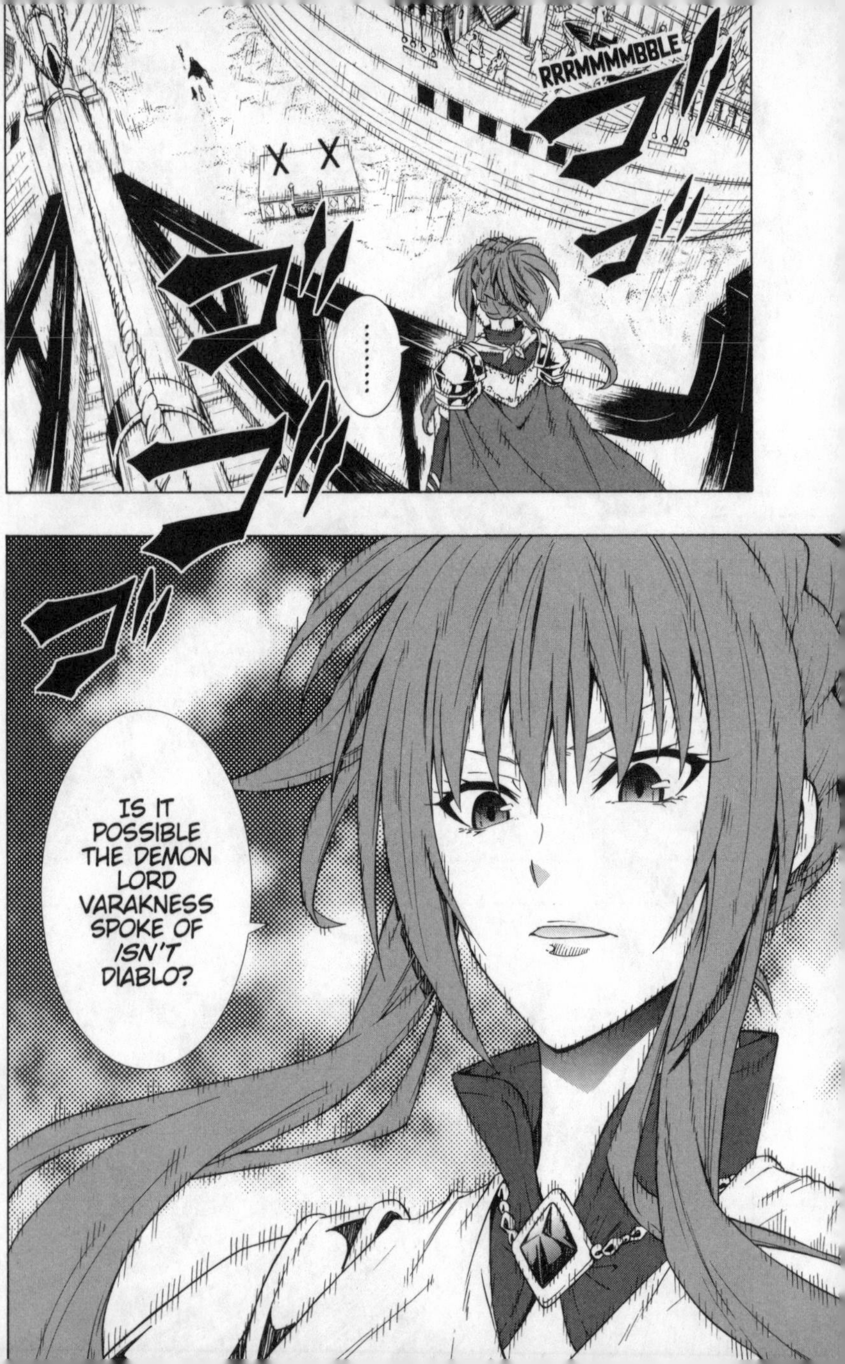
RRRMMMMBBLE
......
IS IT POSSIBLE THE DEMON LORD VARAKNESS SPOKE OF *ISN'T* DIABLO?

HOW NOT TO SUMMON A DEMON LORD

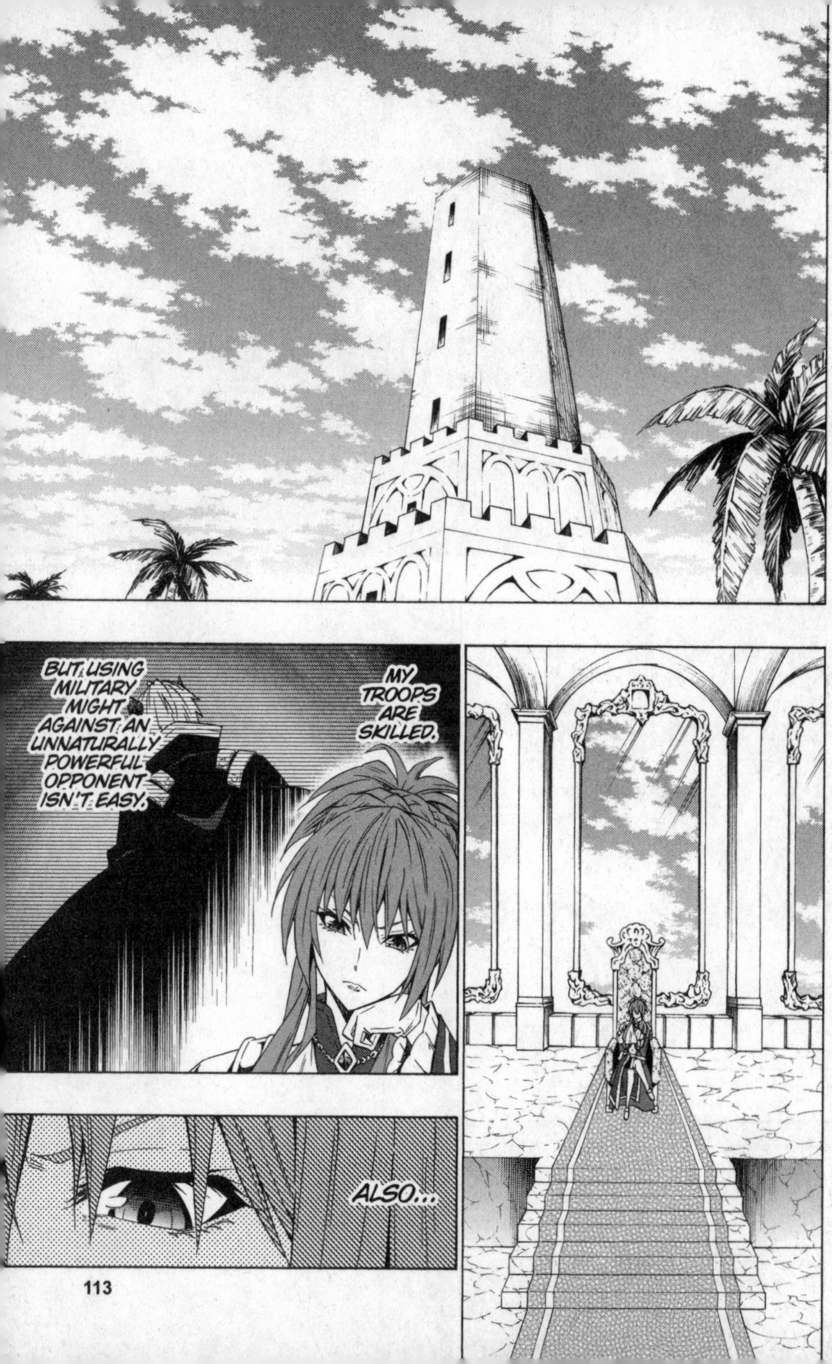
MY TROOPS ARE SKILLED.
BUT USING MILITARY MIGHT AGAINST AN UNNATURALLY POWERFUL OPPONENT ISN'T EASY.
ALSO...

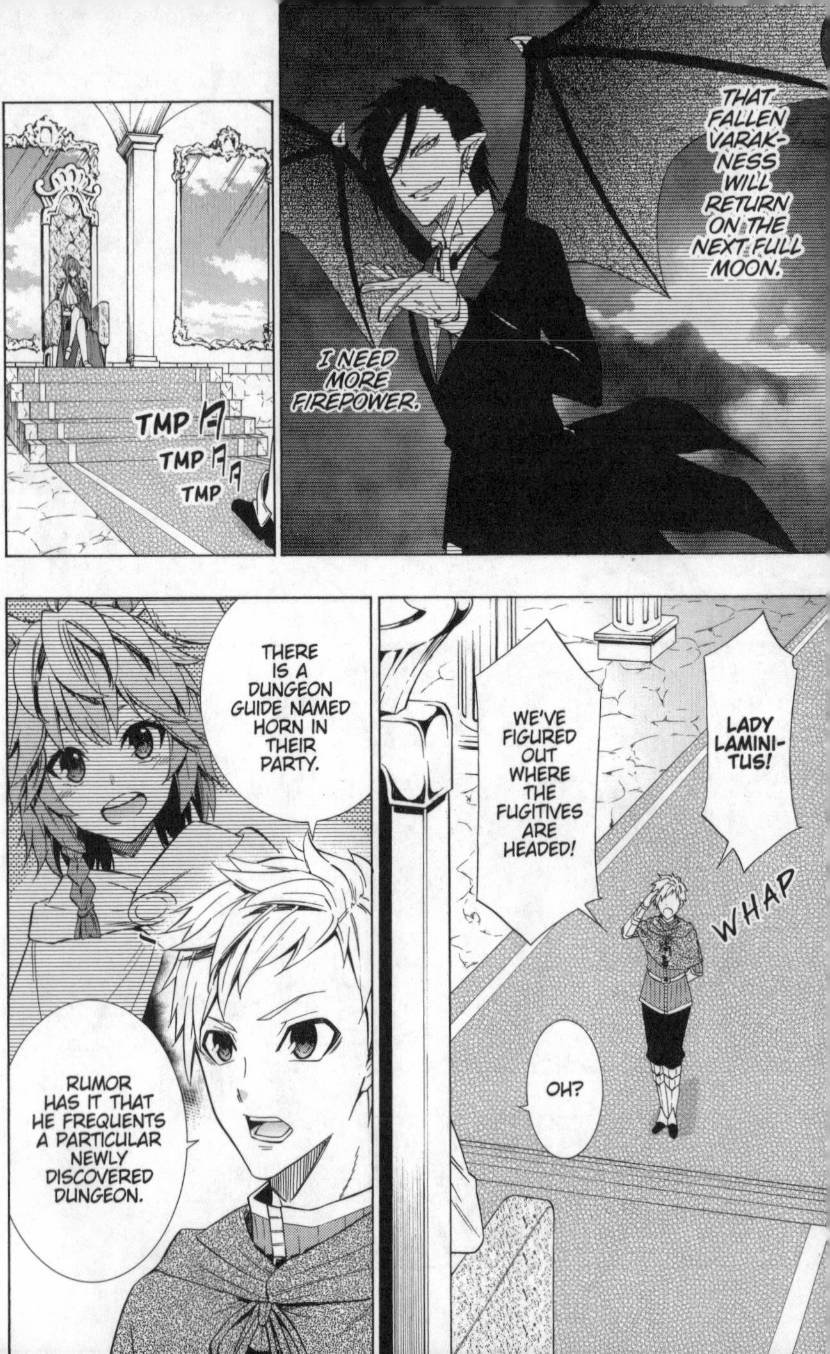
THAT FALLEN VARAKNESS WILL RETURN ON THE NEXT FULL MOON.
I NEED MORE FIREPOWER.
TMP
TMP
TMP
LADY LAMINITUS!
WHAP
WE'VE FIGURED OUT WHERE THE FUGITIVES ARE HEADED!
OH?
THERE IS A DUNGEON GUIDE NAMED HORN IN THEIR PARTY.
RUMOR HAS IT THAT HE FREQUENTS A PARTICULAR NEWLY DISCOVERED DUNGEON.

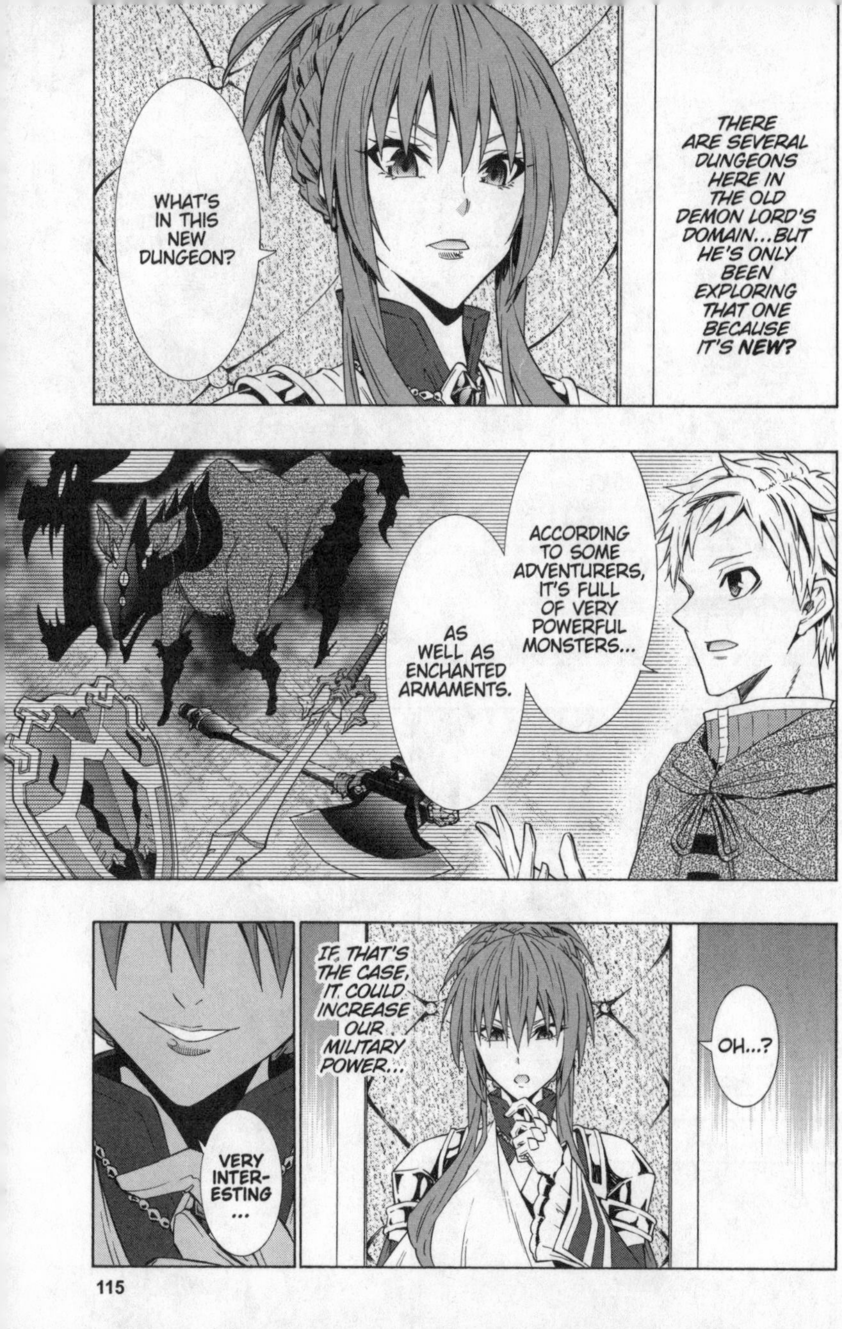
THERE ARE SEVERAL DUNGEONS HERE IN THE OLD DEMON LORD'S DOMAIN...BUT HE'S ONLY BEEN EXPLORING THAT ONE BECAUSE IT'S NEW?
WHAT'S IN THIS NEW DUNGEON?
ACCORDING TO SOME ADVENTURERS, IT'S FULL OF VERY POWERFUL MONSTERS...
AS WELL AS ENCHANTED ARMAMENTS.
OH...?
IF THAT'S THE CASE, IT COULD INCREASE OUR MILITARY POWER...
VERY INTER-ESTING...

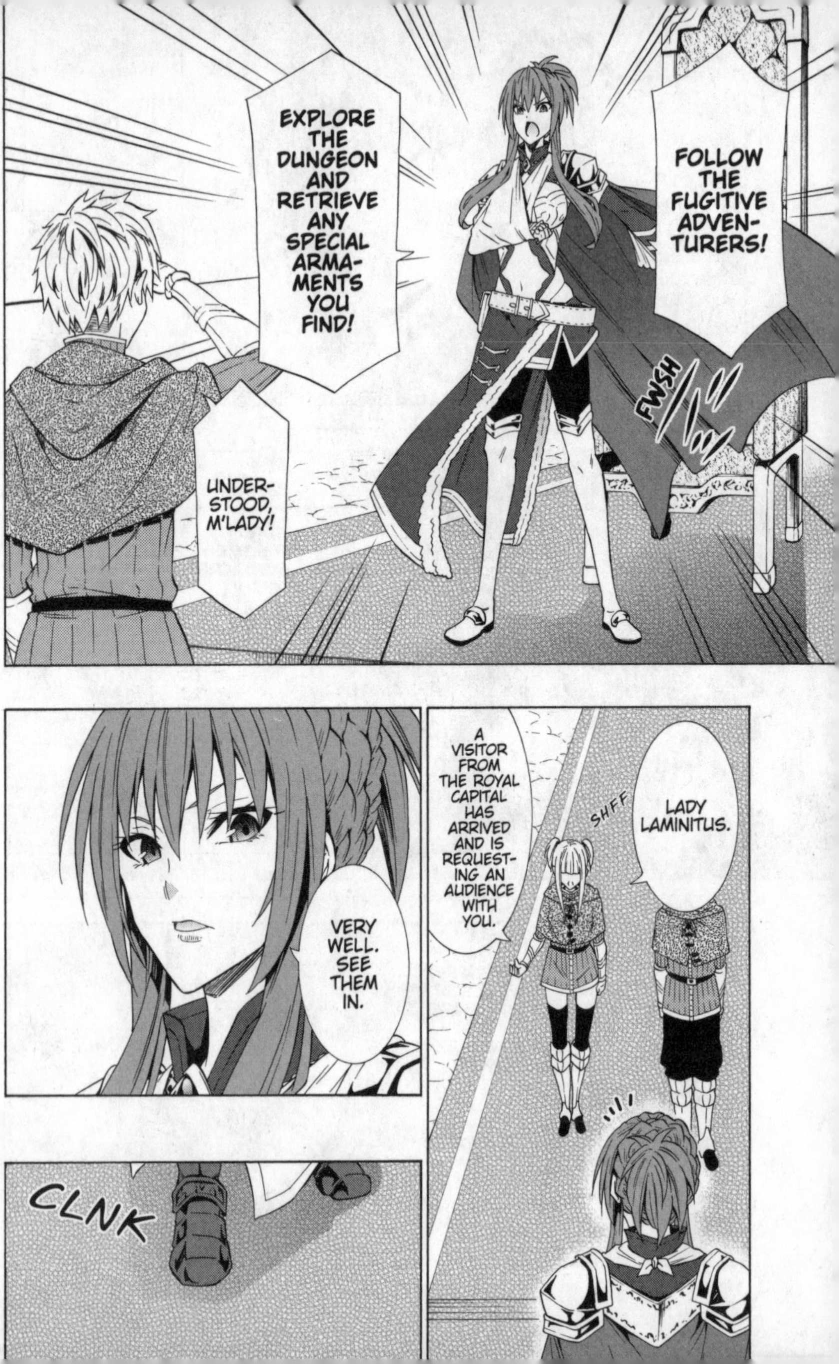
FOLLOW THE FUGITIVE ADVEN-TURERS!
FWSH
EXPLORE THE DUNGEON AND RETRIEVE ANY SPECIAL ARMA-MENTS YOU FIND!
UNDER-STOOD, M'LADY!
LADY LAMINITUS.
SHFF
A VISITOR FROM THE ROYAL CAPITAL HAS ARRIVED AND IS REQUEST-ING AN AUDIENCE WITH YOU.
VERY WELL. SEE THEM IN.
CLNK

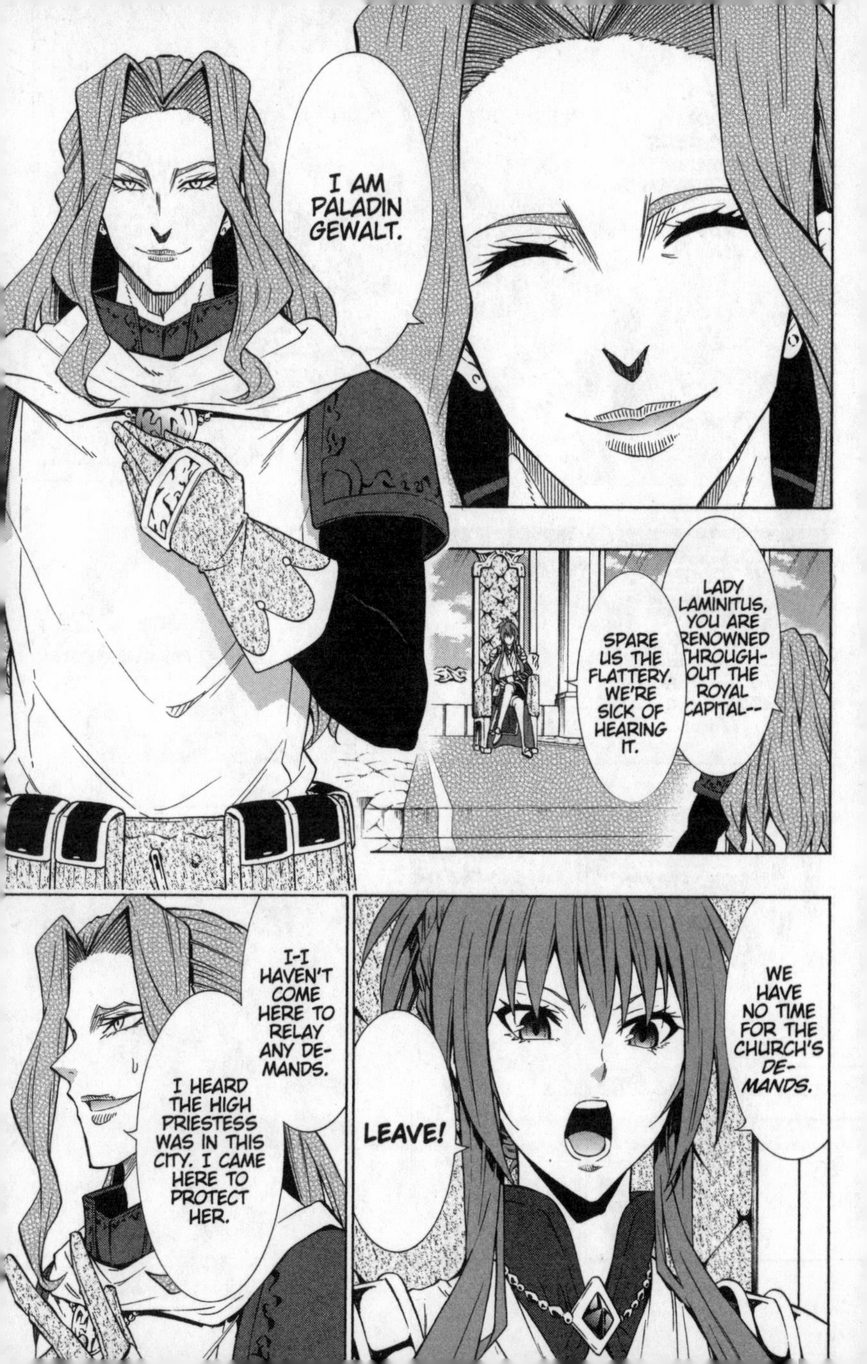
I AM PALADIN GEWALT.
LADY LAMINITUS, YOU ARE RENOWNED THROUGH-OUT THE ROYAL CAPITAL--
SPARE US THE FLATTERY. WE'RE SICK OF HEARING IT.
WE HAVE NO TIME FOR THE CHURCH'S DE-MANDS.
LEAVE!
I-I HAVEN'T COME HERE TO RELAY ANY DE-MANDS.
I HEARD THE HIGH PRIESTESS WAS IN THIS CITY. I CAME HERE TO PROTECT HER.

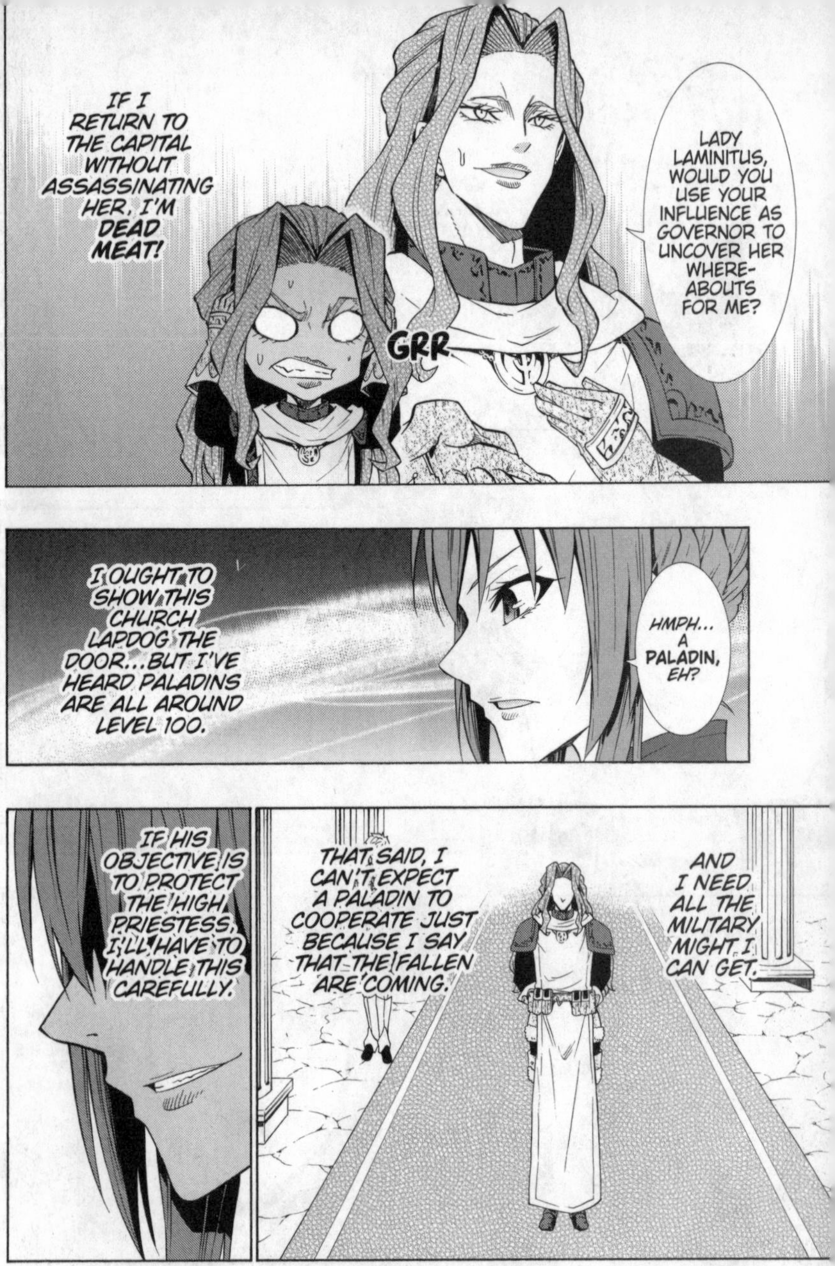
LADY LAMINITUS, WOULD YOU USE YOUR INFLUENCE AS GOVERNOR TO UNCOVER HER WHERE-ABOUTS FOR ME?
IF I RETURN TO THE CAPITAL WITHOUT ASSASSINATING HER, I'M DEAD MEAT!
GRR
HMPH... A PALADIN, EH?
I OUGHT TO SHOW THIS CHURCH LAPDOG THE DOOR...BUT I'VE HEARD PALADINS ARE ALL AROUND LEVEL 100.
AND I NEED ALL THE MILITARY MIGHT I CAN GET.
THAT SAID, I CAN'T EXPECT A PALADIN TO COOPERATE JUST BECAUSE I SAY THAT THE FALLEN ARE COMING.
IF HIS OBJECTIVE IS TO PROTECT THE HIGH PRIESTESS, I'LL HAVE TO HANDLE THIS CAREFULLY.

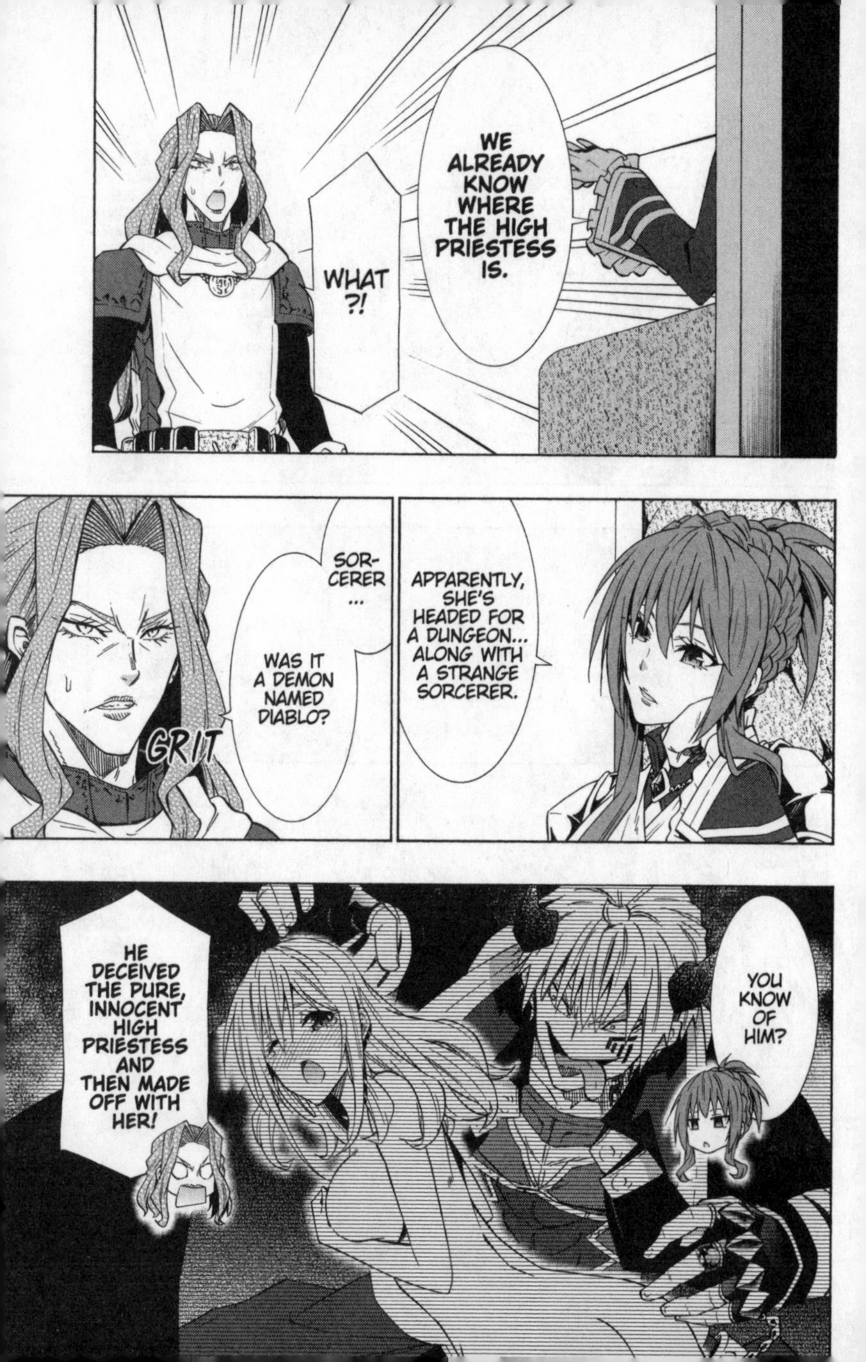
WE ALREADY KNOW WHERE THE HIGH PRIESTESS IS.
WHAT ?!
APPARENTLY, SHE'S HEADED FOR A DUNGEON... ALONG WITH A STRANGE SORCERER.
SOR-CERER ...
WAS IT A DEMON NAMED DIABLO?
GRIT
YOU KNOW OF HIM?
HE DECEIVED THE PURE, INNOCENT HIGH PRIESTESS AND THEN MADE OFF WITH HER!

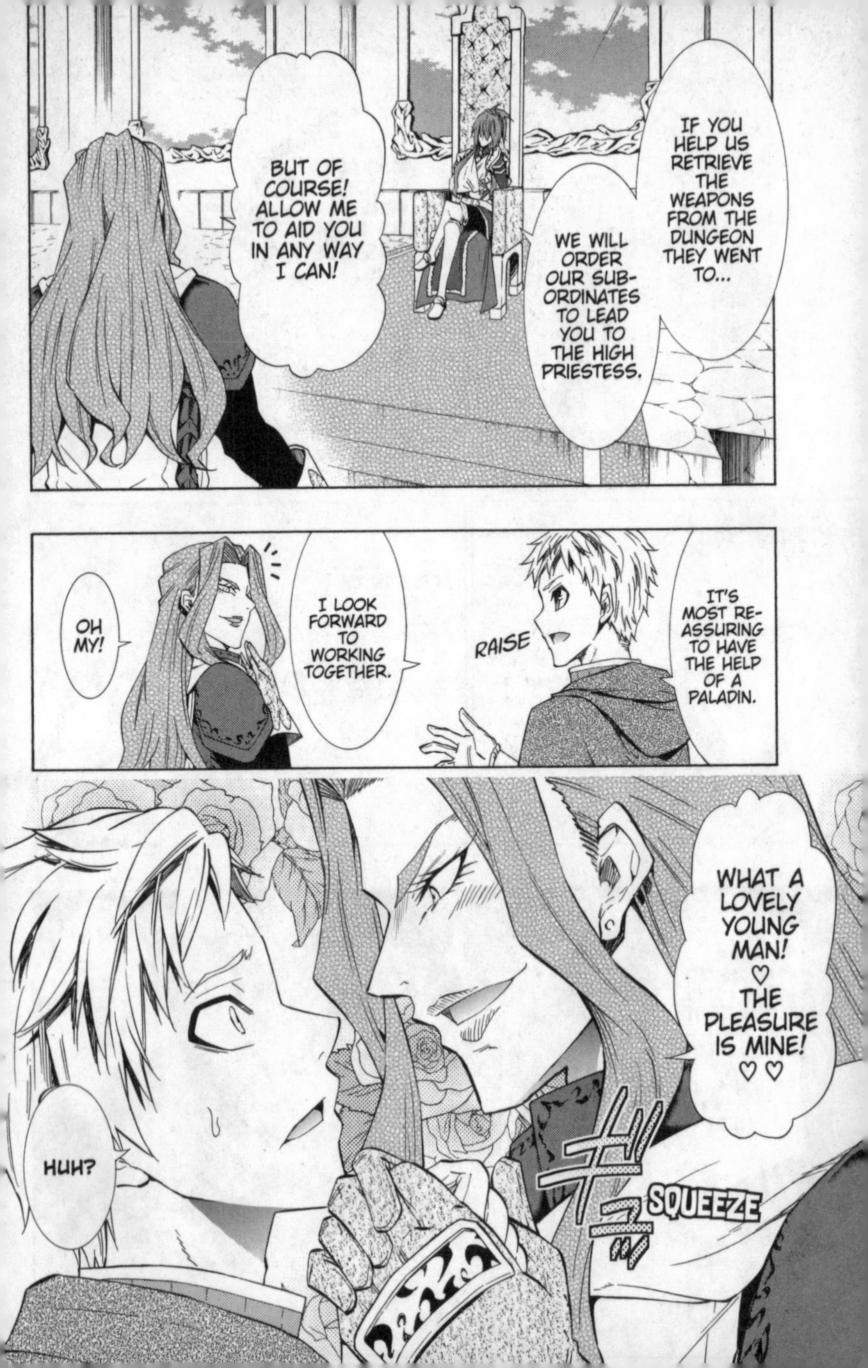
IF YOU HELP US RETRIEVE THE WEAPONS FROM THE DUNGEON THEY WENT TO...
WE WILL ORDER OUR SUBORDINATES TO LEAD YOU TO THE HIGH PRIESTESS.
BUT OF COURSE! ALLOW ME TO AID YOU IN ANY WAY I CAN!
IT'S MOST REASSURING TO HAVE THE HELP OF A PALADIN.
RAISE
I LOOK FORWARD TO WORKING TOGETHER.
OH MY!
WHAT A LOVELY YOUNG MAN! ♡ THE PLEASURE IS MINE! ♡ ♡
SQUEEZE
HUH?

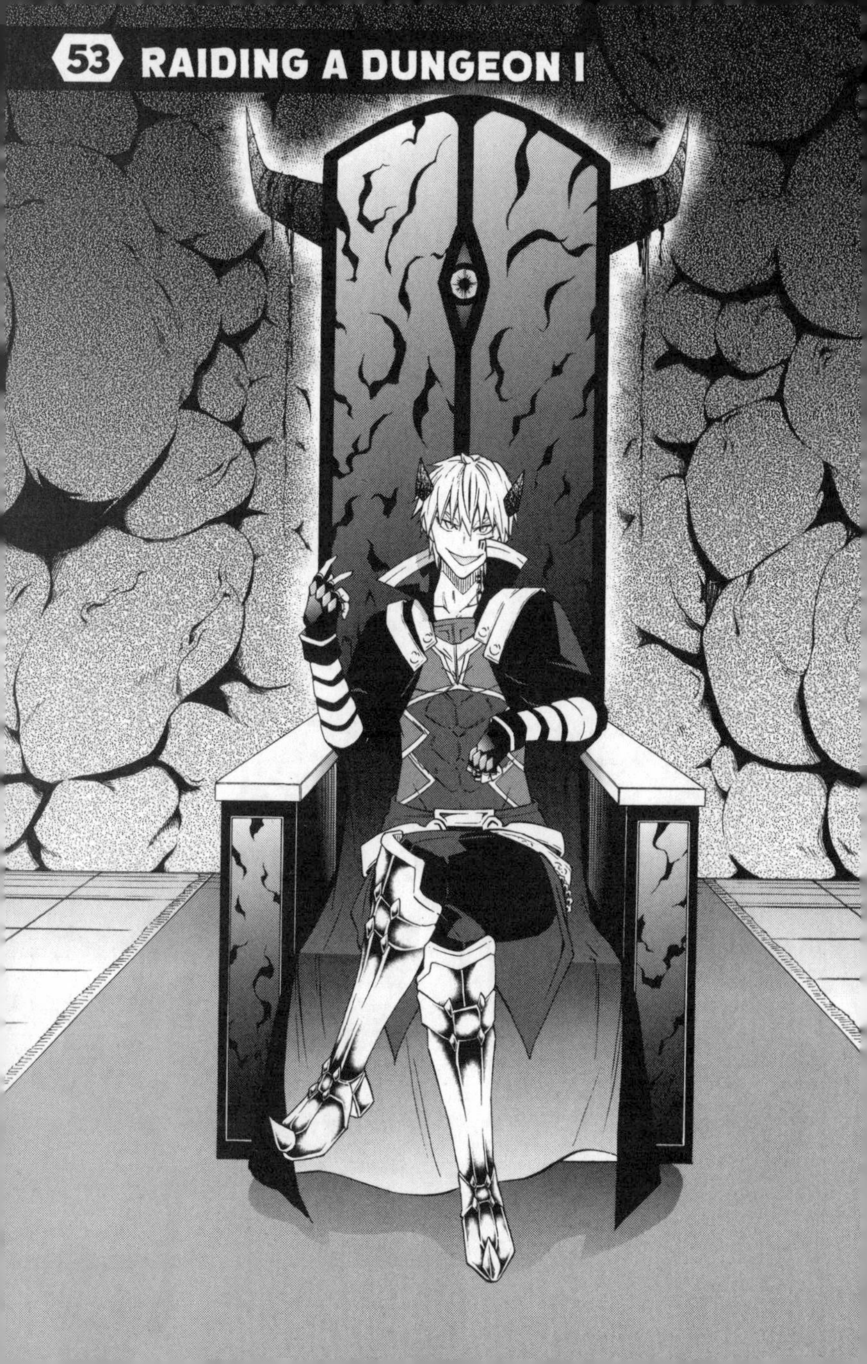
53 RAIDING A DUNGEON I

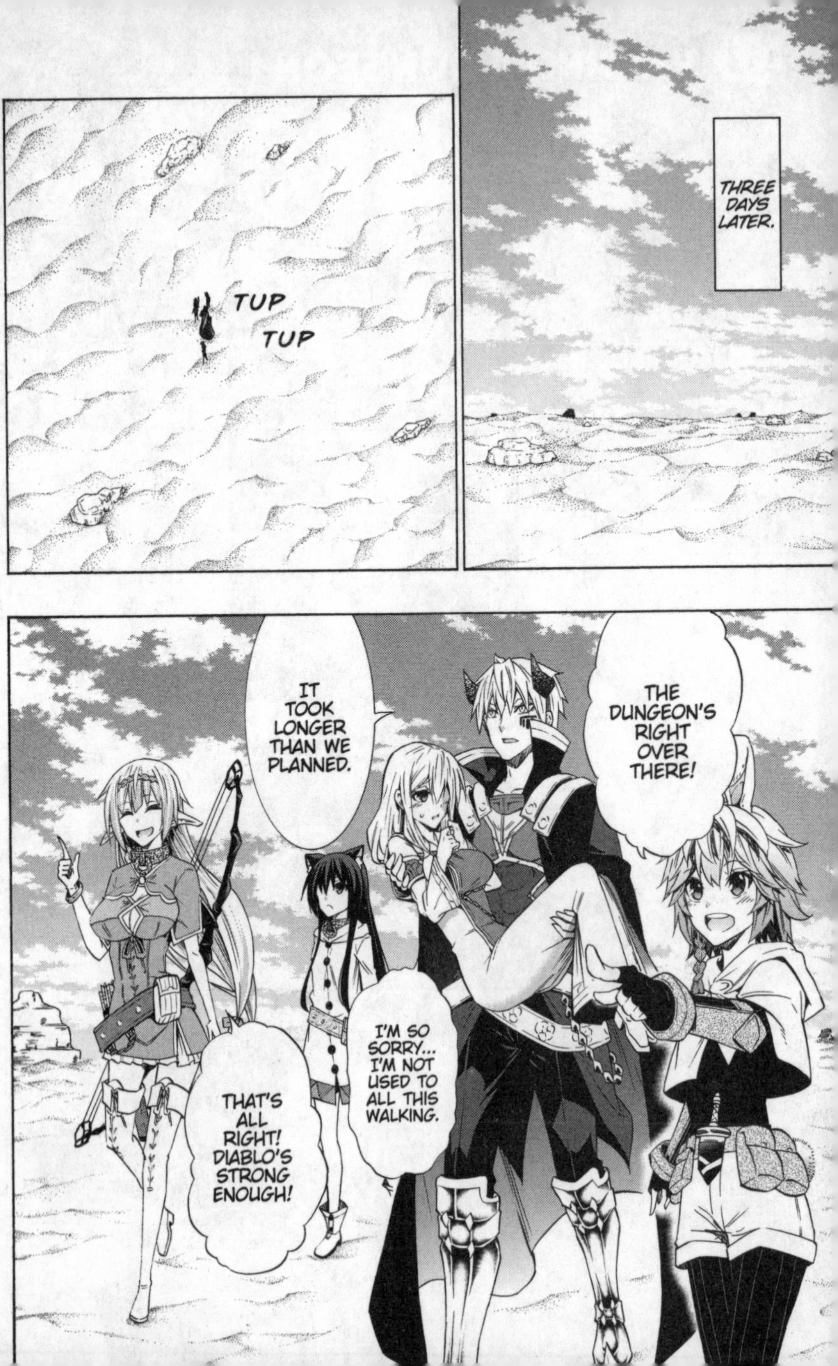
THREE DAYS LATER.
TUP
TUP
THE DUNGEON'S RIGHT OVER THERE!
IT TOOK LONGER THAN WE PLANNED.
I'M SO SORRY... I'M NOT USED TO ALL THIS WALKING.
THAT'S ALL RIGHT! DIABLO'S STRONG ENOUGH!

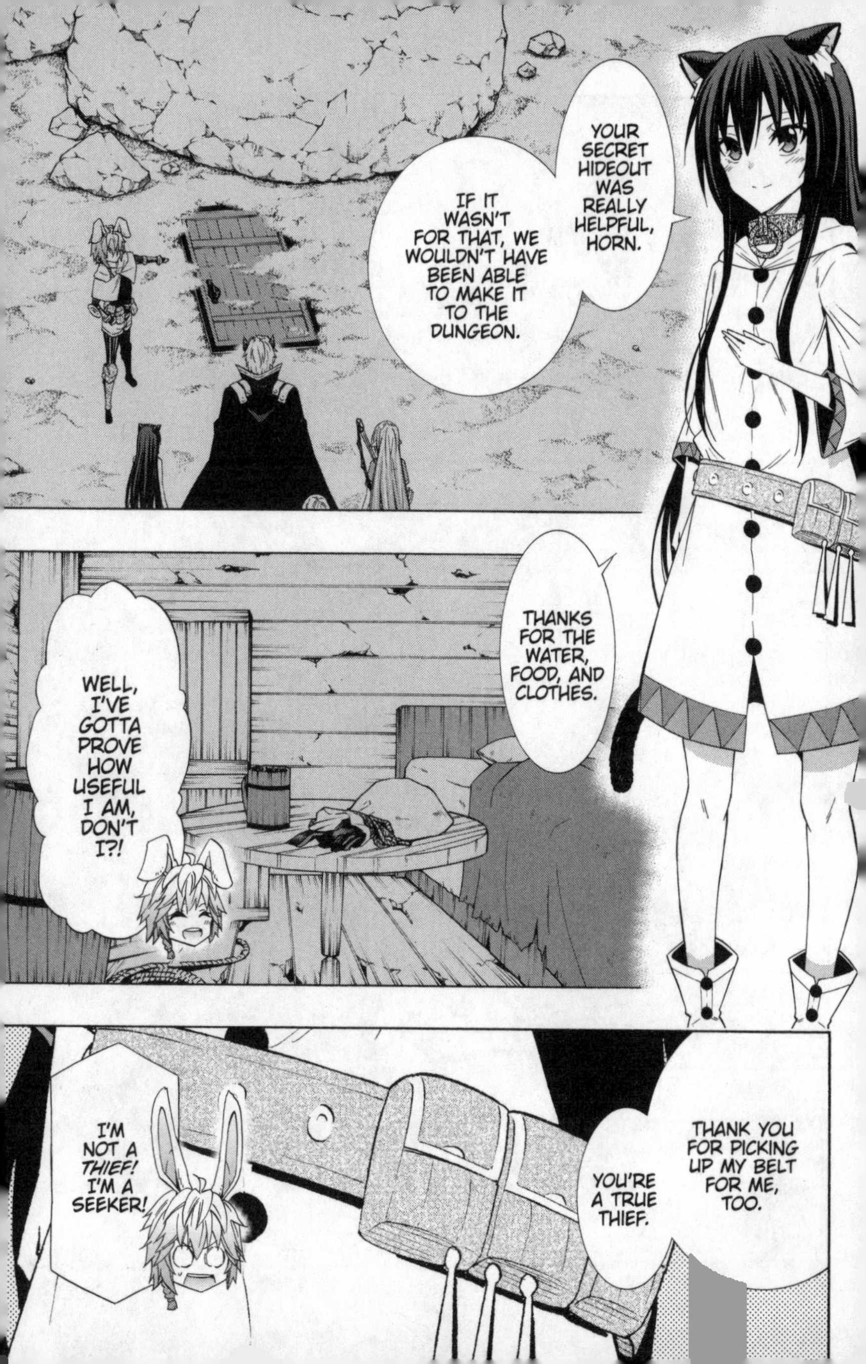
YOUR SECRET HIDEOUT WAS REALLY HELPFUL, HORN.
IF IT WASN'T FOR THAT, WE WOULDN'T HAVE BEEN ABLE TO MAKE IT TO THE DUNGEON.
THANKS FOR THE WATER, FOOD, AND CLOTHES.
WELL, I'VE GOTTA PROVE HOW USEFUL I AM, DON'T I?!
THANK YOU FOR PICKING UP MY BELT FOR ME, TOO.
YOU'RE A TRUE THIEF.
I'M NOT A *THIEF!* I'M A SEEKER!

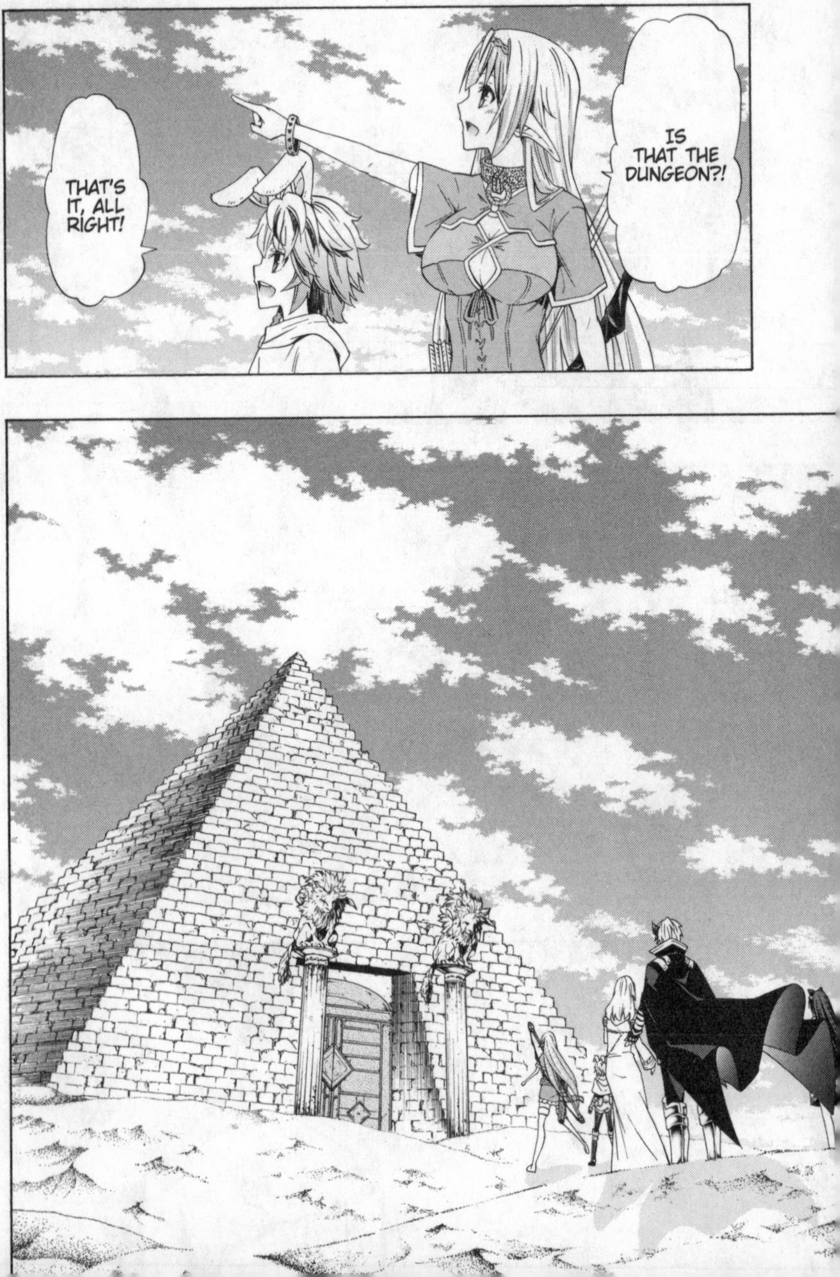
IS THAT THE DUNGEON?!
THAT'S IT, ALL RIGHT!

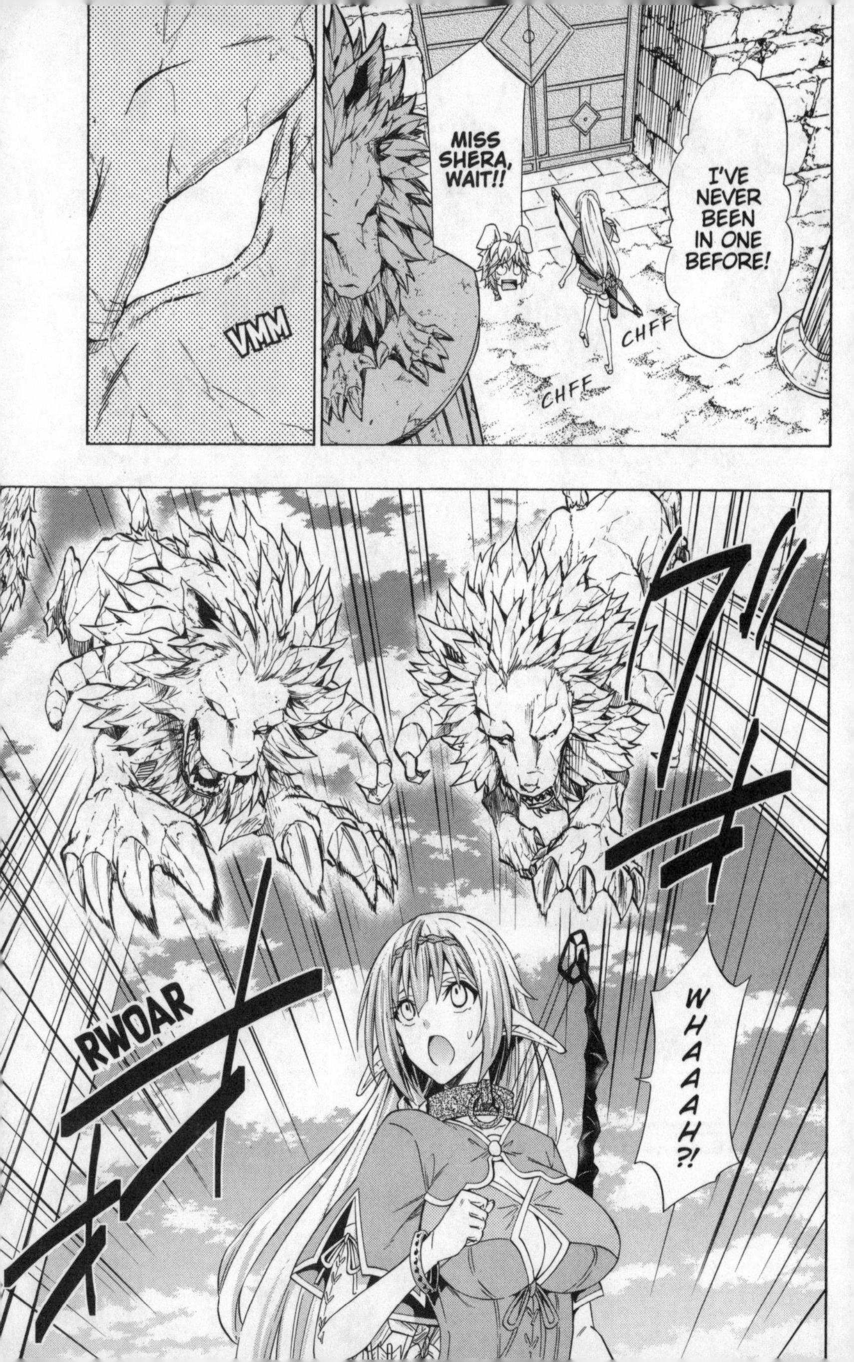
I'VE NEVER BEEN IN ONE BEFORE!
MISS SHERA, WAIT!!
CHFF
CHFF
VMM
WHAAAAH?!
RWOAR

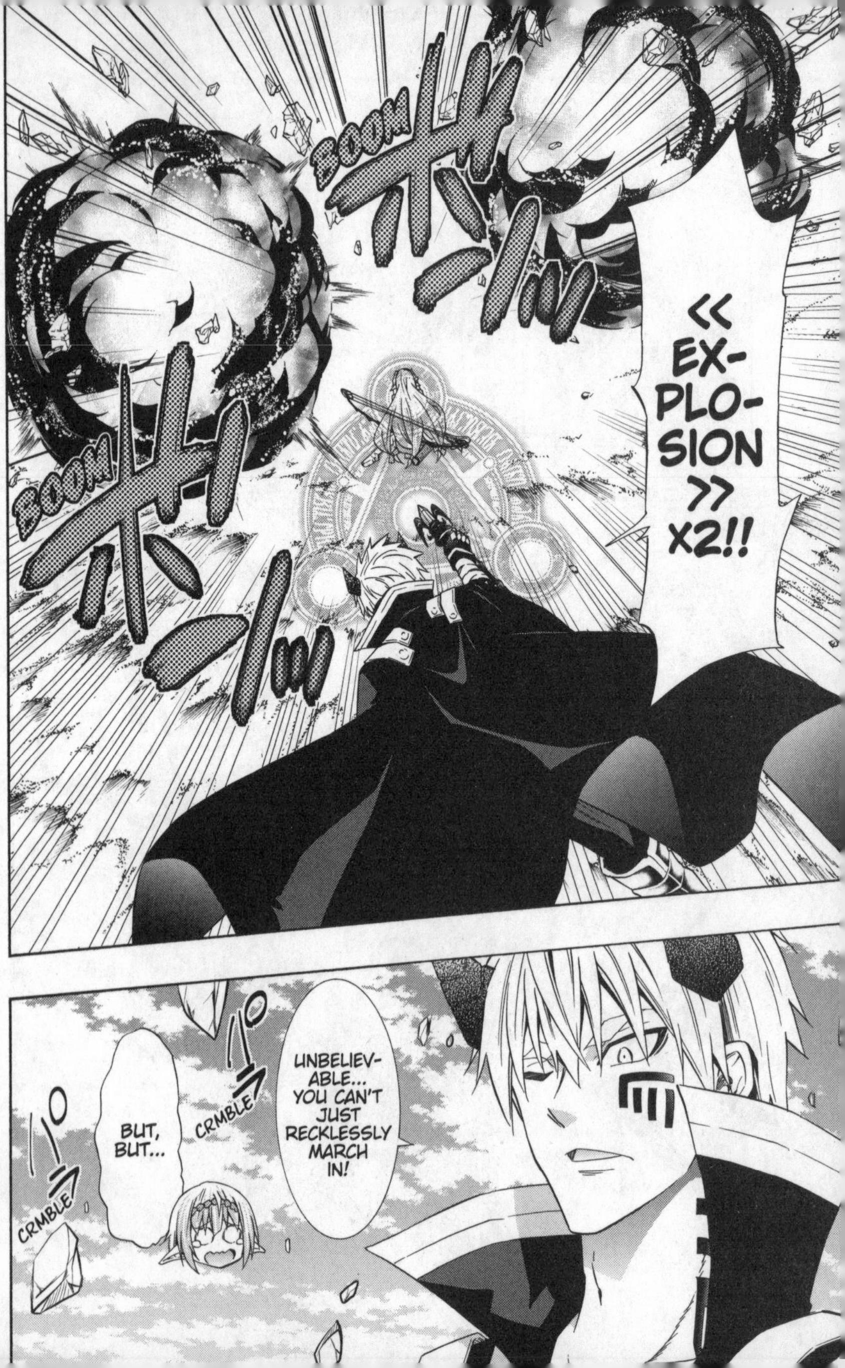
BOOM
«EX-PLO-SION» X2!!
BOOM
UNBELIEV-ABLE... YOU CAN'T JUST RECKLESSLY MARCH IN!
CRMBLE
BUT, BUT...
CRMBLE

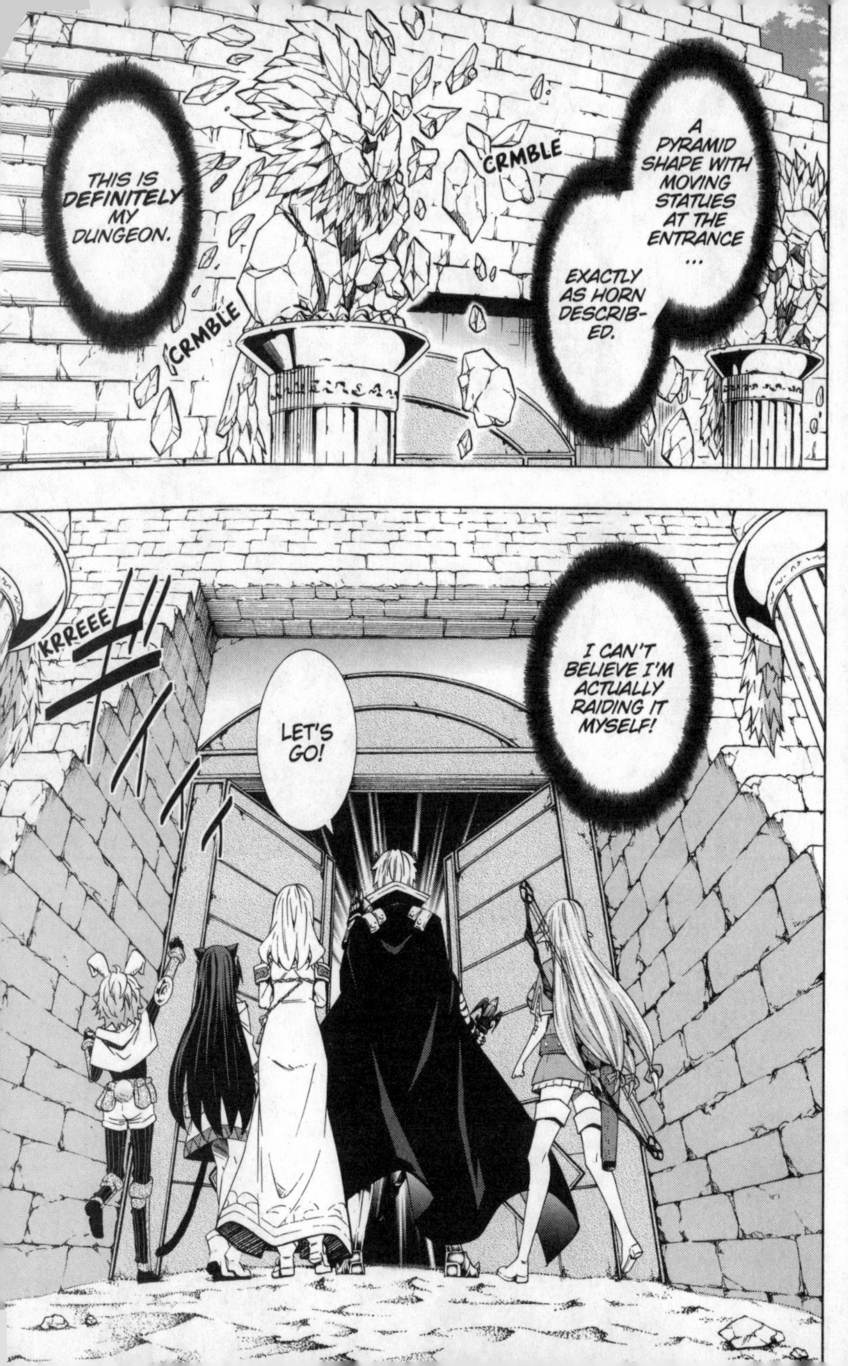
A PYRAMID SHAPE WITH MOVING STATUES AT THE ENTRANCE...
EXACTLY AS HORN DESCRIB-ED.
CRMBLE
THIS IS DEFINITELY MY DUNGEON.
CRMBLE
I CAN'T BELIEVE I'M ACTUALLY RAIDING IT MYSELF!
LET'S GO!
KRREEE

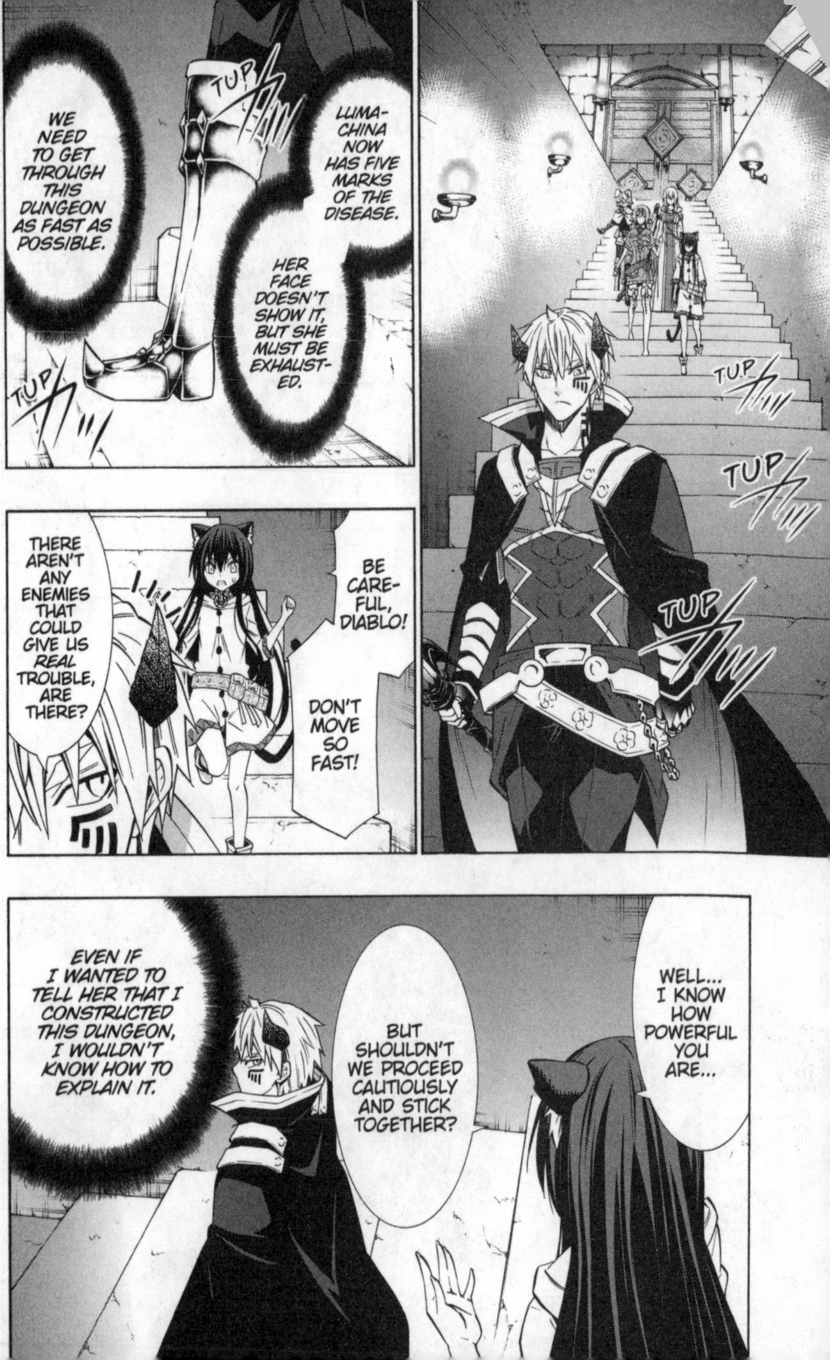
TUP
TUP
TUP
TUP
TUP
LUMA-CHINA NOW HAS FIVE MARKS OF THE DISEASE.
HER FACE DOESN'T SHOW IT, BUT SHE MUST BE EXHAUST-ED.
WE NEED TO GET THROUGH THIS DUNGEON AS FAST AS POSSIBLE.
TUP
BE CARE-FUL, DIABLO!
DON'T MOVE SO FAST!
THERE AREN'T ANY ENEMIES THAT COULD GIVE US REAL TROUBLE, ARE THERE?
WELL... I KNOW HOW POWERFUL YOU ARE...
BUT SHOULDN'T WE PROCEED CAUTIOUSLY AND STICK TOGETHER?
EVEN IF I WANTED TO TELL HER THAT I CONSTRUCTED THIS DUNGEON, I WOULDN'T KNOW HOW TO EXPLAIN IT.

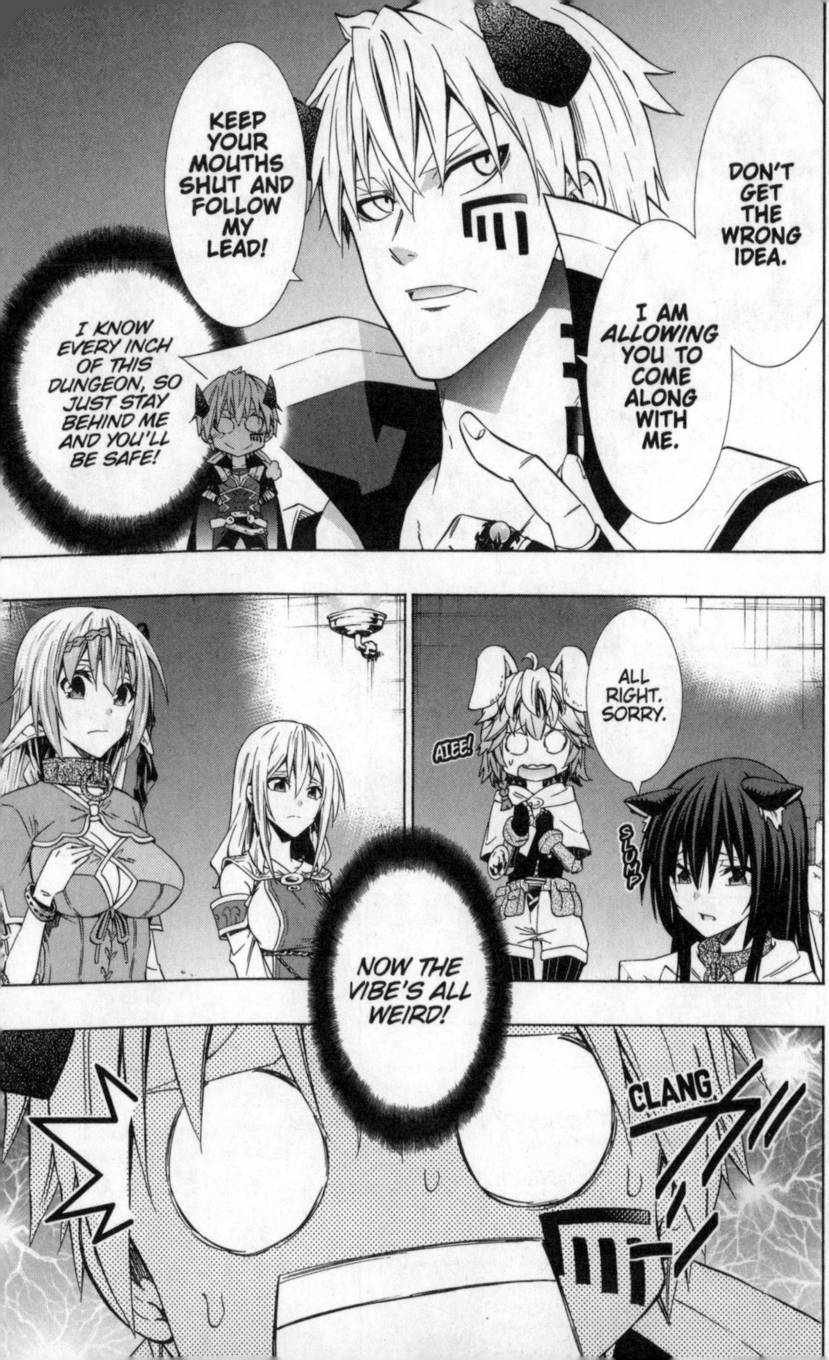
DON'T GET THE WRONG IDEA.
I AM ALLOWING YOU TO COME ALONG WITH ME.
KEEP YOUR MOUTHS SHUT AND FOLLOW MY LEAD!
I KNOW EVERY INCH OF THIS DUNGEON, SO JUST STAY BEHIND ME AND YOU'LL BE SAFE!
ALL RIGHT. SORRY.
SLUMP
AIEE!
NOW THE VIBE'S ALL WEIRD!
CLANG.

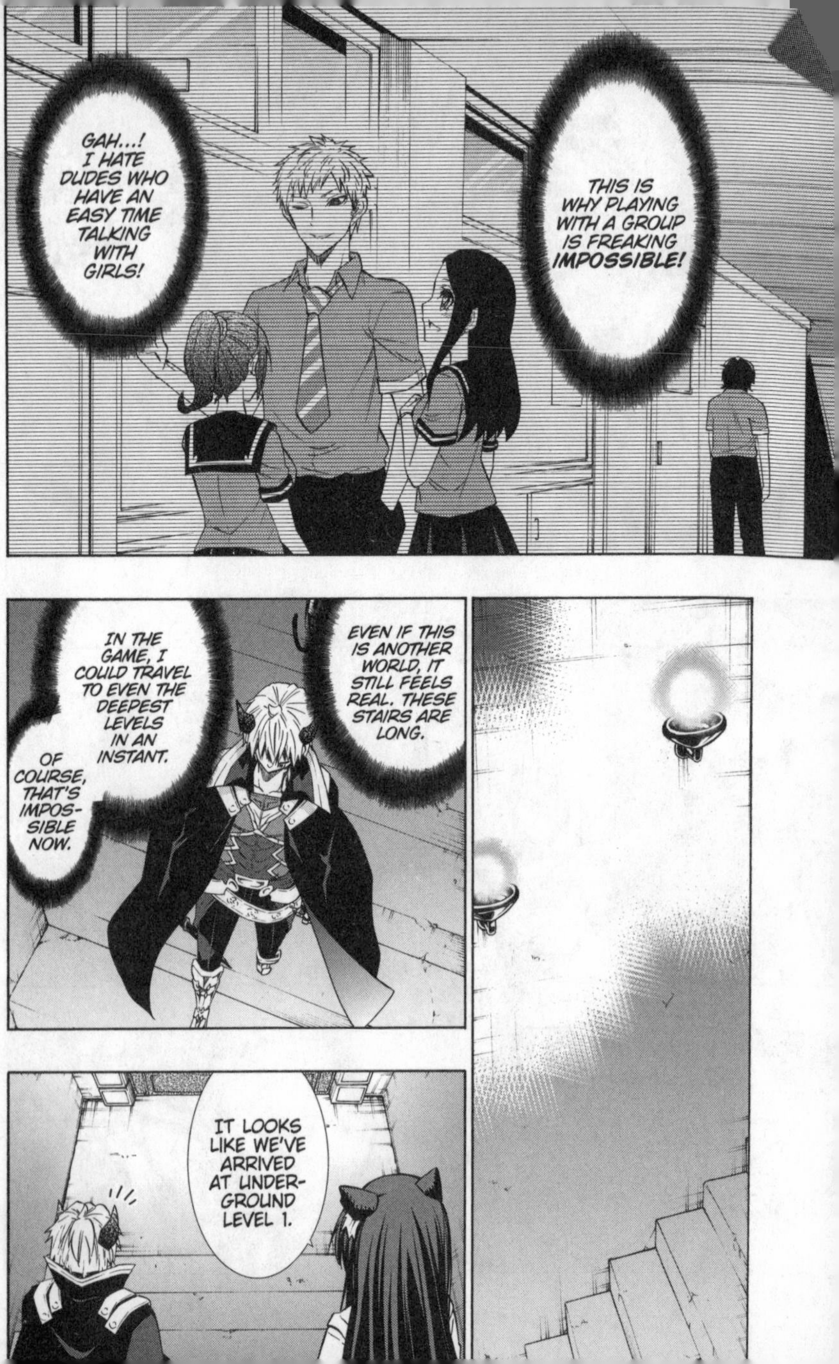
THIS IS WHY PLAYING WITH A GROUP IS FREAKING IMPOSSIBLE!
GAH...! I HATE DUDES WHO HAVE AN EASY TIME TALKING WITH GIRLS!
EVEN IF THIS IS ANOTHER WORLD, IT STILL FEELS REAL. THESE STAIRS ARE LONG.
IN THE GAME, I COULD TRAVEL TO EVEN THE DEEPEST LEVELS IN AN INSTANT.
OF COURSE, THAT'S IMPOSSIBLE NOW.
IT LOOKS LIKE WE'VE ARRIVED AT UNDERGROUND LEVEL 1.

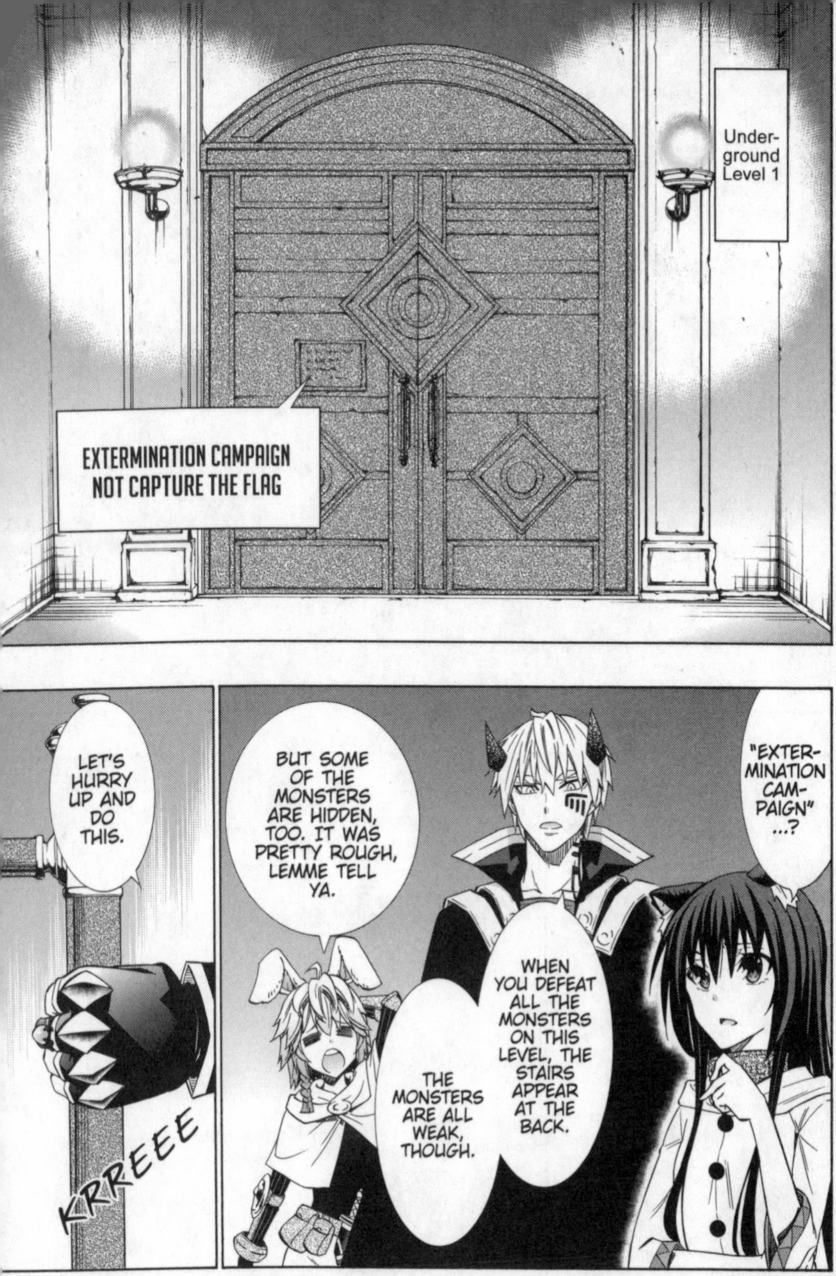
Under-ground Level 1
EXTERMINATION CAMPAIGN NOT CAPTURE THE FLAG
"EXTER-MINATION CAM-PAIGN" ...?
WHEN YOU DEFEAT ALL THE MONSTERS ON THIS LEVEL, THE STAIRS APPEAR AT THE BACK.
THE MONSTERS ARE ALL WEAK, THOUGH.
BUT SOME OF THE MONSTERS ARE HIDDEN, TOO. IT WAS PRETTY ROUGH, LEMME TELL YA.
LET'S HURRY UP AND DO THIS.
KRREEE

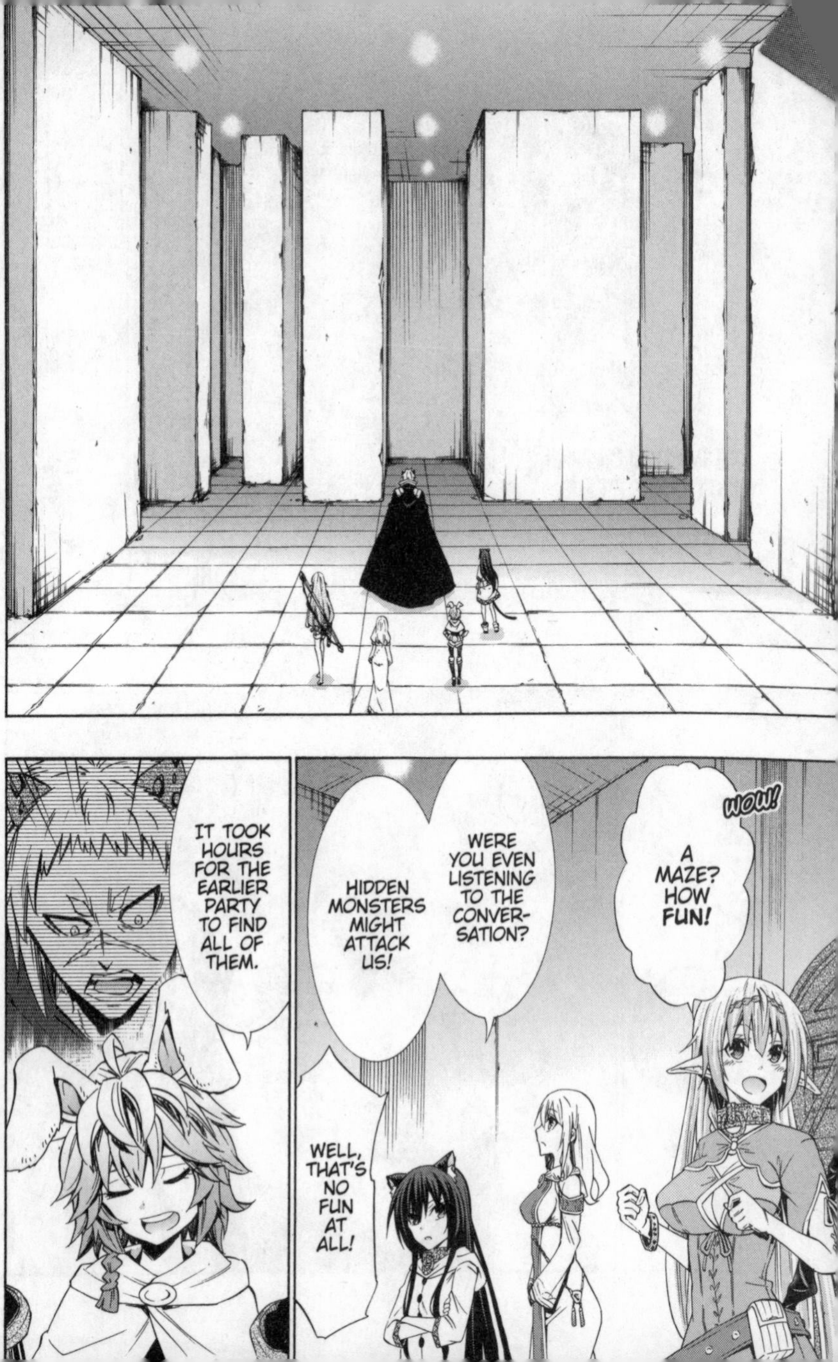
WOW!
A MAZE? HOW FUN!
WERE YOU EVEN LISTENING TO THE CONVER-SATION?
HIDDEN MONSTERS MIGHT ATTACK US!
WELL, THAT'S NO FUN AT ALL!
IT TOOK HOURS FOR THE EARLIER PARTY TO FIND ALL OF THEM.

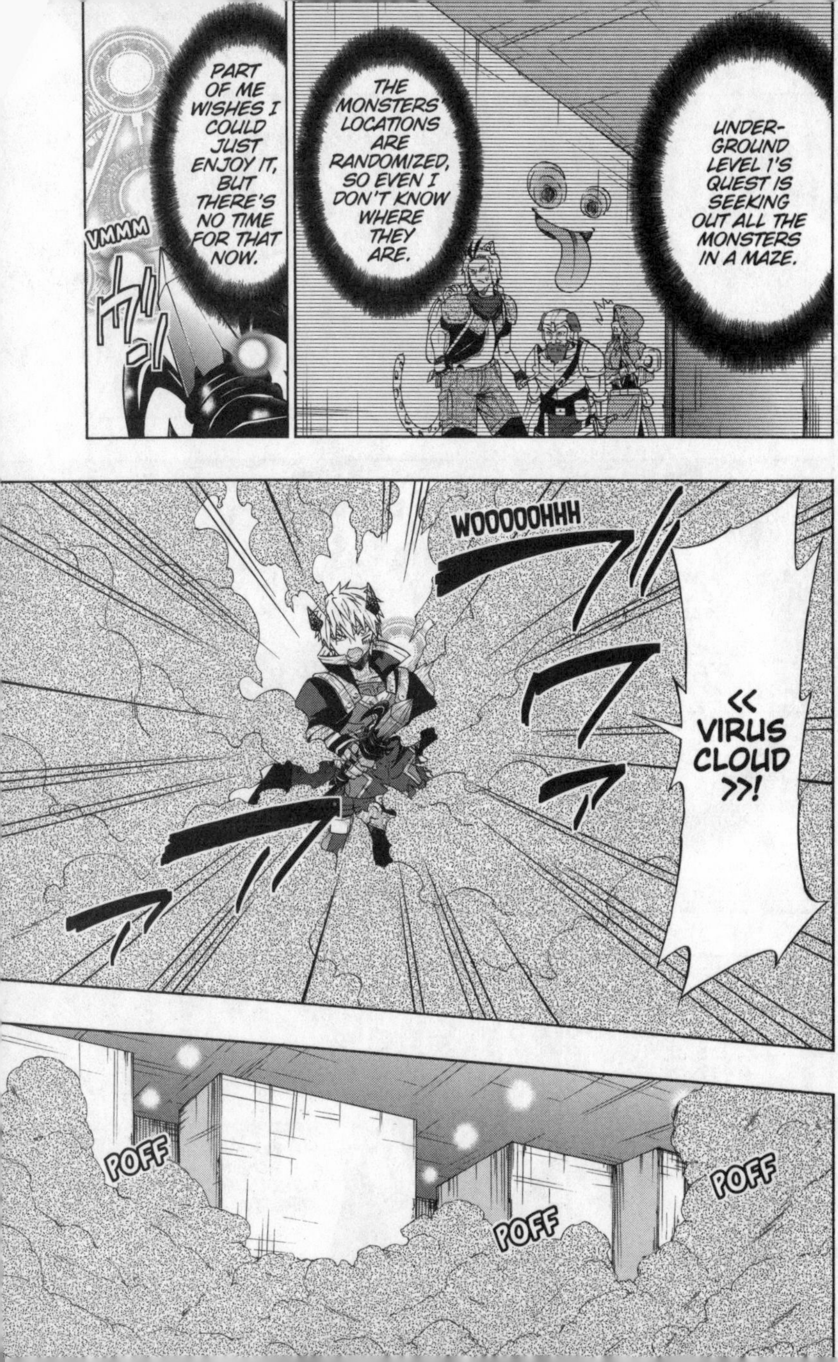
UNDER-GROUND LEVEL 1'S QUEST IS SEEKING OUT ALL THE MONSTERS IN A MAZE.
THE MONSTERS' LOCATIONS ARE RANDOMIZED, SO EVEN I DON'T KNOW WHERE THEY ARE.
PART OF ME WISHES I COULD JUST ENJOY IT, BUT THERE'S NO TIME FOR THAT NOW.
VMMM
« VIRUS CLOUD »!
WOOOOOHHH
POFF
POFF
POFF

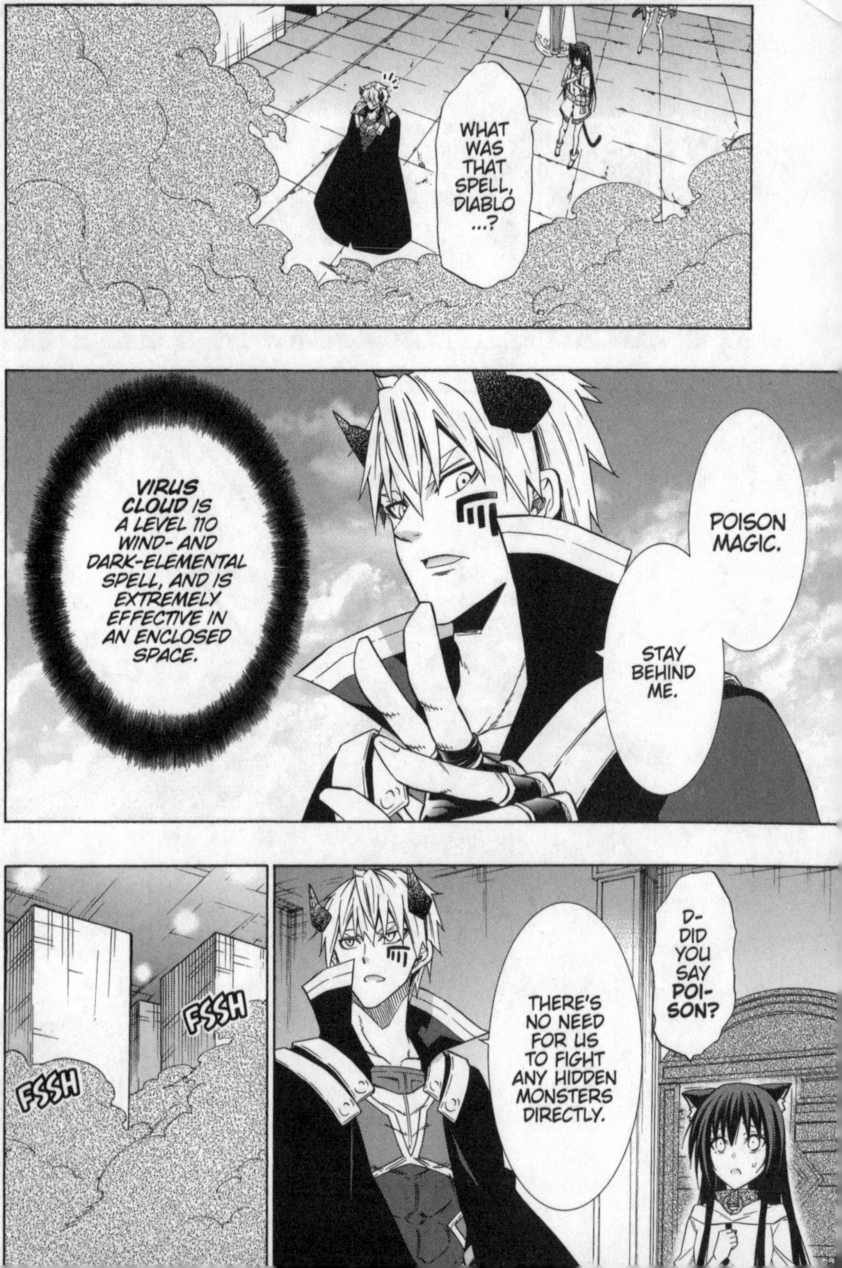
WHAT WAS THAT SPELL, DIABLO ...?
POISON MAGIC.
STAY BEHIND ME.
VIRUS CLOUD IS A LEVEL 110 WIND- AND DARK-ELEMENTAL SPELL, AND IS EXTREMELY EFFECTIVE IN AN ENCLOSED SPACE.
D-DID YOU SAY POI-SON?
THERE'S NO NEED FOR US TO FIGHT ANY HIDDEN MONSTERS DIRECTLY.
FSSH
FSSH

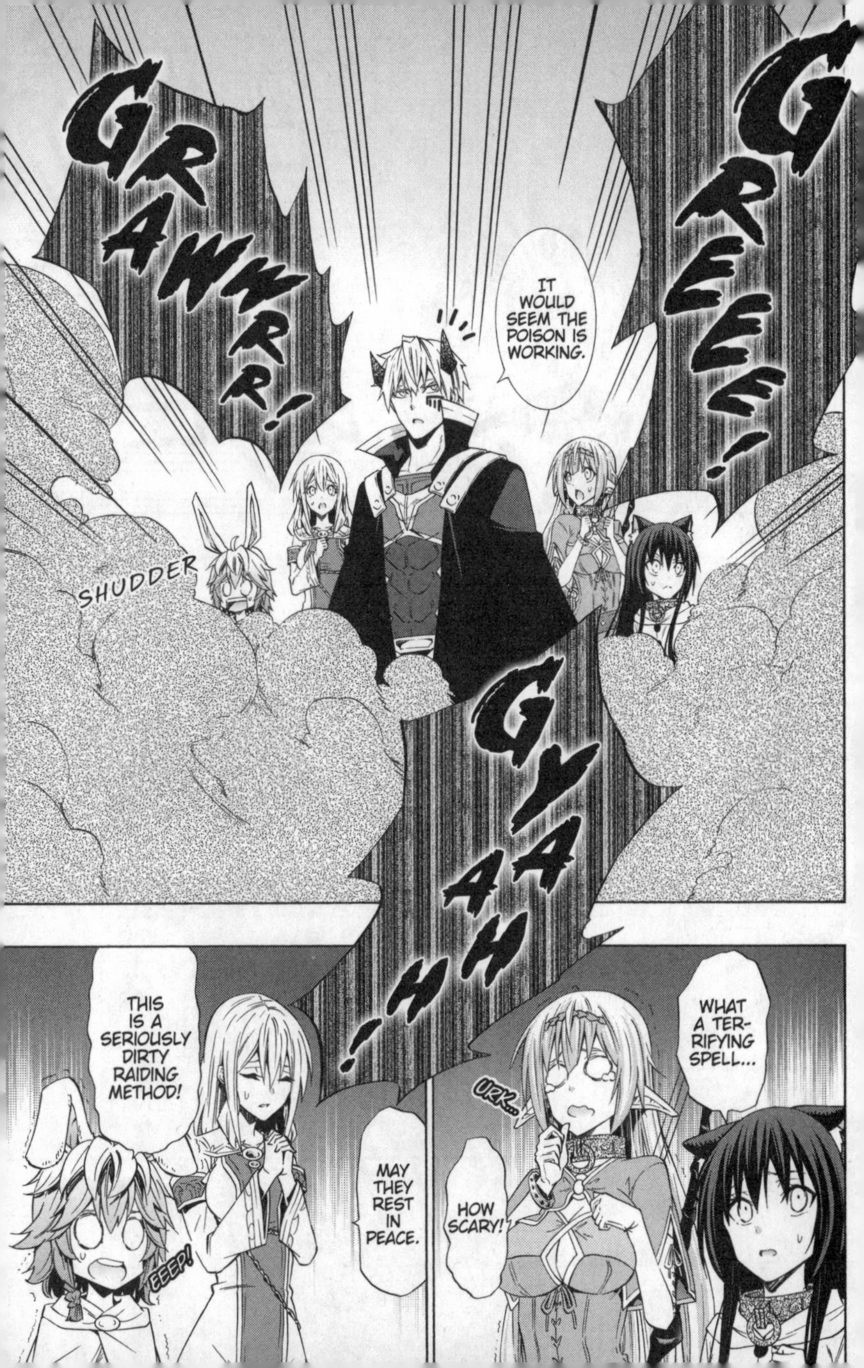
GREEEE!
IT WOULD SEEM THE POISON IS WORKING.
GRAWWRR!
SHUDDER
GYAAAHHH!!
WHAT A TER-RIFYING SPELL...
URK...
HOW SCARY!
MAY THEY REST IN PEACE.
THIS IS A SERIOUSLY DIRTY RAIDING METHOD!
EEEEP!

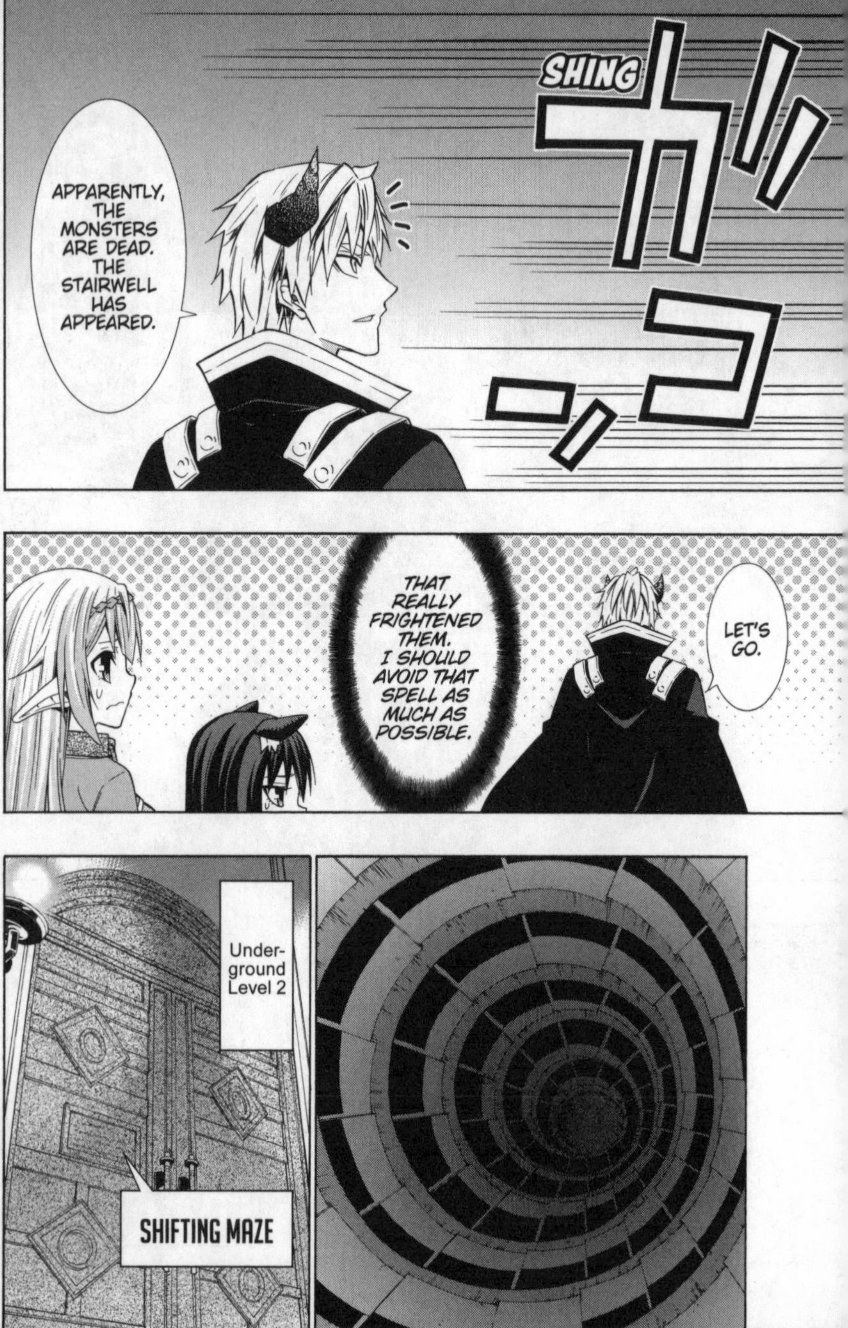
SHING
ガコッ
APPARENTLY, THE MONSTERS ARE DEAD. THE STAIRWELL HAS APPEARED.
LET'S GO.
THAT REALLY FRIGHTENED THEM. I SHOULD AVOID THAT SPELL AS MUCH AS POSSIBLE.
Under-ground Level 2
SHIFTING MAZE

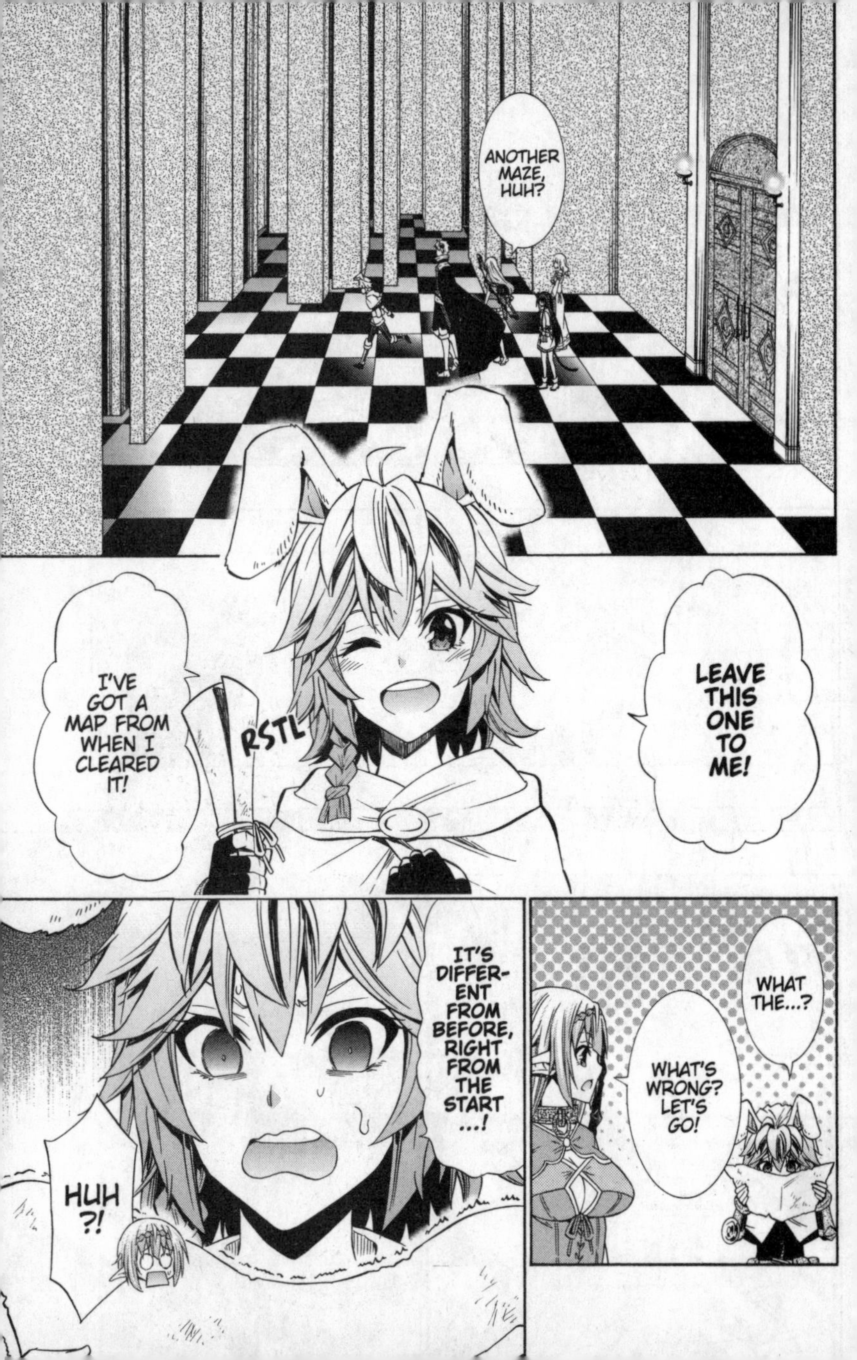
ANOTHER MAZE, HUH?
LEAVE THIS ONE TO ME!
RSTL
I'VE GOT A MAP FROM WHEN I CLEARED IT!
WHAT THE...?
WHAT'S WRONG? LET'S GO!
IT'S DIFFERENT FROM BEFORE, RIGHT FROM THE START...!
HUH?!

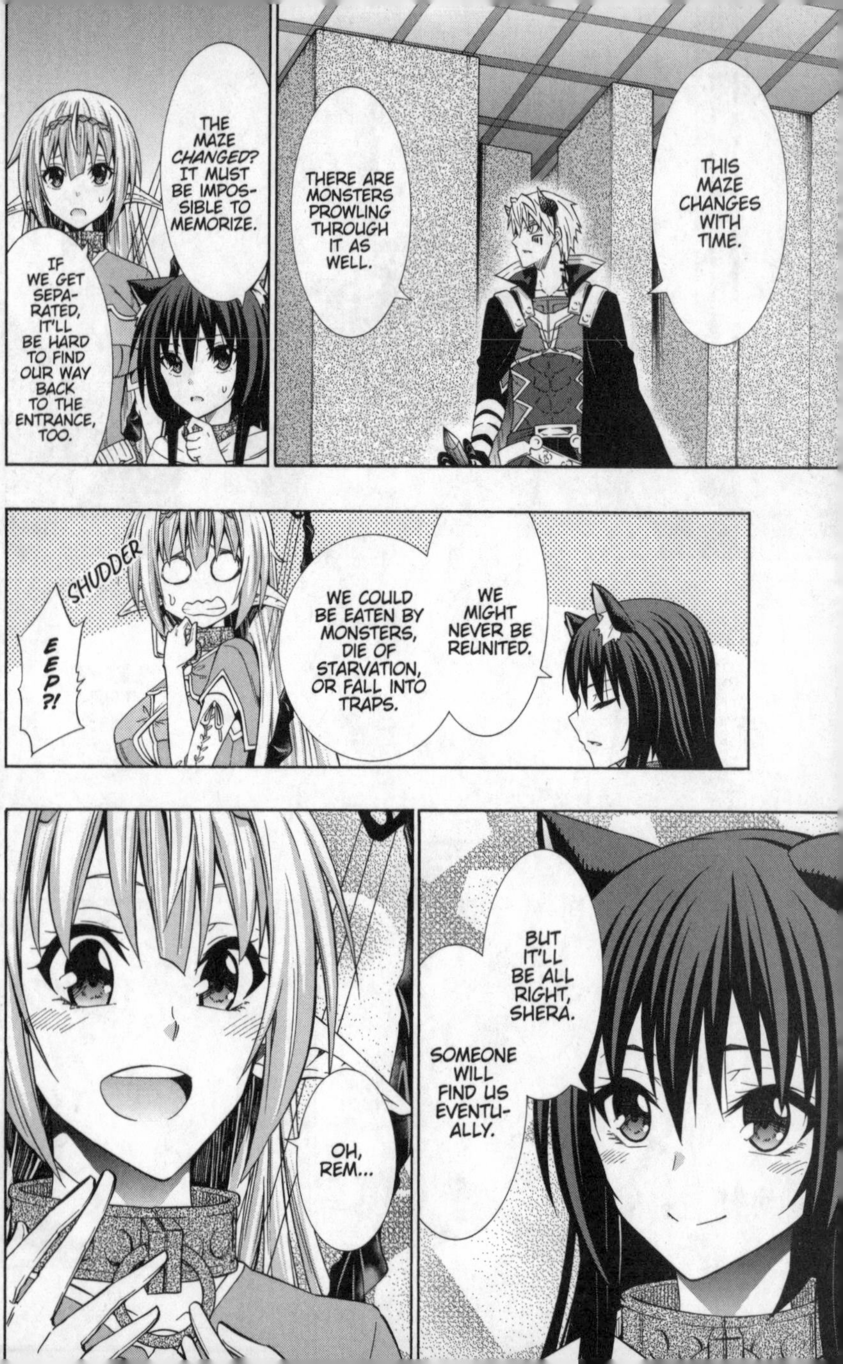
THIS MAZE CHANGES WITH TIME.
THERE ARE MONSTERS PROWLING THROUGH IT AS WELL.
THE MAZE CHANGED? IT MUST BE IMPOSSIBLE TO MEMORIZE.
IF WE GET SEPARATED, IT'LL BE HARD TO FIND OUR WAY BACK TO THE ENTRANCE, TOO.
WE MIGHT NEVER BE REUNITED.
WE COULD BE EATEN BY MONSTERS, DIE OF STARVATION, OR FALL INTO TRAPS.
SHUDDER
EEP?!
BUT IT'LL BE ALL RIGHT, SHERA.
SOMEONE WILL FIND US EVENTUALLY.
OH, REM...

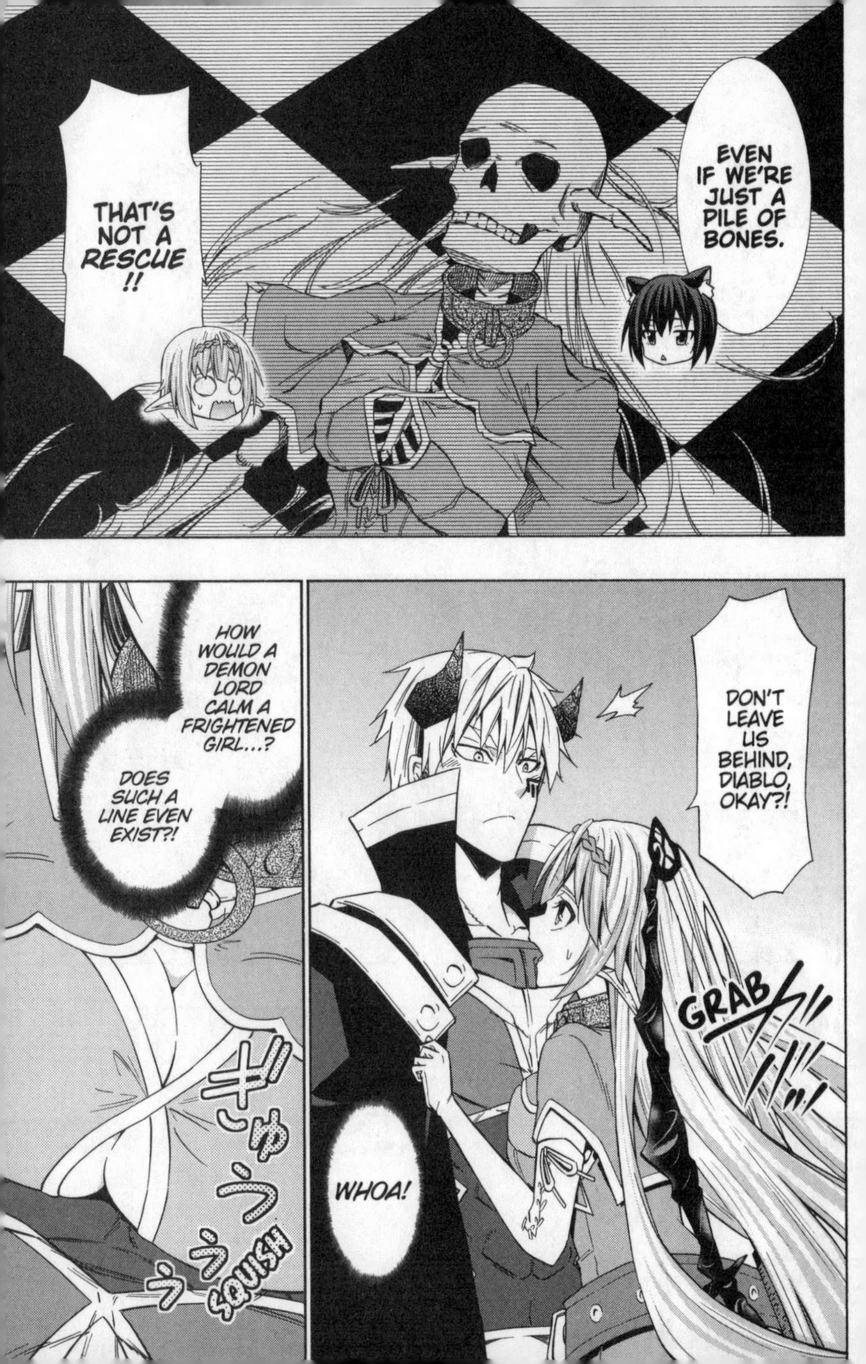
EVEN IF WE'RE JUST A PILE OF BONES.
THAT'S NOT A RESCUE!!
DON'T LEAVE US BEHIND, DIABLO, OKAY?!
GRAB
WHOA!
HOW WOULD A DEMON LORD CALM A FRIGHTENED GIRL...?
DOES SUCH A LINE EVEN EXIST?!
SQUISH

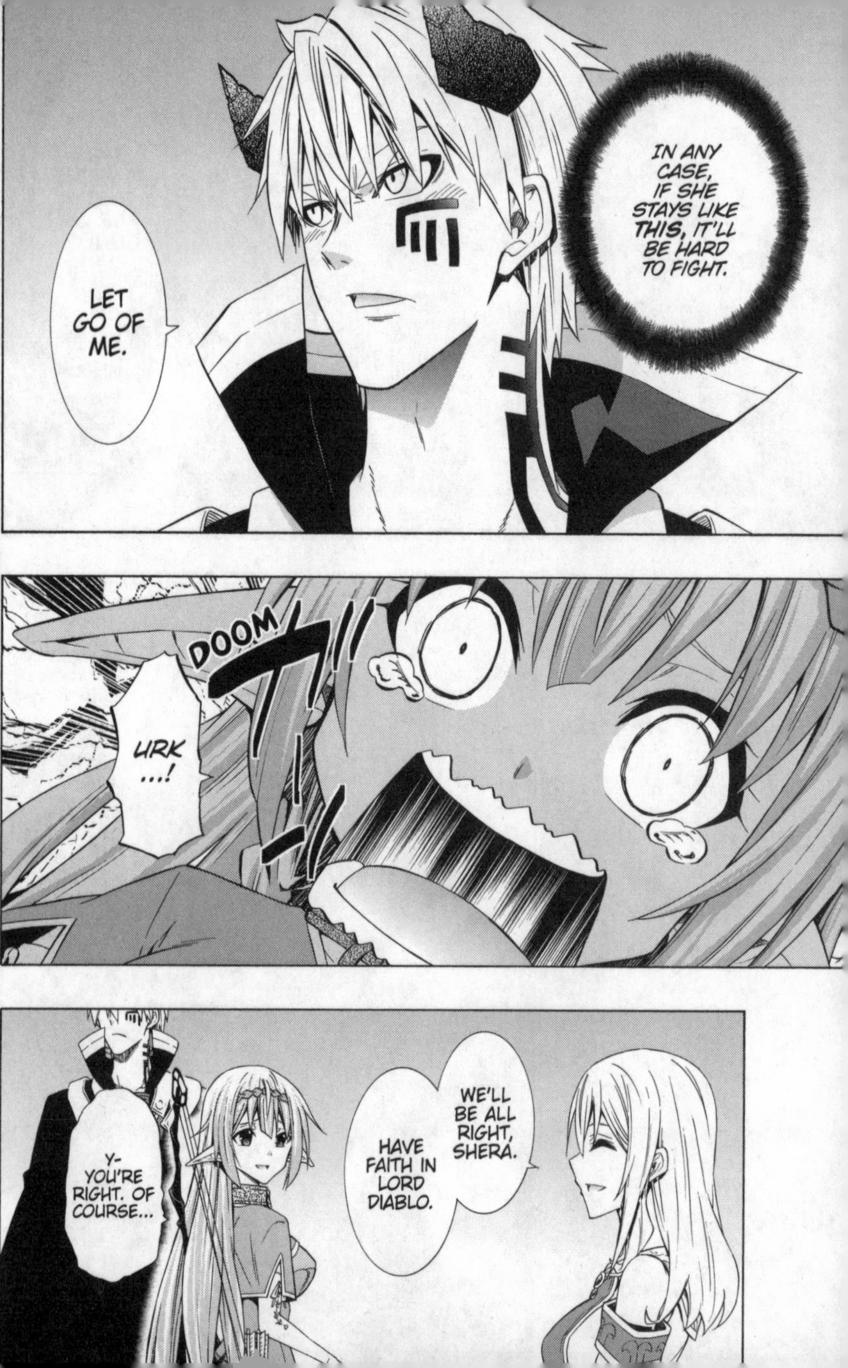
IN ANY CASE, IF SHE STAYS LIKE THIS, IT'LL BE HARD TO FIGHT.
LET GO OF ME.
DOOM
URK ...!
WE'LL BE ALL RIGHT, SHERA.
HAVE FAITH IN LORD DIABLO.
Y-YOU'RE RIGHT. OF COURSE...

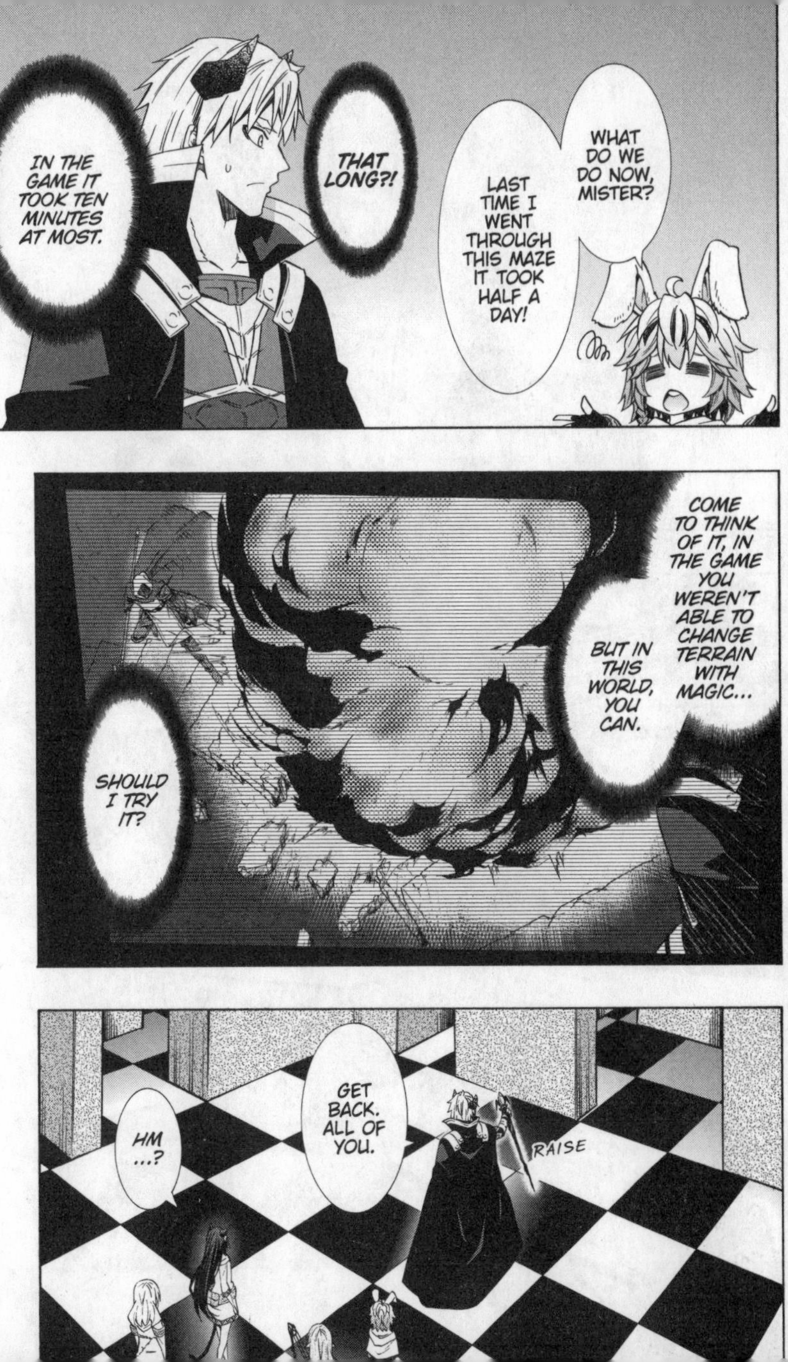
WHAT DO WE DO NOW, MISTER?
LAST TIME I WENT THROUGH THIS MAZE IT TOOK HALF A DAY!
THAT LONG?!
IN THE GAME IT TOOK TEN MINUTES AT MOST.
COME TO THINK OF IT, IN THE GAME YOU WEREN'T ABLE TO CHANGE TERRAIN WITH MAGIC...
BUT IN THIS WORLD, YOU CAN.
SHOULD I TRY IT?
RAISE
GET BACK. ALL OF YOU.
HM ...?

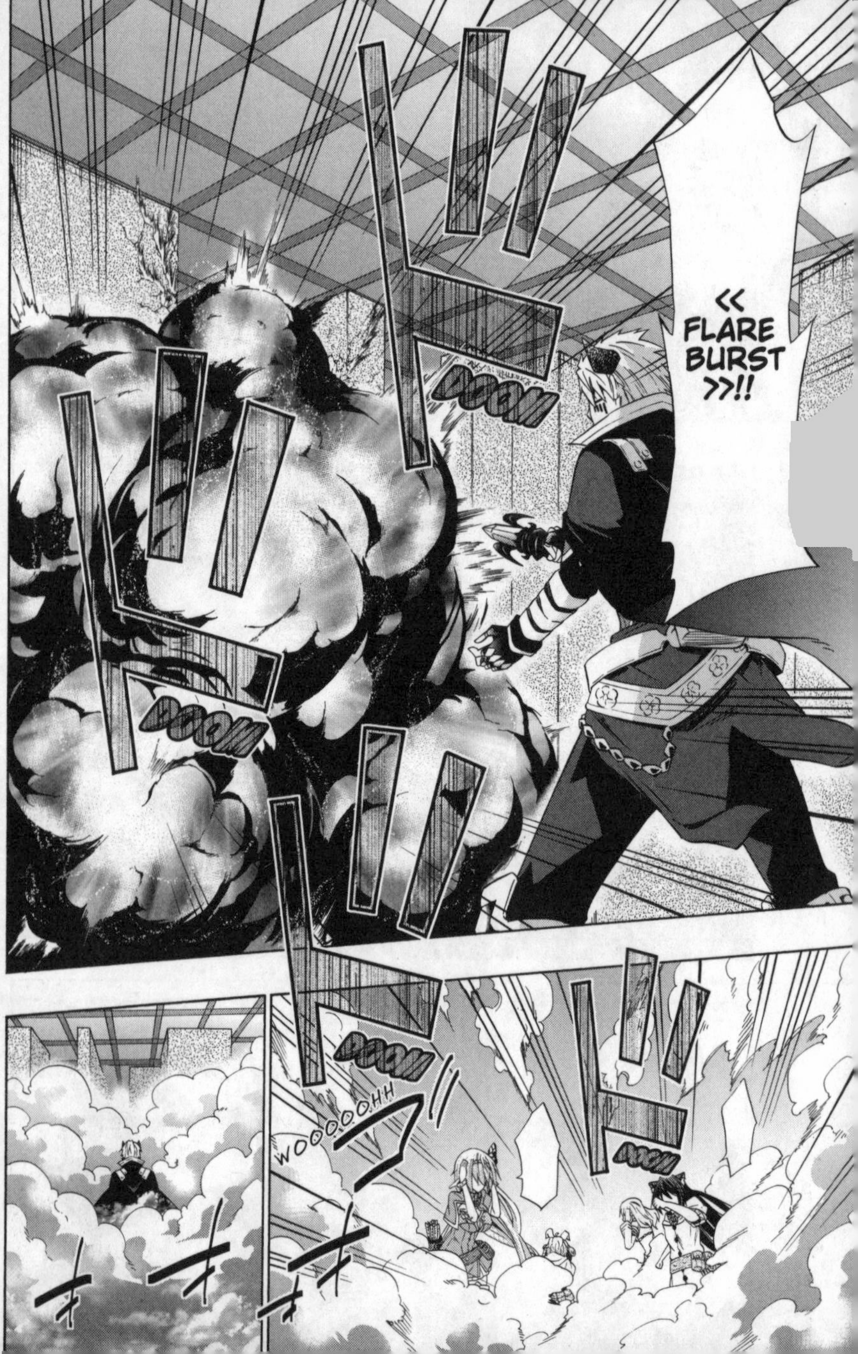
<< FLARE BURST >>!!
DOOM
DOOM
DOOM
WOOOOOOHH

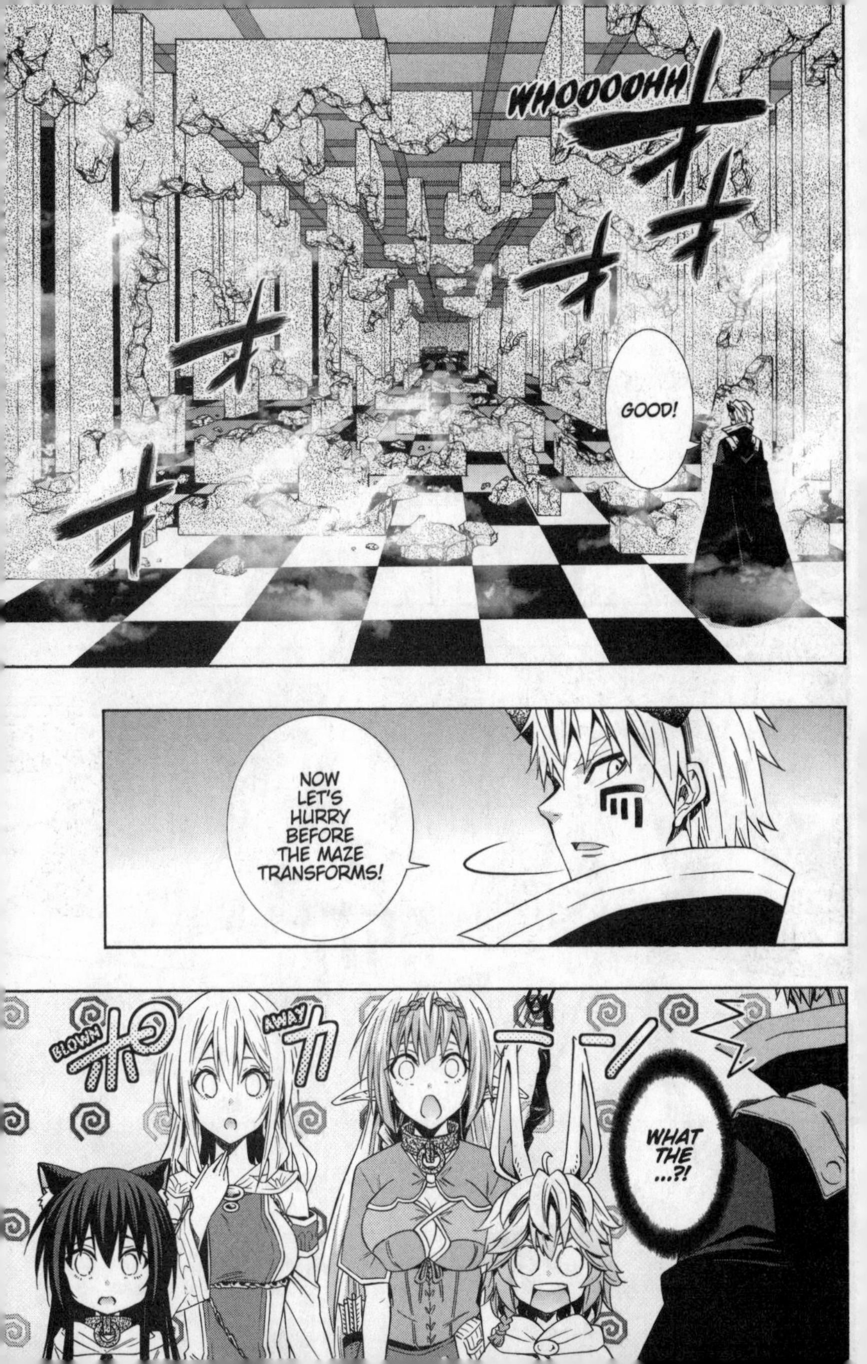
WHOOOOHH
GOOD!
NOW LET'S HURRY BEFORE THE MAZE TRANSFORMS!
WHAT THE ...?!
BLOWN AWAY

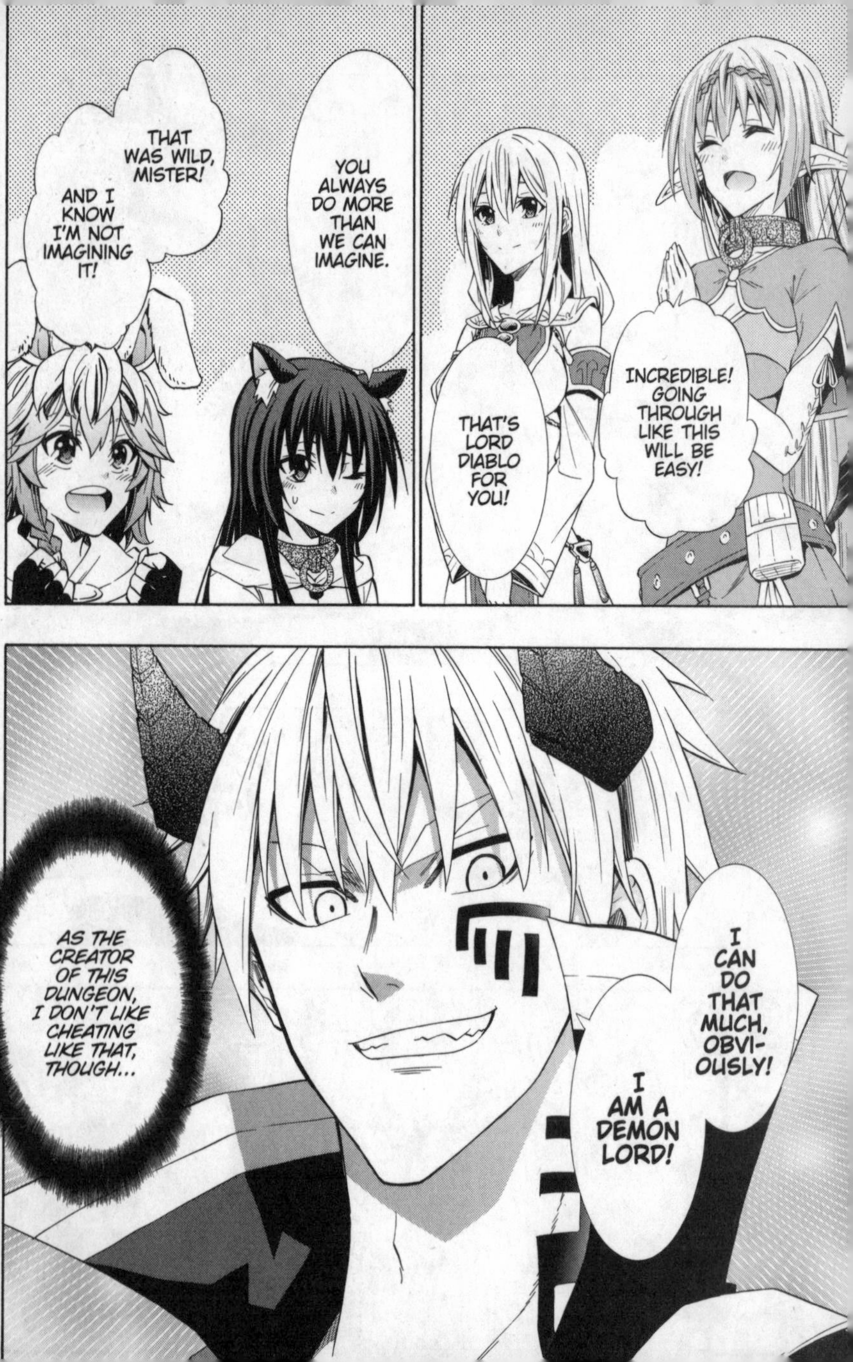
INCREDIBLE! GOING THROUGH LIKE THIS WILL BE EASY!
THAT'S LORD DIABLO FOR YOU!
YOU ALWAYS DO MORE THAN WE CAN IMAGINE.
THAT WAS WILD, MISTER!
AND I KNOW I'M NOT IMAGINING IT!
I CAN DO THAT MUCH, OBVI-OUSLY!
I AM A DEMON LORD!
AS THE CREATOR OF THIS DUNGEON, I DON'T LIKE CHEATING LIKE THAT, THOUGH...

HOW NOT
TO SUMMON A
DEMON LORD

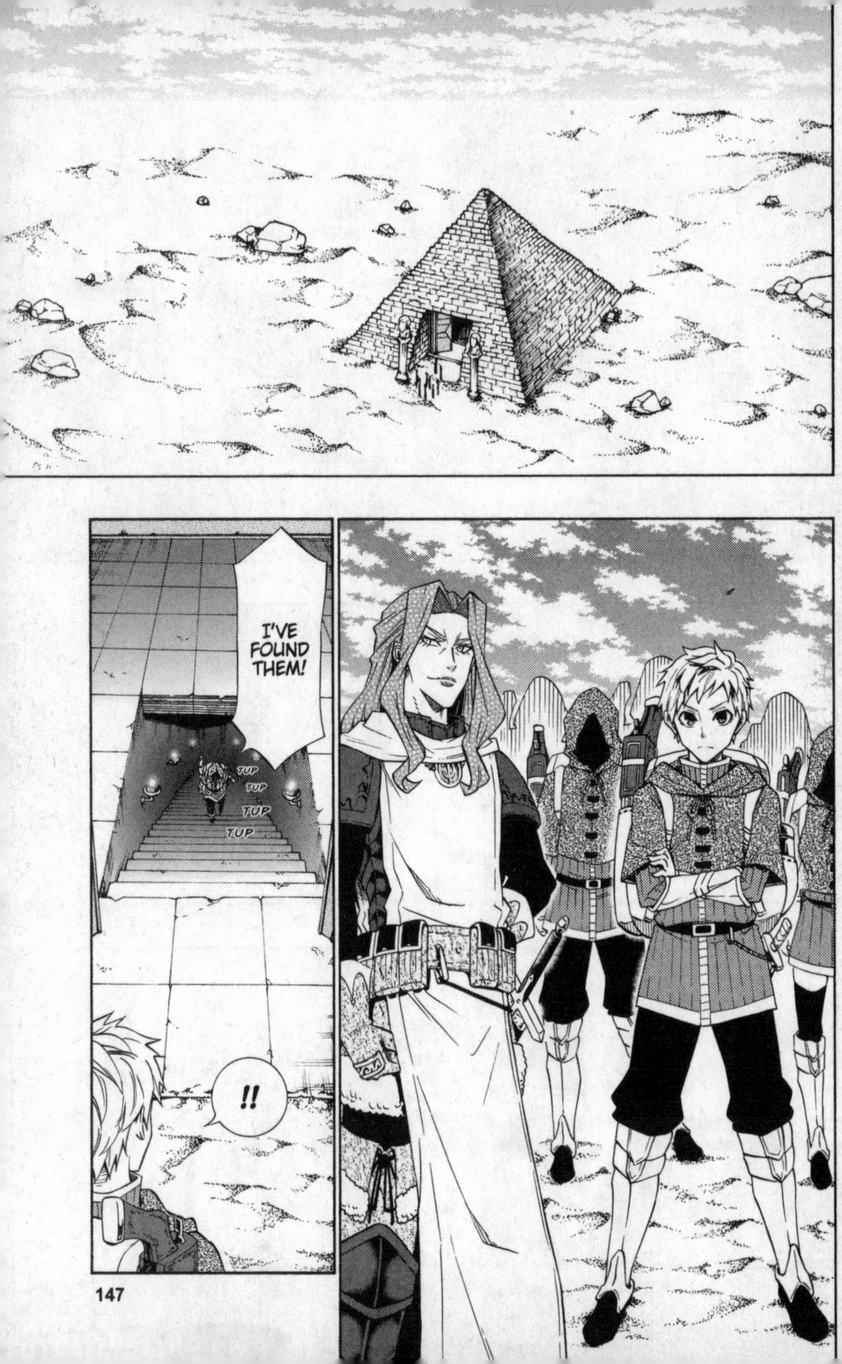
I'VE FOUND THEM!
TUP
TUP
TUP
TUP
!!

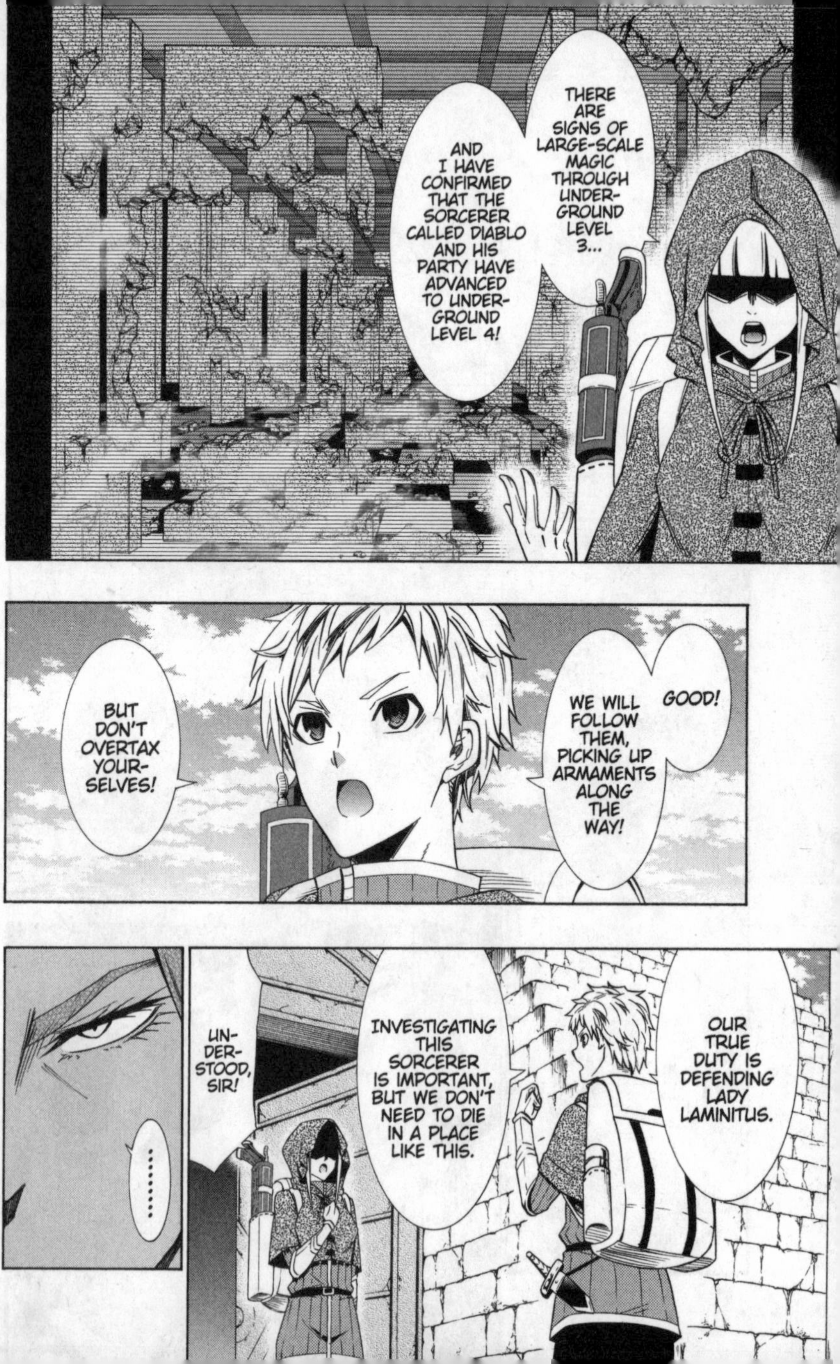
THERE ARE SIGNS OF LARGE-SCALE MAGIC THROUGH UNDER-GROUND LEVEL 3...
AND I HAVE CONFIRMED THAT THE SORCERER CALLED DIABLO AND HIS PARTY HAVE ADVANCED TO UNDER-GROUND LEVEL 4!
GOOD!
WE WILL FOLLOW THEM, PICKING UP ARMAMENTS ALONG THE WAY!
BUT DON'T OVERTAX YOUR-SELVES!
OUR TRUE DUTY IS DEFENDING LADY LAMINITUS.
INVESTIGATING THIS SORCERER IS IMPORTANT, BUT WE DON'T NEED TO DIE IN A PLACE LIKE THIS.
UN-DER-STOOD, SIR!
......

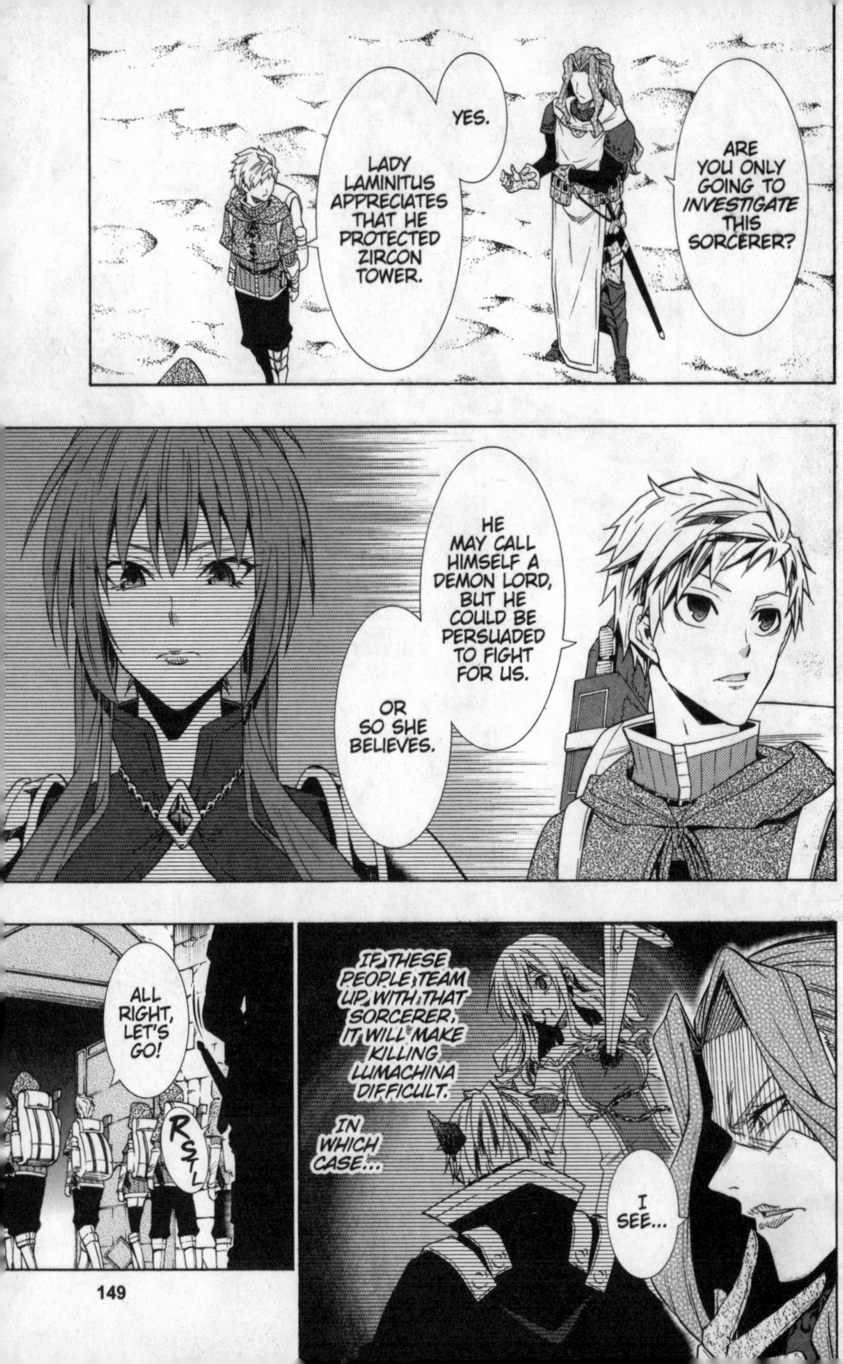
ARE YOU ONLY GOING TO *INVESTIGATE* THIS SORCERER?
YES.
LADY LAMINITUS APPRECIATES THAT HE PROTECTED ZIRCON TOWER.
HE MAY CALL HIMSELF A DEMON LORD, BUT HE COULD BE PERSUADED TO FIGHT FOR US.
OR SO SHE BELIEVES.
IF THESE PEOPLE TEAM UP WITH THAT SORCERER, IT WILL MAKE KILLING LUMACHINA DIFFICULT.
IN WHICH CASE...
I SEE...
ALL RIGHT, LET'S GO!
RSTL

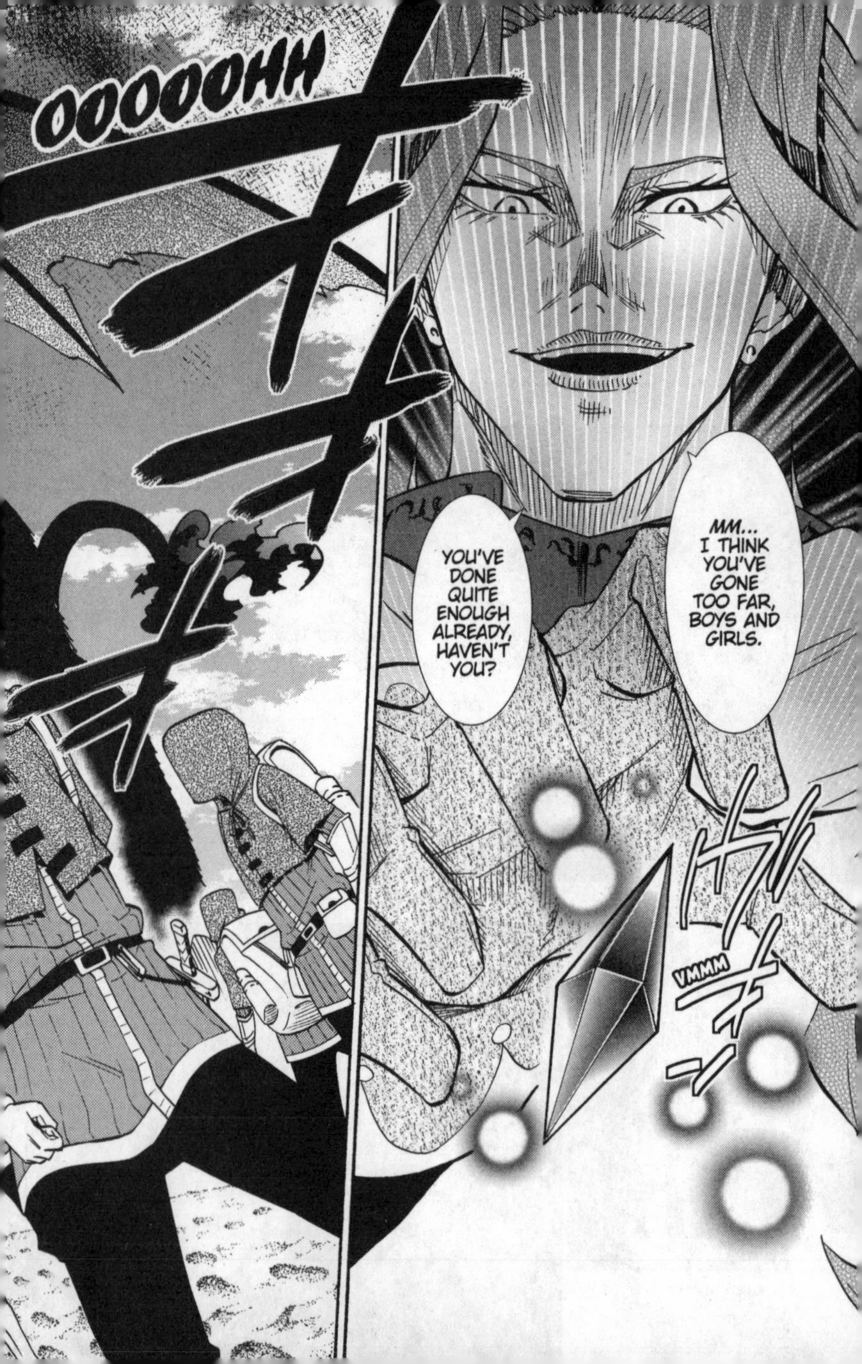
MM... I THINK YOU'VE GONE TOO FAR, BOYS AND GIRLS.
YOU'VE DONE QUITE ENOUGH ALREADY, HAVEN'T YOU?
VMMM
OOOOOHH

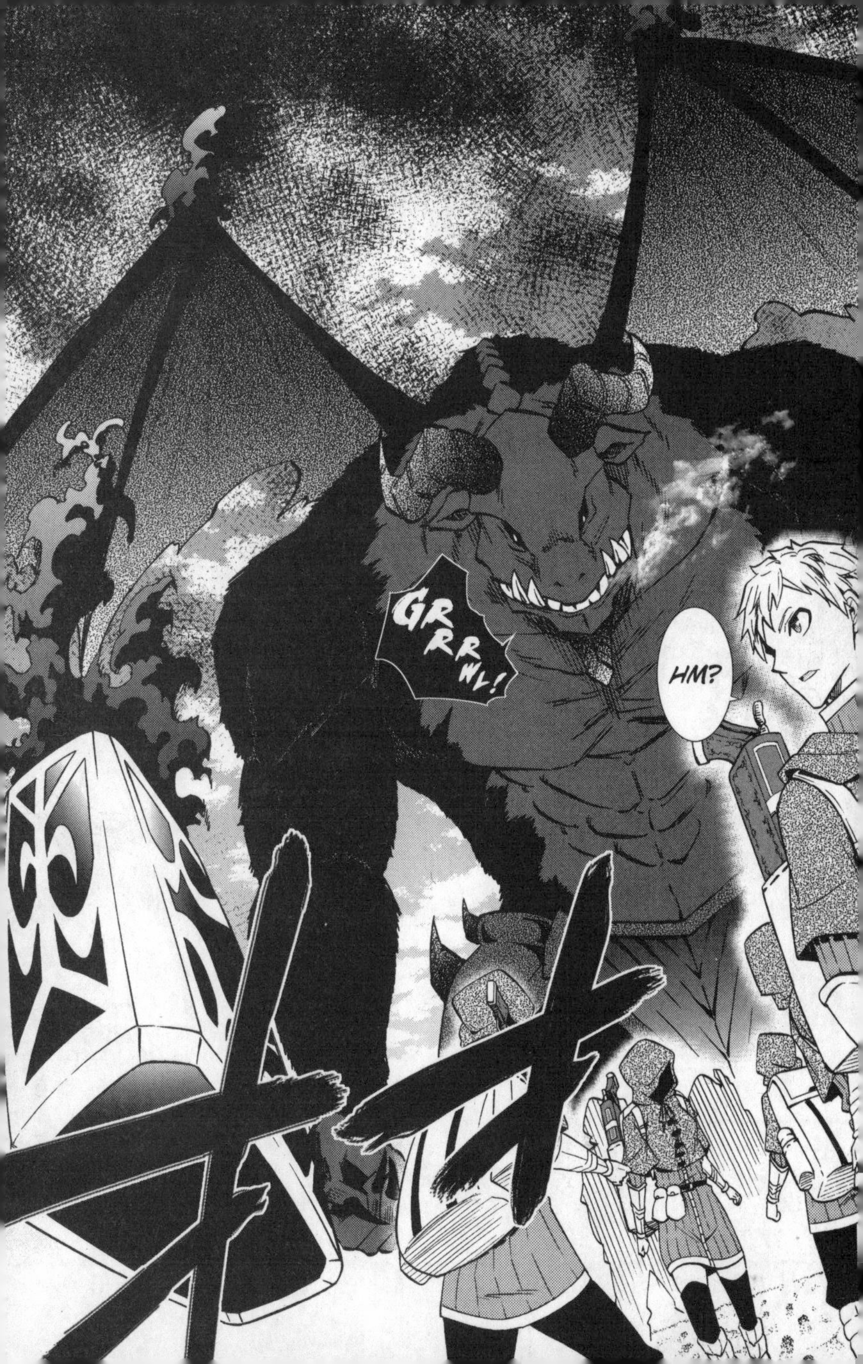
GRRRWL!
HM?

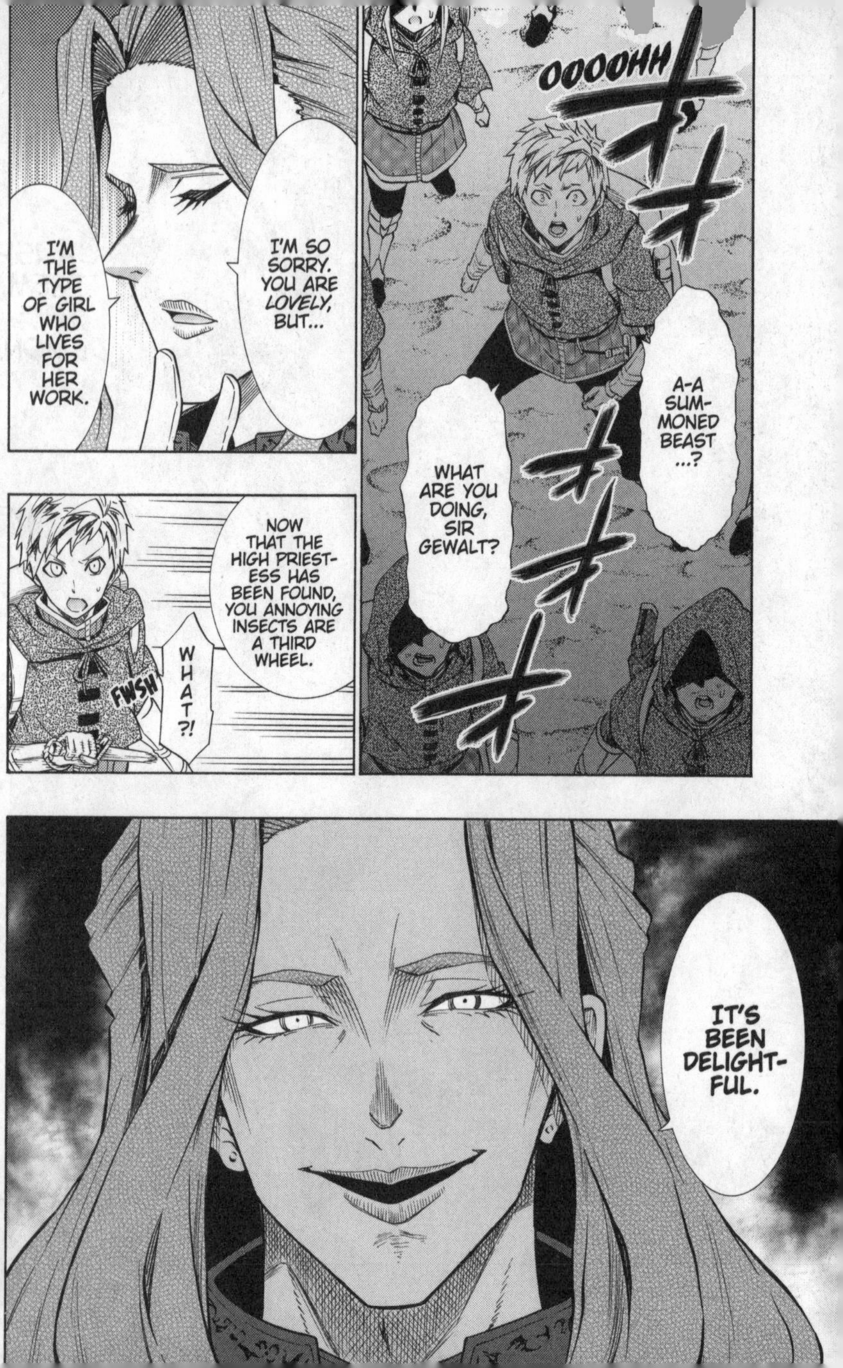
I'M SO SORRY. YOU ARE LOVELY, BUT...
I'M THE TYPE OF GIRL WHO LIVES FOR HER WORK.
NOW THAT THE HIGH PRIESTESS HAS BEEN FOUND, YOU ANNOYING INSECTS ARE A THIRD WHEEL.
FWSH
WHAT?!
OOOOHH
A-A SUMMONED BEAST ...?
WHAT ARE YOU DOING, SIR GEWALT?
IT'S BEEN DELIGHTFUL.

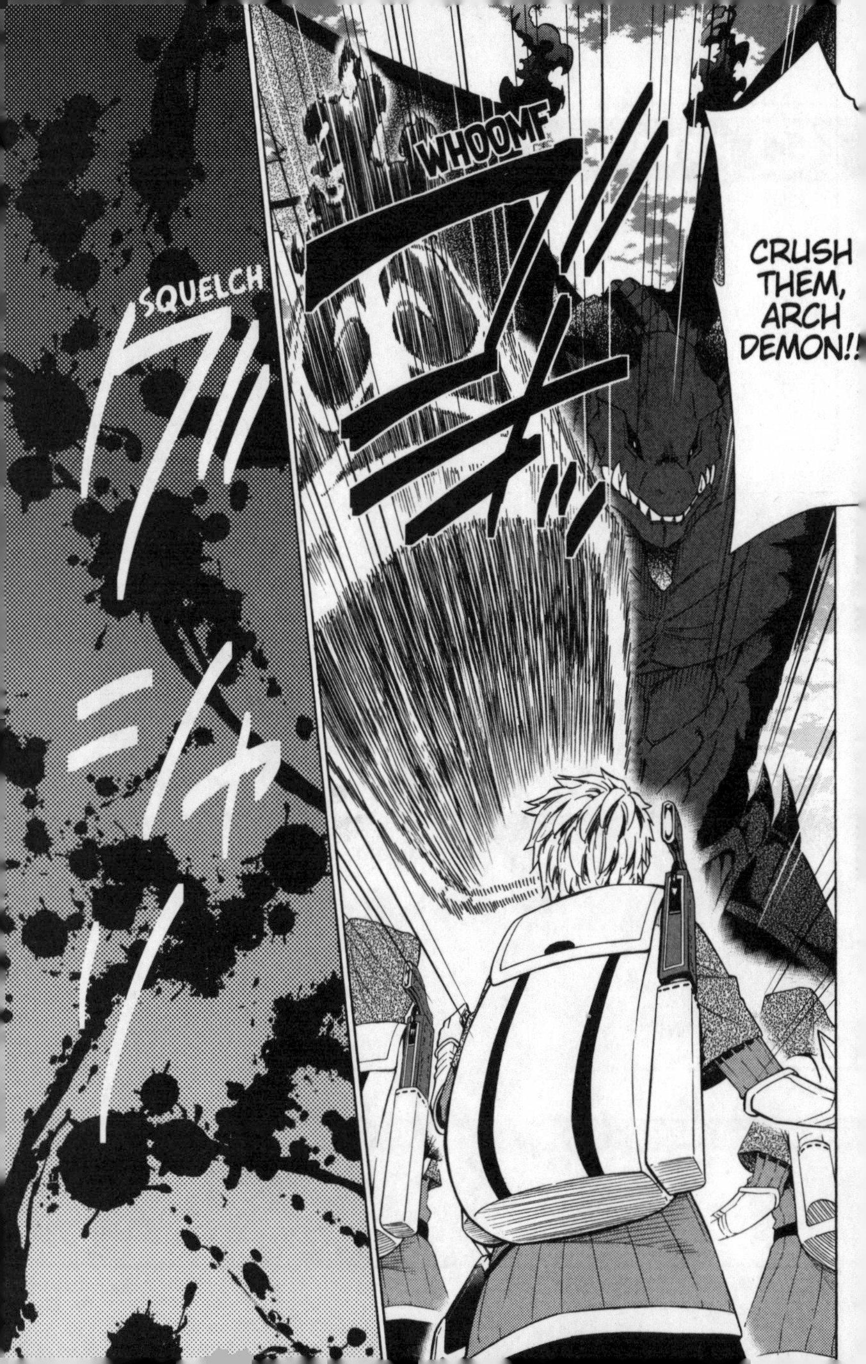
CRUSH THEM, ARCH DEMON!!
WHOOMF
SQUELCH

54 RAIDING A DUNGEON II

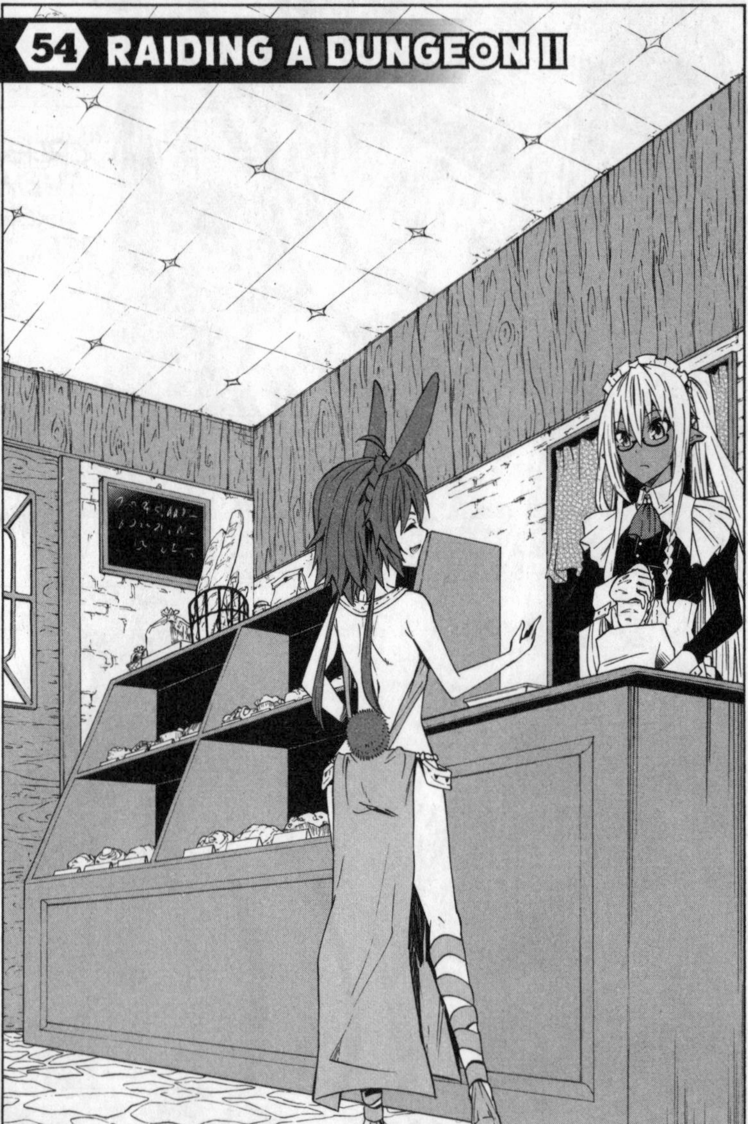

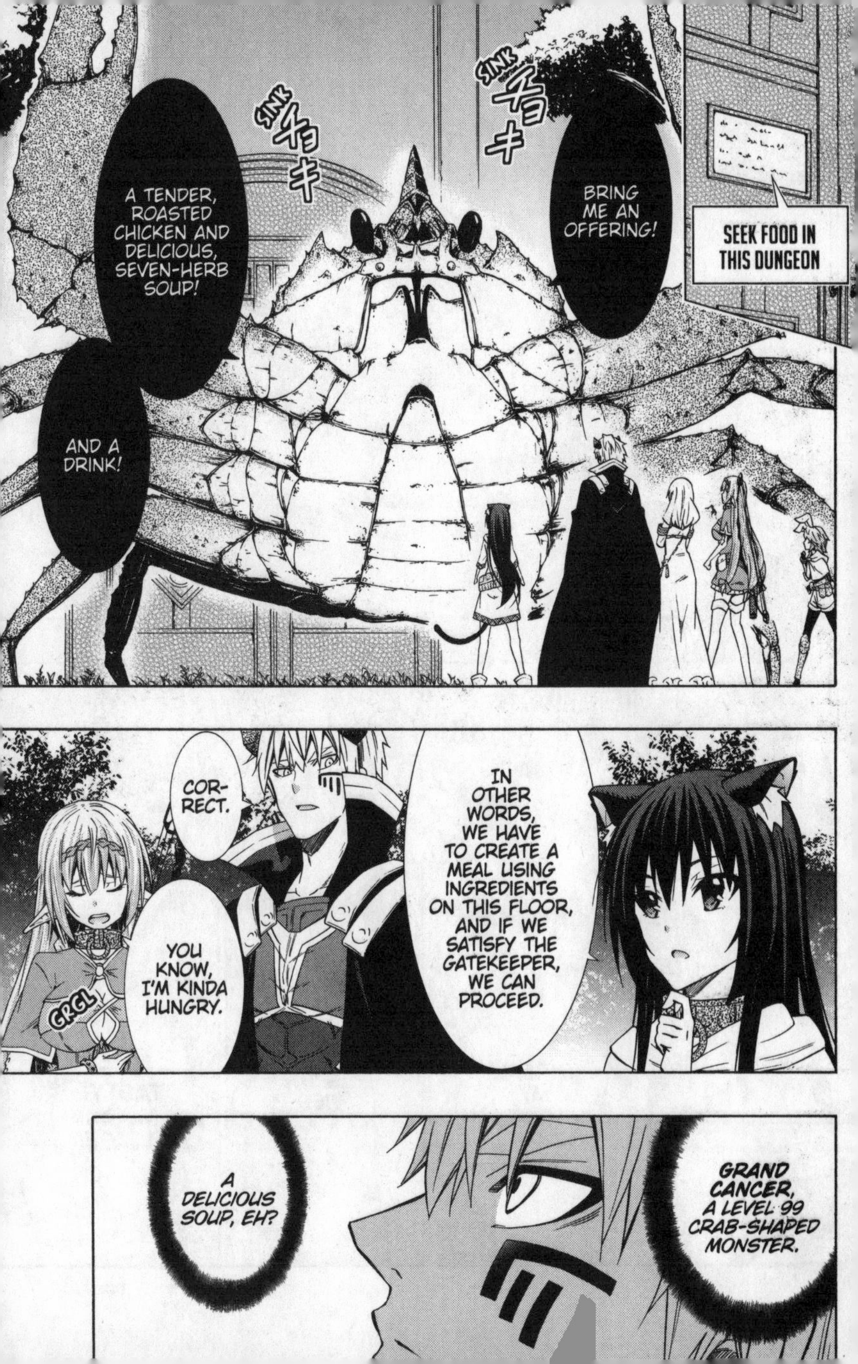
SEEK FOOD IN THIS DUNGEON
SINK
BRING ME AN OFFERING!
SINK
A TENDER, ROASTED CHICKEN AND DELICIOUS, SEVEN-HERB SOUP!
AND A DRINK!
IN OTHER WORDS, WE HAVE TO CREATE A MEAL USING INGREDIENTS ON THIS FLOOR, AND IF WE SATISFY THE GATEKEEPER, WE CAN PROCEED.
COR-RECT.
YOU KNOW, I'M KINDA HUNGRY.
GRGL
GRAND CANCER, A LEVEL 99 CRAB-SHAPED MONSTER.
A DELICIOUS SOUP, EH?

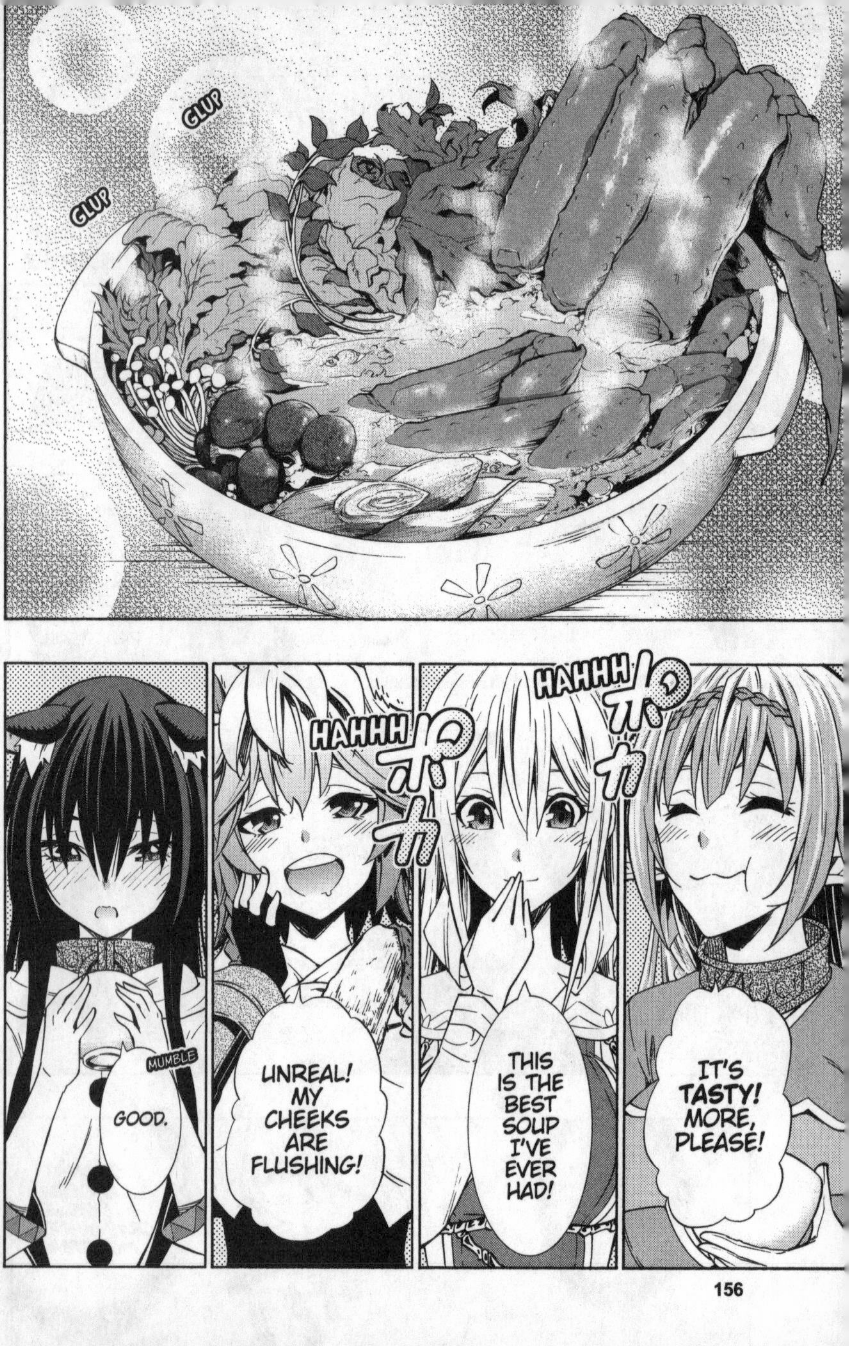
GLUP
GLUP
HAHHH
ポカ
IT'S TASTY! MORE, PLEASE!
THIS IS THE BEST SOUP I'VE EVER HAD!
HAHHH
ポカ
UNREAL! MY CHEEKS ARE FLUSHING!
MUMBLE
GOOD.

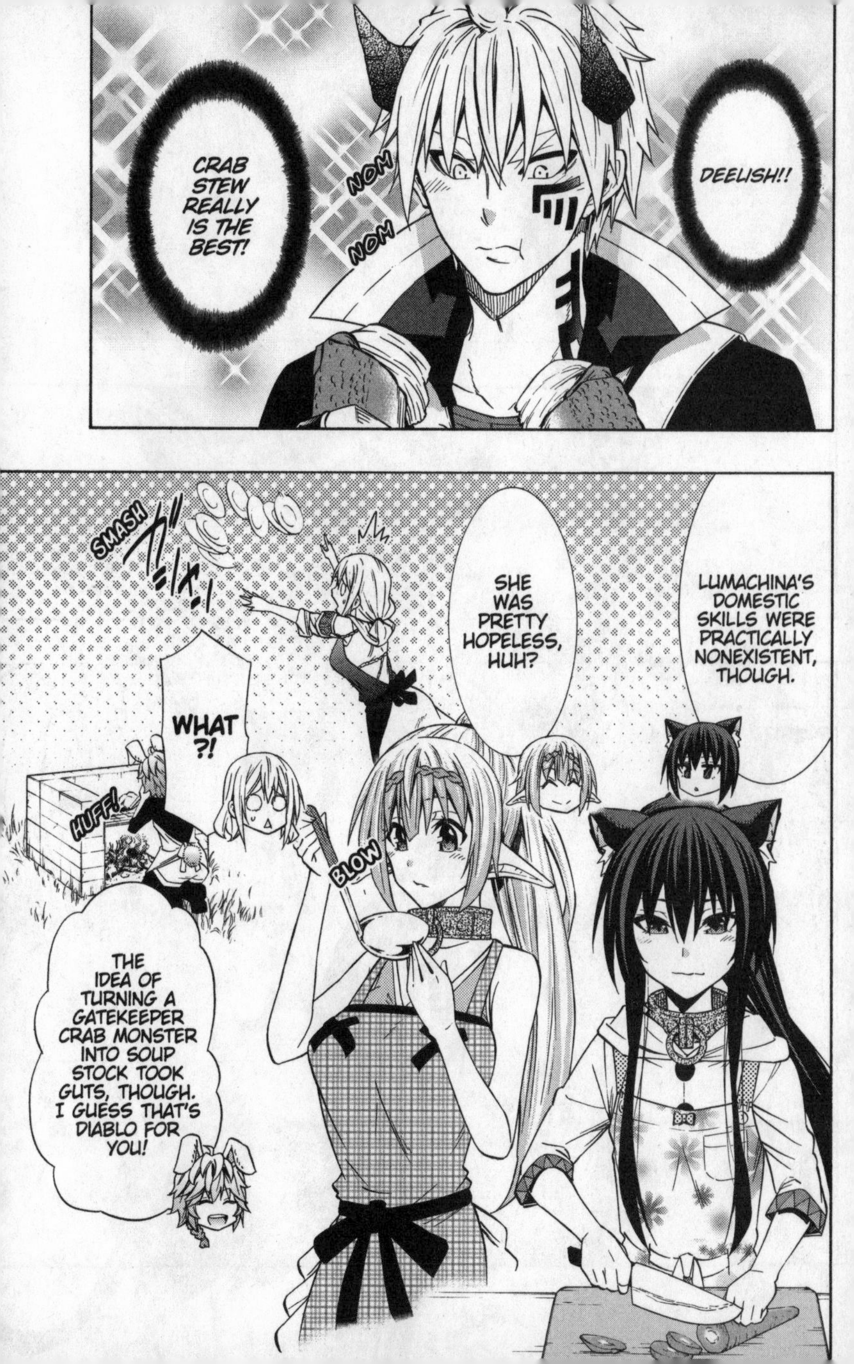
DEELISH!!
NOM NOM
CRAB STEW REALLY IS THE BEST!
LUMACHINA'S DOMESTIC SKILLS WERE PRACTICALLY NONEXISTENT, THOUGH.
SHE WAS PRETTY HOPELESS, HUH?
SMASH
WHAT ?!
HUFF!
BLOW
THE IDEA OF TURNING A GATEKEEPER CRAB MONSTER INTO SOUP STOCK TOOK GUTS, THOUGH. I GUESS THAT'S DIABLO FOR YOU!

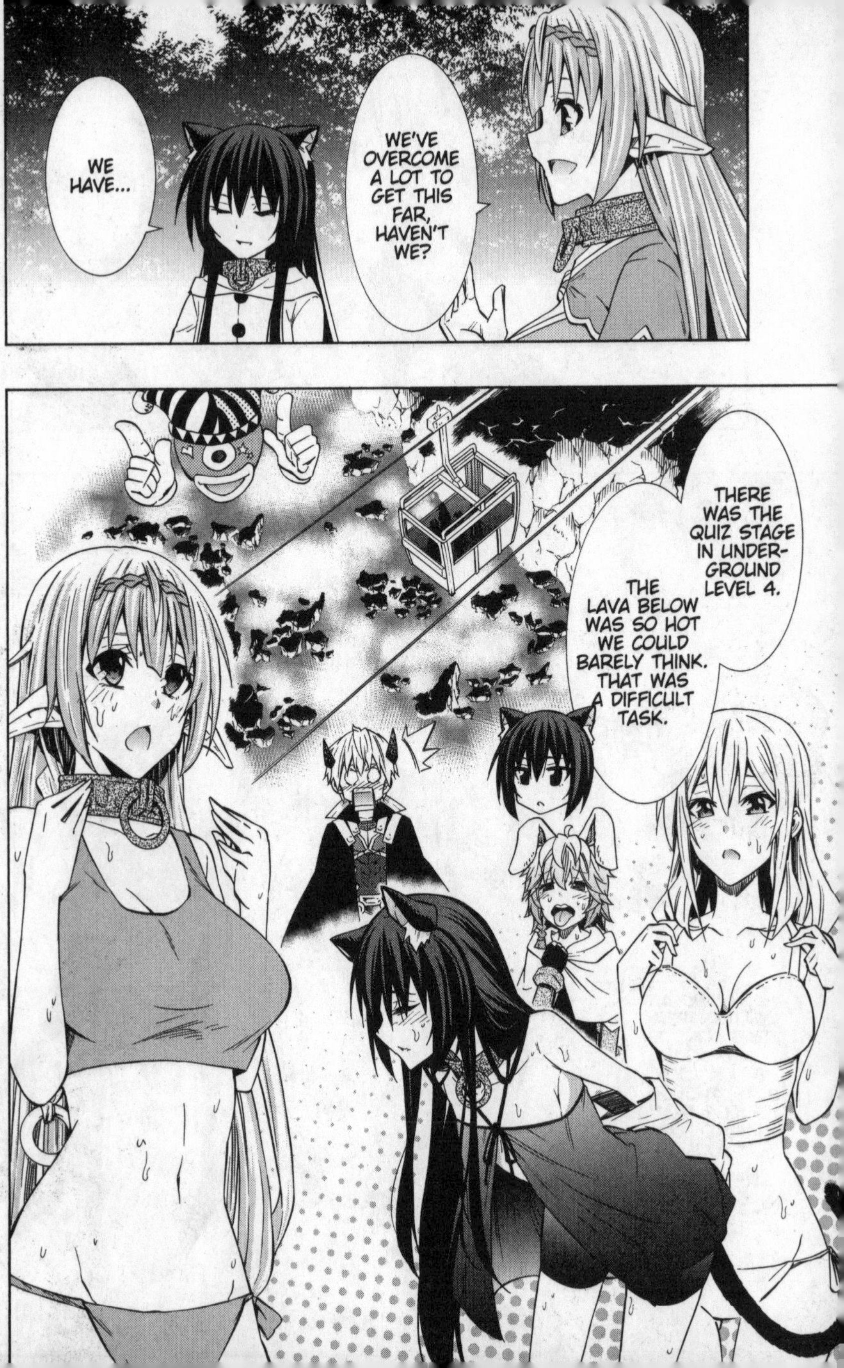
WE'VE OVERCOME A LOT TO GET THIS FAR, HAVEN'T WE?
WE HAVE...
THERE WAS THE QUIZ STAGE IN UNDER-GROUND LEVEL 4.
THE LAVA BELOW WAS SO HOT WE COULD BARELY THINK. THAT WAS A DIFFICULT TASK.

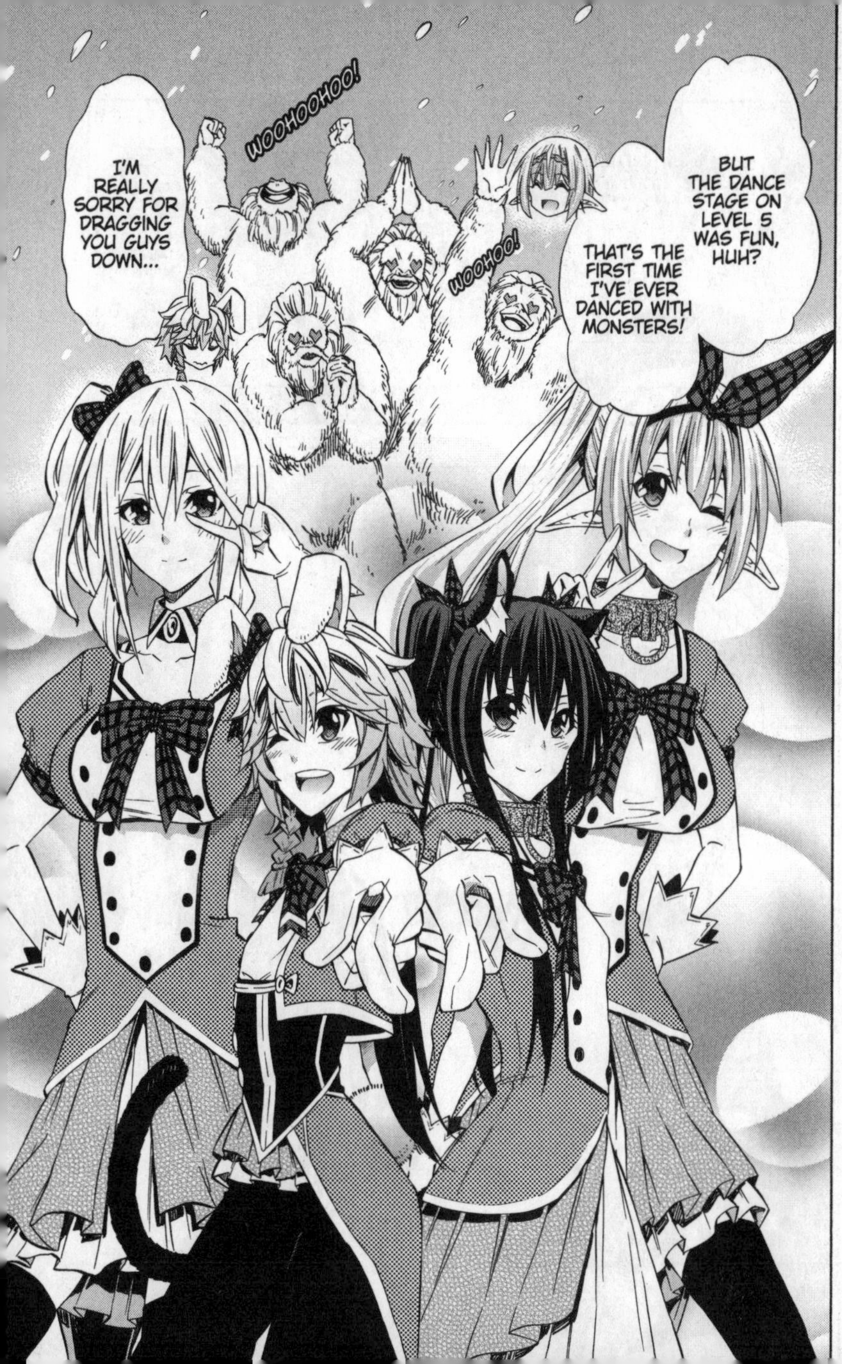
BUT THE DANCE STAGE ON LEVEL 5 WAS FUN, HUH?
THAT'S THE FIRST TIME I'VE EVER DANCED WITH MONSTERS!
WOOHOOHOO!
WOOHOO!
I'M REALLY SORRY FOR DRAGGING YOU GUYS DOWN...

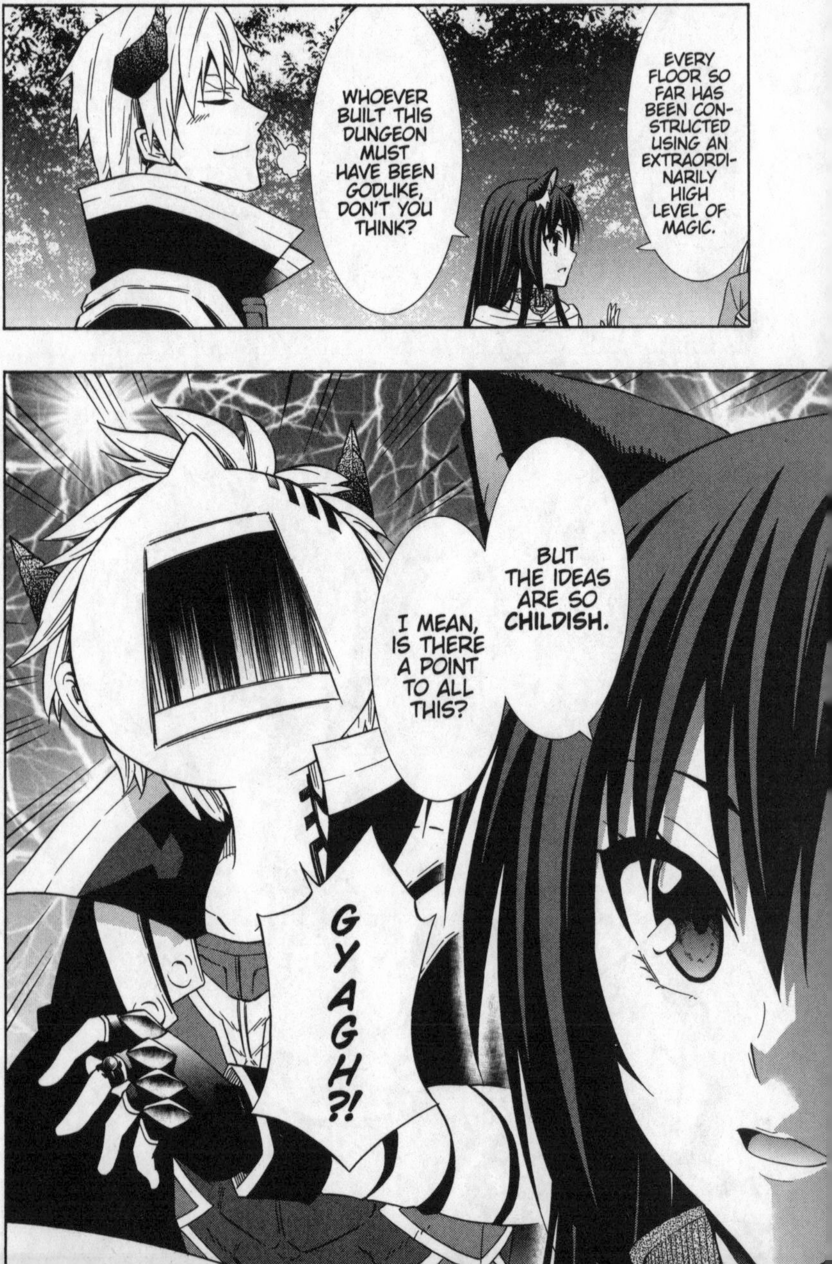
EVERY FLOOR SO FAR HAS BEEN CONSTRUCTED USING AN EXTRAORDINARILY HIGH LEVEL OF MAGIC.
WHOEVER BUILT THIS DUNGEON MUST HAVE BEEN GODLIKE, DON'T YOU THINK?
BUT THE IDEAS ARE SO CHILDISH.
I MEAN, IS THERE A POINT TO ALL THIS?
GYAGH?!

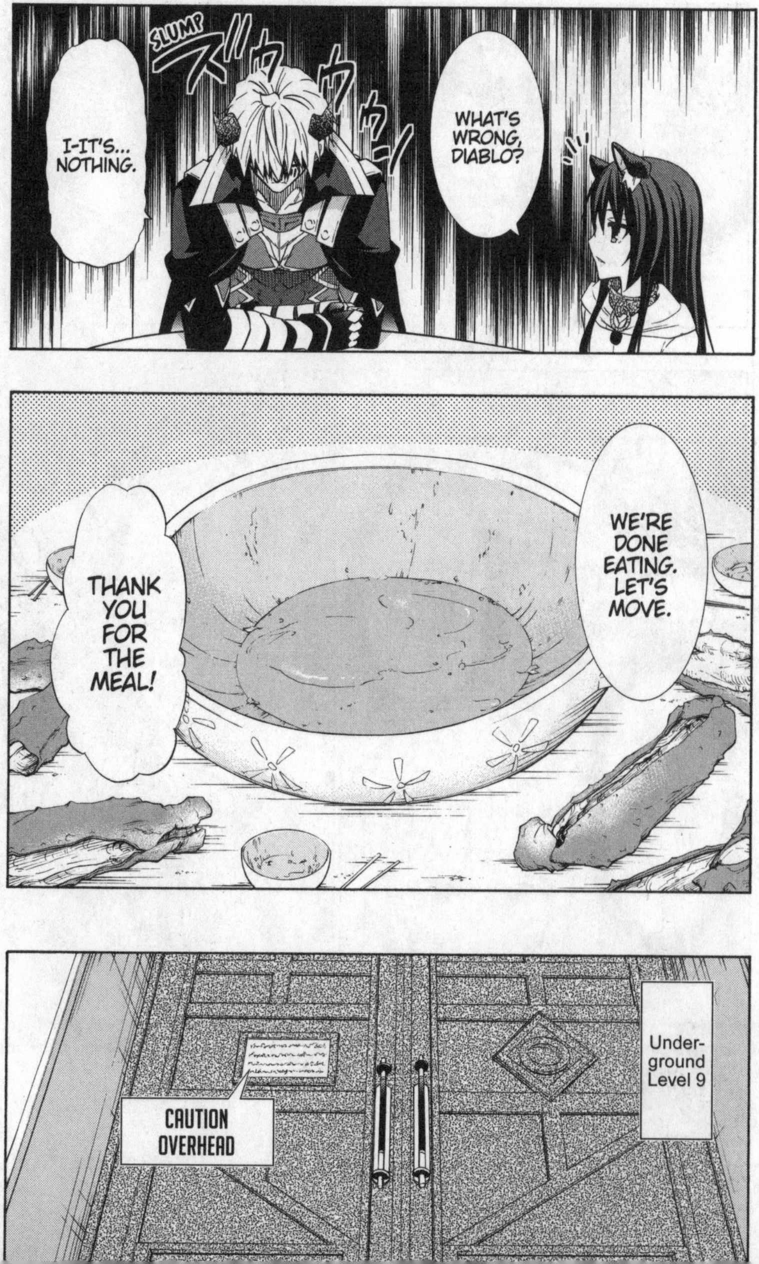
WHAT'S WRONG, DIABLO?
SLUMP
I-IT'S... NOTHING.
WE'RE DONE EATING. LET'S MOVE.
THANK YOU FOR THE MEAL!
Underground Level 9
CAUTION OVERHEAD

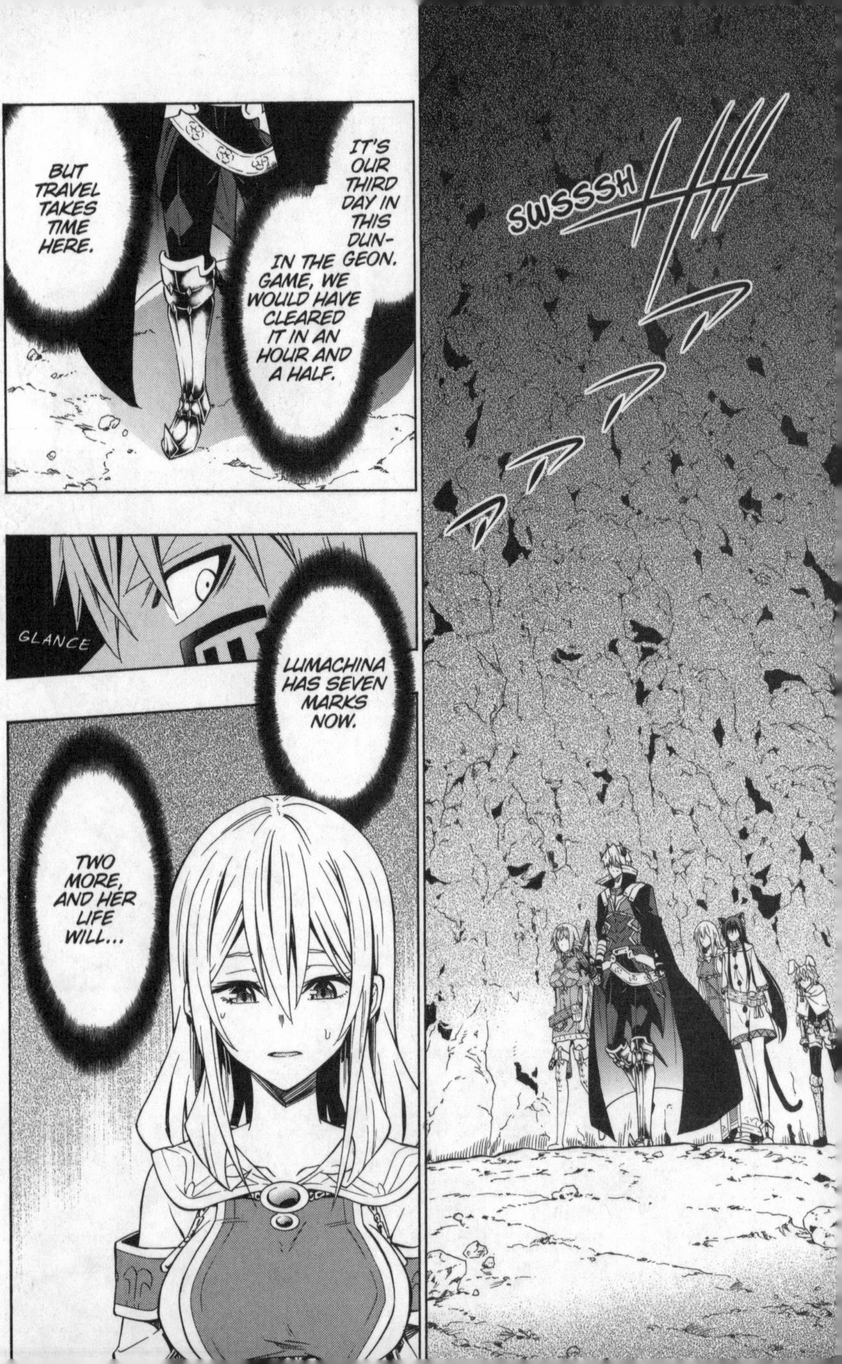
SWSSSH
IT'S OUR THIRD DAY IN THIS DUNGEON.
IN THE GAME, WE WOULD HAVE CLEARED IT IN AN HOUR AND A HALF.
BUT TRAVEL TAKES TIME HERE.
GLANCE
LUMACHINA HAS SEVEN MARKS NOW.
TWO MORE, AND HER LIFE WILL...

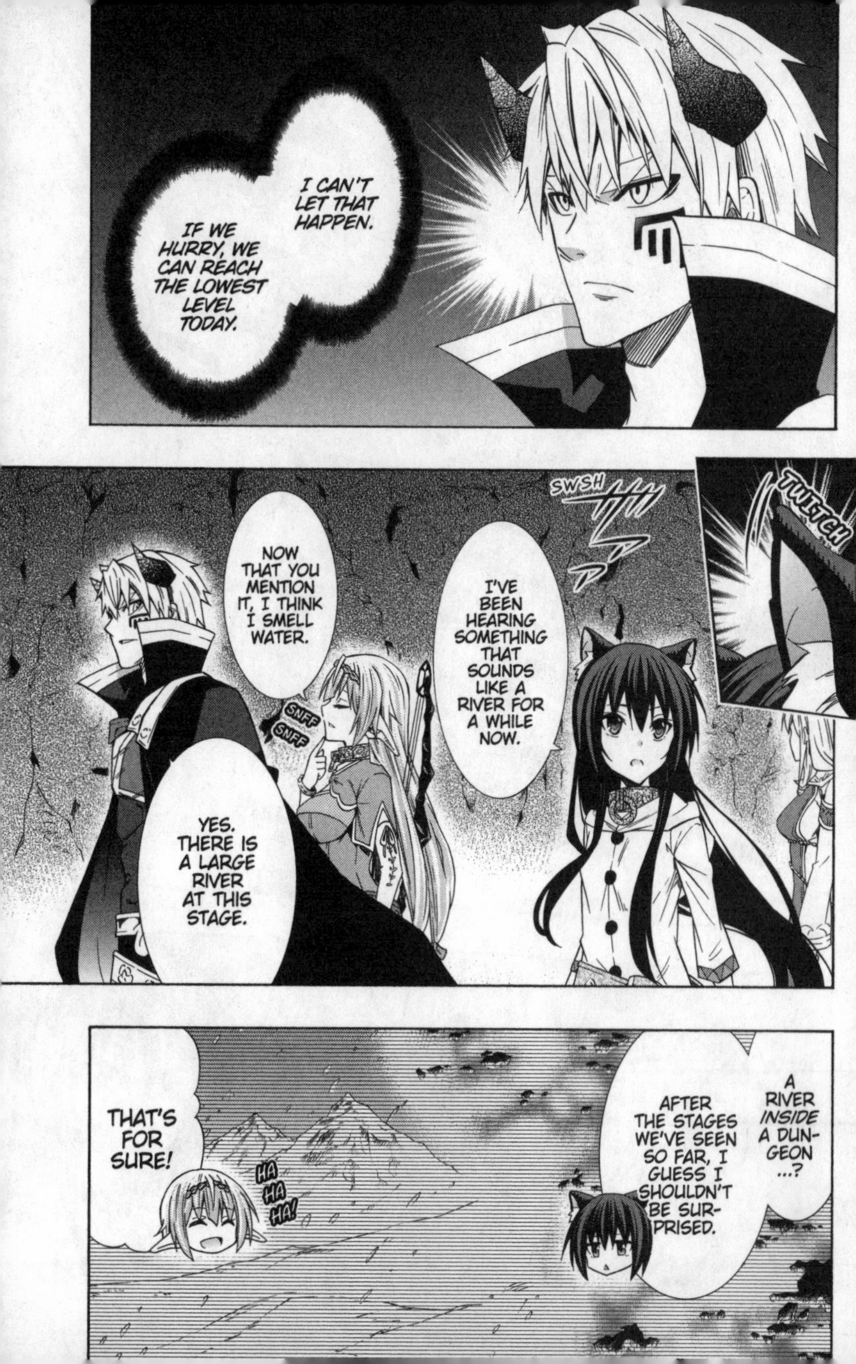
I CAN'T LET THAT HAPPEN.
IF WE HURRY, WE CAN REACH THE LOWEST LEVEL TODAY.
TWITCH
SWSH
I'VE BEEN HEARING SOMETHING THAT SOUNDS LIKE A RIVER FOR A WHILE NOW.
NOW THAT YOU MENTION IT, I THINK I SMELL WATER.
SNFF SNFF
YES. THERE IS A LARGE RIVER AT THIS STAGE.
A RIVER *INSIDE* A DUNGEON ...?
AFTER THE STAGES WE'VE SEEN SO FAR, I GUESS I SHOULDN'T BE SURPRISED.
HA HA HA!
THAT'S FOR SURE!

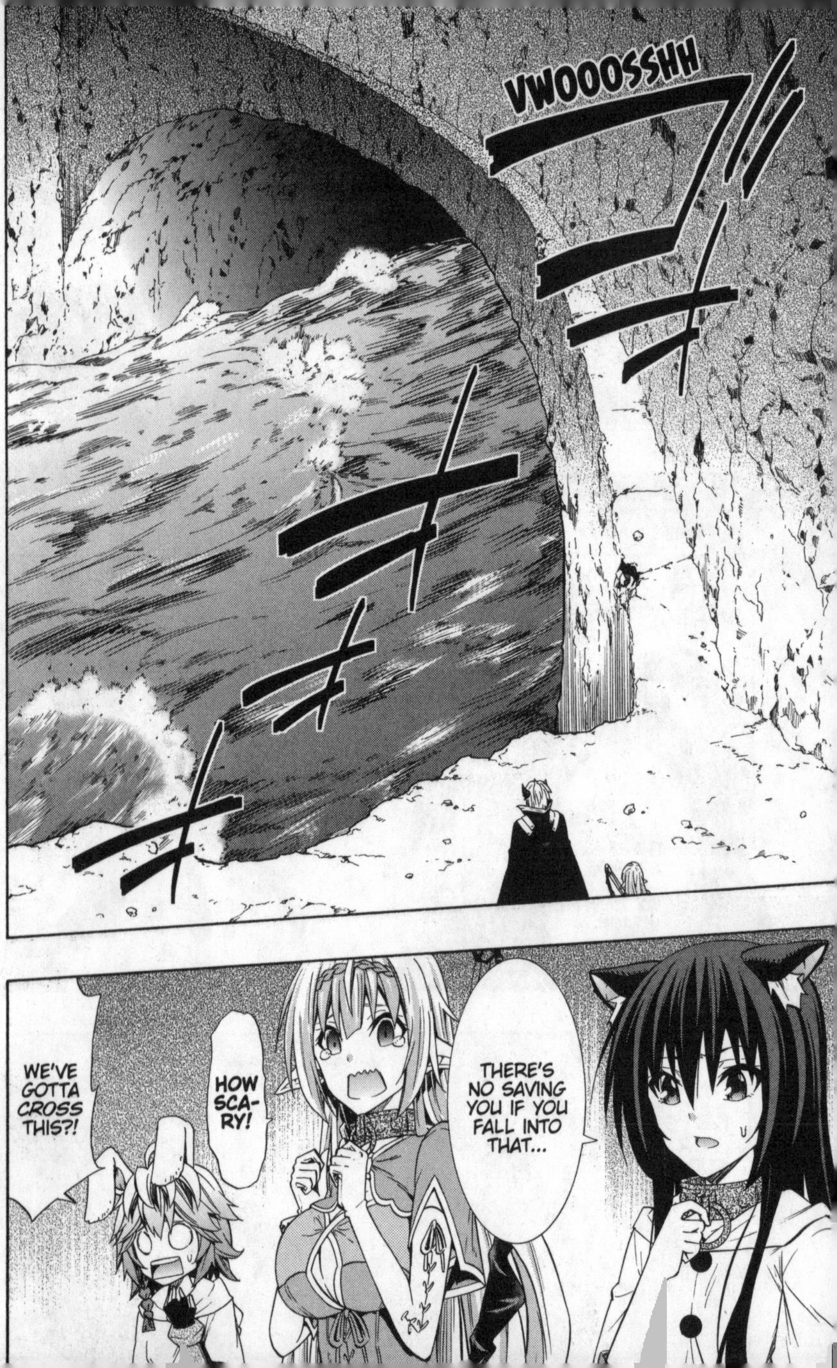
VWOOOSSHH
THERE'S NO SAVING YOU IF YOU FALL INTO THAT...
HOW SCA-RY!
WE'VE GOTTA CROSS THIS?!

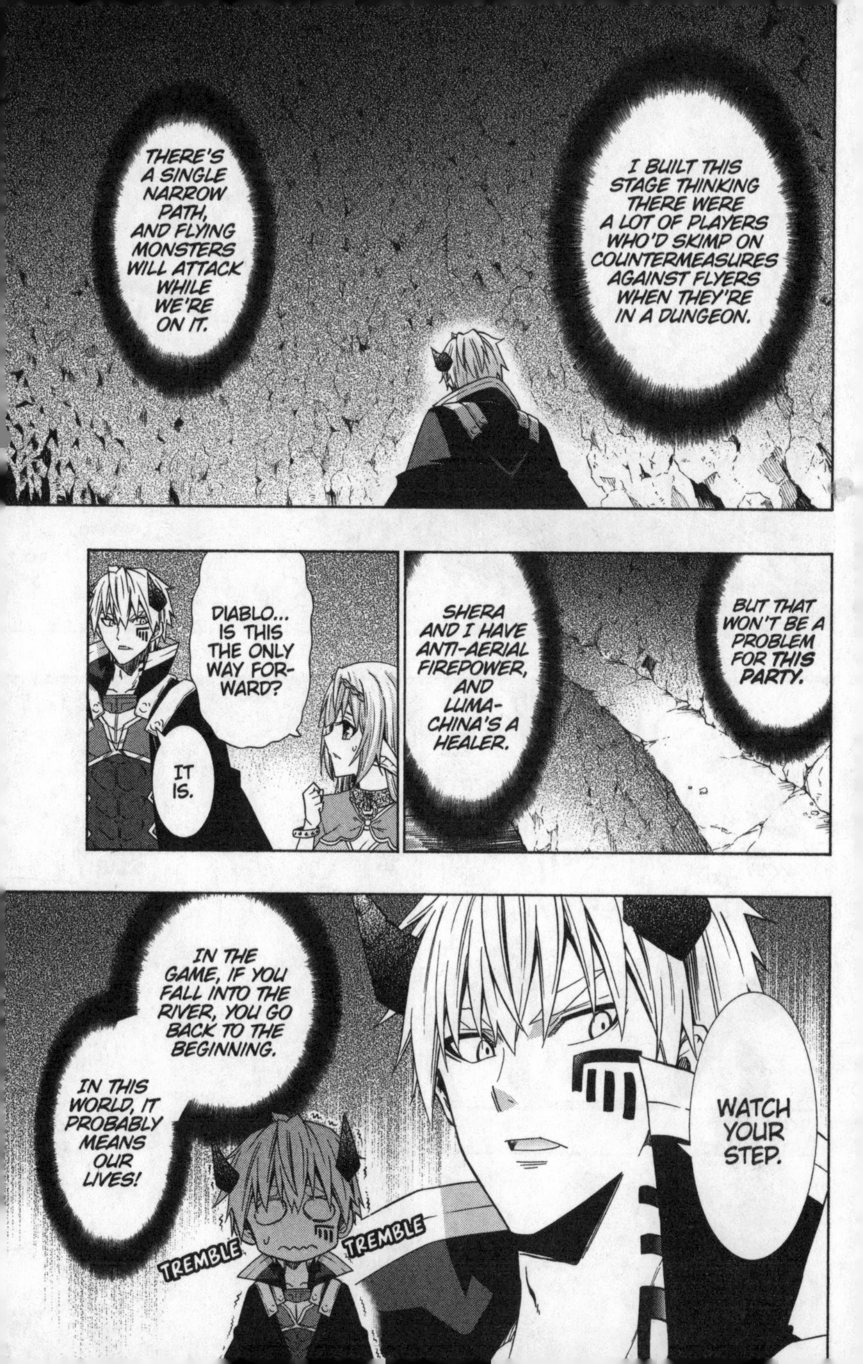
I BUILT THIS STAGE THINKING THERE WERE A LOT OF PLAYERS WHO'D SKIMP ON COUNTERMEASURES AGAINST FLYERS WHEN THEY'RE IN A DUNGEON.
THERE'S A SINGLE NARROW PATH, AND FLYING MONSTERS WILL ATTACK WHILE WE'RE ON IT.
BUT THAT WON'T BE A PROBLEM FOR THIS PARTY.
SHERA AND I HAVE ANTI-AERIAL FIREPOWER, AND LUMACHINA'S A HEALER.
DIABLO... IS THIS THE ONLY WAY FORWARD?
IT IS.
WATCH YOUR STEP.
IN THE GAME, IF YOU FALL INTO THE RIVER, YOU GO BACK TO THE BEGINNING.
IN THIS WORLD, IT PROBABLY MEANS OUR LIVES!
TREMBLE
TREMBLE

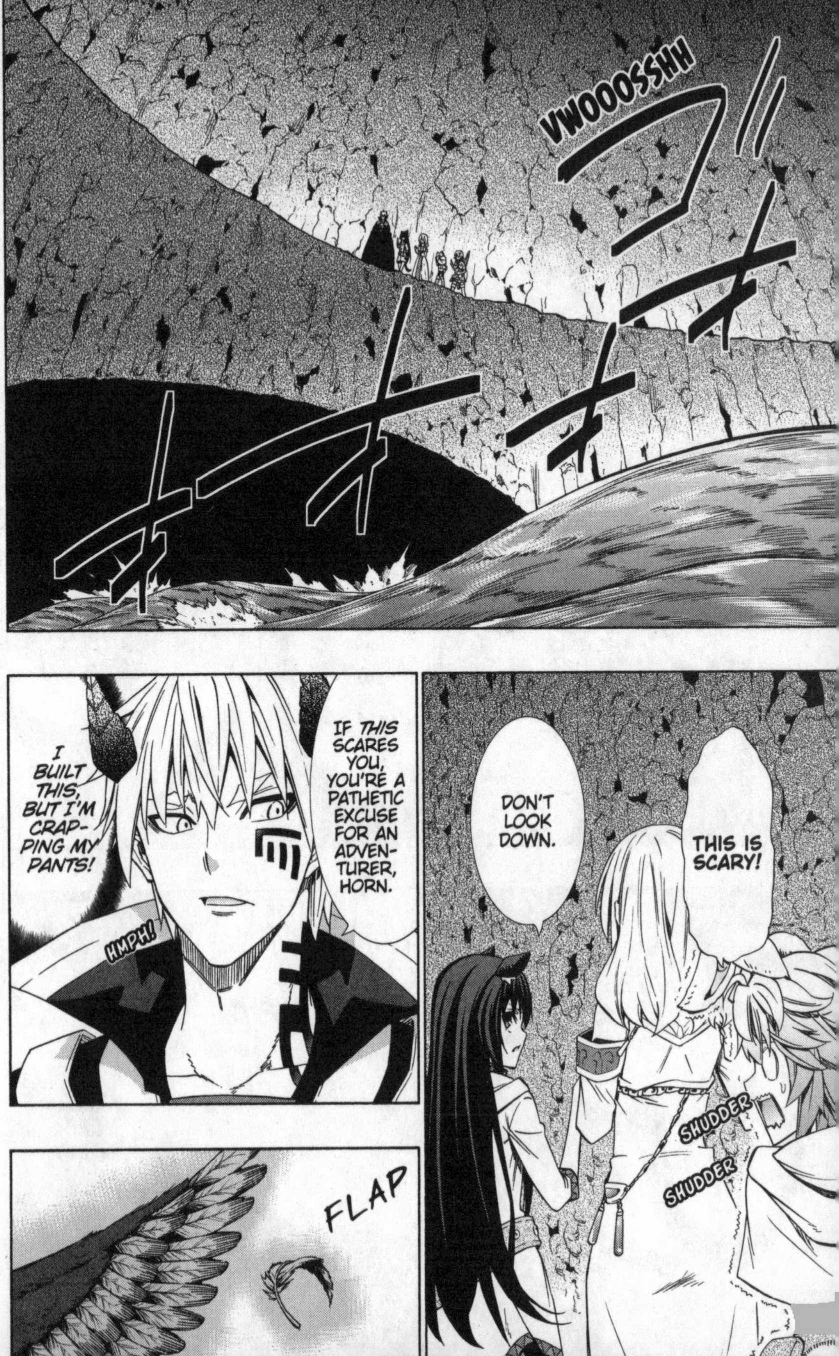
VWOOOSSHH
THIS IS SCARY!
DON'T LOOK DOWN.
SHUDDER
SHUDDER
IF THIS SCARES YOU, YOU'RE A PATHETIC EXCUSE FOR AN ADVEN-TURER, HORN.
HMPH!
I BUILT THIS, BUT I'M CRAP-PING MY PANTS!
FLAP

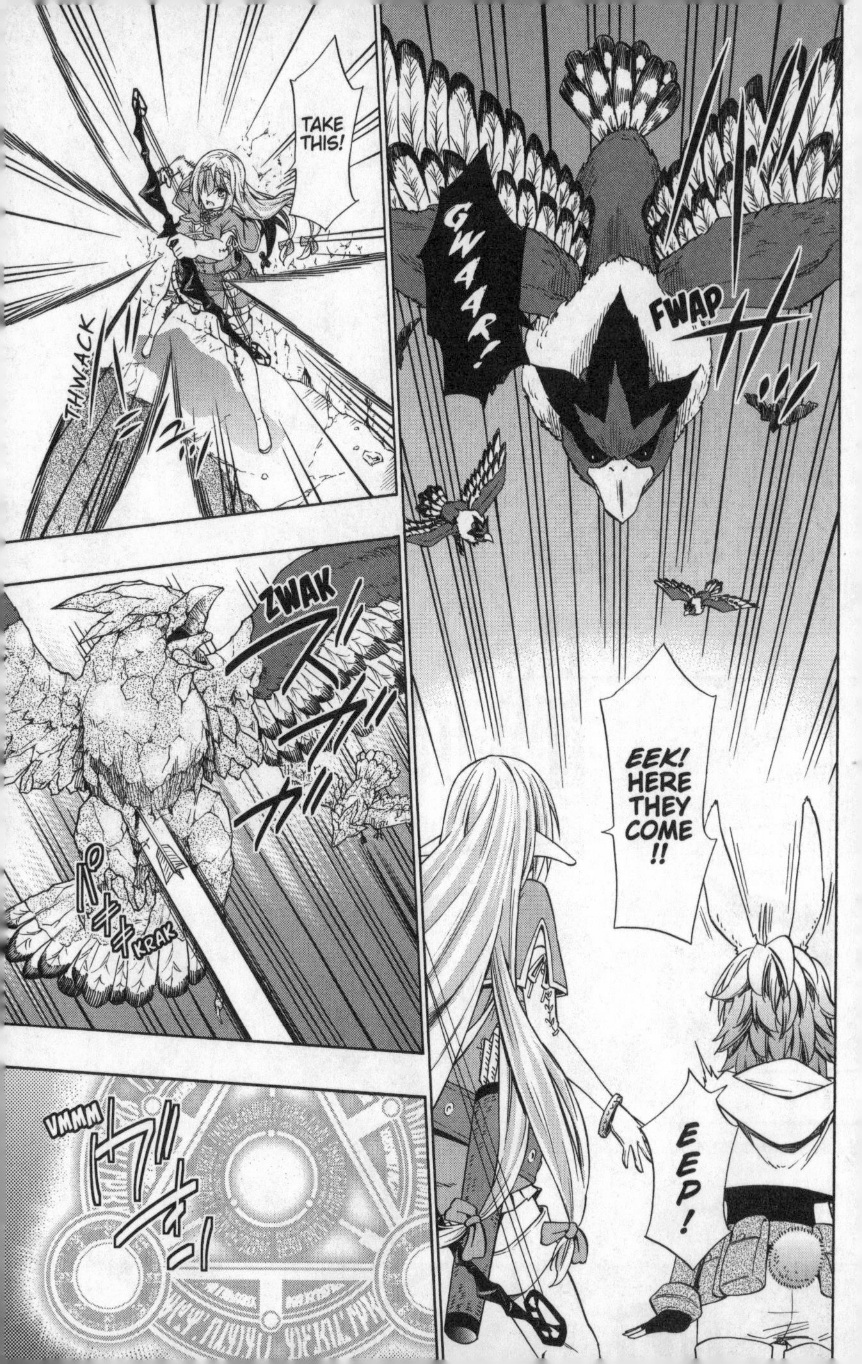
GWAAR!
FWAP
EEK! HERE THEY COME!!
EEP!
TAKE THIS!
THWACK
ZWAK
KRAK
VMMM

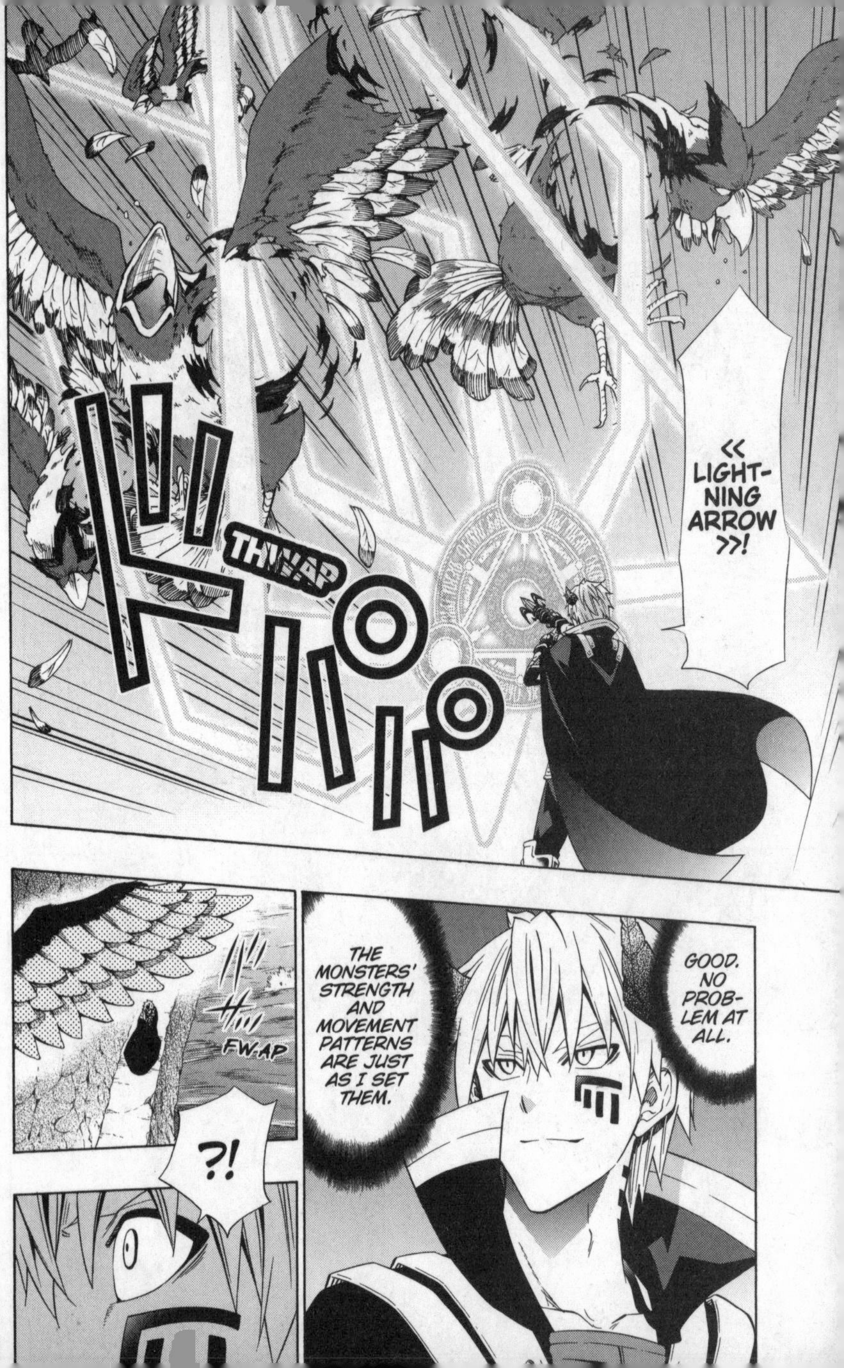
<< LIGHTNING ARROW >>!
THWAP
GOOD. NO PROBLEM AT ALL.
THE MONSTERS' STRENGTH AND MOVEMENT PATTERNS ARE JUST AS I SET THEM.
FWAP
?!

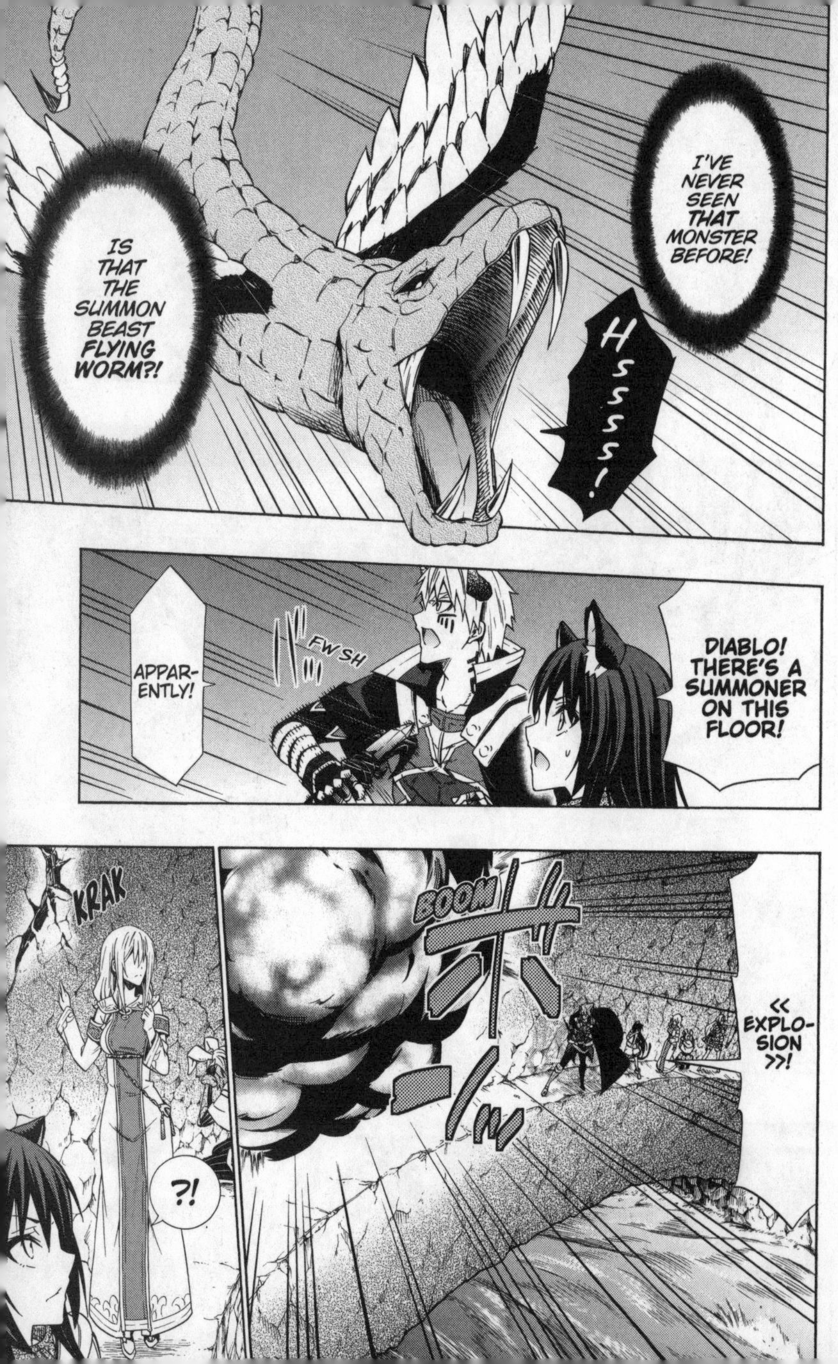
I'VE NEVER SEEN THAT MONSTER BEFORE!
HSSSS!
IS THAT THE SUMMON BEAST FLYING WORM?!
DIABLO! THERE'S A SUMMONER ON THIS FLOOR!
FWSH
APPAR-ENTLY!
<< EXPLO-SION >>!
BOOM
KRAK
?!

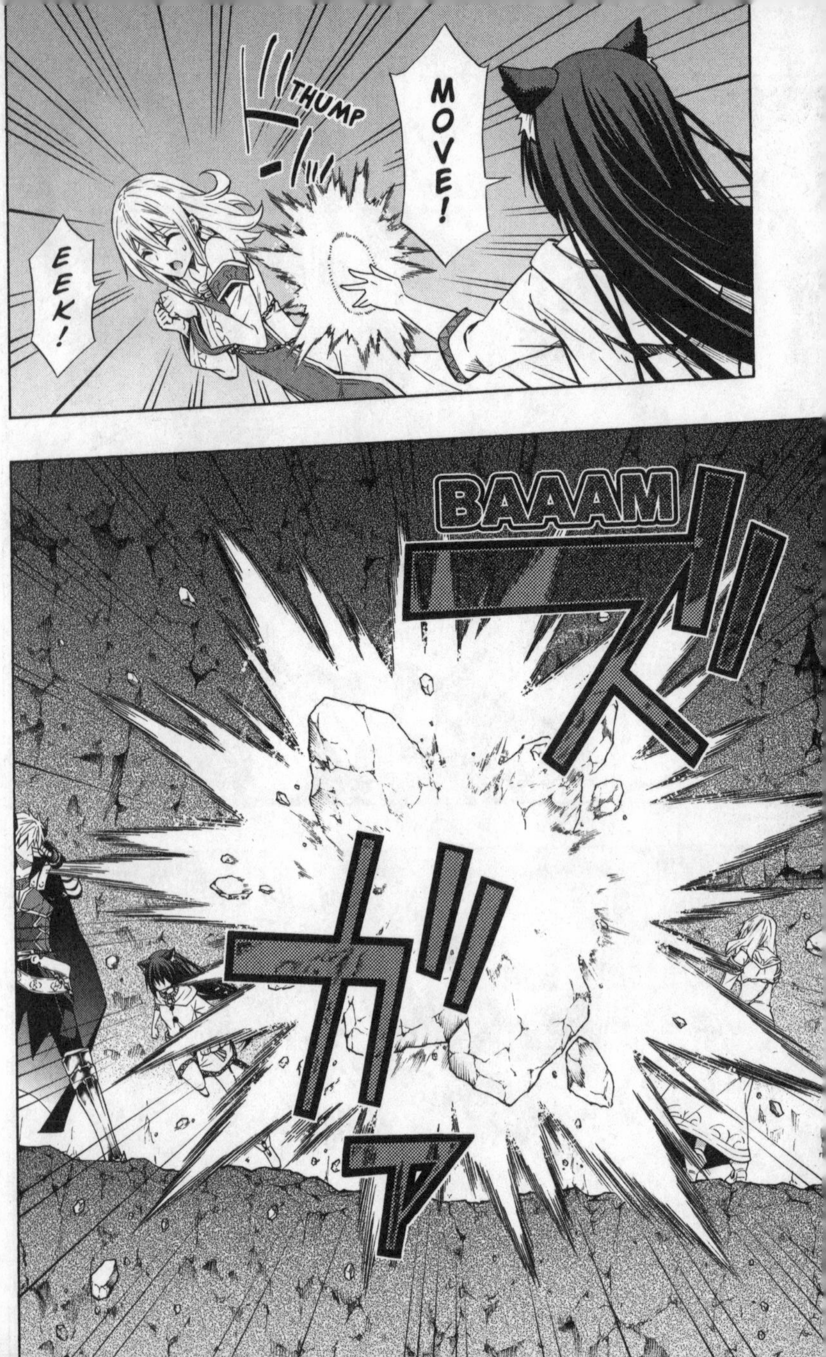
MOVE!
THUMP
EEK!
BAAAM

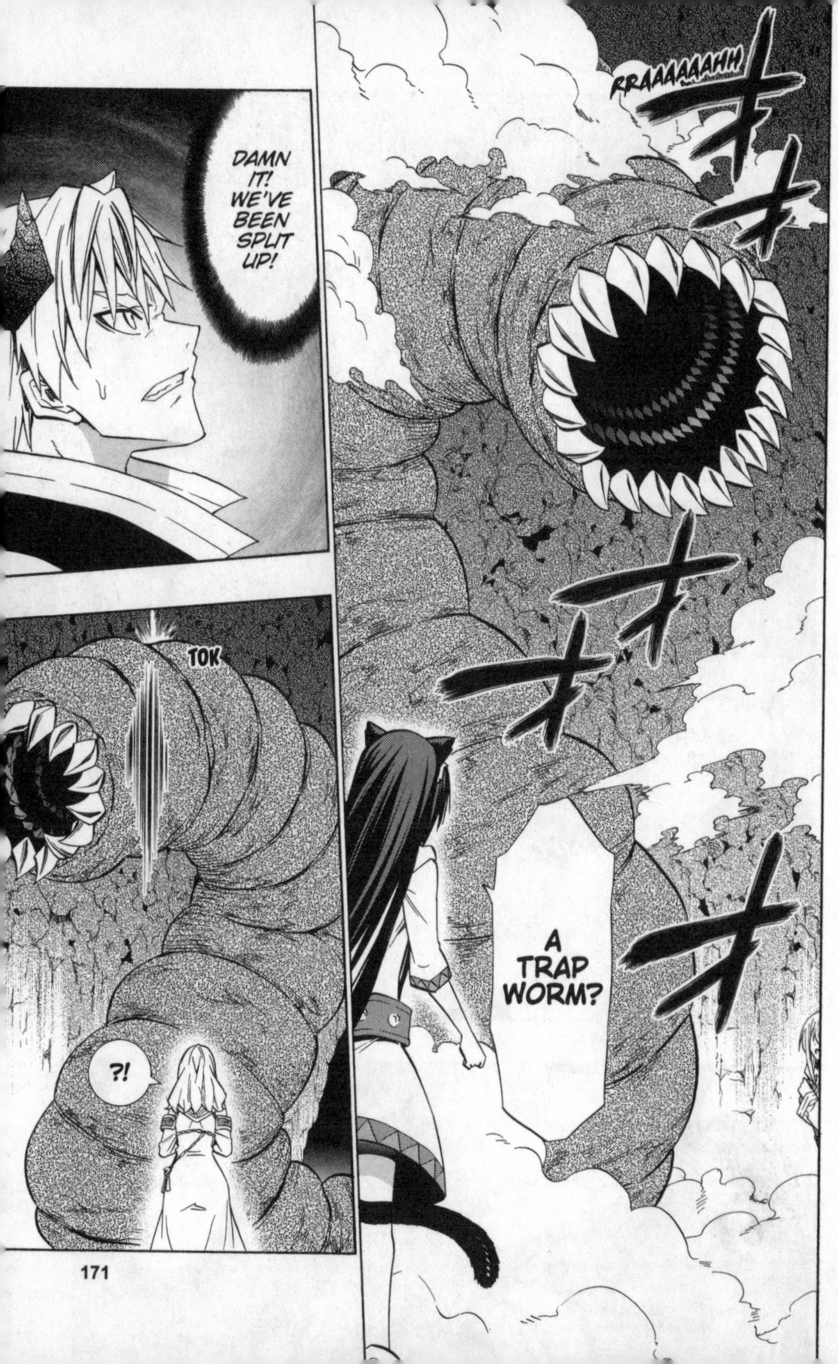
RRAAAAAAHH
A TRAP WORM?
DAMN IT! WE'VE BEEN SPLIT UP!
TOK
?!

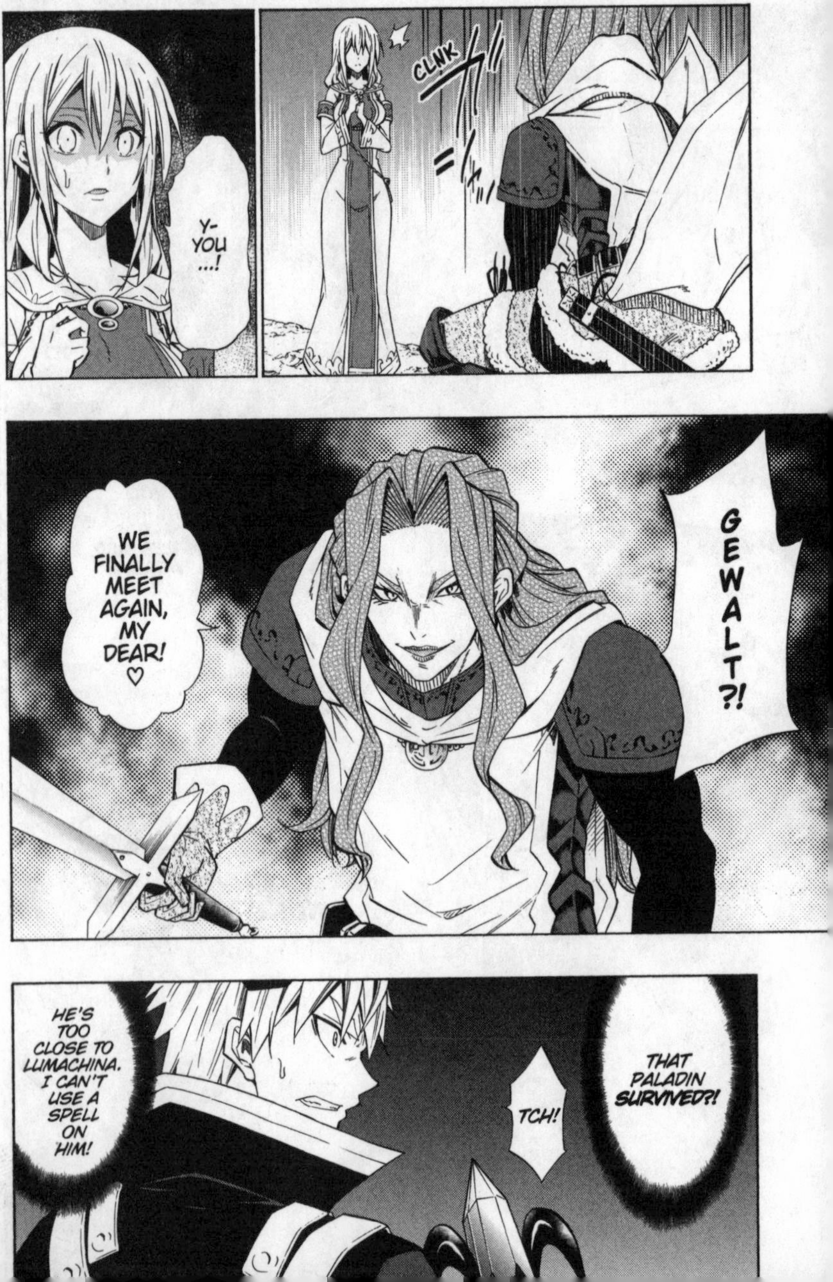
CLNK
Y-YOU...!
GEWALT?!
WE FINALLY MEET AGAIN, MY DEAR! ♡
THAT PALADIN SURVIVED?!
TCH!
HE'S TOO CLOSE TO LUMACHINA. I CAN'T USE A SPELL ON HIM!

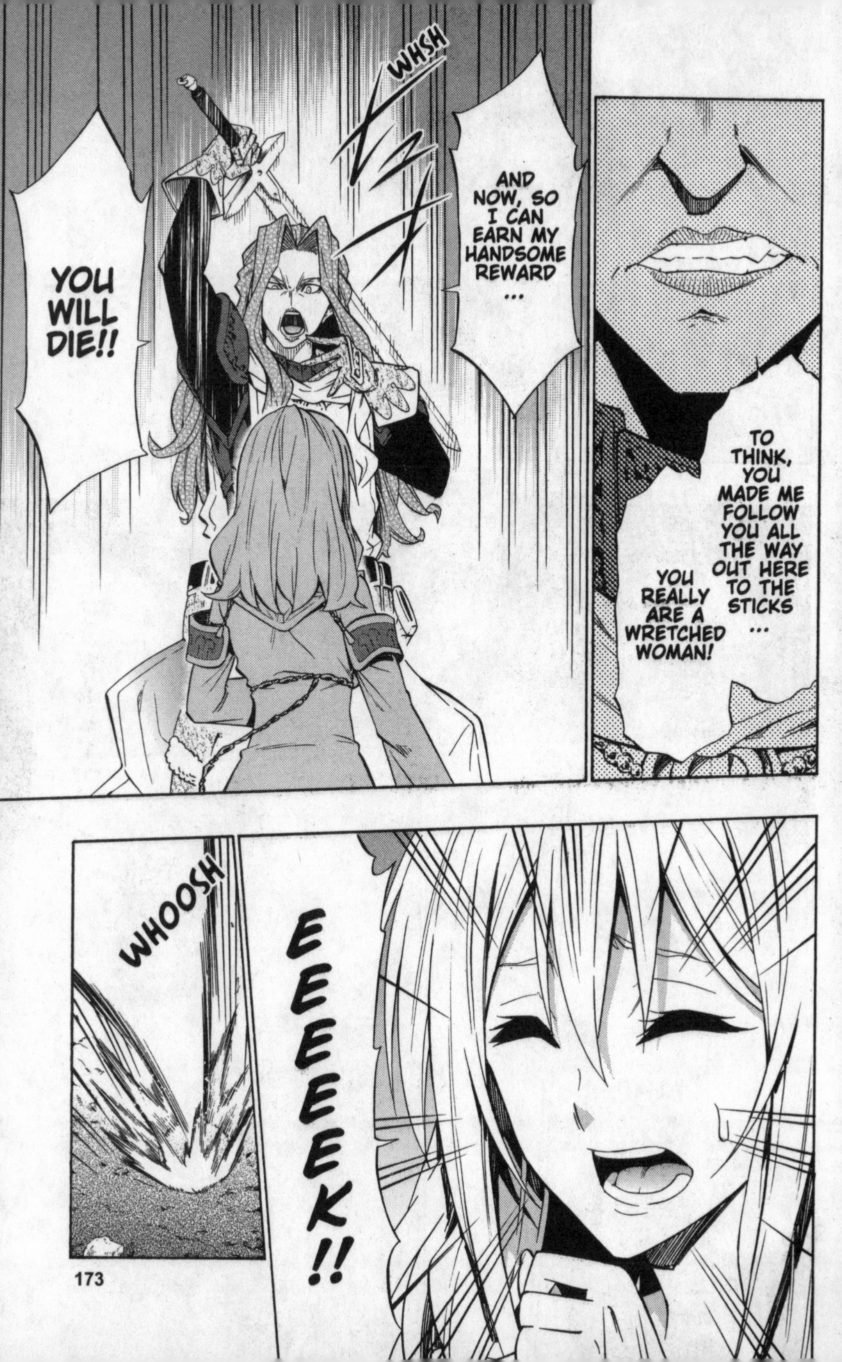
TO THINK, YOU MADE ME FOLLOW YOU ALL THE WAY OUT HERE TO THE STICKS ...
YOU REALLY ARE A WRETCHED WOMAN!
WHSH
AND NOW, SO I CAN EARN MY HANDSOME REWARD ...
YOU WILL DIE!!
EEEEEK!!
WHOOSH

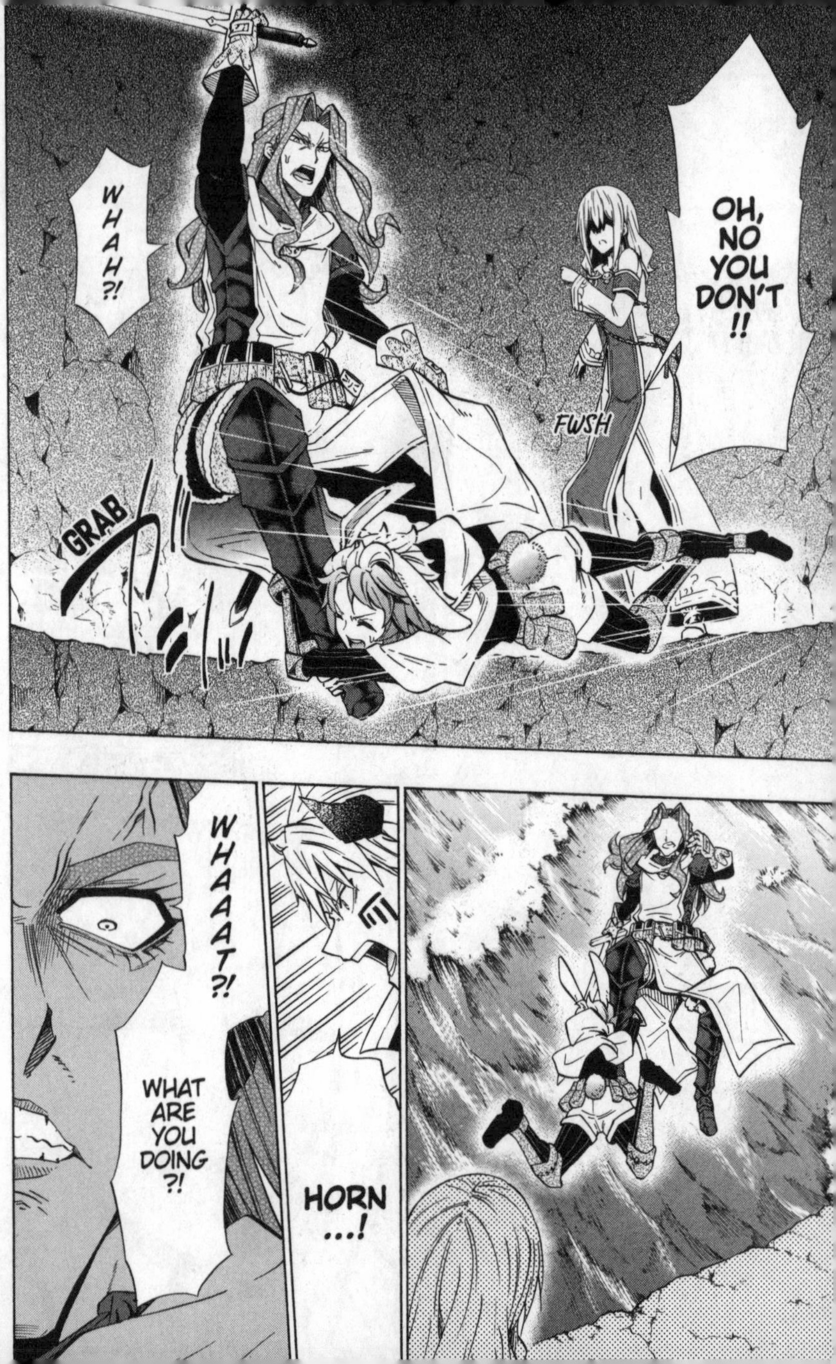
OH, NO YOU DON'T!!
WHAH?!
FWSH
GRAB
HORN...!
WHAAAT?!
WHAT ARE YOU DOING?!

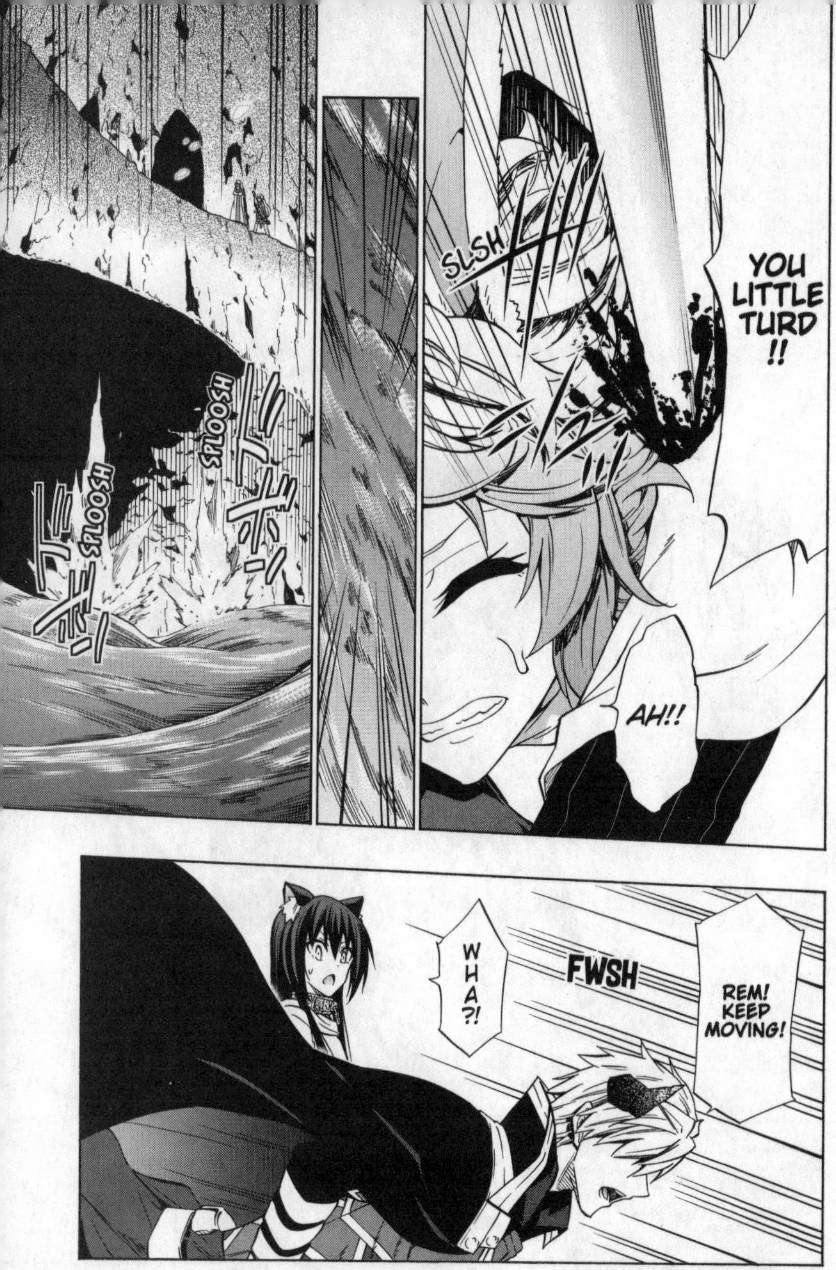
YOU LITTLE TURD!!
SLSH
AH!!
SPLOOSH
SPLOOSH
REM! KEEP MOVING!
FWSH
WHA?!

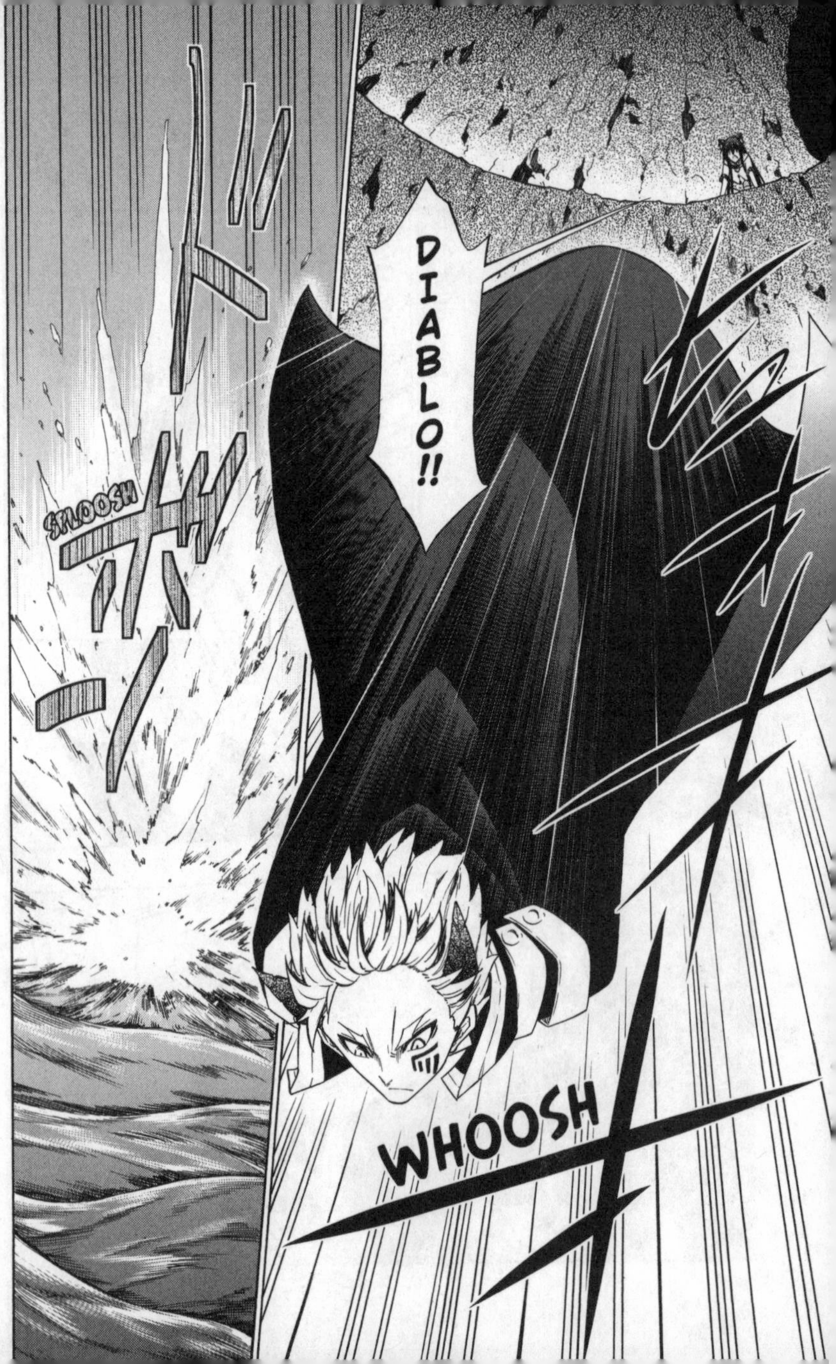
DIABLO!!
WHOOSH
SPLOOSH

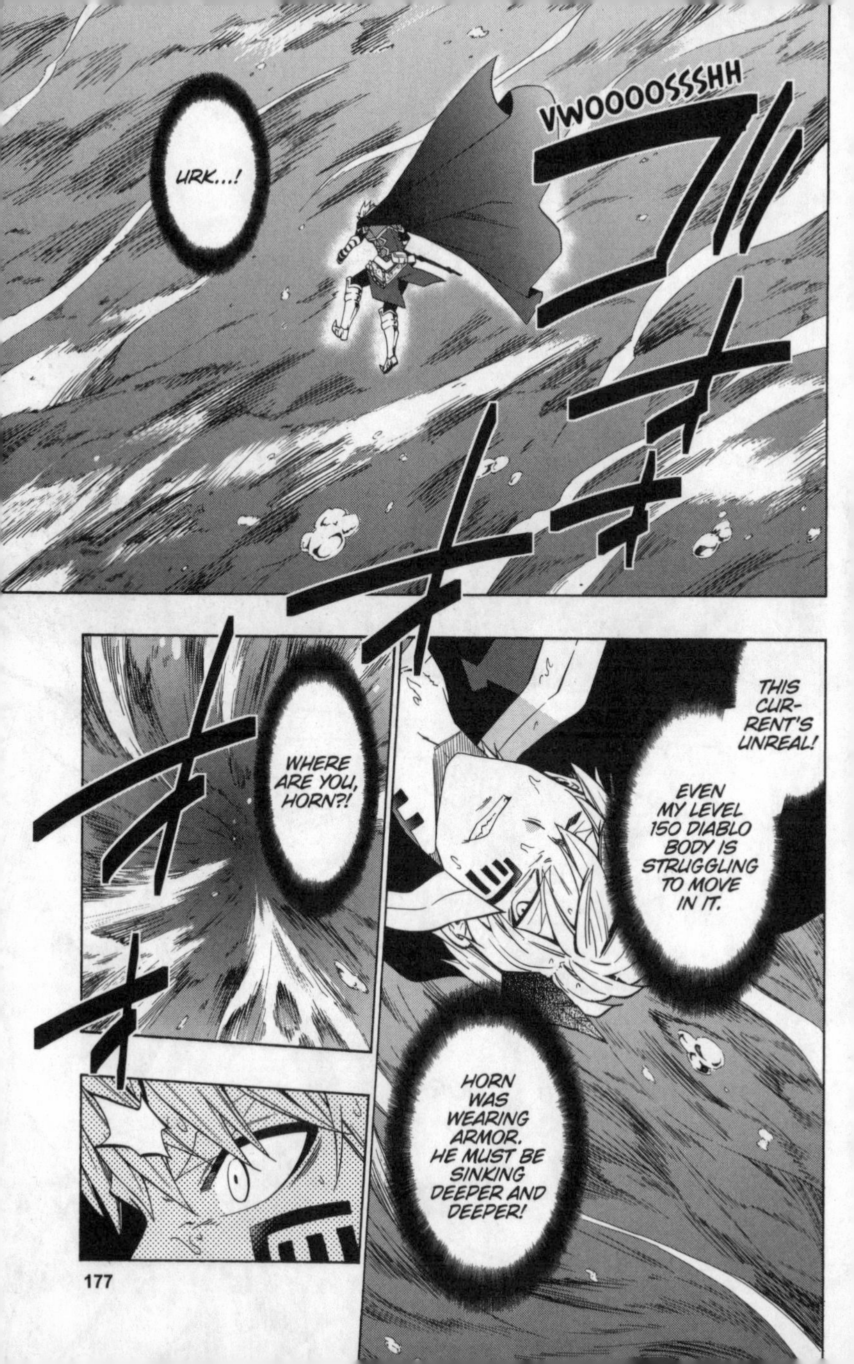
VWOOOOSSSHH
URK...!
THIS CUR-RENT'S UNREAL!
EVEN MY LEVEL 150 DIABLO BODY IS STRUGGLING TO MOVE IN IT.
HORN WAS WEARING ARMOR. HE MUST BE SINKING DEEPER AND DEEPER!
WHERE ARE YOU, HORN?!

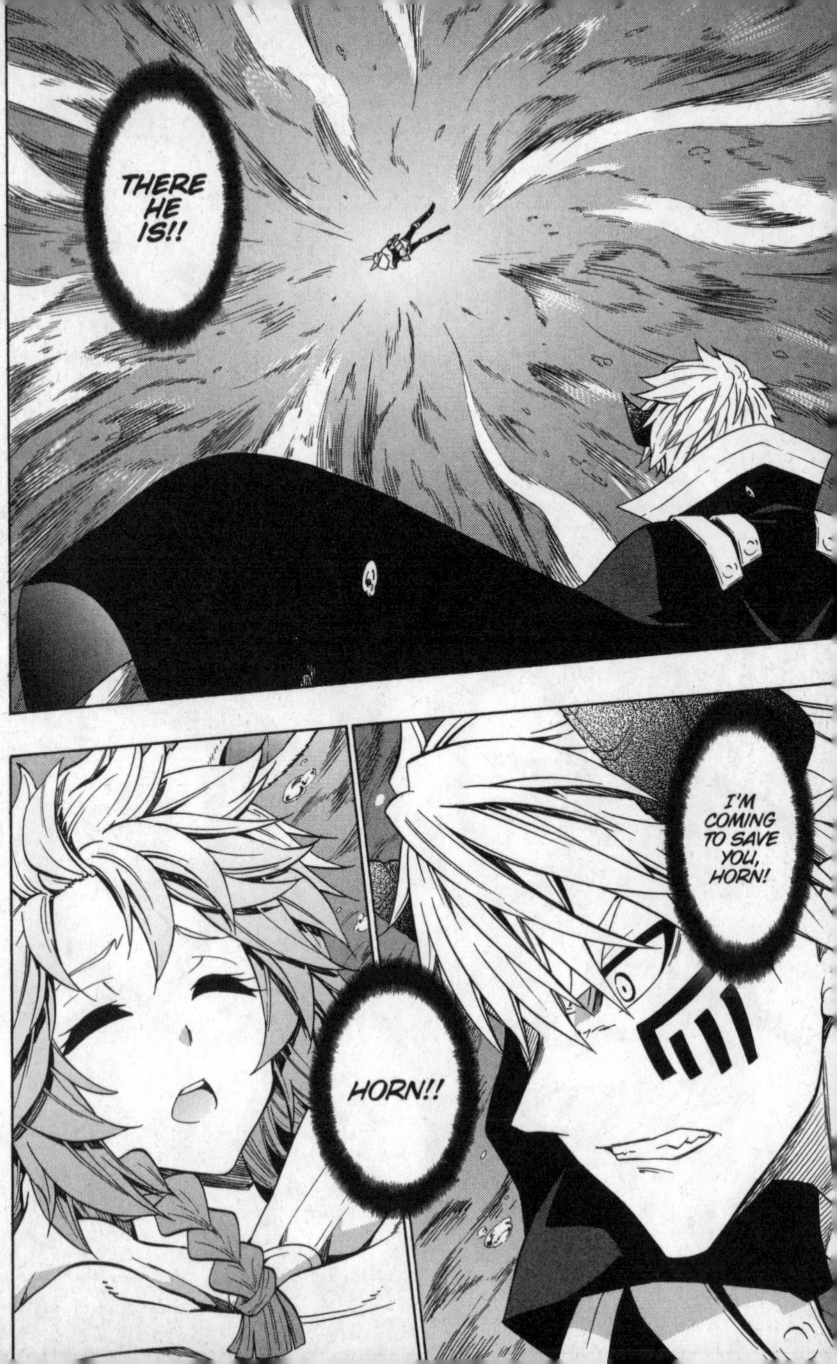
THERE HE IS!!
I'M COMING TO SAVE YOU, HORN!
HORN!!

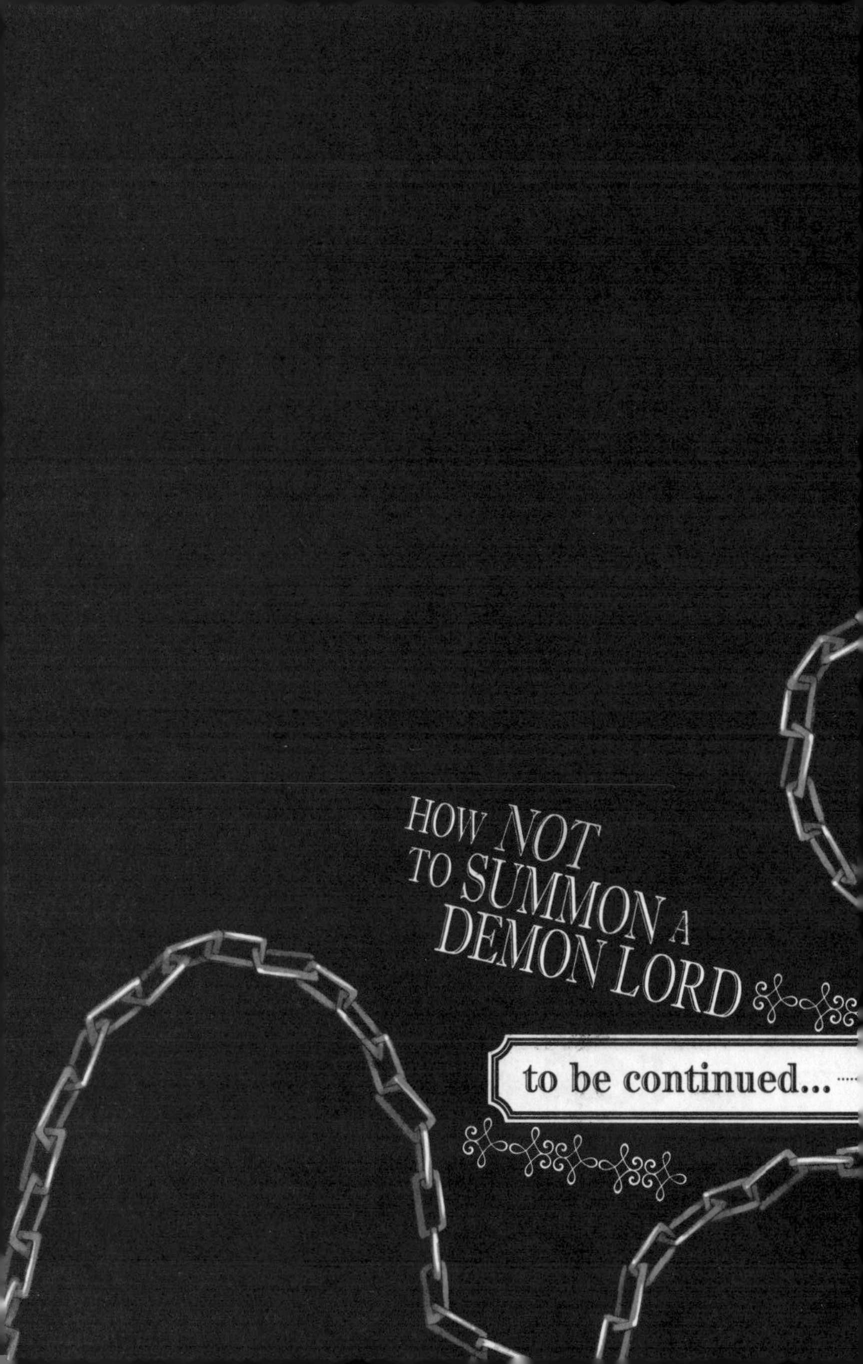
HOW NOT TO SUMMON A DEMON LORD
to be continued...

SPECIAL THANKS FOR VOLUME 11

YUKIYA MURASAKI

TAKAHIRO TSURUSAKI

«ASSISTANTS»
DAIKI HARAGUCHI
YUU TAKIGAWA
MASUMI HIGASHITANI
CHITOSE SAKURA
TAKUYA NISHIDA
DAISUKE MIYAKOSHI

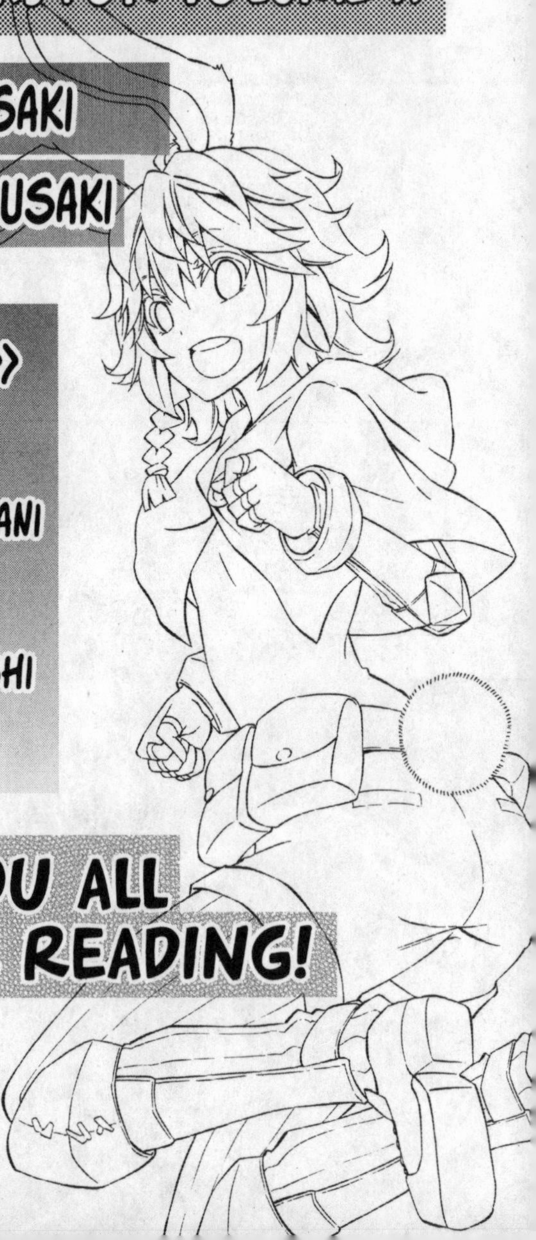

THANK YOU ALL FOR READING!

UNDERGROUND LEVEL 4: DO YOU WANT TO GET TO THE NEXT LEVEL?!

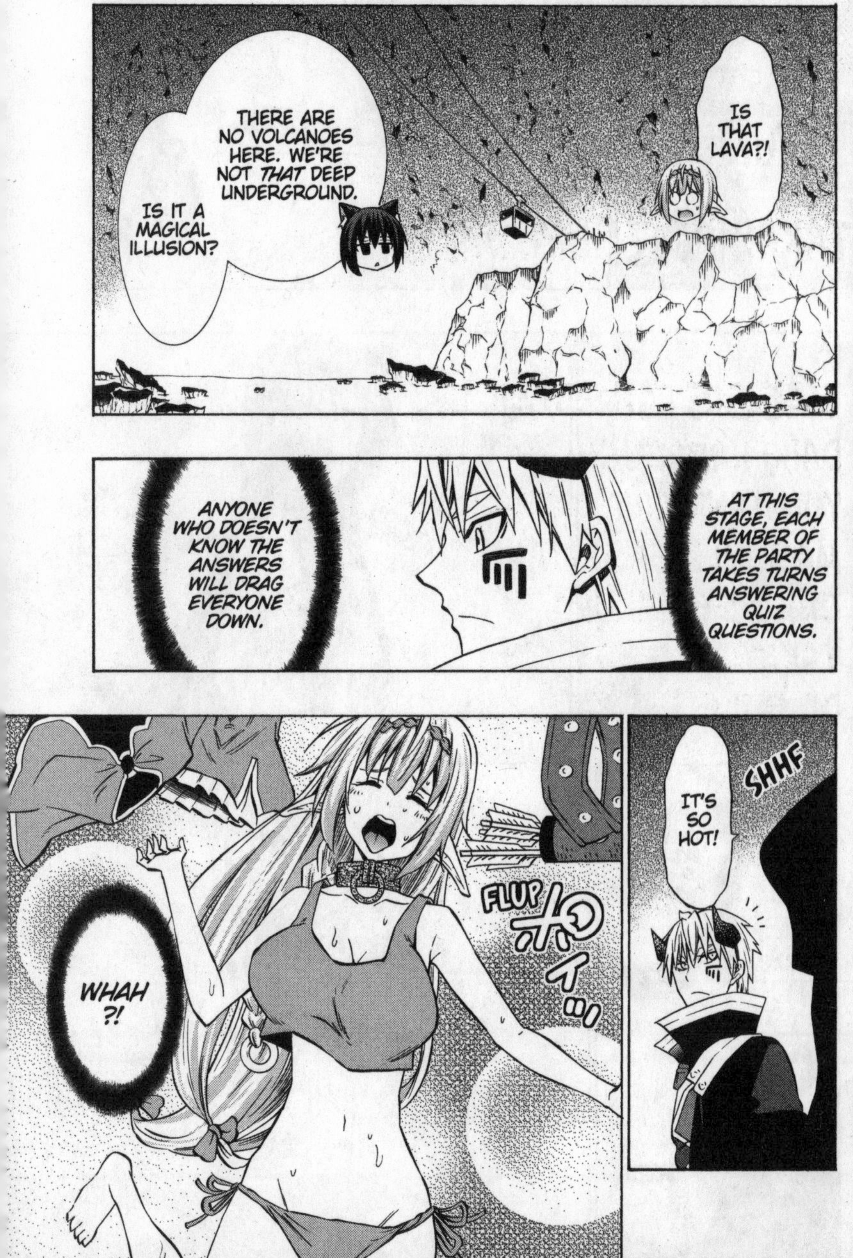
IS THAT LAVA?!
THERE ARE NO VOLCANOES HERE. WE'RE NOT *THAT* DEEP UNDERGROUND.
IS IT A MAGICAL ILLUSION?
AT THIS STAGE, EACH MEMBER OF THE PARTY TAKES TURNS ANSWERING QUIZ QUESTIONS.
ANYONE WHO DOESN'T KNOW THE ANSWERS WILL DRAG EVERYONE DOWN.
SHHF
IT'S SO HOT!
FLUP
ポイッ
WHAH ?!

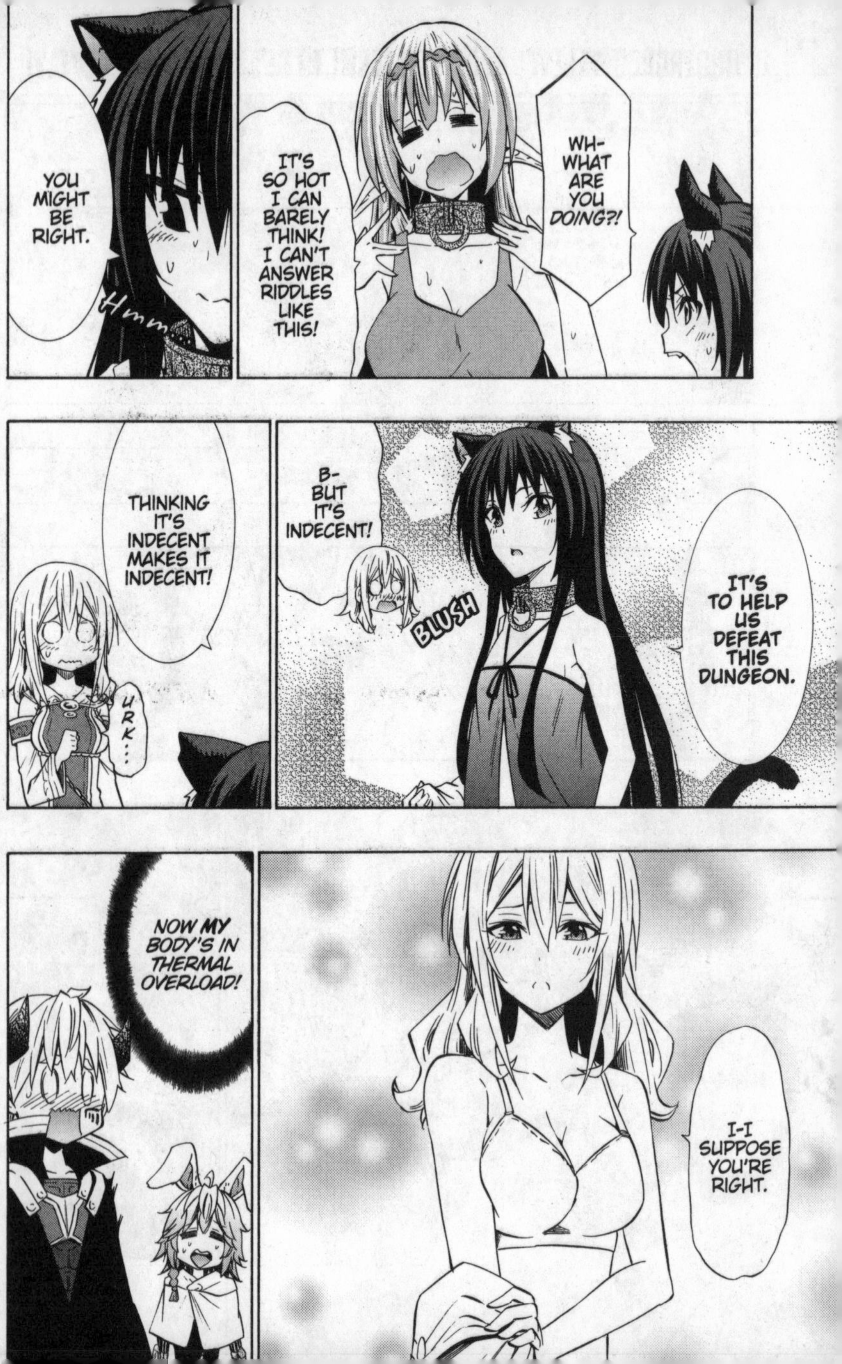
WH-WHAT ARE YOU DOING?!
IT'S SO HOT I CAN BARELY THINK! I CAN'T ANSWER RIDDLES LIKE THIS!
YOU MIGHT BE RIGHT.
Hmm
IT'S TO HELP US DEFEAT THIS DUNGEON.
B-BUT IT'S INDECENT!
BLUSH
THINKING IT'S INDECENT MAKES IT INDECENT!
URK...
I-I SUPPOSE YOU'RE RIGHT.
NOW MY BODY'S IN THERMAL OVERLOAD!

UNDERGROUND LEVEL 5: M@STER, ETC. LOVELY LIVE, ETC.

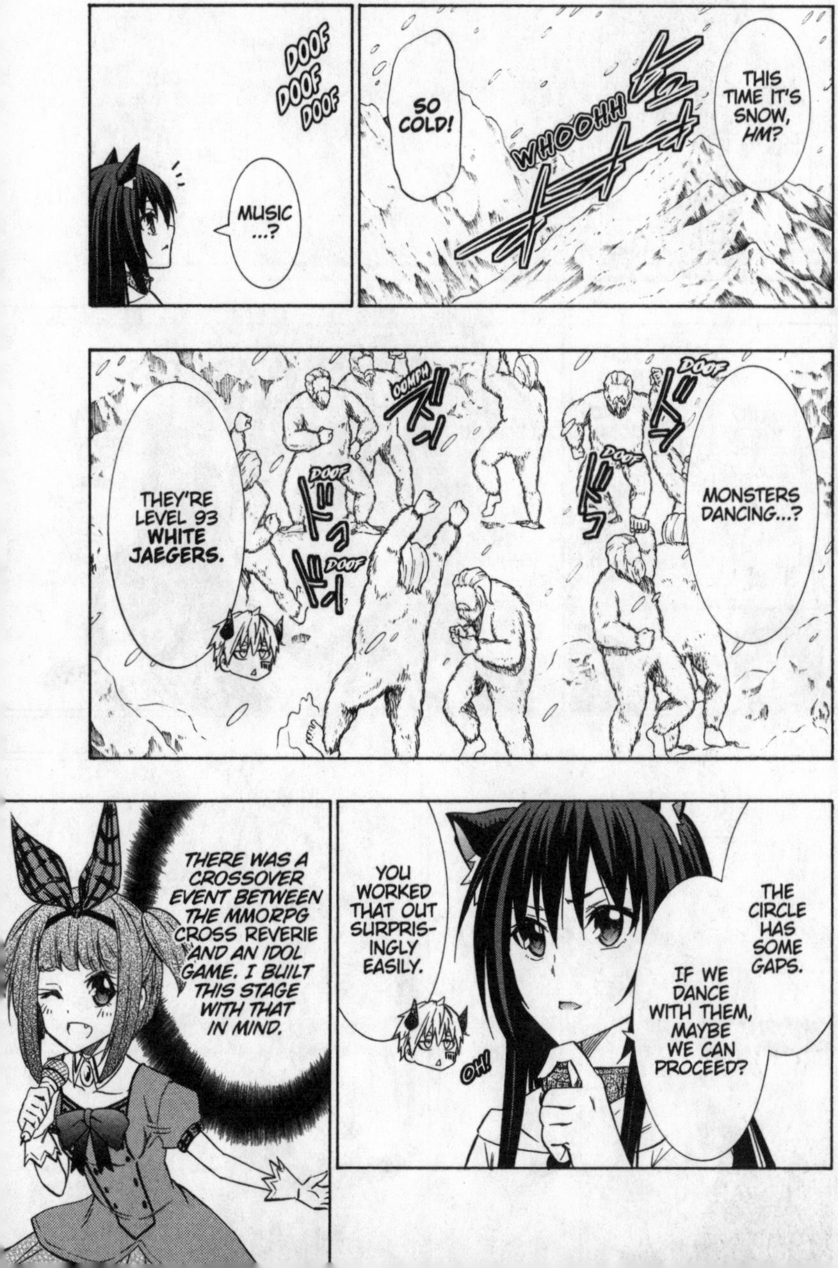
THIS TIME IT'S SNOW, HM?
WHOOHH
SO COLD!
DOOF DOOF DOOF
MUSIC ...?
MONSTERS DANCING...?
DOOF
DOOF
OOMPH
DOOF
DOOF
THEY'RE LEVEL 93 WHITE JAEGERS.
THE CIRCLE HAS SOME GAPS.
IF WE DANCE WITH THEM, MAYBE WE CAN PROCEED?
YOU WORKED THAT OUT SURPRISINGLY EASILY.
OH!
THERE WAS A CROSSOVER EVENT BETWEEN THE MMORPG CROSS REVERIE AND AN IDOL GAME. I BUILT THIS STAGE WITH THAT IN MIND.

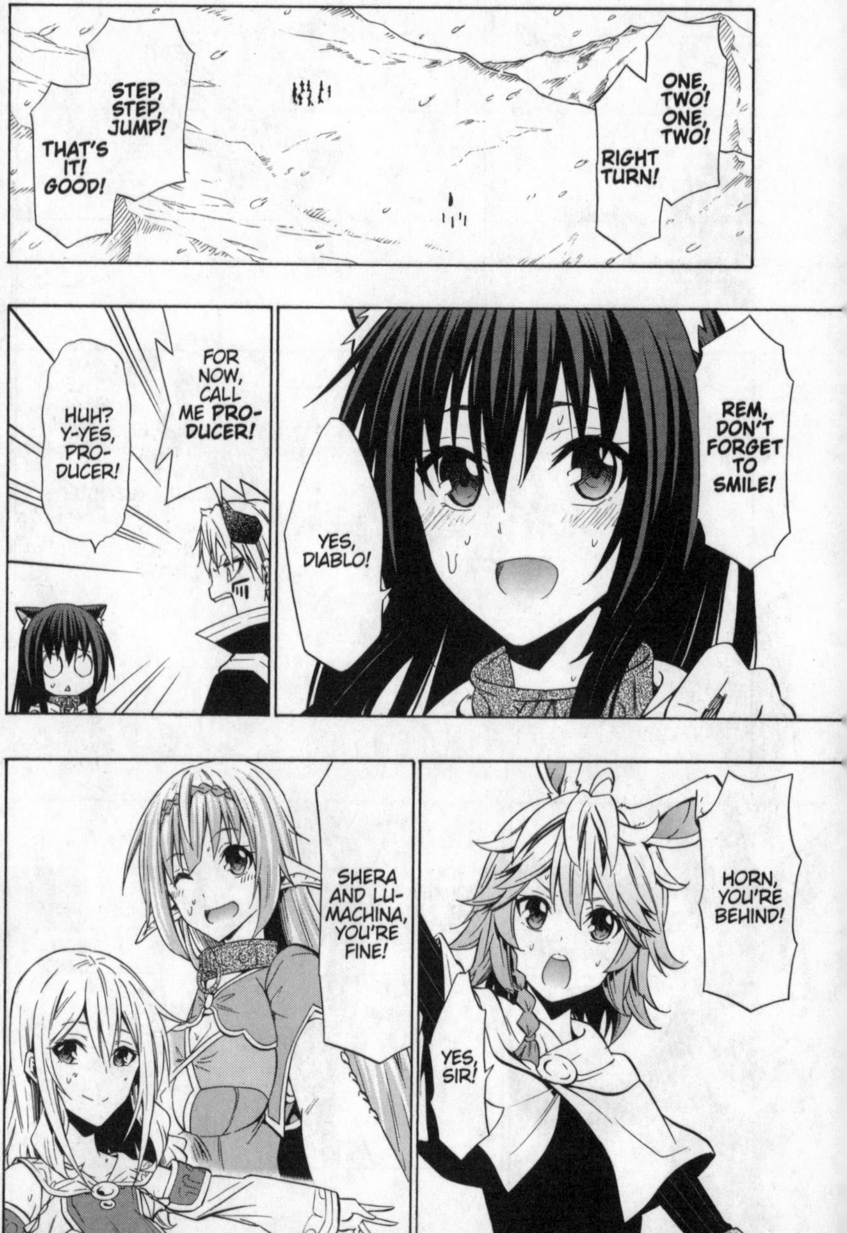
ONE, TWO! ONE, TWO!
RIGHT TURN!
STEP, STEP, JUMP!
THAT'S IT! GOOD!
REM, DON'T FORGET TO SMILE!
YES, DIABLO!
FOR NOW, CALL ME PRO-DUCER!
HUH? Y-YES, PRO-DUCER!
HORN, YOU'RE BEHIND!
YES, SIR!
SHERA AND LU-MACHINA, YOU'RE FINE!

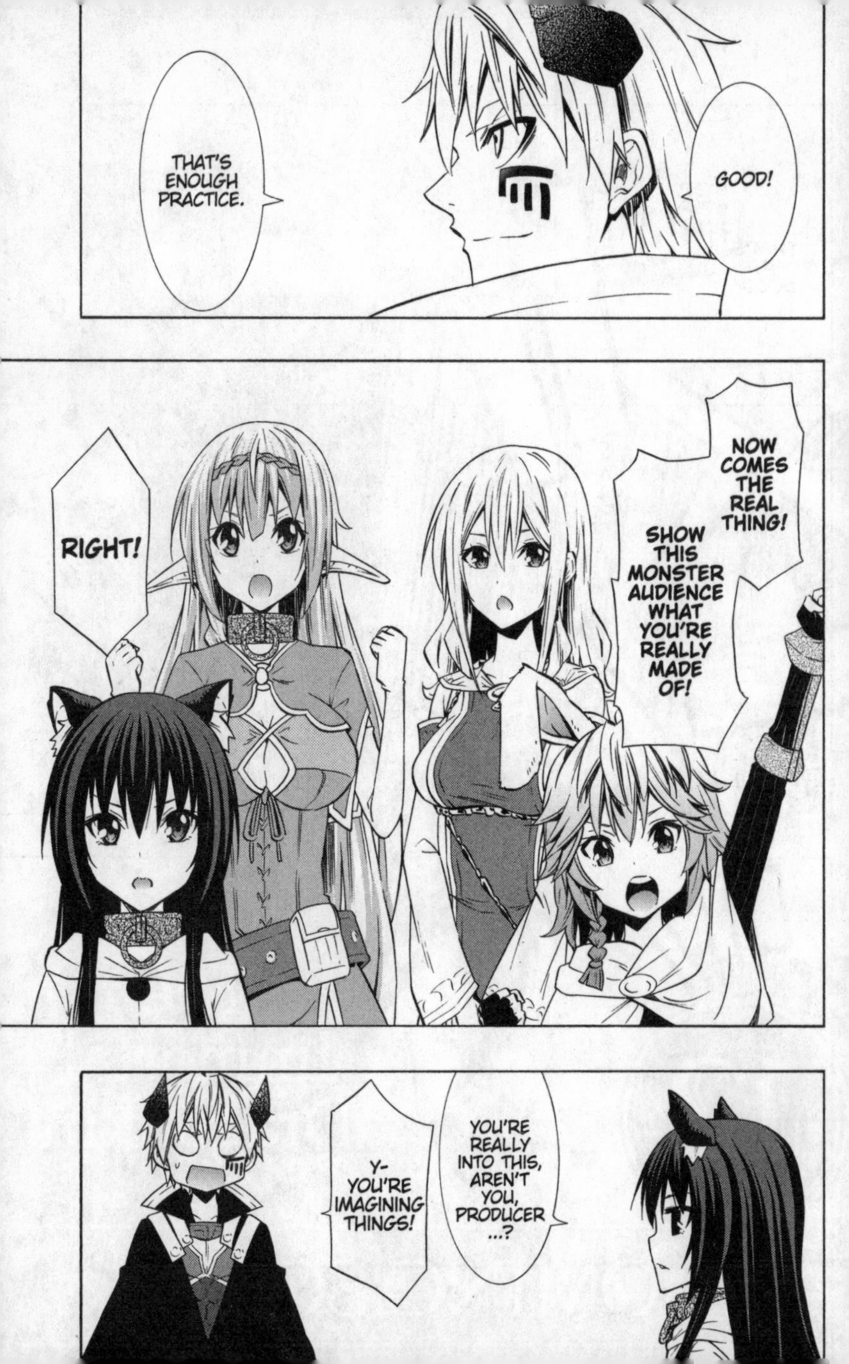
GOOD!
THAT'S ENOUGH PRACTICE.
NOW COMES THE REAL THING!
SHOW THIS MONSTER AUDIENCE WHAT YOU'RE REALLY MADE OF!
RIGHT!
YOU'RE REALLY INTO THIS, AREN'T YOU, PRODUCER...?
Y- YOU'RE IMAGINING THINGS!

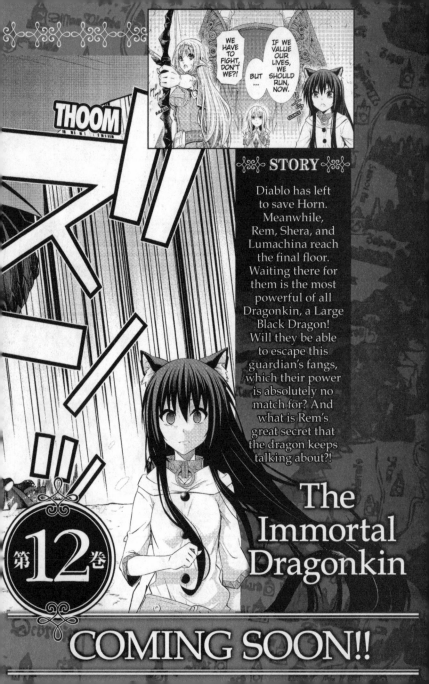

IF WE VALUE OUR LIVES, WE SHOULD RUN, NOW.
GLANCE
BUT ...
WE HAVE TO FIGHT, DON'T WE?!

THOOM

STORY

Diablo has left to save Horn. Meanwhile, Rem, Shera, and Lumachina reach the final floor. Waiting there for them is the most powerful of all Dragonkin, a Large Black Dragon! Will they be able to escape this guardian's fangs, which their power is absolutely no match for? And what is Rem's great secret that the dragon keeps talking about?!

第12巻

The Immortal Dragonkin

COMING SOON!!

A Large Black Dragon Appears!!
A LARGE BLACK DRAGON?!
HOW NOT TO SUMMON A DEMON LORD
THE MEGA-POPULAR OTHER WORLD ADVENTURE

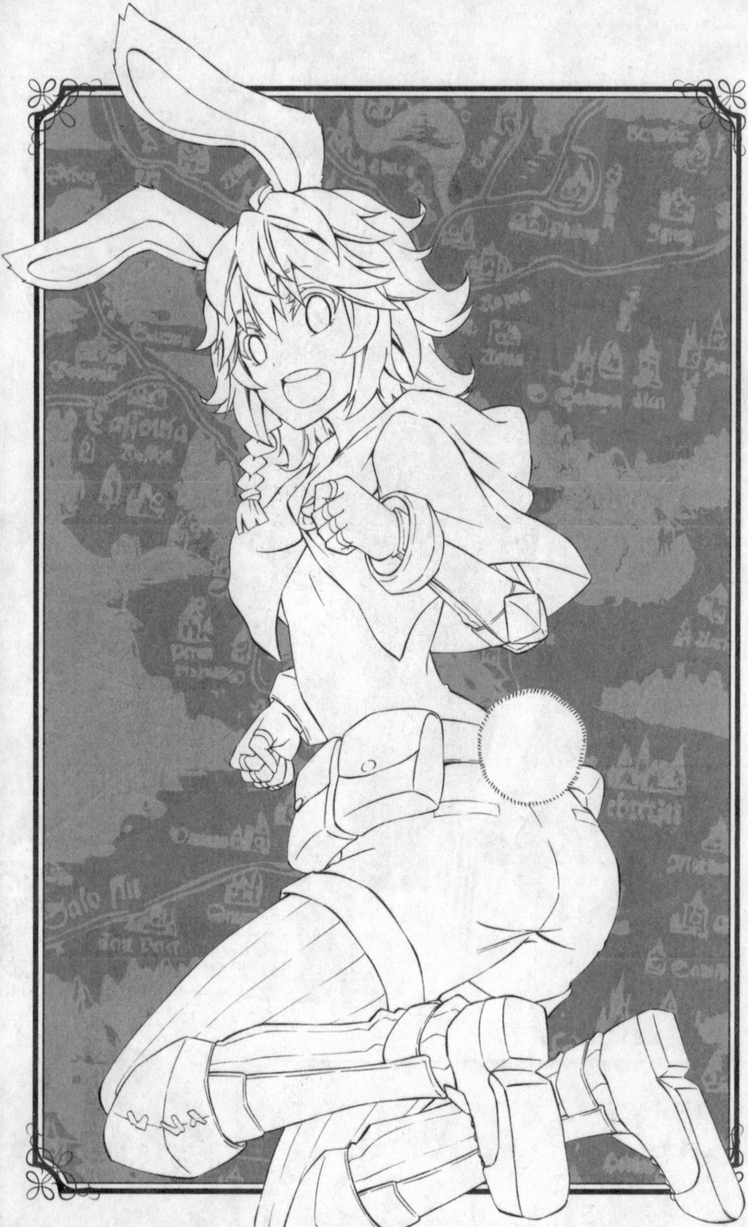

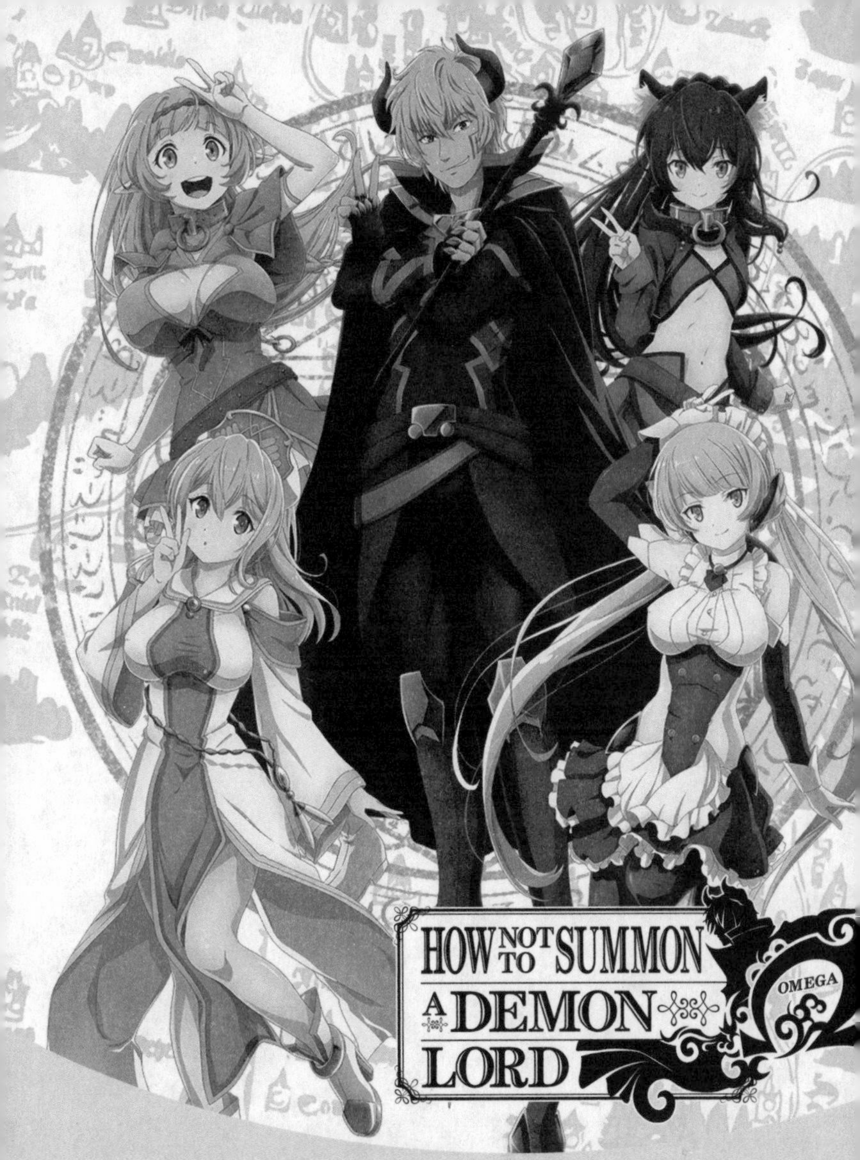
HOW NOT TO SUMMON A DEMON LORD
OMEGA

SEVEN SEAS ENTERTAINMENT PRESENTS

HOW NOT TO SUMMON A DEMON LORD

VOLUME 11

story by **YUKIYA MURASAKI**   art by **NAOTO FUKUDA**

TRANSLATION
Kumar Sivasubramanian

ADAPTATION
Lora Gray

LETTERING AND RETOUCH
Christa Miesner

COVER DESIGN
Kris Aubin

PROOFREADER
Kurestin Armada
Dawn Davis

EDITOR
Peter Adrian Behravesh

PREPRESS TECHNICIAN
Rhiannon Rasmussen-Silverstein

PRODUCTION MANAGER
Lissa Pattillo

MANAGING EDITOR
Julie Davis

ASSOCIATE PUBLISHER
Adam Arnold

PUBLISHER
Jason DeAngelis

ISEKAI MAOU TO SHOKAN SHOJO NO DOREI MAJYUTSU VOL. 11
© 2020 NAOTO FUKUDA, YUKIYA MURASAKI, TAKAHIRO TSURUSAKI.
All rights reserved.
First published in Japan in 2020 by Kodansha Ltd., Tokyo.
Publication rights for this English edition arranged through Kodansha Ltd., Tokyo.

Seven Seas press and purchase enquiries can be sent to Marketing Manager Lianne Sentar at press@gomanga.com. Information regarding the distribution and purchase of digital editions is available from Digital Manager CK Russell at digital@gomanga.com.

Seven Seas and the Seven Seas logo are trademarks of Seven Seas Entertainment. All rights reserved.

ISBN: 978-1-64827-103-8

Printed in Canada

First Printing: May 2021

10 9 8 7 6 5 4 3 2 1

FOLLOW US ONLINE: *www.sevenseasentertainment.com*

READING DIRECTIONS

This book reads from *right to left*, Japanese style. If this is your first time reading manga, you start reading from the top right panel on each page and take it from there. If you get lost, just follow the numbered diagram here. It may seem backwards at first, but you'll get the hang of it! Have fun!!

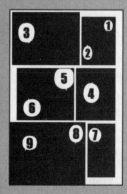